Accounting for Management Decisions

SECOND EDITION

Accounting for Management Decisions

John Arnold

Peat Marwick McLintock Professor of Accounting
University of Manchester

Tony Hope

Visiting Professor of Accounting
INSEAD, Manchester Business School

PRENTICE HALL

New York • London • Toronto • Sydney • Tokyo • Singapore

First published 1983 by
Prentice Hall International (UK) Ltd,
66 Wood Lane End, Hemel Hempstead,

Hertfordshire, HP2 4RG
A division of
Simon & Schuster International Group

Second edition 1990

Typeset in 10/12 English Times by
MCS Ltd, Salisbury.

Printed and bound in Great Britain by
The University Press, Cambridge

British Library Cataloguing in Publication Data

Arnold, John, *1944–*
Accounting for management decisions. -2nd ed
1. Management accounting
I. Title II. Hope, Anthony
658.1'511

ISBN 0-13-004391-5

4 5 94 93 92

For Lynne and Pamela

Contents

Preface to the first edition

We live in a world of scarce resources. Many different economic units from individuals to multinational corporations and governments compete for these scarce resources. How does each economic unit decide how many resources to acquire, at what price, when, and for what purpose? We believe that accountants have a crucial role to play in finding the answers to these and similar questions. In this book we concentrate on one type of accounting information – that which is provided to those responsible for managing economic units to help them make decisions concerning the best allocation of resources. If management accounting information can help to improve the efficiency with which resources are allocated, then it is fulfilling a function which is useful both to the individuals who receive it and to society in general.

This book is directed at students who are approaching management accounting for the first time and at business managers who are interested in developments which have taken place in the management accounting literature in recent years. For the most part, we assume that our readers have no prior knowledge of accounting and no advanced mathematical expertise. We attempt to explain and illustrate the conceptual issues involved in designing useful management accounting information systems for a range of different circumstances. Our main aim is to explain the principles involved in preparing useful information for decisions rather than to present an exhaustive review of all areas in which management accounting is used. For that reason we allocate more space than is usual in management accounting books to the development of a basic framework for management decisions and management accounting. In our view, a sound grasp of basic principles is far more important for any student new to management accounting, than is a detailed description of every aspect of the management accountant's work. This does not mean that we regard applications of the basic principles as unimportant: the second part of the book contains a wide range of these. However, the emphasis in this part is to clarify the principles rather than to describe practical procedures mechanically and uncritically. We make extensive use of numerical illustrations throughout the book.

At the end of each chapter is a list of discussion topics and (where appropriate) a selection of numerical exercises. Each chapter also contains a list of suggested further reading which is provided primarily to enable the interested reader to pursue particular topics in more depth. Some of the references are quite difficult for a reader who is relatively new to the subject. Many of them are original works by writers who have played a major role in the development of management accounting. Although we have tried to reflect the contributions of such writers in the text, there is often no substitute for the original writing. Those who are willing to spend the time necessary to read and understand some of the recommended further readings will be richly rewarded for their efforts.

The book comprises 18 chapters. The role of each one within the overall framework is explained in Chapter 1. For teaching purposes the book should fit neatly into a typical undergraduate course of approximately 20 lectures, with one chapter being covered in each lecture and two lectures being available for revision, review and so on. A teacher should be able to select tutorial/class problems from amongst the discussion topics and exercises provided at the end of each chapter.

Many people have helped in the preparation of the book. We are indebted to Henry Hirschberg and Giles Wright of Prentice Hall International who cajoled us sufficiently often to ensure that we finished; to G. R. Booth, Susan Dev, Angela Filmer, Tom Lee, Michael Mepham, Bob Parker, Peter Sénèque, Alan Southworth and John Whitman who commented critically and helpfully on earlier drafts and again to John Whitman, who prepared the compounding and discounting tables in the appendix. We are also grateful to Maureen Scapens, Imelda Welsby and Colette White who somehow managed to convert our original manuscripts into a form which people other than ourselves could read. We also owe a debt to a succession of first and second year accounting students at the University of Manchester who, over the years, have had to listen to our explanations of management accounting. Their comments, criticisms and questions have hopefully resulted in a more readily understandable book than might otherwise have been the case. We should also like to thank the authors of some of the end-of-chapter exercises. Many of these have been prepared by us as class assignments over a period of years. Others have been 'inherited' from a variety of institutions with which we have been associated, in particular the London School of Economics. Unfortunately, the identities of the original authors of such examples have been lost to us with the passage of time. We are sorry that we cannot acknowledge them by name and hope that they will excuse us for using their material: the book would be poorer without it. Finally, and most importantly, we thank our wives, Lynne (Arnold) and Pamela (Hope) and our children Dan, Anna, Emily and Sophie (Hope), and Kate and Mandy (Arnold), for providing love, enjoyment, encouragement and welcome distractions during the writing of this book.

John Arnold
Tony Hope

Department of Accounting and Business Finance
University of Manchester

Preface to the second edition

It is almost seven years since we wrote the preface to the first edition of this book. In that time, much has changed in the practice of management accounting. In particular, there has been a move away from mechanical management accounting systems which often provided financial data for managers using rules which sometimes failed to recognise the reality of the ways in which management decisions were made. Alternative systems are being developed which recognise new manufacturing procedures such as just in time (JIT) stock control and computer aided design and manufacture (CADCAM). In addition, the research literature in management and management accounting has increasingly emphasised the contribution which accounting can and does make to the effectiveness of organisations. One finding is that the actual contribution is sometimes less than might be expected.

Management is facing a period of rapid change arising, amongst other things, from technological advances in both manufacturing procedures and information processing, the changing nature of the UK economy, new management practices in the public sector and new regulatory regimes in the financial services sector.

In spite of these changes, we believe that much of what we said in the original preface remains as appropriate today as seven years ago. The book continues to be directed at students who are approaching management accounting for the first time and to managers who are interested in recent developments in the management accounting literature. As in the first edition, the book is split into two parts. The first is concerned with the development of a basic framework for management decisions and management accounting, the second with applications of the basic principles to practical issues.

Much of the basic framework which was included in the first edition remains valid and appropriate. We have expanded Chapter 1 to include additional material on the nature of organisations, the organisational context of accounting and the interrelationships between accounting and the other types of information which are available to managers. Chapters 2 to 5 have been revised and clarified in the light of comments we have received from colleagues who have used the book on teaching programmes in universities and polytechnics. The material on scientific method, which previously comprised a chapter in its own right, has been integrated into other chapters where appropriate. We have not on the whole made major changes to the chapters in Part 1.

We have made more substantial changes to the chapters on management accounting applications in Part 2. These include new material on the learning curve in Chapter 7 and, in Chapter 8, additional discussion of the context within which pricing takes place and of the role of pricing as part of an organisation's overall marketing strategy. Chapters 11 and 12, on long-term decisions, include a fuller discussion than previously of the practical difficulties involved in appraising long-term investment opportunities and an introduction to the capital asset pricing model. In Chapter 13, we have expanded and developed our discussions of the advantages of budgets and of their motivational effects. Chapter 16, on divisional performance, has been substantially re-written.

In addition to the modifications outlined above, we have incorporated many detailed changes suggested by reviewers and have included numerous new exercises and further reading references. Many of the new reading references are articles which have contributed to the development of management accounting theory and practice since the first edition was published. A reading of some of them will provide a richer picture of changes in the subject than we are able to offer in a single text. We have tried not to change the basic nature or shape of the book; those who have used the first edition seem, for the most part, to have been reasonably satisfied!

We remain indebted to all the people who helped with the first edition and whom we acknowledged in our original preface. Others have helped in the preparation of the second edition. Maggie McDougall and Cathy Peck of Prentice Hall International have been unreasonably courteous in reminding us that we were behind schedule. They have provided us with encouragement and support beyond the normal call of duty for publishers. We are indebted to Peter Boys, John Piper and Keith Warnock for their constructive criticisms of and suggestions for improvements to the first edition. Amanda Brereton, Angela Jones, Hilary Garraway and Julie Gorton have re-typed successive drafts with their usual cheerfulness and efficiency. As always, our greatest debt is to our wives, Lynne and Pamela, and to our children, Kate and Mandy, and Dan, Anna, Emily and Sophie. They bear the major brunt of our unsociable working hours. The children at least are older and wiser than when we were writing the first edition; but both they and Lynne and Pamela continue to provide the love and encouragement without which the current edition would probably never have seen the light of day.

John Arnold
Tony Hope

Part 1

Basic framework

Chapter 1

The role of management accounting

This is a book about accounting. Specifically it is a book about one area of accounting, often called *management accounting* or *managerial accounting*, which is concerned with the provision of information to those responsible for managing businesses and other economic organisations to help them in making decisions about the future of the organisation and in controlling the implementation of the decisions they make. In this chapter we try to answer some questions which someone embarking on a study of management accounting might naturally ask. Questions such as: What is accounting? What is management accounting and what is its role relative to other branches of accounting? What sorts of decisions do managers have to take and how might accounting information help them?

1.1 What is accounting?

Only in the last few decades has accounting become firmly established as an academic discipline, taught in universities and other educational establishments throughout the world.[1] Accounting traditionally belongs within departments of commerce, or business studies, or within faculties of social science or social studies, along with such other 'applied' subjects as economics, politics, sociology and, sometimes, law. It is not traditionally taught along with medicine or geography or French or Latin or physics. The academic location of the subject as a social science

[1] It should be pointed out that *as a practical discipline* accounting has existed for many centuries. From the earliest times people have kept records of what they own (assets) and what they owe (liabilities), though the *purposes* of keeping such records may not always have been the same. For example, one main purpose of early accounting systems was to expose any losses due to fraud or neglect on the part of the steward or keeper of the records. The record keeper was usually a personal agent or, in Greek and Roman times, a public official of the state. These early forms of record keeping were not concerned with such emotive, modern notions as the measurement of economic efficiency or the determination of income, but rather with the preparation of a statement of receipts and payments relating to a period's transactions, and possibly a listing of assets and liabilities existing at the close of the period. This general form of accounting, which is still practised today, has come to be known as 'stewardship accounting', after the steward who kept the records.

may offer some clues as to the context, or environment, to which accounting belongs.

Most social sciences are concerned primarily with particular aspects of a person's role in society (hence the use of the adjective 'social'). For example, we might view the discipline of *economics* as being concerned with the efficient allocation of society's scarce resources; *law* as being concerned with the framework necessary to regulate individual and corporate behaviour within society; *politics* as being concerned with the political systems under which we live, and *sociology* as being concerned with the interpretation and analysis of individual and group behaviour. There are, as might be expected, some strong links between these various subjects, and these links are frequently recognised in the teaching and content of social science courses – thus some sociology is often taught in politics courses, some economics is taught in law courses, and so on.

So where does accounting fit into this broad spectrum of social science? What is its role, if any, in people's relationship with their environment? We can perhaps begin to envisage a possible role for accounting when we call to mind the notion of commercial activity. In all forms of society, individuals and groups make economic decisions which entail the exchange of property at agreed prices. In order to agree prices, it is necessary to have a unit of measurement or medium of exchange, which is common to all members of the society, and is thus widely understood. In modern societies, this medium of exchange is almost always defined in terms of money – money is used to assign prices or values to property.

Because of its widespread application, the use of a common unit of measurement forms a fundamental role in economic, legal, political and sociological analysis – i.e. because of the continuous need to value and measure objects, all social sciences require quantitative information. This is where accounting comes in. Accounting responds to the need for quantitative and, in particular, financial information. Under this view, accounting is essentially an interdisciplinary subject – it draws on and responds to the other social sciences. Consequently the scope and boundaries of accounting change as society changes and new demands for information emerge. In much the same way, the scope of other social sciences broadens or contracts depending upon society's need for the type of analysis they provide. For example, law, economics and sociology are not static disciplines. They respond to, and indeed help to shape, the needs of society.

The above analysis suggests that a definition of accounting depends upon what is asked of it at any point in time by various groups in society. However, in order to define the scope of a book on one aspect of accounting, we must adopt a more practical philosophy – one which enables us at least to choose some working definitions that we can use as a framework for our future discussions. There are many possible working definitions of accounting. The one that best captures our view of accounting and which we shall in consequence adopt is that formulated by the American Accounting Association (AAA) in 1966.[2] This definition views accounting as

[2] American Accounting Association, *A Statement of Basic Accounting Theory*, American Accounting Association, 1966, p. 1.

> the process of identifying, measuring and communicating economic information to permit informed judgements and decisions by users of the information.

In other words, accounting is a language – the language of economic activity. Like all languages it has its own vocabulary, methods of expression, terminology and conventions – and, because of these, its own difficulties of interpretation and understanding. It is a language which pervades, in some measure, everybody's life, and hence it is a language with which everyone should have some familiarity.

A closer inspection of the terms used in the AAA's definition of accounting reveals some interesting features. To understand accounting, we must understand the nature (and practice) of *measurement* and *communication*, the attributes of (economic) *information*, the theories and practices of *decision making*, and we must try to identify the *users* of accounting information. Each of these features poses its own particular problems, and one purpose of this text is to explore these problems.

We particularly like this definition because it accords with our own philosophy of accounting, which is essentially a philosophy of *providing information to aid good decision making*. However, we should stress that good decision making does not rely solely on accounting information. Rather, accounting information should be seen as a part of the total information set available to decision makers.

1.2 Management accounting and financial accounting

The definition of accounting in the previous section views accounting as a system for providing (primarily financial) information to those who have to make decisions and control the implementation of those decisions. However, the information to be provided by the accounting system depends upon who is making the decision and for what purpose. For example, the sort of information required by the managing director of a large multinational firm such as ICI or the Ford Motor Co. may be very different from the sort of information required by a member of a village cricket club. The former may, for example, require information about the range of products the company is producing and selling; information concerning the quantity, price, cost, competitive position and profitability of each product. The latter may require information about the annual subscription the club will charge its members, the cost of social functions, and so on.

In accounting, a distinction is often made between what is termed 'management accounting' and what is termed 'financial accounting'. (This latter is rather a misleading title as all accounting is, in some respects, financial.) Management accounting is concerned with the provision of information to managers who make decisions about the ways in which an organisation's resources should be allocated. By contrast, financial accounting is concerned with the provision of information to users other than managers, e.g. shareholders, customers and those who have loaned funds to an organisation. The dichotomy between management and financial accounting is, in many ways, both unfortunate and misleading. It implies that there is little, if any, overlap between the information required by managers and that required by others. This is clearly not the case. A shareholder in ICI will probably be as interested as its managers in the future financial prospects of the company. However, it is also the case that shareholders in the company may be interested in information at a level of aggregation different from that required by managers of its factories. Shareholders hope to predict the company's overall future performance as a measure both of the dividends they will receive and of the future value of their shares. Managers will be more concerned with the prospects for their factories because these will affect the decisions they will take concerning the purchase of raw materials, the hiring of labour, the pricing and output levels of products, and so on.

This book is concerned primarily with the provision of accounting information for management decisions. But there are several fundamental notions that are common to all types of accounting information systems. To a large extent, these notions are embodied in our adopted definition of accounting, which is not restricted to any one group of users or type of organisation. We discuss these notions here in Part 1 under the general heading of 'Basic Framework'. Such a framework applies not only to information for management decisions, but also, with very little modification, to the provision of accounting information to other groups of users.

In Chapter 2 we discuss the meaning and importance of a number of the components of our definition of accounting; in particular we examine the nature of information–communication systems, problems of measurement, and theories of individual and group decision making. Chapter 3 is concerned with the meaning, importance and measurement of wealth. Wealth is a vital component of any decision making process as it provides a focal point for the process; the maximisation of wealth, properly defined, provides an objective for decision models and decision makers. The discussion in Chapter 4 of risk and uncertainty in decision making reflects the fact that all decisions relate to alternative future courses of action and that the future is always uncertain. Hence all decisions involve a consideration of the problems posed by the existence of risk and uncertainty. Finally, as part of the basic framework, in Chapter 5 we explain and illustrate the fundamental principles for measuring relevant costs and benefits for decision purposes. The chapters in Part 1 of the book provide a conceptual foundation for Part 2, to which we shall turn shortly. First, however, we investigate further the objectives of organisations and the environments within which they operate.

1.3 The objectives and environments of organisations

Our concern is with the role and design of (management) accounting systems within organisations. An essential first step is to explore the nature of organisations and the procedures which are used to control their progress and development. We should stress at the outset that accounting is but one part of a highly complex decision making and control process in most organisations. An appreciation of its context and limitations is an important prerequisite to the exploitation of its strengths.

What is an organisation?

The answer to this question is not at all obvious! Take, for example, the case of Marks and Spencer plc (although what we will say applies equally to many other organisations, whether in the public or private sector of the economy and whether or not they are profit oriented). When we talk of Marks and Spencer what do we have in mind – its stores and fittings, administrative buildings, stock of merchandise, fleet of vehicles, and so on? Although these are part of the picture, there is almost certainly more. What about the company's reputation and role as an employer, a purchaser of goods, a borrower, a supplier of goods and – more recently – of financial services, and as an investment vehicle for individual and institutional shareholders? All these aspects of the company's activities depend on people and on the nature of their relationships with each other under the umbrella provided by the activities of Marks and Spencer.

This perception suggests that an organisation might be viewed as a group of participants, each of whom makes efforts (*contributions*) on behalf of the organisation and in return receives rewards (*inducements*). The basic criterion for any individual continuing to participate in the organisation is that his or her rewards (inducements) should exceed his or her efforts (contributions). This view of an organisation as an inducement–contribution process is shown in Figure 1.1.

We might illustrate the meaning of some of the boxes in Figure 1.1 by reference to Marks and Spencer. Managers, for example, make contributions to the organisation which are generally non-financial. They contribute mental and physical effort, creativity and other skills. In return they receive both financial and non-financial rewards. The financial rewards will usually include salary payments and bonuses. Non-financial rewards might involve the pleasure that comes from job satisfaction, status and power. Customers contribute financial revenues when they purchase goods from the company. They may also contribute loyalty by preferring to shop at Marks and Spencer even when similar goods are available at a similar or lower price elsewhere. In return, they enjoy the satisfaction which comes from wearing or using the goods which have been purchased.

The shaded area in the middle of Figure 1.1 represents the *transformation process*, where the contributions from the various participants (the *system inputs*) are combined together to provide the *system outputs* which are then used to 'pay' rewards to the various groups of participants.

Several interesting conclusions emerge from analysing the nature of an organisation in this way:

1. All contributions (inputs) are combined and 'transformed' to provide the total inducements (outputs) to be distributed to participants. A contribution change by one group may affect the inducements which can be offered to another. For example, the withdrawal of subsidies by local or national government may affect the wages or other employment prospects of employees.

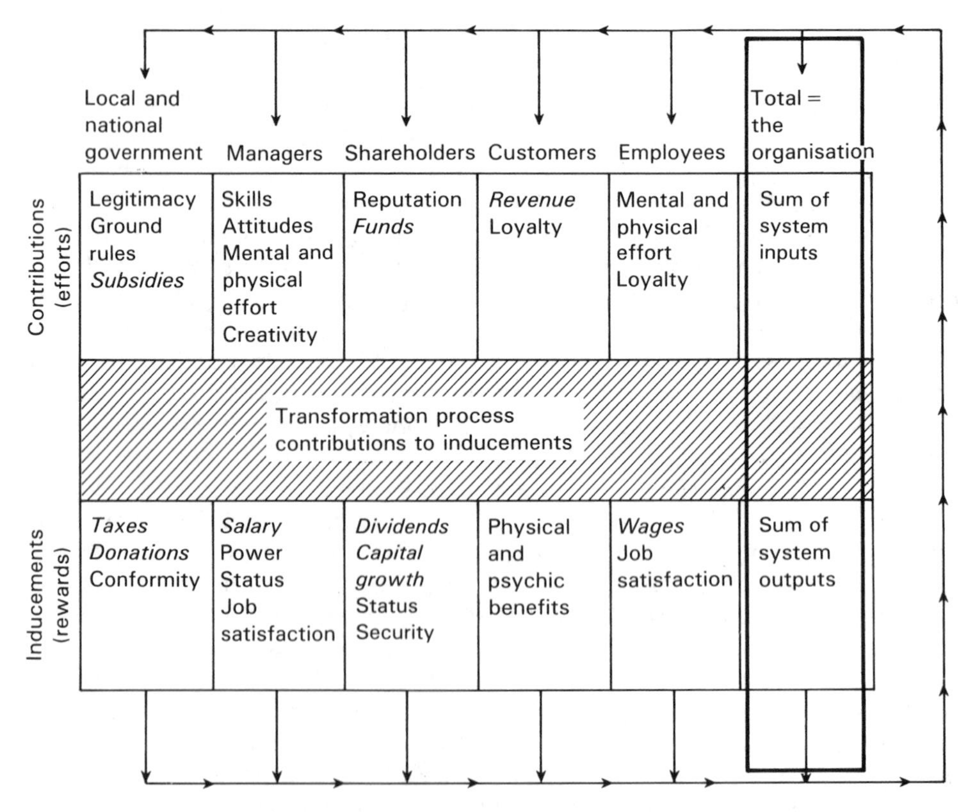

Figure 1.1 Organisation as inducement–contribution process* (based on A. M. Tinker and E. A. Lowe, 'A rationale for corporate social reporting', *Journal of Business Finance and Accounting*, Spring 1980.) *Financial items are in italics.

2. The allocation of total inducements between participants must be such that each participant (or possibly each group of participants) receives inducements which are at least equal to the contributions provided.
3. Contributions and inducements may be either financial or non-financial.
4. The efforts which participants are willing to make will be influenced by the rewards they expect. However, their expectations will be conditioned in part by what has actually happened in the past. Thus, the inducements of one period will influence, to some extent, the contributions of the next period.
5. The managers of organisations have a dual role. First, they must satisfy their own expectations and ensure that their rewards are at least as great as their contributions. Second, they must keep all the other participant groups happy in order to maintain the viability of the organisation. Their ability to achieve the first objective will depend in part on their success in achieving the second! Maintaining the viability of the organisation will involve managers in identifying the minimum inducements required by each participant, in

ensuring that sufficient total inducements are available to meet the needs of each participant and in ensuring that all participants do receive inducements greater than their contributions.

The task of management

The dual role of management, described above, is more easily described than accomplished. An organisation is not a self-contained, isolated entity – it has to operate in an environment which constrains its behaviour.

First, the 'technology' available in the environment affects the ability of the organisation to transform total contributions into total inducements. New equipment and machinery will affect its production process. New marketing and selling techniques will affect the way in which and the success with which it markets and sells its products. New computer developments will affect its administrative procedures. These and other changes in available 'technology' complicate the task of management.

Second, the environment provides alternative opportunities for participants and hence influences the minimum inducements they require from the organisation. For example, the environment provides alternative employment opportunities for employees, alternative investment opportunities for shareholders, alternative sources of supply for customers, and so on.

In both of the above respects, the environment is likely to be dynamic – available alternative technologies and opportunities will be in a continual state of flux. The task facing management may be represented as in Figure 1.2. The organisation operates in, and is affected by, a part (or subset) of the general environment which we might call the substantial environment. Figure 1.2 illustrates management's task if there are four participant groups – government, employees, shareholders and customers *and* if, within each group, the contributions made and the inducements required by each participant are homogeneous. (In practice there will be more groups and the interests of participants within each will not be homogeneous.) Hence the area (or set) described as 'shareholders' defines all points in the environment at which the inducements offered to shareholders are greater than the contributions they make. Any point outside that set will be unsatisfactory and will cause shareholders to withdraw their participation in the organisation. What is acceptable to the shareholders will be influenced by the alternative investment and other opportunities available to them.

Similar sets are defined for the other participant groups. The shaded area, F, is the *feasible set*, the only area within which all participants are satisfied. It is the task of management to make sure that the organisation is located in F – and to keep it there! This task is complicated by a number of factors. Because of their available alternative opportunities, each participant group may be pulling in a different direction from each other group. (Remember that, strictly speaking, each participant within a group may be represented by a different set or region.) Furthermore the environment itself will be changing continuously – what was feasible last week may not be so today – for example, a new competitor may enter the organisation's

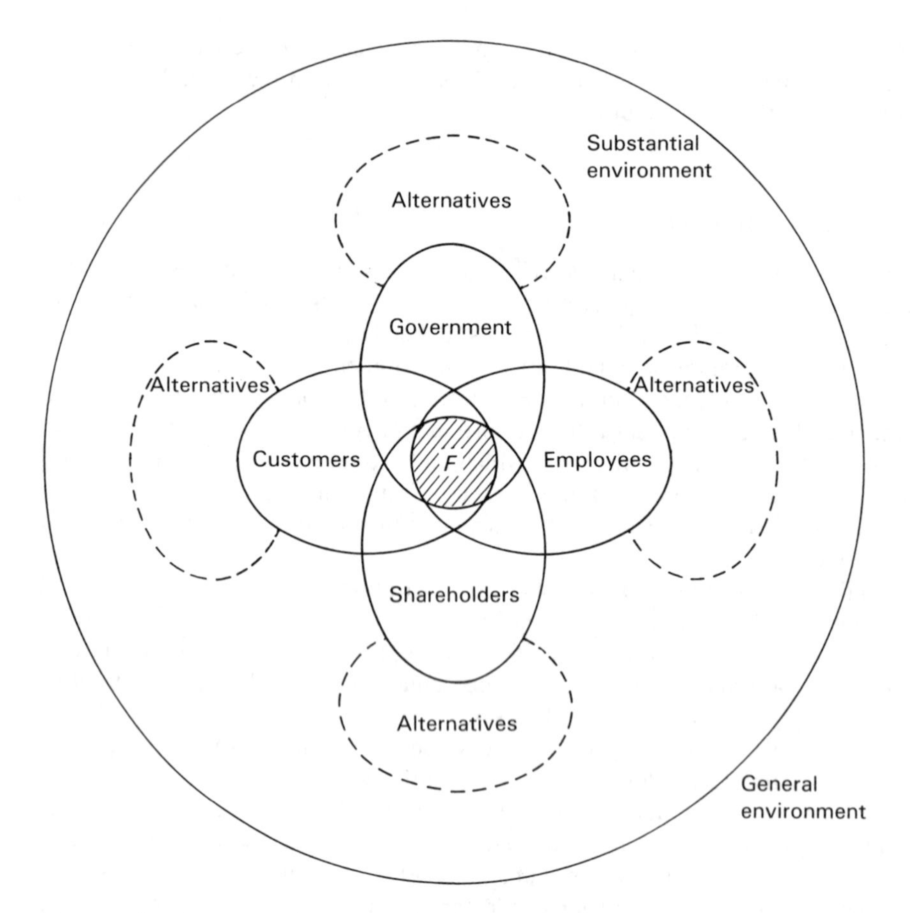

Figure 1.2 Structure of the organisation's environment.

market, a new employer may offer alternative employment opportunities, and so on.

The feasible set is unstable and is influenced by a variety of factors, some of which are *controllable* by managers (for example, the prices the organisation charges for its services or products and the number of staff it employs) and others of which are largely *uncontrollable* (for example, the general economic climate, the prices charged by competitors and government legislation).

It should be apparent from the discussion in this section that the task of controlling an organisation (i.e. of sustaining its viability) is an imposing one. In the next section we outline broadly the role which accounting has to play as part of the process of organisational control.

1.4 The role of accounting

As we have seen, management's task is to make decisions which are likely to ensure the continued viability of the organisation and to control the implementation of those decisions. Where does (management) accounting fit in? It is a part (and only a part) of the total information available to management. It is vital to recognise the partial role of accounting. For example, in considering the desirability of producing a new product, management will consider the costs of making and selling it and the revenues it is likely to produce. This is information which the accounting system should provide. However, management will also consider other aspects of the decision with which the accounting system may not be able to help, such as the technical problems of manufacturing the product, the availability of employees with the necessary production and marketing skills, the nature of the market within which the product will be sold, the extent to which the product fits within the company's existing range, etc. Accounting is only one part of a complicated set of informational and organisational structures. The role of accounting is to provide relevant financial information within those structures. It will rarely provide sufficient information by itself to permit an informed decision to be taken or to control the implementation of organisational plans.

The danger with accounting information is that because it attempts to measure the financial consequences of actions (which are of interest to most participants), because it often looks objective and accurate (but rarely is, as we shall see later), and because it is usually more readily available in quite large quantities than are other sources of information, it is accorded undue importance. An organisation whose managers attempt to make and control decisions entirely on the basis of accounting information is unlikely to remain viable for long.

Nevertheless, this is a book about accounting and about the way in which accounting can assist management in decision making and control. In consequence, our main emphasis will be on the explanation and development of management accounting methods rather than on the broader questions of organisational control. The reader should, of course, remain alert to the need at all stages to consider the non-accounting implications of management actions.

1.5 Information for managerial decision making

Within the context described and explained in the previous sections, in Part 2 we apply the concepts developed in Part 1 to particular decisions facing the managers of organisations. Figure 1.3 presents a simplified, general framework for managerial planning, decision making and control. At this stage we shall examine briefly the individual steps of the framework. Part 2 looks in detail at (sequential) issues raised when the framework is applied to particular situations.

It is important to recognise the role of the feedback mechanism within the general framework. Feedback loops stress interdependences between the various steps of the framework (i.e. the outcome of any one particular step provides information which may influence the formulation of prior steps). As interdependences exist, in some measure, between *all* steps of the framework, feedback is present throughout the entire planning and control system. For illustrative purposes, we have chosen two feedback loops, one linking steps 5 and 1,

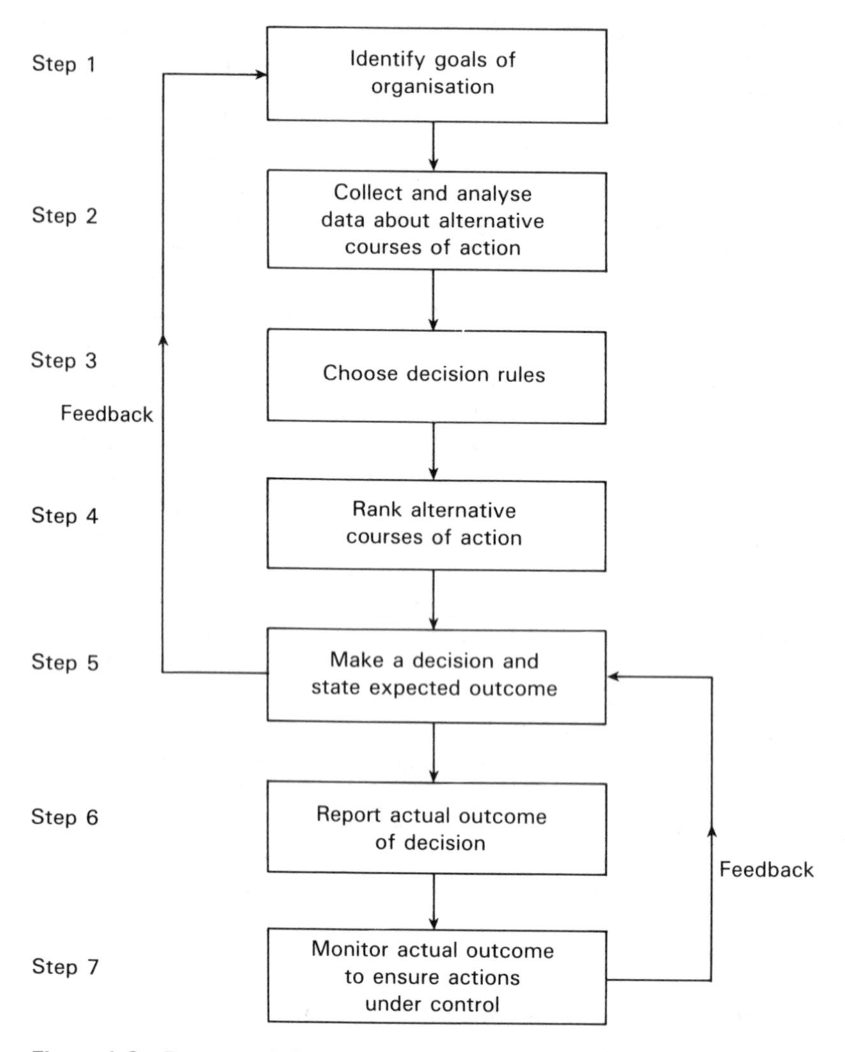

Figure 1.3 Framework for managerial planning, decision making and control.

the other linking steps 7 and 5. The first loop stresses the need to review regularly the goals of the organisation, in the light of the expected outcomes of individual courses of action; the second loop stresses how the control process helps to formulate the planning cycle for the following period (i.e. the differences between expected and actual figures for any period are useful inputs to the prediction of expected outcomes for succeeding periods).

Step 1 – identification of goals

Planning may be defined as the choice of organisational objectives and the means of their attainment. Thus good planning entails a procedure for determining the direction in which the resources of the organisation should be pointed. Formal planning is of particular importance in a large organisation composed of different divisions or sections. Without a knowledge of the objectives of the whole organisation, individual sections may take decisions that are not in the best interests of the whole.

Choice of appropriate organisational goals is one of the most difficult parts of the planning process. It is often blandly stated, as though it were a self-evident truth, that in a capitalist or 'mixed' economy the most appropriate goal for business activity is the making of the maximum possible profit. Profit maximisation or, more precisely, maximisation of the owner's wealth, represents the business objective which is usually assumed in traditional economic theory: indeed it forms the basis of much microeconomic analysis. It is often rephrased vaguely as 'maximisation of long-run growth' or 'maximisation of long-run survival prospects' or even 'maximisation of market share'. All of these possible goals focus in large measure on the maximisation of the owners' wealth, to the exclusion of the interests of other groups. As we have already seen, these goals fail to represent the reality of business planning in organisations with many different participants, each with their own goals.

When constraints of a societal nature (e.g. the employment of disabled workers, the provision of adequate social and recreational facilities) or, indeed, of a legal nature (e.g. the regulation of prices of particular goods, the restriction of monopolies) are superimposed on other disparate goals, we can see readily that the encapsulation of the whole process in terms of 'maximising profit' may in fact be an unrealistic representation of business reality. Yet management must attempt to point the organisation towards some particular goal(s). Without a guiding aim, business decision making would operate in a vacuum; there would be no benchmark against which to assess the desirability of any course of action.

The primary objective of business planning to be adopted in this, and in succeeding chapters, is the maximisation of the present value of the organisation's future cash flows, as we shall explain in Chapter 3. This objective is chosen for a variety of reasons. First, it is quantifiable and thus provides a ready guide for future actions; second, it avoids the imprecision of profit calculations which are based in large measure on the use of often arbitrary accounting conventions; third, it deals directly with one important means (cash) available to individuals to acquire things which give them satisfaction; and last it leaves open the question of how the cash is to be distributed among the members of the coalition of interested groups (i.e. it concentrates on maximising the size of the 'cake' available rather than on how the cake is to be distributed).

Step 2 – collection and analysis of data about alternative courses of action

Management must take a wide range of decisions of varying impact on the firm's (cash) resources. Some decisions will commit the firm's resources for a lengthy period of time and involve major changes in the firm's productive capacity. We might label these *long-term* decisions. Others will be of a more *short-term* nature.[3] Indeed, we would expect different levels of management to be associated with the different types of decisions; for instance, if the building of a large new factory was being contemplated, or if the firm was thinking of setting up operations in a new country, we would expect senior managers to be involved in these long-term decisions, where the level of risk involved is usually high, and the decision less easily reversible once resources have been committed. On a more short-term basis, lower-level managers may concern themselves with such operating decisions as:

1. How many units should be produced of a particular product?
2. How should the selling price of a product be fixed?
3. How many workers should be employed on a particular production process?

Whatever the nature of, and the time period involved in, a particular decision, management must attempt to analyse the costs and benefits to the organisation which are likely to arise. This is seldom easy to do. The difficulties should not be under-estimated. It may seem intuitively to be quite easy to attach particular 'labels' to the more easily quantified aspects of any decision, but in many situations it is those very aspects which are difficult to quantify precisely which may determine the ultimate success or failure of the particular decision. To illustrate this difficulty, let us borrow an analogy from the world of sport. On five or six occasions each summer, certain distinguished gentlemen gather together in London to choose an English cricket team to play against the touring sides. On the basis of the examination of purely quantifiable factors, the deliberations should not take very long; it would simply be necessary to scan the appropriate batting and bowling averages to select the top English performers. Similarly the wicketkeeper with the greatest number of dismissals would be selected. But in fact, the deliberations are not resolved speedily. They last for many hours, and it is by no means obvious at the end of the day that up-to-date statistics form the sole basis for selection of the team. Factors such as leadership quality and the ability to work well with others, though difficult to quantify, may be of equal importance in the ultimate choice. The analogy with managerial decision making should be apparent. Managers will, of course, use the basic quantifiable numbers, the costs and revenues, as the prime inputs to the decision process; but equally they must try to account for the less easily quantified factors inherent in the particular courses of action – factors such as the future economic environment, the strength of competition the firm will face and the uncertainty associated with estimated costs and benefits (discussed in Chapter 4), which may contribute greatly to the ultimate success of any course of action.

[3] Although we shall distinguish between long-term and short-term decisions throughout this book, it is important to recognise that in practice the distinction may often not be clear cut and may, in fact, depend upon the nature of the decision and of the organisation on whose behalf it is being taken. For example, economists often describe the long-term as a period in which all costs are avoidable. This period will probably be longer for a large company manufacturing heavy engineering equipment and having large numbers of factories, plant and employees than for a sole trader selling fruit from a market stall.

Steps 3 and 4 – choice of decision rules and ranking of alternative courses of action

In order to make effective decisions, managers need to understand two fundamental requirements:

(i) the appropriate *basis* for decision making;
(ii) the *types of data* to use in decision making and, by implication, the types of data not to use.

Decisions involve choices, and decision making entails making choices between alternative, competing courses of action. If no alternative courses of action exist, no decisions need to be made. In effect, the nature of a decision is of the kind 'What difference would it make if we chose to do X instead of not doing X?' More specifically, when we ask this question, we are asking for an assessment of the impact of either doing or not doing X on the organisation's cash resources.

In practice there may be many possible courses of action available to decision makers, each having different potential cash consequences. Furthermore, the alternatives available will change continually over time. The question then becomes 'How is management to choose from among these many possible alternatives so as to maximise the present value of the expected future cash flows?' If alternatives exist, there must be differences between them, and a first step in decision making is to analyse these differences. We might term this analysis *differential* or *incremental* analysis. Differential analysis involves an assessment of the advantages and disadvantages that might arise from the choice of alternative actions, and as it is necessary to express these advantages and disadvantages in a quantifiable form, we attach cash costs and benefits to them. The option showing the greatest net cash benefit to the firm represents, under the principle of differential analysis, the preferred alternative. (Because of the impact of non-cash factors, it may not always be the alternative which is actually accepted.)

These themes are developed in Chapters 5 and 6, where were consider in detail some general rules for determining the costs and benefits attaching to managerial decisions, and in Chapters 8–12 where we examine some specific types of short- and long-term decisions.

Steps 5, 6, and 7 – decision making and control

Having evaluated alternative courses of action in the light of the organisation's goals, the managers are now in a position to decide which action to take. The final steps in the framework cover the control of the implementation of the decision. A forecast (Step 5) is made of the likely outcome of the decision, usually expressed in the form of a *budget*. The budget is prepared on the basis of the differential costs and revenues associated with the particular course of action which has been adopted, and may incorporate probabilities or ranges of estimates. The difficulties of predicting costs and revenues are examined in Chapter 7. They relate both to the ranking of alternative courses of action and to the preparation of budgets reflecting the decisions taken. The budgets for all decisions undertaken by management are then gathered together into a single unified statement of the organisation's expectations for future periods. This statement is known as the *master budget*. It is a formalised document serving as a written intention of management's plans and is usually drawn up for a period of one year, although it may cover a shorter period (as in an organisation manufacturing and selling fashion goods) or a longer one (as in an organisation building oil tankers). We discuss budgeting in Chapters 13 and 14.

To increase the chances of meeting the budget targets (and therefore reaching the desired goals), and to generate information for subsequent planning, actual performance must be regularly monitored (Steps 6 and 7). The monitoring of performance is known as the firm's *control process*. This process is helped by the use of regular control reports which relate the costs and revenues actually incurred to those expected; they provide *feedback* to help management to decide if any corrective action is required.

The regularity of the issue of the control reports is an important issue. Management will wish to know as speedily as possible if there is a need for corrective action, and therefore the earlier it receives the information, the swifter will be the cure. The regularity of reporting depends primarily upon the position of the manager; for example, top management may see shop floor production reports only at quarterly intervals, whereas factory supervisors, who are much closer to actual operations, may require daily reports of levels and costs of production. We discuss control systems in Chapters 15 and 16.

We conclude this chapter by summarising the objectives we hope to achieve in this book. They are:

1. To provide a framework for the analysis of accounting problems, i.e. problems of identifying information which should be communicated to the users of accounting statements to aid their decision making processes.
2. To use the framework to identify principles which can be applied in order to identify the particular information that should be made available to decision makers.
3. To apply the principles identified to a variety of decision making problems facing business managers, and to suggest methods for solving those problems.
4. To describe accounting procedures used by practising management accountants and to compare them with the procedures implied by our analysis. In many ways, this is the most difficult of our objectives because relatively little is known about the information actually used by managers or about the reasons as to why they prefer one type of information to another.

Discussion topics

1. Explain the role of accounting in the context of the resolution of social problems.
2. Can you think of any decisions with which you have recently been concerned which have involved the use of accounting information? Explain how the accounting information helped (or hindered) your decision process.
3. Distinguish between management accounting and financial accounting. Do you think that the distinction is helpful?
4. Outline the main stages in a managerial planning, decision making and control process, and give a brief description of each stage.
5. Explain what you understand by feedback. Do you think feedback is important to accounting information systems?

Further reading

Arnold, J. and Scapens, R., 'The British contribution to opportunity cost theory', in Bromwich, M. and Hopwood, A. (eds), *Essays in British Accounting Research*, Pitman, 1981.

Chatfield, M., *A History of Accounting Thought*, The Dryden Press, 1974.

Cooper, D., 'A social and organizational view of management accounting', in Bromwich, M. and Hopwood, A. (eds), *Essays in British Accounting Research*, Pitman, 1981.

Ginter, P. M., Rucks, A. C. and Duncan, W. J., 'Planners' perceptions of the strategic management process', *Journal of Management Studies*, November 1985.

Hales, C. P., 'What do managers do? A critical review of the evidence', *Journal of Management Studies*, January 1986.

Hopper, T. and Powell, A., 'Making sense of research into the organizational and social aspects of management accounting: a review of its underlying assumptions', *Journal of Management Studies*, September 1985.

Parker, R. H., 'History of accounting for decisions', in Arnold, J. Carsberg, B. and Scapens, R. (eds), *Topics in Management Accounting*, Philip Allan, 1980.

Solomons, D., 'The historical development of costing', in Solomons, D. (ed.), *Studies in Cost Analysis*, 2nd edn., Sweet & Maxwell, 1968.

Wells, M. C., 'Some influences on the development of cost accounting', *The Accounting Historians Journal*, Fall, 1977.

Chapter 2

Accounting and decision making

In Chapter 1 we defined accounting as 'the process of identifying, measuring, and communicating economic information to permit informed judgements and decisions by users of the information',[4] and we stated that subsequent chapters would examine each of the major issues thrown up by our definition. The aim of this chapter is to introduce briefly the important concepts underlying the definition so as to understand better the problems of accounting as discussed in Part 2. In particular we discuss the nature of *information*, and some procedures for its *communication*; we also consider the meaning and importance of *measurement* and, finally, we focus attention on a general description of *decision making procedures*, with specific reference to some differences between individual and group decision making. Our discussion will deal with these concepts both in a general way, and also in the context of their application to accounting.

2.1 The meaning of information

Information is a fashionable word. We are often said to live 'in a world of information'. One of the most important changes in our environment during the past decade has been the development of information technology, in the form of advances in both computer hardware and software. The widespread use of the computer and in particular the development and introduction of inexpensive and powerful micro-computers has made the gathering and dissemination of information a relatively easy task. We receive information from a variety of different sources – from 'indirect' sources such as television, radio, books, newspapers, and computer printouts, and from more 'direct' sources such as conversation. But what is information? How can we distinguish between information and non-information? How do we know when we are 'informed'?

We need here to draw a distinction between data and information. The two words do not mean the same thing, though they are often used synonymously. The

[4] American Accounting Association, *A Statement of Basic Accounting Theory*, American Accounting Association, 1966; p. 1.

Oxford English Dictionary defines data, the plural of datum, as 'facts of any kind'. We cannot define information in such a broad way. Information has a more particular meaning. It is a subset of data. An item of data is usually classed as information only if it changes the expectations of the person receiving it, or, more specifically, if it changes the probabilities which the receiver attaches to future events or outcomes. For example, suppose that a traveller is told that the 8.12 a.m. train from Manchester to London will leave at 8.12 a.m., and that, before receiving this message, the traveller fully expected the train to leave on time. This statement possesses no information content, as it does not change the traveller's expectations about the train's departure time. If, however, the traveller is told that the 8.12 a.m. train will leave at 9.00 a.m., this is information, as it changes prior expectations of the departure time.

A further distinction is important for decision making. Not all information is *valuable*. If our traveller is about to embark on a train journey from Manchester to Glasgow, information about a change in the departure time of the Manchester–London train is of no value. Although it changes expectations of the departure time of the London train, and is hence 'information', *it does not cause the traveller to change his or her planned course of action*. If, on the other hand, the traveller is intending to catch the 8.12 a.m. train to London, a message that the train's departure time has been delayed may be valuable information as it may result in a change in the planned course of action; for example, the traveller may now choose to visit a public library in the intervening 48 minutes!

The distinction between valuable and valueless information is of crucial importance for accounting; accounting should be concerned primarily with the provision of valuable information, otherwise it will be a rather sterile area for study and research. In view of its importance, let us consider a further example of the distinction. Suppose an accounting student is told that last year's accounting examination included a question on the history of accounting. This statement has some information content, unless, of course, the student already knew last year's questions. But the information may be of little value unless the student believes that the examiner's choice of questions for this year's paper will be influenced by the questions in last year's examination. However, suppose the student is told that this year's examination paper will include a question on the history of accounting. If this statement is from a reliable source, it presumably has information content and, almost certainly, is of value to the student. Why is this? Because it will change what the student does; he or she will now spend more (scarce) time in revising the subject matter of accounting history and less on other topics, in the expectation of being able to answer at least one question reasonably well. The value of the information derives from the fact that it enables the student to allocate a scarce resource, time, more efficiently than before.

2.2 The value of information

Let us explore further this idea of the value of information. If the value of a piece of information is dependent upon its impact on future decisions, it follows that the value is personal to the decision taker, the user of the information. In assessing the value of information, we must consider who is going to use the information, and for what purpose. We shall return to these issues later in this section.

The provision of information is not, generally speaking, free. Information has a cost, and one kind of information may be more costly to provide than another. Thus cost is an important factor in the choice of alternative sources of information. Someone who wishes to inform a friend in the USA that his wife has recently given birth may, if the timing of the message is not critical, prefer to send a letter, rather than send a telegram or make a telephone call, because the cost of sending a letter is cheaper than either alternative.

We can formalise these practical cost considerations in the following way. Suppose we make a particular decision which we regard as optimal on the basis of existing information. Then suppose we are given an extra piece of information, which causes us to revise our previous view of the optimal decision. The difference between the net benefits (or 'value') we expect from the revised decision and the net benefits we would now expect from the original decision, represents the 'value' of the extra information. Information is valuable only if the decision maker's best action with the information is different from his or her best action without the information. This 'value' of the extra information is usually termed its *gross value*, and the difference between the gross value and the cost of providing the information is called the *net value* of the information. We can use the notion of the net value of information to aid two kinds of (important) decisions which involve the production of information:

1. Decisions as to whether a piece of information is worth producing. Production is worthwhile if the net value of the information is positive.
2. Decisions concerning the choice of alternative information production methods. The method with the highest positive net value should be chosen.

Suppose that a land speculator has the opportunity to buy land for possible resale a development site. The cost of the land is £500,000. Its resale value depends upon whether the speculator will be able to obtain planning permission for development. If planning permission is obtained, the resale value of the land will be £800,000; without planning permission it will be worth only £300,000. The speculator believes that there is a 50:50 chance of obtaining planning permission.

The 'expected' value of the land (i.e. the weighted average of its possible values) is 50% of £800,000 plus 50% of £300,000, which equals £550,000. In Chapter 4 we discuss the nature of expected values and their role in decision making. At this stage we assume that the speculator's decision will be based on the expected value of the land. As the expected value of £550,000 is greater than the cost of £500,000, the speculator will purchase the land. The expected surplus is £50,000, comprising a 50% chance of a gain of £300,000 (if planning permission is obtained) and a 50% chance of a loss of £200,000 (if planning permission is refused).

Suppose now that the speculator is able to buy for £80,000 information about whether or not planning permission will be granted and suppose, for simplicity, that the information is certain to be correct. What is the value of the information? If the information says that planning permission will be granted, the resale value of the land will be £800,000 and the speculator will buy it and realise a gain of £300,000. If the information says that planning permission will not be granted, the speculator will not buy the land (as to do so would result in a loss) and will realise neither gain nor loss. As each message is equally likely in this case, the expected value of the possible outcomes (ignoring the cost of the information) is 50% of £300,000 plus 50% of zero, which equals £150,000.[5]

We may now calculate the gross and net value of the information. The *gross value* is the expected value of the speculator's best action *with* the information (£150,000) minus the value of his or her best action *without* the information (£50,000), i.e. £100,000. The *net value* of the information is its gross value (£100,000) minus the cost of obtaining it (£80,000), which equals £20,000. In other words, the information is worth purchasing as the expected surplus is increased from £50,000, without the information, to £70,000 with it.

2.3 Information and accounting

These ideas of information value and cost may well be of general interest and importance, but what is their relevance to accounting? Recall our definition of accounting which we set down at the start of the chapter. This definition suggests that accounting is concerned with the provision of information to aid decisions, i.e. with the provision of valuable information. 'Valuable' information in an accounting sense is that which relates to the decisions taken by users of such information. And these decisions are likely to vary from user to user. Many groups might be interested in information produced by a large industrial organisation such as BP or ICI. In order to illustrate the nature of the information provision problem facing such organisations, consider the following groups of users and some of the possible decisions for which each group requires information:

User group	*Example of decision for which information is required*
Shareholders	Buy, sell or hold shares
Lenders/creditors	Increase, reduce or keep constant levels of credit and loans
Employees	Submit claim for wage increase; change employment
Government	Raise taxation; examine the impact of the firm on the environment
Customers	Buy the firm's products
Managers	Determine the level at which to conduct operations
General public	Assess the economic and 'social' impact of the firm

[5] 50% of £300,000 is the probability that the information will confirm that planning permission will be granted; 50% of zero is the probability that the information will indicate that such permission will *not* be granted.

It is clear that these different users may not always require the same information. For example, information on the number of prosecutions suffered by a firm for failure to meet safety requirements may affect decisions of employees, but is likely to be of less interest to customers. Differing user information needs present a major difficulty for the accountant or other provider of information who may have to attempt to satisfy them in a single report (or at least in a small number of reports).

Whatever the possible conflicting needs of users of accounting information, it remains necessary to devise suitable channels for communicating information from the reporting entity to those who are interested in its performance and prospects. It is to this issue that we now turn.

2.4 The meaning of communication

The process of communication is at the heart of the accounting information system. To make good decisions it is necessary that those who possess valuable information should be able to communicate this information successfully to those who do not have it. Thus there is a need for accountants to study the process of communication. Most communication systems comprise at least five elements, which we denote as Stages A to E in Figure 2.1.[6]

The intention of the system is that the message sent by the sender (Stage A) should influence in an appropriate manner the actions of the receiver (Stage E). This will occur only if the substance of the message which reaches the receiver is the same as that intended by the sender. Because the message must go through intermediary stages B, C and D, there may be problems of '*noise*' (i.e. distortion) within the system which prevent the intention of the sender from being satisfied. Explanation of these intermediary stages may reveal the nature of such problems.

Suppose that the accountant of a limited company is preparing annual information concerning one of the company's divisions for circulation to managers. Thus the sender of the message (Stage A) is the company's accountant, and the receiver (Stage E) is its managers. In order to present the message in a comprehensible language, the accountant uses a form of code (Stage B). For effective communication to take place the nature of this code must be understood and agreed by the receiver. The specialised notation which attaches to the accountant's balance sheet and income statement represents a form of code. For example, words like depreciation, profit, current asset, and indeed balance sheet and income statement themselves, are code words which are intended to convey specific meanings.

Having encoded the message, the sender must ensure that it is transmitted properly to the receiver (Stage C). For example, accounting reports may be transmitted in the form of printed words or numbers, by computer, or verbally by telephone or in 'face-to-face' conversation.

[6] The model in Figure 2.1 is an adaptation of the communication model first suggested by C. E. Shannon and W. Weaver in *The Mathematical Theory of Communication*, University of Illinois Press, 1964.

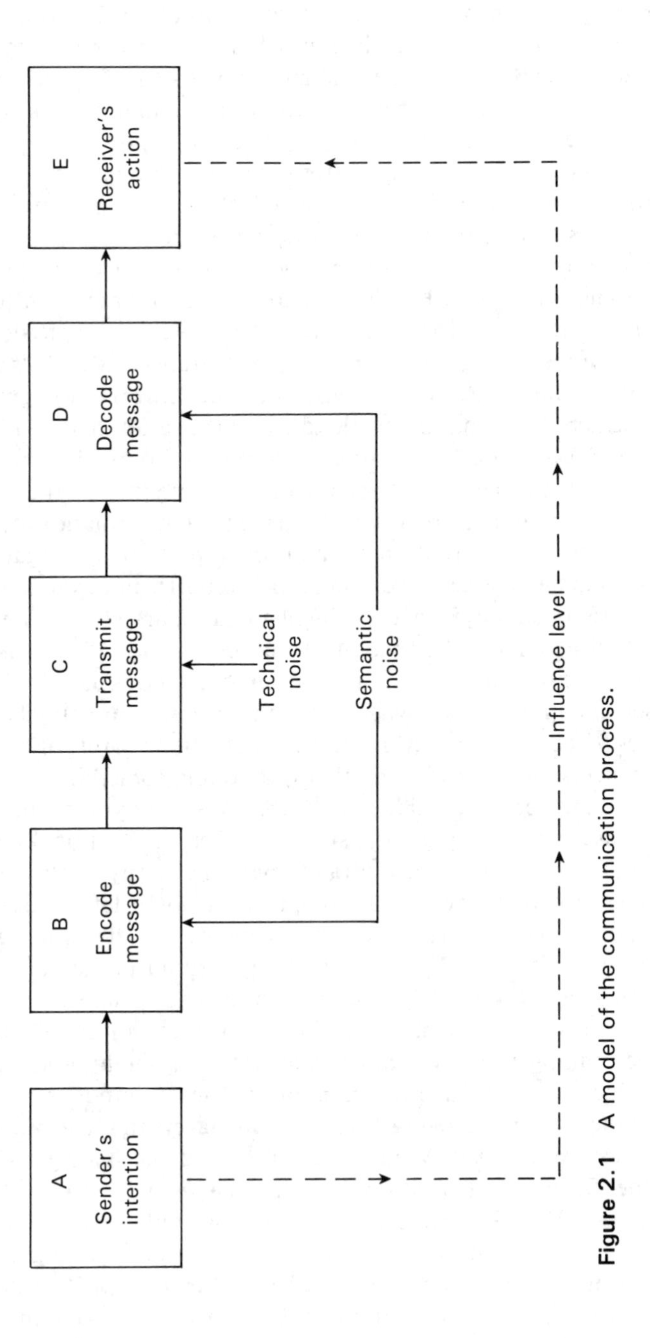

Figure 2.1 A model of the communication process.

Distortions to the intended message (*system noise*) may occur either at the encoding/decoding stage – when they are termed *semantic noise* – or at the transmission stage – when they are termed *technical noise*. Broadly speaking, semantic noise occurs when the receiver attaches a different meaning to a message from that intended by the sender, and technical noise stems from distortions arising from the technical or mechanical functioning of the communication equipment. We now consider some examples of technical and semantic noise.

In the context of telephone systems (the dialling of wrong numbers) or computer systems (flaws in the computer program), technical noise can be a major problem. In accounting systems, this kind of 'mechanical' noise may be slight, and involve such relatively minor problems as correct typing, printing and circulation of balance sheets and income statements. However, there is a further aspect of technical noise that may be more significant for accounting. This relates to the physical *capacity* of the receiver to process all the information being transmitted. This is a common problem in many communication systems. Too much information given in any one message may lead to 'information overload', with the result that the most important aspects of the message are lost, buried in a mass of other information and the ultimate action of the receiver is different from that intended by the sender. It is for this reason that accountants reporting management information often include a separate short summary of the most important aspects of an organisation's or a division's results in a prominent position in their reports. For example, profit, sales, and return on assets employed may be highlighted separately in the report.

Semantic noise arises at the encoding or decoding stage if there is confusion in meaning between sender and receiver in relation to the terms used in the message. In particular, semantic noise arises where different meanings are attached to the same word, or series of words. Semantic noise is common in all forms of communication, not least in conversation. How many times, on doing something for which we are criticised, do we answer 'Oh, I didn't know that was what you meant!'? The extent of semantic noise can be very great, especially when international communication takes place. For example the word 'estate' might mean any of the following to an English speaker: a manor house and grounds, an amount left on death, a housing development, an industrial site, or a type of motor car. Thus a message from a manager to a subordinate to 'buy an estate' might result in the purchase of a large motor car rather than the intended purchase of an industrial site!

Semantic noise presents major problems in accounting. If the sender and receiver of accounting messages cannot concur at the semantic level (the level of meaning), influential and effective communication is impossible. Suppose, for example, that the accountant tells a company's managers that machinery is shown in the balance sheet at £50,000. What meaning should the managers attach to this message? Does it mean that a similar machine would now cost £50,000 (its replacement cost)? Does it mean that the company would receive £50,000 if it sold the machine now (its resale value)? Does it mean that the original cost of the machine less a provision of 'wear and tear' is £50,000 (its written-down historical cost)? Each of these alternative meanings might be used in accounting reports. Each involves a different accounting *measurement*, i.e. at the root of the problem of semantic noise in accounting lies the issue of measurement, which we now consider.

2.5 The issue of measurement

The *Oxford English Dictionary* defines the verb 'to measure' as:

> ascertain extent or quantity of (thing) by comparison with fixed unit or with object of known size.

Two important facets of measurement emerge from the definition. First, measurement is *relative* – it is related to something else whose size is known. Second, measurement is *numerical* – it involves putting numbers on things. Measurement is fundamental to all aspects of society, primitive and modern.

To illustrate the use and importance of measurement in a somewhat different society from our own, consider the case of Robinson Crusoe. In particular consider his situation before the appearance of Man Friday. Robinson Crusoe, stranded on his desert island, is faced with a dilemma. He has to eat, and he has two immediate choices in terms of the provision of his food. He can either spend his time fishing with his bare hands, by which method he can catch two fish per day indefinitely, or he can devote one week to the making of a fishing rod which will allow him to catch three fish per day. During the week set aside for the making of the fishing rod he can catch only one fish per day, which is barely enough to live on. Robinson Crusoe has no means of storing fish, i.e. he has no freezer!

He is faced with a fundamental investment decision (not different in kind from that facing a large company deciding whether to buy a new machine or to recruit more labour). He can either have more fish during the following week (two per day), and the same amount later, or he can have fewer fish for the first week (one per day), but the expectation of three per day thereafter. His choice is between more present consumption and more future consumption. The answer to Robinson Crusoe's dilemma depends largely upon an estimate of the costs and benefits associated with each alternative. In order to choose, Robinson Crusoe must *compare* the alternatives. To compare the alternatives he must use some unit of measurement. Because money is non-existent in his society, he cannot measure in *financial* terms. He may decide to use *fish* as his basis of measurement. We might say that Robinson Crusoe's fishing rod would be 'worth' one extra fish per day for the indefinite future, and that its cost would be one fish per day for the week, which would have to be sacrificed immediately. Robinson Crusoe's decision about whether to make the rod will depend upon his relative preferences for early rather than later consumption of fish.

Accountants do not, of course, usually measure in terms of fish, but they do measure in terms of the medium of exchange demanded by the society in which they operate. Just as fish might be used as an appropriate medium of exchange in Robinson Crusoe's unique society, so modern society demands that money is used as a medium of exchange to compare alternatives. Money is used by accountants to measure costs, values, benefits, profits, and so on. British accountants measure in pounds sterling, French accountants in francs, and Russian accountants in roubles. When organisations trade in many different countries and thus pay for and are paid for goods and services in different currencies, special problems arise when it becomes necessary to translate these foreign currencies into the currencies of the 'home' countries. And yet if the organisation desires to express the results of its world-wide transactions in one common measuring unit, it must ensure that these translations are carried out.

The use of money involves other problems which are not necessarily of an international nature. The greatest problem concerns its stability as a unit of measurement. Stability is an important attribute of all measuring units, whether of distance, weight, liquidity or money. It is essential for architects and builders to know that their measurement of a metre or of a ton is a 'correct' measure. If not, a bridge may collapse or a house fall down. If architects were unsure as to whether their measurement of a metre was correct, they could take their metre rules to the planetarium in Paris and measure them against a metre length of platinum. Accountants do not have such safeguards. Their unit of measurement cannot be viewed independently of what it can buy. A pound sterling (or a franc or a rouble) is only as stable as the prices of the goods it can buy. Thus if prices rise (as happens during a period of inflation) or drop (as during a period of deflation) the purchasing power of the unit of measurement becomes unstable. Because of this instability, it becomes difficult for the accountant to compare assets, liabilities and profits arising in one period with assets, liabilities and profits arising in any other period. Thus adjustments to the accountant's unit of measurement have been advocated as a way of overcoming this basic problem.

But which adjustments? How should the accountant deal with changes in the measuring unit? Should it be adjusted for changes in the general rate of inflation? Or should it be adjusted to reflect only those price changes that are specific to the reporting organisation's assets and liabilities? This is really the essence of the accountant's measurement problem. There is no agreed 'best' basis for measurement in accounting. We shall return to this issue in later chapters.

Thus far we have discussed the need for *stability* of the measuring unit. Other attributes are also of importance. The measuring unit should be *understandable* to users. It should be *cost-effective*, i.e. the benefits from adopting it should be greater than the costs of so doing. It should be *precise*. (But illusory precision should be guarded against. The story of the shepherd and his accountant is salutary. When asked by a shepherd to 'measure' the number of sheep the shepherd owned, the accountant took a swift look and replied immediately '2,007'. 'How did you count them so quickly?' asked the shepherd. 'Well,' said the accountant, 'there are 7 by the river and about 2,000 in the far field'!)

Most important of all, the measurement should be *relevant*. As we have seen when discussing the meaning of information, the object of measurement depends upon the decision to be taken by the user of the information. Thus the basis of measurement should also be relevant to the decision.

In the coming chapters we will consider alternative measurement bases available to the accountant and discuss the extent to which they possess the attributes of measurement bases outlined in this section.

2.6 Theories of decision making

We have now examined briefly the information, communication and measurement issues arising from our adopted definition of accounting. It remains for us to look at the final concept in the definition – the concept of decision making. We will first consider a very general model for decision making and then look at its possible application to decisions taken by individuals and by groups. Throughout we shall stress the contribution of accounting to the model. We differentiate between individual and group decision making because the latter is more complex, primarily as a result of conflicts between individuals in a group and the consequent need for compromise.

Figure 2.2 presents an example of a general model for decision making. A model is a simplified approximation or simulation of real world conditions, constructed from assumed or observed relationships. Accounting models may take the form of verbal expressions, geometric diagrams or, most frequently, mathematical expressions. All of these forms of models may be expressed in computer language, a characteristic of particular importance in the modern world. The model in Figure 2.2 is similar to the first five steps of Figure 1.3 (p. 12). Figure 1.3 related particularly to management accounting whereas Figure 2.2 relates to decision making in general. A model is an abstraction of the real world which, to be of any use, must relate ultimately to how people or things behave, i.e. it must have some descriptive validity. The six stages of our general decision model are as follows.

Stage 1 involves the establishment of the decision maker's objectives or goals; in order to use the model as a route map, the decision maker must know the intended destination. Objectives are expressed in terms of some desired level of performance (e.g. the decision maker may wish to be earning £30,000 per annum by the age of 30). Stage 2 entails a regular review of expected performance. If expected performance is up to or beyond the desired level, the decision maker may either increase the level of aspirations (e.g. raise the desired level of earnings to £40,000 per annum by the age of 30), or continue on the present course to attain the original target. If expected performance is less than desired (i.e. it is unsatisfactory) the decision maker should move to Stage 3, and search for alternative courses of action (e.g. alternative employment) which might offer a better chance of reaching the goal. This search for alternative courses of action involves the need to acquire information concerning future opportunities and future environments. *It is the most difficult stage in the whole process.*

In order to aid choice from among the alternative courses of action which have been sought (and found) the decision maker constructs a model (Stage 4). This model will predict the effects of the various alternatives on the measures represented in the stated objectives under the various environments that might exist. For example, the model might predict the chance of the decision maker earning £40,000 per annum by the age of 30 in different employments and under different possible environmental circumstances.

Before the model is used to select the opportunity, or combination of opportunities, that seems to satisfy best the decision maker's objectives it should be

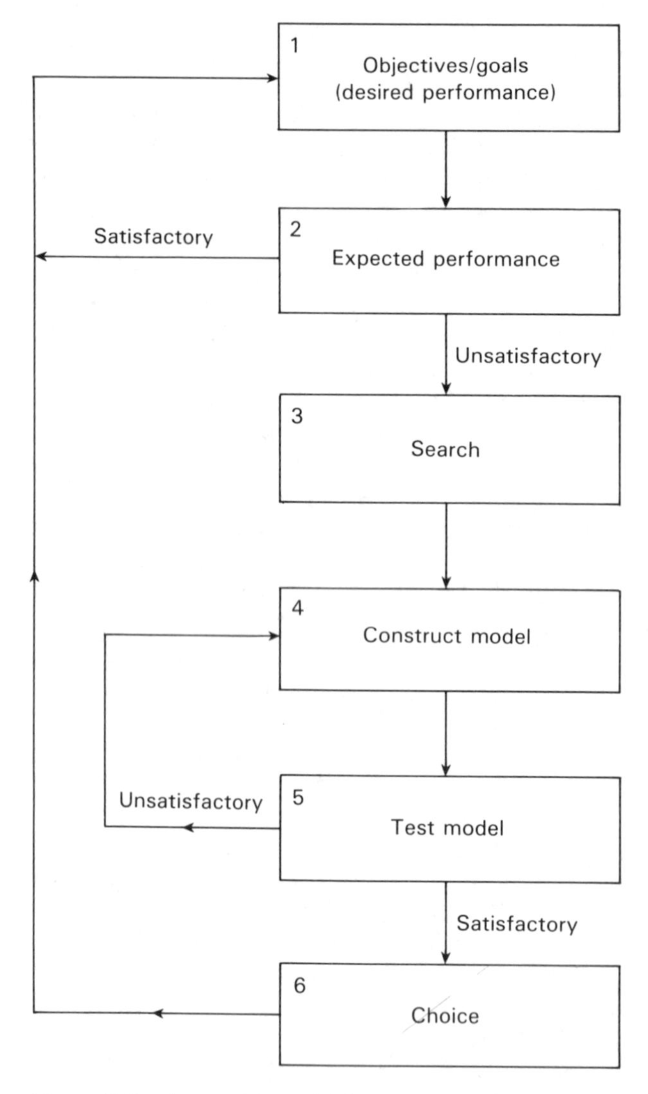

Figure 2.2 A general model for decision making.

critically tested to discover whether it is appropriate for the particular decision maker and whether it predicts efficiently when applied to the decision maker's affairs. The testing of models in the social sciences is very difficult, precisely because such models deal with human behaviour, which is notoriously difficult to predict. If the testing of the model appears satisfactory, the decision maker will be in a position to use the model to choose the course of action which best satisfies the objectives (Stage 6). Information about decision alternatives and future environments is fed into the model and the combination of opportunities is selected which the model reveals to be in best accord with the decision maker's objectives.

The arrowed lines in Figure 2.2, which link various stages of the process, are of particular importance. These are known as 'feedback loops' and they signify that the entire process is continuous and dynamic. In other words, the decision maker should continually review actual performance, expected performance, objectives, available alternatives and the state of the immediate operating environment. A change in any one of these may signal the need for further decisions.

Where does accounting fit into this general model? Accounting is concerned directly with Stages 2, 4 and 6 – where quantitative information is required about performance currently expected and about future alternative courses of action. It is, however, important to understand equally well the other stages in order to appreciate the contribution of accounting information to the whole decision making process.

The following two chapters are concerned essentially with concepts which are fundamental to the general decision model in Figure 2.2. Chapter 3 looks at wealth and wealth maximisation as one possible objective of decision makers and Chapter 4 deals with risk and uncertainty as a necessary component of all decision making.

2.7 Individual decision making

The basic notion implied by the general decision model in Figure 2.2 is that an individual decision maker will consider *all* possible alternative actions and choose the one which best satisfies the objectives. Phrased in the jargon of economics, the model assumes that individuals will choose rationally from among all alternatives so as to maximise their own (i.e. subjective) expected utility or satisfaction. The model is thus sometimes referred to as the '*subjective expected utility*' (SEU) model. The SEU model emphasises the ultimate choice or outcome rather than the process of choosing. Its importance rests on the influence it has exerted on much of the thinking in management science. The model depends for its validity upon four key assumptions about the decision maker's process:

1. Information is available about all possible alternatives.
2. The decision maker has sufficient mental capacity to evaluate all alternatives, including the capacity to make the necessary forecasts about future outcomes.
3. The decision maker will behave consistently in choosing between alternatives (e.g. if alternative A is preferred to alternative B, and alternative B is preferred to alternative C, then alternative A should be preferred to alternative C).
4. The decision maker will always seek to maximise utility or satisfaction.

These are very demanding assumptions. How adequately do they reflect the real situation of decision making? The main problem with the SEU model is its failure to recognise that an individual's rationality may be constrained or 'bounded' by, among other things, environment and education, and particularly by limited mental capacity. Thus the notion of '*bounded rationality*' is often thought to be a more appropriate description of individual decision making.

Bounded rationality implies that individuals have limited mental capacities for making complex choices and therefore adopt simplified decision models which are characterised by:

(i) satisficing, rather than maximising, behaviour;
(ii) a restricted search for alternatives;
(iii) a tendency to 'block out' alternatives which require substantial changes to the existing position;
(iv) the use of 'filters' to reduce the possibility of information overload. (The filter should however ensure that as far as possible 'good' information is not discarded along with 'bad' information.)

As an example of the application of the concepts of bounded rationality, consider the case of an individual who owns and runs a small greengrocery. According to our general decision model, the greengrocer ought *strictly* to be evaluating continuously the possibility of taking over Marks and Spencer or Sainsburys, or of expanding activities to Australia, the United States, and so on. Such diversifications are not impossible, although they may be highly unlikely. Most individuals who run small greengroceries are likely to devote their time to different, and more immediate, problems: which vegetables to purchase, where to find the money to pay next month's rent, and when to replace the delivery van.

There are messages for accountants in the notion of bounded rationality. If accounting is to provide useful information for decision making, as our definition states, it should recognise the constraints under which the users of information actually operate, and provide information accordingly. In particular, accountants should attempt to avoid information overload (which might result, for example, from the generation of piles of computer printout), by filtering out and discarding what they consider to be non-relevant information; they should present information in an easily understandable form; and should be aware of the users' objectives so as to present information in a way that is easily related to such objectives. These are difficult targets for accountants. The provision of relevant information that relates to decision makers' objectives implies that the accountant knows who uses accounting information and why and how they use it. It is by no means obvious that such knowledge currently exists.

2.8 Group decision making

The provision of information to groups of users poses further problems for the accountant. A group may be viewed as a coalition or collection of individuals (e.g. a trades union, a board of directors or a students union). If all individuals within the same group have similar objectives and similar power in decision making, conflicts may not arise in the running of the group, and in this case the general decision model of Figure 2.2 may be applicable to group decision making in much the same way as to individual decision making.

If, as is more likely, conflicts between objectives exist within the group, problems arise over and above those encountered in individual decision making. For example, suppose that two doctors combine in partnership and agree to share profits equally. Prior to the setting up of the partnership, Doctor A has divided the week between work and golf on the basis of four days' work and three days' golf, whereas Doctor B has worked for six days and played golf on one day. The solution to the work/leisure problem will ultimately be a compromise, but the outcome of the compromise is likely to reflect the relative bargaining power of the two partners. The outcome may be an agreed five days' work and two days' leisure, or it may be four or six days' work if one partner can impose his or her will on the other and bring about a change in the other's personal preferences. The conflict might also be resolved by a change in the profit sharing ratio. Imagine this 'conflict situation' transposed to a large industrial organisation whose decision makers (users of accounting information) include such groups as managers, trade unions, shareholders, creditors and customers. If these groups have conflicting objectives, both for themselves and for the organisation, then both decisions and the information needed to make decisions will involve trade-offs which reflect the power of the particular groups.

Finally, we should note that group decision making involves the delegation of decision taking. This in turn may lead to the possibility of suboptimisation within the organisation, meaning that different groups (or individuals) take decisions which maximise their own satisfaction in a way which conflicts with the objectives of the organisation. For example, suppose that a firm makes two products, muesli and honey, and that the objective of the firm is to maximise total cash available from the production and sale of its two products. It may happen that the muesli division undertakes an extensive advertising campaign as a result of which sales of muesli expand and the division's cash surplus increases. However, many of the new consumers of muesli previously ate toast and honey for breakfast and, in consequence of their new-found taste for muesli, their demand for honey declines. The result is that sales of the firm's honey fall and the cash surplus of the honey division decreases, possibly by a larger amount than the increase in the cash surplus of the muesli division. Hence, the muesli division, by maximising *its* cash surpluses, has caused a decrease in the cash surplus of the firm as a whole. It is one role of accounting information, as we explain in Chapter 16, to resolve this kind of suboptimisation problem.

Discussion topics

1. Discuss the differences between 'valuable' and 'valueless' information. Give examples from your own personal experience to illustrate the differences.
2. The problem of 'information overload' is common to many communication systems. Explain the nature of the problem and discuss some possible ways of overcoming it.

3 Give some examples of semantic noise, and explain how incorrect decisions may be taken because of its existence.

4 Why might different users of accounting statements require different information? Can you envisage situations in which different users might require the same information?

5 Discuss the importance of measurement in accounting. Which characteristics of the measuring unit are essential for accounting purposes? Do these characteristics still apply when measurements are used for non-accounting purposes?

6 Discuss the possible impact of inflation on the accountant's measuring unit. What difficulties does this present for the accountant? (Relate your answer to the user needs discussed in Question 4 above).

7 Is 'rationality' a quality which most of us apply to our decision making? If not, why not? Give examples from your own experience.

8 Discuss the essential differences between individual and group decision making. Do these differences have significance for the accountant?

Further reading

Ackoff, R. L., 'Management misinformation systems', *Management Science*, December 1967.

Anton, H., 'Some aspects of measurement and accounting', *Journal of Accounting Research*, Spring 1964.

Bird, P. A., 'Standard accounting practice', in Edey, H. C. and Yamey, B. S. (eds), *Debits, Credits, Finance and Profits*, Sweet & Maxwell, 1974.

Cooper, D., 'Models for personal choice', in Arnold, J., Carsberg, B. and Scapens, R. (eds), *Topics in Management Accounting*, Philip Allan, 1980.

Cyert, R. M. and March, J. G., *A Behavioral Theory of the Firm*, Prentice Hall, 1963.

Demski, J. S., *Information Analysis*, 2nd edn, Addison Wesley, 1980.

Feltham, G. A., 'The value of information', *The Accounting Review*, October 1968.

Mace, J. R., 'Value of information', in Arnold, J., Carsberg, B. and Scapens, R. (eds), *Topics in Management Accounting*, Philip Allan, 1980.

March, J. G., 'Ambiguity and accounting: the elusive link between information and decision making', *Accounting, Organizations and Society*, Vol. 12, No. 2, 1987.

Mock, T. J., 'Concepts of information value and accounting', *The Accounting Review*, October 1971.

Ryan, R. J., 'Scientific method', in Arnold, J., Carsberg, B. and Scapens, R. (eds), *Topics in Management Accounting*, Philip Allan, 1980.

Simon, H. A., *The New Science of Management Decision*, Harper & Row, 1960.

Sterling, R. R., 'On theory construction and verification', *The Accounting Review*, July 1970.

Chapter 3

Wealth and wealth maximisation in decision making

In Chapter 2 we discussed a general model for decision making and control. We now turn to the problem of applying the decision model and to a consideration of its implications for accounting. In particular, we consider the meaning of 'wealth' and the important role it plays in the decision making process. We also discuss the need to take account of the time value of money and the role of discounted present values in the measurement of wealth. We conclude this chapter with a discussion of the importance and treatment of non-financial data in decision making. In an appendix to this chapter we explain the use and relevance of compound interest tables.

3.1 The meaning and importance of wealth and wealth maximisation

In general, all individuals are concerned with planning their lives in order to achieve the pattern of 'consumption' over time which gives them the most satisfaction. We use 'consumption' here, and indeed throughout the book, in its normal economic sense, i.e. to include all goods, services and other 'experiences' that provide satisfaction to the recipient. The above statement of individuals' objectives is self-evident – in order to apply it to a decision making process we must identify and measure those elements of an individual's life which provide satisfaction, and develop a means of comparing the relative importance of the various elements. It is perhaps helpful to start with a simplified version of the general decision model introduced in the previous chapter. The main steps in the model are:

(i) set objectives;
(ii) enumerate available alternatives;
(iii) choose alternatives that best satisfy objectives.

The role of accounting is to provide information that clarifies the available alternatives and helps to quantify their effects on objectives. Thus, in order to do their job properly, accountants should be aware of the existence and consequences of available courses of action and of the objectives of the individual, or group of individuals, for whom they are providing accounting information.

In the previous chapter we considered various groups of users of accounting reports, and the sort of decisions for which they might require information. In order to illustrate the diverse nature of the information that may be needed by just one individual to achieve the preferred pattern of consumption over time, we consider the case of a college student making plans for the coming year. For simplicity, we restrict the time horizon to one year. The information required by the student depends upon his or her objectives and on the entities which will affect his or her life during the coming year. Some possible entities, and the sort of information that might be required from them, are shown in Table 3.1 below. The list is by no means exhaustive, and will vary from student to student. However, it serves to demonstrate that every individual is likely to require a variety of information from a large number of different sources. Table 3.1 also draws attention to two further points. The first is that, as we are considering only a one year decision horizon, the information required relates to the coming year. For example, the student is interested in returns from investments (if any!) and grant income next year, the prices of books, food, clothes, alcohol, etc. next year, train and bus timetables for next year, and so on. As we shall see later in the book, published (accounting) information about an entity generally relates to past periods (for example as regards

Table 3.1 Information a student might require for decision making

Entities affecting student	*Information required*
Government	Levels of grant available
Local authority	Levels of grant available
College	Scholarships available
Parents	Financial support available
Companies, etc. in which student has invested/may invest	Returns on investment
Bank	Overdraft and loan facilities available
College	Course details
	Tuition fees
	Costs of residence, meals, etc.
Electricity and gas corporation	Lighting and heating costs
Oil companies	Petrol prices
Post Office	Telephone and postage charges
Local bookshop	Prices of academic books
Supermarkets	Food prices
Department stores	Clothes prices
Railway and bus corporations	Train and bus fares
	Train and bus timetables
Local hostelries	Drink prices
	Types of drink available
Local sports stadia	Admission prices
	Fixture lists
Local theatres and concert halls	Programme of future events
	Admission prices

returns on investment) or to the present (as, for example, with commodity prices). Thus it is often necessary for an individual decision maker to make predictions from information available about the past and the present. This is one of the fundamental problems involved in using and evaluating accounting information, and one to which we shall return.

The second point highlighted by Table 3.1 is that the information required is not exclusively financial. For example, in order to plan for the coming year, the student requires course details from the college, train and bus timetables, concert programmes, and so on. We consider the importance of non-financial information further at the end of this chapter. Although non-financial factors have an impact on an individual's decisions, it is often the case that the goods and services of which consumption consists are available only in return for the payment of a cash price. Consequently, while acknowledging the importance of non-financial factors, we shall initially consider the concept of wealth in terms of expected costs and benefits expressed in cash terms.

Individuals are faced with three basic financial decisions:

1. The *investment* decision. How much of the individual's resources should be committed to investment, that is, sacrificed immediately in return for the expectation of increased resources being available at some time in the future? Which particular opportunities should be undertaken with the amounts available for investment?
2. The *financing* decision. How much finance should individuals raise to enable them to undertake their investment and consumption policies? From what sources should this finance be obtained?
3. The *consumption* decision. How much of the individual's resources should be spent on immediate consumption? On what should the resources be spent?

The same three decisions also face firms of all sizes, except that the consumption decision becomes a distribution decision, i.e. how much should be distributed to the firm's owners by way of dividend or otherwise? The three decisions are interdependent. The amount committed to investment will depend upon the return available on investment opportunities and also on the cost and availability of finance and the individual's personal consumption preferences. The financing decision will depend upon the cost of finance and upon available investment opportunities and desired patterns of consumption. The consumption decision will depend upon consumption preferences and on available investment and financing opportunities.

Let us consider again the case of a college student. Suppose the student expects to receive in the coming year a local authority grant of £4,000 plus an amount to cover college course fees, a parental gift of £1,600 and a college scholarship of £400. These amounts, totalling £6,000, represent part of the finance available to be spent. Suppose also that the student estimates costs of £4,800 during the year for essential residence, food, travel, clothes and books. This sum represents part of the amount that will be spent on consumption. Thus after paying essential costs, the student expects to have a cash surplus of £1,200. He or she must decide how much of it to spend on consumption, i.e. on goods, services and so on that will not provide benefits in future years, and how much to invest. For example, the student may decide to spend £1,000 during the year on alcohol and on tickets for pop concerts and on clothes (i.e. on additional consumption) and to invest £200 in a bank deposit account providing an amount of £200 plus interest in *future* years. In deciding how much to consume and how much to invest, the student will have to weigh the benefits from immediate consumption against the benefits from investment which provides funds for future consumption. This is partly a matter of personal preference and will be influenced by many factors including the pleasure derived from early rather than delayed consumption, the returns available on investment, and the funds the student expects to have available from other sources in future years. The decisions in respect of the coming year are, in fact, more complicated than we have so far implied. Many students may decide to increase current consumption or investment by borrowing additional funds, for example from the bank or from their parents. This is part of their financing decision.

What sort of information is necessary for decision makers to decide which set of alternatives (investment, financing and consumption) provides most satisfaction or, in other words, which set of alternatives maximises their wealth? It is apparent from the above discussion that when we talk of wealth as a measure of the current value of future satisfaction we do not mean only the cash resources and other possessions of an individual at the present time. Consider an example. Who is the better off – an accounting student with little immediate cash and the prospect of very high earnings in the future or an unskilled worker with some immediate cash resources and little prospect of ever earning much more than basic living expenses? If we consider only the current cash resources of the student and the unskilled worker, we ignore the future cash and other prospects of both, which undoubtedly contribute to the satisfaction they will obtain throughout their respective lives. Thus in order to measure wealth we need to consider both current resources and future prospects. The importance of such a measure of wealth, which incorporates present position and future prospects, is that it may be used as a criterion in evaluating alternative courses of action – a course of action which increases wealth is worthwhile, one which decreases wealth is not. The measurement of wealth in this sense is not easy, however, even if we restrict our consideration to the cash consequences of alternatives. The basic problem is that we cannot simply add cash expected at different times in the future in order to obtain a measure of present wealth. Few of us would be indifferent between the receipt of £1,000 now and the (certain) receipt of £1,000 five years from now. Such differences between the desirability of £1 at different times in the future give rise to the concept of the time value of money, to which we now turn.

3.2 The time value of money

In the previous section we suggested that £1 now is worth more than £1 at some time in the future. Why is this so? The time value of money is the result of the existence of investment, lending and borrowing opportunities, of the preference that many individuals have for immediate rather than future consumption, and of expected inflation. These factors mean that those who wish to have cash for consumption sooner rather than later incur a cost (pay a price) in so doing, and that those who are willing to defer having cash available for consumption enjoy a benefit (receive a price). The prices paid or received are normally expressed in terms of interest rates which represent the costs or benefits of transferring money from one period to another, in much the same way as costs or benefits arise when other resources are acquired or disposed of.

In practice, a spectrum of interest rates exists at any time in the capital market (i.e. the market in which funds are borrowed and loaned). Rates of interest vary from borrower to borrower and from lender to lender, depending upon the amounts involved, the status of the individual or entity concerned, and so on. In order to simplify our discussion of the role of interest rates in the measurement of wealth we make two rather unrealistic assumptions at this stage. (Some of the implications of relaxing these assumptions are discussed in Chapter 11.) First, we assume that there are perfect markets for borrowing and lending funds, i.e. perfect capital markets. Three conditions must be satisfied if this assumption is to hold:

1. No lenders or borrowers are large enough for their transactions to affect the ruling market price for funds (the interest rate).
2. All traders in the market have equal and costless access to information about the ruling price and all other relevant information.
3. There are no transactions costs involved in using the market and no taxes that would alter economic decisions.

Second, we assume that the future is known with certainty. If these two assumptions hold, there will be a unique market rate of interest, which we shall call i, at which all users of the capital market are able to borrow or lend as much as they wish. Under the conditions assumed, competitive forces are likely to eliminate opportunities to lend or borrow at any interest rate other than i. The assumption of a unique market rate of interest leads to a useful simplification in the measurement of wealth: cash flows which arise at different points in time may be compared without the ambiguities which might arise if a number of different possible interest rates existed.

Given the unique market rate of interest, i, an individual presently in possession of £C could lend it to yield £$C(1 + i)$ after one year, i.e. the return of capital, £C, plus interest £$C \times i$. (In these expressions and all relevant subsequent ones in this chapter, i should be interpreted as the rate of interest expressed as a decimal of 1. Thus, for example, an interest rate of 6% would be written as 0.06 and one of 20% as 0.20.) If capital and interest are lent for a further year the total returns at the end of the second year will be £$C(1 + i)(1 + i)$, which equals £$C(1 + i)^2$. In general, if an amount £C is invested for n years at an annual compound rate of interest, i, the amount to which it will have accumulated after n years will be £$C(1 + i)^n$. (The word 'compound' indicates that once the interest for a period has been earned, that interest itself earns interest during subsequent periods. Nowadays this practice is virtually universal in lending and borrowing.) This process is known as *compounding*, and enables us to re-express present values in terms of equivalent future values. A rational individual should be indifferent between £$C(1 + i)^n$ after n years and £C immediately, because possession of the latter could be converted to the former by lending at the market rate of interest.

For purposes of measuring present wealth we are interested not so much in re-expressing present values in terms of equivalent future values as in the opposite process of re-expressing expected future cash flows in terms of equivalent present values. This process is known as *discounting*, and provides us with a common basis for measuring wealth, in terms of (discounted) present values.

Suppose an individual expects to receive £C after one year. What is the present value (PV) of the expected receipt? Let us think of PV as the immediate amount the investor would have to lend in order to accumulate £C after one year. Then:

$$\text{PV}(1 + i) = £C, \text{ and}$$

$$\text{PV} = \frac{£C}{(1 + i)} \text{ (sometimes written as } £C(1 + i)^{-1}\text{)}$$

By similar reasoning, it may be shown that the present value of £C receivable or payable after two years is £$C/(1 + i)^2$ and, in the general case, that the present value of £C receivable or payable after n years is £$C/(1 + i)^n$. A rational investor should be indifferent between any expected future amount and its present value. For example, in the general case, an individual expecting to receive £C after n years could convert it to £$C/(1 + i)^n$ immediately by borrowing, and an individual with £$C/(1 + i)^n$ could convert it to £C after n years by lending.

The equivalence between an expected cash receipt or payment and its discounted present value enables us to measure the impact of a future cash flow on an individual's or firm's present wealth. It also provides us with a means of calculating the total wealth of an individual or firm, provided we can estimate the amount and timing of all relevant future cash flows; the process is to estimate the future cash flows, discount them to present values and sum the present values. Although we have assumed the existence of a unique interest rate for discounting purposes, the procedure described is often valid in an environment where multiple interest rates exist. Of course, such environments create the additional problem of selecting a discount rate or rates which reflect the individual's or firm's particular borrowing and lending opportunities and the risk associated with expected cash flows. We discuss these problems briefly later, for example in the next chapter, although a detailed consideration of them is beyond the scope of an introductory text.

Let us suppose, as an illustration, that an individual expects to receive net cash inflows (i.e. cash receipts from salary, investment, etc. less essential living expenses) of £3,000 immediately, £5,000 after one year, £7,000 after two years, £8,000 after three years and zero per annum (p.a.) thereafter. In this context, essential living expenses may be regarded as equivalent to the operating expenses of a business. They may be thought of roughly as the expenses of maintaining an 'acceptable' living standard and, in consequence, may vary depending upon the individual's place of work and residence. The relevant interest rate, i, is 10% (0.10) p.a.

Assuming that the individual expects no other cash flows and has no other resources, what is his or her present wealth? Following the process described above, we may calculate the individual's wealth as the discounted present value (PV) of the expected net cash inflows:

$$PV = 3{,}000 + \frac{5{,}000}{(1+i)} + \frac{7{,}000}{(1+i)^2} + \frac{8{,}000}{(1+i)^3}$$

$$PV = 3{,}000 + \frac{5{,}000}{(1.1)} + \frac{7{,}000}{(1.1)^2} + \frac{8{,}000}{(1.1)^3} = £19{,}341$$

The individual's present wealth is £19,341.

This concept of wealth is extremely important in decision making; it provides a cornerstone for the decisions of individuals and firms who wish to measure the impact of alternative courses of action on their wealth. In the next section we consider the role of wealth in the evaluation of alternative courses of action.

3.3 The role of present values

So far in this chapter we have discussed the role and importance of wealth measurement primarily as it relates to individuals. It is important to recognise that the discounted present value concept discussed is equally applicable to other economic units, for example businesses or machines. When we apply the concept to such other economic units we do not generally talk about their wealth, but rather about their value and, in particular, about their 'economic value'.

Take the case of a firm which expects to receive, and distribute to its owners, net cash inflows (i.e. cash receipts from sales, etc. less operating costs) of £50,000 after one year, £65,000 after two years and £100,000 after three years, and nothing thereafter. The relevant interest rate, i, is 15% (0.15) p.a. What is the present economic value (EV) of the firm? Calculating the discounted present value of expected net cash inflows and summing gives:

$$EV = \frac{50{,}000}{(1+i)} + \frac{65{,}000}{(1+i)^2} + \frac{100{,}000}{(1+i)^3}$$

$$EV = \frac{50{,}000}{(1.15)} + \frac{65{,}000}{(1.15)^2} + \frac{100{,}000}{(1.15)^3} = £158{,}379$$

The present economic value of the firm is £158,379.

Let us now consider the role of discounted present values in evaluating new opportunities. Suppose that the firm in the above illustration is offered the opportunity of investing in a new project. The investment cost would be £10,000, payable after one year, and the project would produce additional net cash inflows of £8,000 after two years and £9,000 after three years. If the firm's owners wish to increase their wealth, the new opportunity should be accepted if it increases the firm's present economic value. The new value (EV′) would be:

$$\text{EV}' = \frac{(50{,}000 - 10{,}000)}{(1.15)} + \frac{(65{,}000 + 8{,}000)}{(1.15)^2} + \frac{(100{,}000 + 9{,}000)}{(1.15)^3} = £161{,}650$$

The new project appears worthwhile – its acceptance would increase the present economic value of the firm by £3,271 (£161,650 – £158,379). This increase in the discounted present value of the firm's future cash flows is called the *net present value* (NPV) of the project, and may be calculated more directly by discounting the cash flows of the new opportunity:

$$\text{NPV} = -\frac{10{,}000}{(1.15)} + \frac{8{,}000}{(1.15)^2} + \frac{9{,}000}{(1.15)^3} = +£3{,}271$$

A positive net present value implies that acceptance of the project being considered will increase the firm's value (by the amount of the net present value). A negative net present value implies a decrease in the firm's value, and a zero net present value implies no change in the firm's value. Thus net present value provides a useful decision rule for firms whose owners wish to increase the firm's economic value: new investment opportunities should be accepted if their net present values are positive and rejected if they are negative. The firm should be indifferent between acceptance and rejection of projects with zero net present values. This is a most important decision rule which is developed further in Chapter 11.

The meaning and interpretation of net present value may be further clarified in simple cases by regarding it as an additional amount which could be made available for immediate distribution (or consumption) if the opportunity was accepted. In the case of the illustration above, suppose that the firm decides to accept the project and distribute its net present value immediately. As the firm has no cash on hand it decides to borrow the amount required (£3,271) from its bank at 15% p.a. interest, the rate of interest assumed to be relevant. It also decides to borrow the amount needed to invest in the project, in order not to disturb existing distributions to its owners. Table 3.2 shows the firm's loan account with the bank. The investment opportunity provides just sufficient cash to repay the two loans with interest. In other words, the interest adjustment incorporated in the discounting process takes exact account of the actual money interest cost involved.

For interested readers we now provide a symbolic representation of the measures used so far in this chapter for calculating economic value (wealth) and net present value. Economic value, or wealth, may be described by the expression:

$$\text{EV}_0 = \frac{C_1}{(1+i)} + \frac{C_2}{(1+i)^2} + \frac{C_3}{(1+i)^3} + \cdots + \frac{C_n}{(1+i)^n}$$

where: EV_0 is the economic value at time 0 (i.e. the present time),
C_1 is the net cash inflow expected at time 1 (i.e. after one year),
C_2 is the net cash inflow expected at time 2, and so on,
n is the last time at which a cash flow is expected to arise,
i is the appropriate interest rate.

Table 3.2 Firm's loan account with the bank

	£
Immediately: Borrow project NPV for distribution to owners	3,271
After one year: Interest at 15%	491
: Borrow for investment in project	10,000
Loan outstanding at the end of one year	13,762
After two years: interest at 15%	2,064
	15,826
: Use first cash inflow from project to repay part of loan	8,000
Loan outstanding at the end of two years	7,826
After three years: Interest at 15%	1,174
	9,000
: Use second cash inflow from project to repay balance of loan	9,000
Loan outstanding at the end of three years	0

This expression may be more conveniently written:[7]

$$\mathrm{EV}_0 = \sum_{j=1}^{n} \frac{C_j}{(1+i)^j}$$

The net present value (NPV) of a project may be described by:

$$\mathrm{NPV} = \sum_{j=0}^{n} \frac{F_j}{(1+i)^j}$$

where: F_j is the net cash inflow expected at time j,[8]
n is the last time at which a cash flow is expected from the project,
i is the appropriate interest rate.

3.4 The importance of non-financial data

So far in this chapter we have concentrated on the application of financial data to the measurement of wealth. We now turn to a brief consideration of the importance

[7] The Greek letter Σ (sigma) is convenient mathematical shorthand, meaning the sum of all values in a particular series. By introducing lower and upper limits (written below and above Σ) we may define the summation of a particular series between certain limits. So:

$$\sum_{i=1}^{i=n} x_i \left(\text{or} \sum_{i=1}^{n} x_i\right) = x_1 + x_2 + x_3 + \cdots + x_n$$

[8] Usually, the first cash flow (at least) associated with a project will be negative, i.e. the investment cost. The introduction of negative signs before some of the F_j values does not affect the validity or application of the NPV expression.

of non-financial data. Although accounting reports are traditionally concerned with financial data, the wealth of those who use the reports, and in consequence their decisions, may also be influenced by factors which are generally not expressed in money terms, i.e. by non-financial factors. Indeed for some decisions, particularly in the public sector, concerned for example with health and education services, non-financial factors may be much more important than financial ones. We discuss first some decisions which may be affected by non-financial factors, and then consider the extent to which accountants might help in the provision of information about such factors.

In Chapter 2 we considered a variety of users of accounting reports. Such users may use non-financial as well as financial information in their decision processes. Investors in quoted companies, for example, make decisions about buying, holding and selling shares and about the extent to which they should intervene in the management of companies in which they hold shares. In addition to financial factors, non-financial information may be of interest to them. Their decisions may be influenced by the prestige of a company and by the investors' political and moral beliefs (for example, some investors may not wish to hold shares in tobacco companies). They will require information about such aspects of the company, and about the extent to which their actions as shareholders might affect the company's behaviour.

The employees of an organisation may also require non-financial information in making decisions about whether to stay with their present employers or change jobs, and in negotiating wage and salary claims. Like shareholders, they may be conscious of the prestige differences between organisations (some journalists, for example, may prefer to work for a national rather than a local newspaper) and about their different political and moral behaviour. They may also be interested in conditions of work (health and safety regulations, the length of the working week, holiday entitlements, and so on) and in job satisfaction (most university teachers, for example, probably regard this as a major attraction of their employment).

Government is also likely to require non-financial information from organisations. For example, if it wishes to formulate legislation designed to protect the environment, government will require information from public and private sector organisations about the extent of pollution and other factors harmful to the environment, caused by the organisation's activities. A company's potential customers will be interested, amongst other things, in the quality of the company's products. A student, in deciding which courses to take, will require information about staff–student ratios and the quality of staff in different departments, and about the interest level of different courses.

The above examples illustrate the sort of non-financial information that might be required from organisations by those who have dealings with them. It is apparent that such information will often have a significant impact on the eventual decision. The questions we now need to ask are: 'should accountants attempt to provide this sort of information?' and 'are they in a position to provide it?'

As we noted earlier, the role of the accountant is traditionally restricted to the provision of financial information. However, if decisions are to be taken in the light of the maximum possible relevant information, someone ought to be providing information about non-financial factors and accountants would seem to have as strong a claim to this role as has any other group. (Whether accountants would welcome this additional burden is another question!) As accountants are already responsible for providing a substantial part of the information required for decisions, i.e. the financial part, there would seem to be some sense in their providing at least some of the remaining information.

Accountants also appear to be in a good position to provide non-financial information. In some cases it may be possible and helpful to assign financial values to items which, at first sight, appear non-financial. For example, various studies evaluating the worthwhileness of constructing the Victoria Line on the London Underground system included attempts to put financial values on the time that would be saved by commuters and others if the line was built.[9] Even if financial values cannot be imputed, it will often be possible for wealth measurement and decision making to adopt a different unit of measurement, for example the number of students to each member of staff in a college department, the number of hours in a working week at a particular organisation, or the quantity of chemicals introduced into a river by a particular production process. If accountants are to assume some responsibility for the provision of non-financial information, their eventual aim should probably be to use financial measurements wherever reasonable and feasible, and to quantify other factors using the most appropriate available unit of measurement. In this way, those responsible for making decisions will have available to them the maximum possible amount of quantitative data. They must then use their own judgement to weigh financial and non-financial factors in arriving at a final decision.

In the remainder of this book we recognise the traditional role of the accountant as being primarily a provider of financial information. Nevertheless, where non-financial items arise in subsequent examples and discussions, we attempt to suggest ways in which they might be handled.

[9] See, for example, Foster, C. D. and Beesley, M. E., 'The Victoria Line: social benefit and finances', *Journal of the Royal Statistical Society*, Series A, **128**, (1), 1965; and 'Estimating the social benefit of constructing an underground railway in London', *Journal of the Royal Statistical Society*, Series A, **126** (1), 1963.

Chapter 3 Appendix

Use of compound interest tables

Earlier in this chapter we introduced the ideas of compounding and discounting, particularly for purposes of calculating economic values and net present values. Such compound interest methods are now widely used in accounting and will be referred to again in the remainder of this book. In practice, the calculations involved may be quite complex and for this reason they are often undertaken by use of a computer. Where a more simple calculator is used special tables, known as compound interest tables, are available to facilitate the calculations. The purpose of this appendix is to explain and illustrate the use of compound interest tables, and to deal with a number of other problems frequently encountered when discounting or compounding calculations are undertaken.

A full set of compound interest tables is provided at the end of the book (pp. 385–406). Each table is based on a different interest rate. For simplicity, we will use only one interest rate, 8%, in this appendix. Each table consists of seven columns. The first column (headed n) relates to the number of years involved in the calculation to be performed. The remaining six columns give either compounded or discounted values, under various circumstances, for a basic unit of £1 or £1 per annum (or for basic units of 1 dollar, 1 franc, 1 yen, 1 mark, etc.). We now provide an explanation of each of these six columns. Throughout the appendix i means the annual compound interest rate and n means the relevant time period.

The meaning of each column in compound interest tables

$(1 + i)^n$

In words, each figure in this column represents the amount to which £1 invested now at a compound rate of interest i, will accumulate *after n years*. We use annual periods for ease of exposition. Periods of other lengths may be used, provided that the interest rate is expressed as a rate per the appropriate period. This is the column to be used to compound the value of a single sum.

Illustration: An individual invests £100 in a bank deposit account at a compound interest rate of 8% p.a. To what amount will the £100 have grown by the end of seven years?

Terminal value $= 100(1 + i)^7 = 100(1.08)^7$

From the table, $(1 + i)^n = 1.7138$ for $n = 7$ and $i = 8\%$

Terminal value $= 100(1.7138) = £171.38$

Now suppose that the £100 is invested in a bank deposit account at a compound interest rate of 3% per *quarter*. To what amount will the £100 have grown by the end of three years (i.e. by the end of 12 quarters)?

Terminal value $= 100(1 + i)^{12} = 100(1.03)^{12}$

From the table, $(1 + i)^n = 1.4258$ for $n = 12$ and $i = 3\%$

Terminal value $= 100(1.4258) = £142.58$

$V_{\overline{n}|}$ (pronounced 'V angle n')

In words, each figure in this column represents the value *now* (the present value) of £1 expected in n years' time, at a compound rate of interest i. Each value given is the reciprocal of the equivalent figure in the $(1 + i)^n$ column, i.e. each figure is calculated from the expression $1/(1 + i)^n$. This column should be used to discount the value of a single sum.

Illustration: An individual expects to receive £700 after five years. What is the present value of the expected receipt, assuming an annual compound interest rate of 8%?

$$\text{Present value} = \frac{700}{(1 + i)^5} = \frac{700}{(1.08)^5}$$

$$\text{From the table, } \frac{1}{(1 + i)^n} = V_{\overline{n}|}\, i = 0.680583 \text{ for } n = 5 \text{ and } i = 8\%$$

Present value $= 700(0.680583) = £476.41$

In other words, £476.41 now should grow to £700 after five years. We may check this answer by using the previous column:

$476.41(1.08)^5 = 476.41(1.4693) = £700$

$S_{\overline{n}|}$ (pronounced 'S angle n')

In words, each figure in this column represents the value *at the end of n years* of £1 p.a. payable or receivable for n years. The first payment or receipt arises at the *end* of year 1 and the last one at the end of year n. A series of annual receipts or payments of identical amount is known as an annuity. Thus this column is used to find the future or terminal value of an annuity. Each value given is based on the expression:

$$S_{\overline{n}|} = \left(\frac{(1 + i)^n - 1}{i}\right)$$

This expression is the summation of the geometric progression:

$$1 + (1 + i) + (1 + i)^2 + \cdots + (1 + i)^{n-1}$$

where the first term (1) is the terminal value of the last receipt or payment (of £1), the second term $(1 + i)$ is the terminal value of the penultimate receipt or payment (of £1) and so on.

Illustration: An individual intends to invest £50 in a bank deposit account at the end of each of the next seven years. What amount will be accumulated in the deposit account at the end of year 7, assuming an annual compound rate of interest of 8%?

$$\text{Terminal value} = 50(1 + i)^6 + 50(1 + i)^5 + \cdots + 50(1 + i) + 50$$

$$= 50\left[(1 + i)^6 + (1 + i)^5 + \cdots + (1 + i) + 1\right]$$

$$\text{From the table, } \left[1 + (1 + i) + \cdots + (1 + i)^{n-2} + (1 + i)^{n-1}\right]$$

$$= S_{\overline{n}|}\,i = 8.9228 \text{ for } n = 7 \text{ and } i = 8\%$$

$$\text{Terminal value} = 50(8.9228) = £446.14$$

$S_{\overline{n}|}^{-1}$ (pronounced '*S* angle *n* minus 1')

In words, each figure in this column represents the annual sum that it is necessary to invest at the end of each of the next *n* years in order to accumulate £1 *at the end of year n*. Each value given is the reciprocal of the equivalent figure in the $S_{\overline{n}|}$ column i.e. each figure is calculated from the expression $1/S_{\overline{n}|}$. This column should be used to convert a single future sum into an annuity.

Illustration: An individual wishes to accumulate £5,000 in four years from now in order to purchase a motor car. How much is it necessary to invest at the end of each of the next four years, assuming an annual compound rate of interest of 8%?

If we call the annual amount to be invested *a*, then:

$$5{,}000 = a(1 + i)^3 + a(1 + i)^2 + a(1 + i) + a$$

$$5{,}000 = a\left[(1 + i)^3 + (1 + i)^2 + (1 + i) + 1\right]$$

$$a = 5{,}000\left[\frac{1}{(1 + i)^3 + (1 + i)^2 + (1 + i) + 1}\right]$$

$$= 5{,}000\left[\frac{1}{S_{\overline{n}|}\,i}\right]$$

$$\text{From the table, } 1/S_{\overline{n}|}\,i = S_{\overline{n}|}^{-1}i = 0.221921 \text{ for } n = 4 \text{ and } i = 8\%$$

$$\text{Annual amount} = 5{,}000(0.221921) = £1{,}109.60$$

Obviously, the same answer could be obtained by dividing the required terminal amount by the relevant factor in the $S_{\overline{n}|}$ column:

$$\text{Annual amount} = \frac{5{,}000}{S_{\overline{n}|}\,8\%} = \frac{5{,}000}{4.5061} = £1{,}109.60$$

The sort of calculation involved in this illustration is usually called a 'sinking fund' calculation.

$A_{\overline{n|}}$ (pronounced '*A* angle *n*')
In words, each figure in this column represents the value *now* (the present value) of £1 p.a., payable or receivable for n years. The first payment or receipt arises at the *end* of year 1 and the last one at the end of year n. This column is used to find the present value of an annuity. Each value given is based on the expression

$$A_{\overline{n|}} = \left(\frac{1 - \dfrac{1}{(1+i)^n}}{i}\right)$$

This expression is the summation of the geometric progression:

$$\frac{1}{(1+i)} + \frac{1}{(1+i)^2} + \cdots + \frac{1}{(1+i)^n}$$

where the first term is the present value of the first receipt or payment, and so on.

Illustration: An individual expects to receive £50 at the end of each of the next seven years. What is the present value of the expected receipts, assuming an annual compound interest rate of 8%?

$$\text{Present value} = \frac{50}{(1+i)} + \frac{50}{(1+i)^2} + \cdots + \frac{50}{(1+i)^7}$$

$$= 50\left[\frac{1}{(1+i)} + \frac{1}{(1+i)^2} + \cdots + \frac{1}{(1+i)^7}\right]$$

$$\text{From the table, } \left[\frac{1}{(1+i)} + \frac{1}{(1+i)^2} + \cdots + \frac{1}{(1+i)^n)}\right] = A_{\overline{n|}}\, i = 5.2064$$

for $n = 7$ and $i = 8\%$

Present value = 50(5.2064) = £260.32

In the above illustration we used the same basic annuity data as in the $S_{\overline{n|}}$ illustration. Both $A_{\overline{n|}}$ and $S_{\overline{n|}}$ columns sum annuity values to a single amount – the former at the start of the annuity period and the latter at the end. The relationship between the figures in the two columns is as follows:[10]

$$A_{\overline{n|}} = S_{\overline{n|}} \times V_{\overline{n|}}$$

[10] This relationship may be easily proved, using the definitions of $A_{\overline{n|}}$, $S_{\overline{n|}}$ and $V_{\overline{n|}}$ given earlier:

$$A_{\overline{n|}} = S_{\overline{n|}} \times V_{\overline{n|}}$$

$$\left(\frac{1 - \dfrac{1}{(1+i)^n}}{i}\right) = \left(\frac{(1+i)^{n-1}}{i}\right) \times \frac{1}{(1+i)^n}$$

Multiplying each side by $(1+i)^n$ gives

$$\left(\frac{1(1+i)^n - \dfrac{(1+i)^n}{(1+i)^n}}{i}\right) = \left(\frac{(1+i)^n - 1}{i}\right)$$

Using the annuity in the above illustrations:

$$260.32 = 446.14 \times V_{\overline{7}|}8\% = 446.14 \times 0.583490$$

$A_{\overline{n}|}^{-1}$ (pronounced 'A angle n minus 1)
In words, each figure in this column represents the annual sum that it is necessary to pay at the end of each of the next n years in order to repay *an immediate loan of £1*. Each value given is the reciprocal of the equivalent figure in the $A_{\overline{n}|}$ column, i.e. each figure is calculated from the expression $1/A_{\overline{n}|}$. This column is used to convert a single immediate sum into an annuity.

Illustration: An individual borrows £16,000 from a building society to be repaid, with compound interest at 8%, by equal annual instalments over the next twenty years. What is the amount of the annual payment that will have to be made at the end of each of the next twenty years?

If we call the annual amount to be paid a, then:

$$16{,}000 = \frac{a}{(1+i)} + \frac{a}{(1+i)^2} + \cdots + \frac{a}{(1+i)^{20}}$$

$$16{,}000 = a\left[\frac{1}{(1+i)} + \frac{1}{(1+i)^2} + \cdots + \frac{1}{(1+i)^{20}}\right]$$

$$a = 16{,}000 \quad \frac{1}{\frac{1}{(1+i)} + \frac{1}{(1+i)^2} + \cdots + \frac{1}{(1+i)^{20}}}$$

$$= 16{,}000\left[\frac{1}{A_{\overline{20}|}i}\right]$$

From the table, $1/A_{\overline{n}|}i = A_{\overline{n}|}^{-1}i = 0.101852$ for $n = 20$ and $i = 8\%$

Annual amount $= 16{,}000(0.101852) = £1{,}629.63$

The same answer could be obtained by dividing the amount borrowed by the relevant factor in the $A_{\overline{n}|}$ column:

$$\text{Annual amount} = \frac{16{,}000}{A_{\overline{20}|}\,8\%} = \frac{16{,}000}{9.8181} = £1{,}629.63$$

Perpetuities

We saw in the previous section that the present value of an annuity may generally be calculated using the $A_{\overline{n}|}$ column of the compound interest tables. We now consider a particular type of annuity, known as a perpetuity, for which this treatment is inappropriate. A perpetuity is an annuity which is expected to last indefinitely, for example undated government stocks on which a fixed amount of interest is paid each year but on which the capital is unlikely ever to be repaid. The figures in the compound interest tables are all based on finite time periods, and in consequence are unsuitable for streams of receipts and payments which are expected to last indefinitely. Fortunately, a very simple formula is available for calculating the present value of a perpetuity. Let us consider again the expression for calculating the present value of an annuity of £1 p.a., described above:

$$A_{\overline{n}|} = \left(\frac{1 - \dfrac{1}{(1+i)^n}}{i} \right)$$

As the value of n increases, i.e. as the life of the annuity lengthens, the value of the term $1/(1+i)^n$ in the above expression becomes smaller. As n tends towards infinity (i.e. as the annuity tends to become a perpetuity), the value of $1/(1+i)^n$ tends towards zero and the value of the whole expression tends towards $1/i$. Thus:

$$\text{Present value of perpetuity of £1 per annum} = \frac{1}{i}$$

It follows that the present value of any perpetuity is given by the annual receipt or payment divided by the relevant rate of interest. So the present value of a perpetuity of £100, at an annual compound rate of interest of 8% is:

$$\text{Present value} = \frac{100}{0.08} = £1{,}250$$

Looked at another way, £1,250 invested at 8% p.a. will produce a return of £100 each and every year.

Deferred and advanced annuities and perpetuities

The tables and formulae discussed so far for calculating the present values of annuities and perpetuities are based on the assumption that the first annual receipt or payment is due after one year (i.e. at time 1). In other words, the formulae give the lump sum value of the annuity one year before the first receipt or payment is due. Adjustments are necessary if the annuity being considered does not comply with this pattern, that is if its starting date is deferred or advanced.

Consider first the case where the first receipt or payment is deferred. For example, suppose that an individual expects to receive five annual amounts of £100, the first receipt being after two years (i.e. at time 2). What is the present value (at time 0) of the annuity, assuming an annual compound interest rate of 8%? If we simply apply the five year $A_{\overline{n}|}$ factor from the 8% table to the annuity, we get the value one year before the first receipt, i.e. at time 1. We require the value at time 0. The necessary adjustment may be achieved in one of two ways. The first is to discount the calculated time 1 value to time 0, using the $V_{\overline{n}|}$ factor for one year:

$$\begin{aligned}\text{Present value} &= 100 \times A_{\overline{5}|}\ 8\% \times V_{\overline{1}|}\ 8\% \\ &= 100(3.9927)(0.925926) = £369.70\end{aligned}$$

The second is to take the annuity factor for the period from the present to the time of the last annual receipt (time 6 here), subtract from it the annuity factor for the period of deferral (one year here), and multiply the difference by the annual amount

$$\text{Present value} = 100 \times (A_{\overline{6}|}\ 8\% - A_{\overline{1}|}\ 8\%)$$
$$= 100(4.6229 - 0.9259) = £369.70$$

Consider now the case where the first annual receipt or payment is advanced. For example, suppose that an individual expects to receive five annual amounts of £100, and that the first receipt is due immediately. What is the present value of the annuity, assuming an annual compound rate of interest of 8%? It is necessary now to split the annuity into two parts; the immediate first instalment (due at time 0) and the remaining instalments (due at times 1, 2, 3 and 4) which comply with the pattern assumed in the annuity formula:

$$\text{Present value} = 100 + 100 \times A_{\overline{4}|}\ 8\%$$
$$= 100 + 100(3.3121) = £431.21$$

Further comments

We conclude this appendix with two further comments which may be of use to the student with little previous experience of compound interest methods. The first is that of the six columns described earlier, two ($V_{\overline{n}|}$ and $A_{\overline{n}|}$) are used much more frequently in accounting than are the remaining four. The mastery of these two columns in particular will greatly facilitate the understanding of a number of subsequent sections of this book.

The second comment is that a mechanical application of the factors in the tables to uncertain estimates will often result in an answer which appears extremely precise. Suppose that a new project costs £100 and is expected to produce one net cash inflow of roughly £200 at the end of seven years. We may calculate the net present value of the project, assuming an interest rate of 8%, as:

$$\text{NPV} = -100 + 200 \times V_{\overline{7}|}\ 8\%$$
$$= -100 + 200(0.583490) = +£16.698$$

The precision implied by the net present value is illusory, given the approximate nature of the net cash inflow estimate. It may be sensible to round the answer to the nearest £1, £5 or £10 if the decision maker is not to be confused. We consider in the next chapter some more refined methods of dealing with risk and uncertainty!

Discussion topics

1 What do you understand by 'wealth'?

2 Discuss the role of wealth in the decision making process.

3 Describe the factors that might contribute to an individual's wealth. Illustrate by referring to your personal position and attempt to measure your own wealth.

4 Outline the three basic financial decisions which face most entities and illustrate the interdependences between the decisions.

5 Explain what is meant by the 'time value of money' and discuss its importance in the measurement of wealth.

6 Define the 'economic value' of an enterprise.

7 Define the 'net present value' of a project and explain its relationship with an entity's economic value.

8 Discuss, giving examples, the importance of non-financial data to the measurement of wealth.

9 Consider the extent to which accountants should be responsible for the provision of non-financial information.

Exercises

3.1 Mr Bizet expects to receive net cash inflows (i.e. cash receipts from salary, investment and pension less essential living expenses) of £2,000 immediately. £8,000 after one year, £3,000 at the end of each of the subsequent twenty years and zero thereafter. He assesses his relevant discount rate at 15% p.a. He expects no cash flows other than those described above and has no other resources.

Estimate Mr Bizet's present wealth.

3.2 Dvorak plc expects to make the following cash distributions (dividend payments) to its owners:

Time	*Dividend payment* (£000)
After 1 year	500
After 2 years	550
After 3 years	600
At the end of *each* subsequent year, continuing indefinitely	700

The directors of Dvorak plc estimate that the return required by the company's owners is 20% p.a.

(a) Estimate the value of Dvorak plc to its owners, based on expected future dividend payments.

(b) Discuss any other factors which might influence the value of Dvorak plc to its owners.

3.3 Byrd Ltd has recently undertaken a feasibility study at a cost of £20,000 to assess the desirability of adding a new product, the blake, to its existing range. The new product would have a life of five years and the feasibility study suggests that 10,000 units could be sold annually at a price of £3 each.

The production manager of Byrd Ltd estimates that variable cost per unit would be £1.50 during each year of the product's life. He also argues that the blake would have to bear its 'fair share of fixed costs' and suggests an allocated cost of £1 per blake. The total fixed costs of Byrd Ltd (excluding depreciation on the special machine required) would be the same whether or not blakes were manufactured.

Manufacture of blakes would require the purchase of a special machine for £50,000, payable immediately. The machine has an expected economic life of five years, at the end of which it could be sold for scrap for £2,000. Byrd Ltd can lend and borrow money at a compound interest rate of 10% p.a. Assume that all cash inflows and outflows will arise at the end of the year to which they relate, with the exception of the initial cost of the machine.

(a) Prepare calculations showing whether Byrd Ltd should manufacture blakes.

(b) Justify the appraisal method you have used in (a), and note any reservations you have about your advice.

3.4 *Compound interest problems*

Assume a relevant interest rate of 10% in each of the following problems. Show your workings.

(a) Mr Baldovinetti wishes to purchase a twenty year annuity. He has available a sum of £10,000 to spend on the annuity. What annual amount should he expect to receive?

(b) An investment is expected to produce annual cash returns of £3,000 indefinitely. The first receipt is expected to arise in one year's time. What is the present value (PV) of the investment?

(c) How would your answer to (b) differ if the first receipt was expected immediately?

(d) How would your answer to (b) differ if the first receipt was expected after two years?

(e) Klee Ltd has the opportunity to invest in a project which will produce only one cash return: £7,000 after six years. What is the maximum amount Klee Ltd should be willing to pay immediately to undertake the investment?

(f) Berg Ltd has just purchased a new machine for £50,000. The machine is expected to last for four years. The company wishes to set aside and invest a constant annual amount at the end of each of the next four years which, together with accumulated interest, will provide for replacement of the machine at the end of its life. The cost of a replacement machine in four years is expected to be £75,000. How much should the company set aside each year?

(g) How would your answer to (f) differ if the annual amount was to be set aside and invested at the beginning of each of the next four years?

(h) Mrs Ives buys a car on hire-purchase. She pays a cash deposit of £1,000 and agrees to pay the balance by four annual instalments of £800. The first instalment is due one year after the purchase date. What is the 'cash price' of the car (i.e. the price if Mrs Ives paid in full at the time of purchase)?

(i) Mr Arne decides to provide for his retirement (eighteen years from now) by investing £500 at the end of each of the next eighteen years. What lump sum will he have available on retirement?

3.5 It is 31 March 19X1 and Papageno is presently employed looking after the birds in the local zoo for which he was paid £10,000 for the twelve months to 31 March 19X1. His employers have assured him that his post with the zoo is safe for the next five years and that his salary will be increased to keep pace with general inflation levels. However, Papageno feels that he may be able to improve his position if he buys a pet shop business which has just come up for sale. The pet shop owner has provided the following details for the year ended 31 March 19X1.

Pet sales	£30,000	(expected to increase at 8% p.a.)
Feed and other costs	£6,000	(expected to increase at 13% p.a.)
Site rent	£2,000	(fixed for the next five years and payable at the start of each year)

The pet shop owner is asking £100,000 for his business and has estimated that if the business is managed in a proper fashion then Papageno should be able to sell it 'for a minimum of £140,000 in five years' time'.

Papageno is only interested in looking five years into the future and conducts his affairs in such a way that it is a reasonable approximation to assume that all his cash flows (with the exception of site rent) arise at the end of each year. The bank manager has offered to lend Papageno £100,000 at a fixed rate of interest of 12% for the next five years. The bank manager has also told Papageno that his best estimate of the rate of general inflation for the next five years is 10%.

(a) Prepare calculations to show whether Papageno should buy the pet shop business.

(b) Explain to Papageno any reservations you have about the calculations performed in part (a).

(c) Discuss what other factors should be considered by Papageno.

Further reading

Carsberg, B. V., *Analysis for Investment Decisions*, Chapters 1 and 2, Haymarket, 1974.

Hicks, J. R., *Value and Capital: Inquiry into some Fundamental Principles of Economic Theory*, 2nd edn., Oxford University Press, 1946.

Layard, R. (ed.), *Cost–Benefit Analysis*, Penguin, 1972.

Mishan, E. J., *Elements of Cost–Benefit Analysis*, Allen & Unwin 1972.

Prest, A. R. and Turvey, R., 'Cost–benefit analysis: a survey', in *Surveys of Economic Theory*, Vol. III, *Resource Allocation*, Macmillan, 1968.

Chapter 4

Risk and uncertainty in decision making

A main feature of the approach to accounting adopted in this book is the emphasis on deriving accounting information *which is useful for decision making*. This emphasis applies to all types of accounting information – whether for use by managers within the organisation, or for external use by shareholders, government and other interested parties.

Information for decision making invariably possesses both quantitative and qualitative characteristics. Decisions are rarely taken on the basis of numbers alone. Intuition, experience and judgement often constitute a major element of the decision process. But there is one facet of decision making which is always present, irrespective of the nature of the decision. That facet is the need to make a *prediction*. Every decision entails making a prediction.

Decisions are characterised by their orientation to the future. Past events in themselves are virtually never relevant to current decisions, as they cannot be affected by any decision which is taken. (Although, as we discuss later, they may play an important role in the prediction of relevant future events.) But prediction is a notoriously difficult task. We are never able to predict the future with certainty – it would indeed be a dull world if we could. Thus we might say that the very essence of decision making, in our personal lives as in business situations, lies in the making of predictions which try to accommodate the many uncertainties that the future holds.

We note at this stage that a distinction is often drawn between risk and uncertainty. Risk is defined as a situation in which there are several possible outcomes and there is material statistical evidence relating to them. Risks are normally capable of being insured. Uncertainty is said to exist where there are again several possible outcomes, but where there is little previous statistical evidence to guide the decision maker in predicting them. Most business decisions fall into this category. The distinction between risk and uncertainty in decision making seems to be of little practical assistance and henceforth the terms will be used interchangeably.

4.1 'Probably' statements

When speaking of future intentions or outcomes we frequently use the word 'probably'. We use it to qualify the chosen verb, because we cannot know precisely what will happen in the future. For example, looking at next weekend's football fixtures, we might say that 'Bolton Wanderers will probably lose on Saturday'. We cannot be absolutely sure about this, but as we see that they are playing Arsenal then we believe there is a good chance that we are right.

Predictions, or 'probably' statements, do not in themselves mean a great deal. The mere making of a prediction does not imply the making of a decision. If however we choose, on the basis of a prediction, to take a decision which involves us in a subsequent course of action, then the prediction itself assumes importance. For example, if we say that 'As it will probably rain tomorrow (prediction), we will go to the cinema in the afternoon (decision)' we are, in effect, saying that it is the probability of rain which determines the cinema visit. In summary, although we can make a prediction without making a decision, we cannot make a decision without making a prediction.

4.2 Predictions and probabilities

Our discussion of predictions has not so far involved us in any refined attempt at quantifying the likelihood of a particular event occurring. Our examples have involved intuitive guesses (perhaps based on past experience of similar situations) which express our opinion that there is a good chance that a particular outcome will occur. In many situations, however, decisions may be based on a more mathematically ordered prediction of future outcomes. For example, we might say that 'As there is a 90% chance that Bolton Wanderers will lose to Arsenal, we will not go to the game'. The percentage figure expresses our personal degree of confidence in the outcome of our prediction.

In mathematical terms a probability of outcome is usually represented by a decimal number on a scale from 0, which denotes a nil likelihood of occurrence, to 1, which signifies absolute certainty – a definite occurrence. For example, a 70% chance of rain tomorrow is expressed as a probability of 0.7.

Probabilities are based on mathematical laws which depend for their validity upon the existence of a large number of situations. (This observation will assume more importance as we develop our explanation of probabilities in a business situation.) The application of probability theory is intended to give decision makers two important pieces of information. First, it provides a notion of the *range* of possible outcomes of the decision, and second, it offers information on the *likelihood* and *size* of deviations of actual outcomes from the expected outcome. Probabilities are used to calculate, not the *specific* value or outcome of any particular decision, but rather the *expected* value or outcome. The terms 'expected value' and 'expected outcome' will be used widely in our subsequent discussion of business decisions, so we should be quite clear as to their meaning. In a statistical sense, the word 'expected' refers to the 'average' or 'mean' outcome of a decision.

Strictly speaking the expected value of a decision represents the *long-run average outcome, expected if a particular course of action is undertaken many times.* For example, the assertion that there is an equal probability of a tossed coin landing 'heads' or 'tails' really means that if the coin is tossed a large number of times it will come down heads about half of the time, and tails about half of the time.

4.3 Business decisions and expected values

The attachment of probabilities to expected outcomes is of fundamental importance in business life. Business decision makers do not live in a deterministic (certain) world. They live, as we all do, in a world of uncertainty – a world of probabilities. For example, a business manager contemplating the purchase of a large expensive machine which is intended to increase a firm's productive capacity will try to predict (amongst other things) the additional yearly cash flows which will accrue to the firm because of the decision to buy the machine. These cash flows will be uncertain, both in their timing and their amount, and the manager may use probabilities to determine their expected values. The expected (present) value of these uncertain future cash flows may well influence the purchase decision. Alternatively, the manager may be contemplating an addition to the firm's existing range of products. In this case he may use probabilities to estimate the level of market share he can expect on the basis of alternative pricing policies. Equally, shareholders might wish to estimate the likely level of dividends receivable from their shareholdings. The use of probabilities may help in this estimation.

Expected values can be derived in a variety of ways which use different levels of intuition, experience and formal mathematical analysis. Indeed most derivations of probabilities use *all* of these qualitative and quantitative factors, although the 'proportions' of each may vary depending on the particular decision. Probabilities will normally be determined in the light of past experience. For example, shareholders may choose to invest in a particular company on the basis that its ability to earn profits and pay dividends in the future will reflect its proven ability to earn profits and pay dividends in the past. Managers who are considering whether to undertake a new investment may base their predictions of the likely net benefits from the investment on the results of similar investments undertaken previously. The degree of formality employed in any decision will usually be determined on a cost–benefit basis, i.e. the extra costs involved in pursuing a more rigorous approach to the determination of expected values should not be viewed in isolation, but rather in relation to the benefits obtained from the extra information provided by the more rigorous analysis.

In the remainder of this chapter we look in more detail at two possible methods of incorporating uncertainty into decision making: expected value analysis and portfolio analysis.

Expected values – illustration 1

Suppose that a company, Ninian Ltd, is considering whether to undertake a new project, of similar size and characteristics to a project which has been undertaken one hundred time previously. The results of the previous projects, expressed in terms of the present value of the cash surplus (or deficit) are as follows:

(1) *Result cash surplus/(deficit)* (£)	(2) *Number of times the result has occurred*	(3) *Probability of occurrence*
(20,000)	8	0.08
(5,000)	22	0.22
3,000	40	0.40
7,000	18	0.18
10,000	12	0.12
	$\Sigma = 100$	$\Sigma = 1.00$

Column 1 reveals that there have been five different outcomes from the previous hundred projects, varying from a deficit of £20,000 to a surplus of £10,000. Column 1 thus gives information on the *range* of outcomes which have occurred in previous situations. Column 2 of the table shows the *frequency* with which the five outcomes have occurred. The total of column 2 (expressed by the Greek symbol Σ) must equal the number of observed outcomes – in this case 100. Column 3 translates the absolute numbers from column 2 into probabilities, expressed as decimals, on the assumption that past outcomes are a good basis for predicting future results. Each figure in column 3 is equal to the figure on the same row of column 2 divided by the total number of outcomes (100). Thus the probability of a deficit of £20,000 is 8 divided by 100, which equals 0.08. The total of column 3 must sum to 1, as the sum of the probabilities of occurrence must always equal unity. If the total is less than 1, all possible outcomes are not included. If it is greater than 1, one or more of the probabilities assigned to individual outcomes is incorrect.

We are now in a position to calculate the expected value of the new project. The expected value is represented by the sum of each possible outcome multiplied by the probability of its occurrence. Thus we have an expected value of:

$$\begin{aligned} & -20{,}000\ (0.08) - 5{,}000\ (0.22) + 3{,}000\ (0.40) + 7{,}000\ (0.18) \\ & + 10{,}000\ (0.12) \\ = & -1{,}600 - 1{,}100 + 1{,}200 + 1{,}260 + 1{,}200 \\ = & +\text{£}960 \end{aligned}$$

On the basis of the numbers produced by application of the expected value technique, it appears that Ninian Ltd should undertake the new investment. *On past experience* the average expected value of the new project is a cash surplus of £960. Is this an adequate analysis of the uncertainty associated with the project? Before we answer this question let us consider a more complex business decision.

Expected values – illustration 2

Suppose Ninian Ltd, is now considering the purchase of a new machine for £350. The directors feel very confident that they can sell the goods produced by the machine so as to yield a yearly cash surplus of £100. There is, however, some uncertainty as to the machine's working life. A recently published Trade Association survey shows that members of the association have between them owned 250 of these machines, and have found the lives of the machine to vary as follows:

Number of years of machine life	*Number of machines having given life*
3	20
4	50
5	100
6	70
7	10
	$\Sigma = 250$

In order to decide whether to purchase the machine Ninian Ltd might proceed as follows. First, calculate the present value of the cash surplus or deficit arising if the machine lasts 3, 4, 5, 6 or 7 years. The present value of the cash surplus or deficit is represented by the difference between the *discounted* annual cash flows of £100 and the cost of the machine, which is £350.[11] If we assume a discount rate of 10%, the net present value for each different machine life is as follows:

Machine life	*Net present value* (£)
3	(101)
4	(33)
5	29
6	86
7	137

As the machine life lengthens from 3 to 7 years, and Ninian Ltd. receives a greater number of yearly cash flows, the net present value of the machine changes from −£101 (i.e. a situation which does not warrant purchase) to +£137 (i.e. a situation which favours purchase).

In order to calculate the expected value of these different net present values we need to perform two further calculations. First, each individual net present value is multiplied by its probability of occurrence; and second, the totals derived are added together. Table 4.1 shows both sets of calculations.

[11] This technique of project appraisal, which involves the discounting of future cash flows, is usually referred to as the 'net present value' method. It was described briefly in Chapter 3 and will be discussed in more detail in Chapter 11.

Table 4.1 Calculation of the expected net present value of purchasing a machine

(1) *Machine's life in years*	(2) *Net present value* (£)	(3) *Number of machines having given life*	(4) *Probability of occurrence*	(5) *Expected net present value* (£)
3	(101)	20	$\frac{20}{250} = 0.08$	(8.1)
4	(33)	50	$\frac{50}{250} = 0.20$	(6.6)
5	29	100	$\frac{100}{250} = 0.40$	11.6
6	86	70	$\frac{70}{250} = 0.28$	24.1
7	137	10	$\frac{10}{250} = 0.04$	5.5
		$\Sigma = 250$	$\Sigma = 1.00$	26.5

Column 5 of Table 4.1 shows the expected net present value of purchasing the machine. The individual values appearing within column 5 are calculated by multiplying the net present values in column 2 by the probability of their occurrence, as shown in column 4. On the basis of the expected value calculation, supported by 250 previous observations, it appears that Ninian Ltd should go ahead with the purchase of the machine as it yields a positive expected net present value of £26.5.

4.4 Some problems with the expected value criterion

Let us now return to the question we asked previously. Is the expected value method a sufficient treatment of the problem of uncertainty? In other words, should an enterprise always accept projects with positive expected values and reject those with negative expected values? To answer these questions we need to understand what lies behind the expected value approach. The approach is based upon the application of probabilities, however derived, to a specific situation, in order to produce a 'long-run average' solution. It does not accommodate the decision taker's risk preferences. It does not indicate whether the decision taker is prepared to take the chance of incurring the various possible outcomes which contribute to the 'average' solution.

Let us digress to reinforce this point. Suppose that Mr X and Mr Y are considering whether to play a coin tossing game. They agree that the rules of the game will be as follows. The coin will be tossed only once. If it turns up 'heads' Mr X gives Mr Y £10,000, whereas if the coin turns up 'tails' Mr Y gives Mr X £10,000. The expected value of Mr X's cash flows, assuming an unbiased coin, are:

Event	*Outcome* (£)	*Probability*	*Expected outcome* (£)
Heads	−10,000	0.5	−5,000
Tails	+10,000	0.5	+5,000
		Expected value	0

Mr X's expected value (i.e. his expected gain or loss) on this gamble is zero, but that will not be the actual outcome. In fact, he might gain or lose £10,000. The crucial question is whether (as the expected value criterion suggests) Mr X would be indifferent to playing the game or not, knowing that although he could win £10,000, he could also lose the same amount. In this situation the expected value would be an appropriate basis for choice only if the two gamblers were neutral to risk, i.e. if they were prepared to take the chance of winning or losing £10,000 with equal probability. Note that if the two players agree to play the game not just once but a number of times, the chance of a zero average outcome will become progressively more likely the more times the coin is tossed. This is the basis of probability theory to which we referred earlier. The principle is known as the *law of large numbers.* Hence probability is strictly defined as the long-run relative frequency of a particular event; it may be used to provide a calculation of expected outcome or expected value, that is, the long-run average outcome or value expected if a particular course of action is undertaken many times.

With these ideas in mind let us return to our two earlier examples. In the first, concerning the undertaking of a new project, the application of the expected value method suggested acceptance of the project on the basis of a positive expected value of £960. Note that this 'average' figure has never actually been achieved. The most likely (or *modal*) result is in fact a surplus of £3,000. When we explore in more detail what underlies the expected value of £960 we see that, on the basis of the previous hundred observations, there is an 8% probability that the project will incur a loss of £20,000 and a 22% probability that the project will lose £5,000 – i.e. there is a 30% chance that a deficit will occur. The broad question then becomes 'is the management of Ninian Ltd willing to run the 30% risk of a loss in return for a 70% chance of generating a cash surplus?' It may be, for example, that a loss of £20,000 or even £5,000 would be so significant in terms of the firm's size and current position, that its occurrence would force the firm out of business. Many managers would be unwilling to run the risk of such an outcome, even though it was more likely that the project would generate a surplus.

In the second example, concerning the purchase of a new machine, there is an 8% chance of showing a negative net present value of £101 and a 20% chance of a negative net present value of £33, depending upon whether the new machine lasts for three or four years. These results are based on a sample of 250 similar observations. The number of observations used as the basis for attaching probabilities may affect the confidence we have in the expected value results; the more observations we take the more confident we are likely to be in the results. In this case Ninian Ltd must determine whether the 28% chance of incurring some loss is compensated by the 72% chance of earning surpluses. In this example, the amounts involved are small. A deficit of £101 or £33 is unlikely to bankrupt the firm, and the management may decide that the high probability of some surplus makes purchase of the machine worthwhile.

The crucial factor which will eventually determine the decision in each of the above cases is the decision maker's attitude to risk. This is the critical variable which is excluded from the expected value calculations, and yet it is the variable that may weigh most heavily in any decision. The level of risk which any of us will be willing to bear in our own decisions cannot be simply plucked out of the air. It depends upon many different aspects of our personal situations including our individual nature – whether we are risk-takers or risk-avoiders – and on the resources we possess (i.e. on the amount of money we can afford to lose). We cannot evaluate levels of risk independently of available resources. The same is true for management decision making: the level of acceptable risk depends upon many factors, including the nature of the particular decision, the amount of funds available to management, the return demanded by and the risk acceptable to providers of funds, and the attitudes to risk possessed by managers – the actual decision makers.

The practical limitations of the expected value technique should now be clearer. Because it ignores the risk attitudes of the decision maker(s) it is appropriate as a basis for choice only in limited situations. We might characterise these situations as follows:

1. The decision involves an opportunity which can be undertaken many times under independent conditions, i.e. the outcome of each opportunity is independent of the outcomes of all others. (These conditions form the basis of insurance transactions.)
2. The decision involves amounts that are small in relation to the total size of an organisation.
3. Decision makers are neutral to risk.

In the likely event that none of these characteristics holds, a more sophisticated method has to be found to incorporate risk and uncertainty into decision making. One such approach, which has received wide support both in theory and practice, is the method of *portfolio analysis*.

4.5 Portfolio analysis – introduction

Among the criticisms we might level at the expected value method is its ignorance of the possible relationship between the outcome of any one decision and the outcomes of other decisions taken by the same individual. This is a serious shortcoming. Few firms put all their (financial) eggs in one basket; rather they try to minimise the level of risk by spreading it around a variety of projects. This spreading of risk is known as *diversification*, and diversification lies at the heart of portfolio analysis.

Portfolio analysis is the study of the interrelationships between the different financial elements which in total make up a portfolio (for example, a portfolio of shares or of projects). Basically it is a term to describe a common-sense activity in which most of us engage. If we were given a particular endowment of resources, and a degree of choice as to how we use the endowment, most of use would try to spread our risks in such a way that if one decision proved to be a loser then others would turn out to be winners. For example, an individual with available funds to invest might consider a variety of possible uses for them, such as the purchase of 'risky' shares, 'safe' shares and government stocks, deposits in building societies and banks, and a regular gamble on the football pools or the tote. It is unlikely that the returns from all these investments will fail simultaneously.

Portfolio analysis helps to explain why, for example, it is more likely that a substantial and risky project, promising either an excellent or a disastrous pay-off, will be more acceptable to a large organisation than to a small one. The consequences of a few failures out of a wide portfolio of projects are likely to be less catastrophic than the failure of an organisation's single project.

The principles underlying the portfolio approach also help to explain why so many large companies engage in such diversified and divergent activities. Some of the very large UK-based multinational companies such as Unilever and ICI, produce and sell a variety of different products in order to help minimise the levels of risk associated with business life. For example, Unilever sells soap powder and cereals. Perhaps a more immediately recognisable example of this type of business diversification is the huge increase that has taken place in the sale of food and drink as a proportion of the total activities of Marks and Spencer. Marks and Spencer can no longer be thought of simply as a company which sells clothes through its retail stores. It may also be pointed out that there has been an equally impressive increase in the contribution of Marks and Spencer's total profits which has been provided by its sales of food and drink. Whatever the economic climate we must still eat and drink!

An ideal form of diversification and risk minimisation is to place funds in sources which have 'negatively correlated' returns, i.e. the returns from some sources are high when the returns from others are low and vice versa. Let us take a simple example to illustrate this point. Suppose an investor decides to place 50% of her funds in the shares of an umbrella manufacturer and 50% in the shares of an ice-cream manufacturer. Also suppose that returns from the investment in the umbrella manufacturer will drop when the weather is fine but that those from investment in the ice-cream manufacturer will rise and that the situation will be reversed when the weather is bad. The investor is hedging her bets by spreading the risk inherent in the investment. The risk of the portfolio depends not upon the variability of the returns from the shares in the individual companies but rather on the effect on the *total* portfolio returns of the various economic (and climatic) circumstances. Even investments that are susceptible to large variations in their returns may be good (risk) choices for the use of funds provided that they are *negatively correlated* with other investments within the portfolio. It is this notion of negative correlation which is important in minimising the level of risk in any business situation.

Table 4.2 Mr Filbert: returns from investment

State of the world	A	B	C
Probability of state of the world	0.4	0.3	0.3
Returns from investment of £1,000:	(£)	(£)	(£)
Company D	1,200	800	1,600
Company E	1,200	1,100	1,300
Company F	1,200	1,700	700

We now use a simple example to explain the principles of portfolio analysis. At this stage, we restrict ourselves to a summary of basic concepts. In the next section we explain in greater detail the mechanics of portfolio analysis.

Mr Filbert possesses £1,000 cash and no other assets. He has the opportunity of investing his cash in one of three companies, or in a combination of any two of the three companies. No other investments are available now or in the foreseeable future. Mr Filbert is a risk-averse investor; he wishes to achieve the lowest possible level of risk for a given expected return. An investment in each company produces a single return after one year, but the size of the return depends upon which of three sets of economic circumstances (known as states of the world) prevails. The possible returns from an investment of £1,000 in each company are shown in Table 4.2.

The first step in Mr Filbert's investment decision is to calculate the expected value of investing in each company. The expected value calculations are set out in Table 4.3. The weighted average of the returns expected from an investment of £1,000 is £1,200 in each case. On the basis of the expected value criterion Mr Filbert would be indifferent between the investments. However, as we noted earlier, the expected value criterion may be an inadequate decision rule. Mr Filbert is interested in minimising the level of risk associated with his investment.

Table 4.3 Mr Filbert: expected value calculations

State of the world	*Return* (£)		*Probability* (£)		*Expected value*
Company D:					
State A	1,200	×	0.4	=	480
State B	800	×	0.3	=	240
State C	1,600	×	0.3	=	480
			Expected value		1,200
Company E:					
State A	1,200	×	0.4	=	480
State B	1,100	×	0.3	=	330
State C	1,300	×	0.3	=	390
			Expected value		1,200
Company F:					
State A	1,200	×	0.4	=	480
State B	1,700	×	0.3	=	510
State C	700	×	0.3	=	210
			Expected value		1,200

Table 4.4 Mr Filbert: returns from investment in companies E and F

State of the world	A	B	C
Probability of state of the world	0.4	0.3	0.3
	(£)	(£)	(£)
Investment of £833.33 in company E and £166.67 in company F:			
Return from company E (83.333% of returns shown in Table 4.2)	1,000	917	1,083
Return from company F (16.667% of returns shown in Table 4.2)	200	283	117
Total return	1,200	1,200	1,200

Observation of the figures in Table 4.2 suggests that the returns from company E are less volatile (i.e. vary less depending upon which environment prevails) than are the returns from either of the other companies. For example, returns from company E will be in the range £1,100 to £1,300, compared with £800 to £1,600 for company D and £700 to £1,700 for company F. If Mr Filbert could invest in only one company he would, as a risk-averse investor, choose company E. However he is not restricted to investment in only one company; he may, if he wishes, spread his cash between two of the companies. Again, observation of the figures in Table 4.2 reveals that the returns of company D and company E are positively correlated; both companies do relatively badly under state B and relatively well under state C. The returns of company D and company F, and of company E and company F are negatively correlated; company F does relatively well under state B whereas companies D and E do relatively badly, and vice versa under state C.

The above observations suggest that investment in companies D and F or in companies E and F offers more scope for reducing the risk of Mr Filbert's portfolio than does investment in companies D and E or in one of the three companies alone. In fact, by investing 83.333% of his funds in company E and 16.667% in company F, Mr Filbert may eliminate risk completely. The results of this strategy are shown in Table 4.4, which demonstrates that whichever state of the world obtains, Mr Filbert will receive a return of £1,200. In the next section we explain in more detail the formal analysis which will lead to this result.

4.6 Portfolio analysis – further considerations

As we noted in the previous section, Mr Filbert is a risk-averse investor, interested in minimising the level of risk associated with his investment. He is thus interested in determining the extent to which the return from each company *covaries* with the return from each of the others, i.e. to what extent the return from company D covaries with that from company E, company E with company F, and company D with company F. Although the analysis in this section involves some basic statistics, that in itself is no bad thing. Statistical manipulations in many different guises confront us every day of our lives. It is, however, important not to lose sight of the message we are trying to convey, by becoming too immersed in the statistics. The message, which was demonstrated simply in the previous section, is that one (and possibly the best) method of dealing with business risk is not to look at the risks of individual projects and investments in isolation, but rather at how these risks move together or covary with the risk attached to other projects and investments.

The preferred combination of investments for a risk-averse investor will be that combination in which the expected returns offset each other, i.e. that combination which has the highest negative correlation coefficient. Correlation coefficients lie in the range from -1 to $+1$. A correlation coefficient of -1 (perfect negative correlation) means that risk can be diversified away completely: poor returns from one project are offset exactly by good returns from the other. A correlation coefficient of $+1$ (perfect positive correlation) means that no risk diversification is possible; good returns from one project are accompanied by good returns from the other and bad returns from one by bad returns from the other. All other correlation coefficient values mean that some risk can be diversified away, and the nearer is the value of the correlation coefficient to -1, the greater is the amount of risk that can be eliminated.

The correlation coefficient (r) for any two projects (x and y) is found by dividing the joint risk of the two projects (the covariance) by the product of the individual risks. The most popular measure of individual risk used in statistical analysis is given by the standard deviation (σ). We can express the correlation coefficient for two projects (x and y) as follows:

$$r_{x,y} = \frac{\text{covariance}(x, y)}{\sigma_x \times \sigma_y} \tag{4.1}$$

We have not yet explained how we derive the standard deviation, nor why we use it as a measure of individual risk. The standard deviation gives a *monetary* indication to decision makers as to how confident they can be in the occurrence of the expected (average) outcome, by providing information about the likely *dispersion* (or range) of outcomes around the expected outcome and about the size of the possible deviations of the actual outcome from the expected outcome. In statistical terms the standard deviation is the square root of the variance. To derive the standard deviation of a project we thus need first to calculate the variance (or σ^2). We may calculate the variance in four simple stages:

Stage 1 Calculate the deviation of each possible outcome (x_n) from the expected outcome (E_x), i.e. $(x_n - E_x)$.

Stage 2 Square this answer to make all the values positive, i.e. $(x_n - E_x)^2$.

Stage 3 Multiply this term by the probability (P_n) of actually getting the outcome x_n, i.e. $P_n(x_n - E_x)^2$.

Stage 4 Sum the results of stage 3 to give a measure of the variability of the likely outcomes, the variance, i.e. $\sigma^2 = \Sigma\ P_n(x_n - E_x)^2$.

The above symbols represent a straightforward set of calculations. Let us return to the figures in our example to illustrate them. To calculate the standard deviations

Table 4.5 Mr Filbert: calculation of the standard deviation of each investment

State of the world	*Return* x_n	*Expected value of return* E_x	*Deviation* $(x_n - E_x)$	*Deviation squared* $(x_n - E_x)^2$	*Probability* P_n	*Sum* $P_n(x_n - E_x)^2$
Company D:						
State A	1,200	1,200	0	0	0.4	0
State B	800	1,200	− 400	160,000	0.3	48,000
State C	1,600	1,200	+ 400	160,000	0.3	48,000
					Variance $(\sigma^2) = \Sigma =$	96,000
Standard deviation = $\sqrt{96{,}000}$ = £309.84						
Company E:						
State A	1,200	1,200	0	0	0.4	0
State B	1,100	1,200	− 100	10,000	0.3	3,000
State C	1,300	1,200	+ 100	10,000	0.3	3,000
					Variance $(\sigma^2) = \Sigma =$	6,000
Standard deviation = $\sqrt{6{,}000}$ = £77.46						
Company F:						
State A	1,200	1,200	0	0	0.4	0
State B	1,700	1,200	+ 500	250,000	0.3	75,000
State C	700	1,200	− 500	250,000	0.3	75,000
					Variance $(\sigma^2) = \Sigma =$	150,000
Standard deviation = $\sqrt{150{,}000}$ = £387.30						

or measures of risk for each of the three investments we proceed as in Table 4.5. The standard deviation calculations in Table 4.5 show that the return from company E varies less, depending upon which state of the world prevails, than do the returns from investment in company D or company F (i.e. investment in company E produces the same average return and lower variability of return than investment in either of the other companies). Does this mean that Mr Filbert should apply his £1,000 entirely to investment in company E? So far we have calculated separately the variability of the returns from each company. We now need to see if Mr Filbert's level of risk can be reduced by investing in a combination of any two of the companies.

Suppose Mr Filbert invests his total capital equally in the shares of two companies (i.e. £500 is invested in each company). Which two companies should he choose? The three possible combinations, or portfolios, of returns from this strategy are shown in Table 4.6, and the standard deviation of each is shown in Table 4.7. (Each return is one-half of the total return shown in Table 4.2.)

Tables 4.6 and 4.7 show that by investing in a diversified portfolio Mr Filbert can obtain the same return with a lower level of risk than was possible by investing in the shares of one company alone. Each portfolio and each company offer an expected return of £1,200. However, the calculations in Table 4.5 demonstrated that the lowest standard deviation possible from investment in only one company (company E) is £77.46. The figures in Table 4.7 show that this standard deviation

Table 4.6 Mr Filbert: possible combinations of returns

State of the world	A	B	C
Probability of state of the world	0.4	0.3	0.3
	(£)	(£)	(£)
Portfolio 1 – equal investment in company D and company E			
Return from company D	600	400	800
Return from company E	600	550	650
Total return	1,200	950	1,450
Expected value of returns		1,200	
Portfolio 2 – equal investment in company E and company F			
Return from company E	600	550	650
Return from company F	600	850	350
Total return	1,200	1,400	1,000
Expected value of returns		1,200	
Portfolio 3 – equal investment in company D and company F			
Return from company D	600	400	800
Return from company F	600	850	350
Total return	1,200	1,250	1,150
Expected value of returns		1,200	

Table 4.7 Mr Filbert: calculations of the standard deviation of each portfolio

State of the world	*Return* x_n	*Expected value of return* E_x	*Deviation* $(x_n - E_x)$	*Deviation squared* $(x_n - E_x)^2$	*Probability* P_n	*Sum* $P_n(x_n - E_x)^2$
Portfolio 1						
State A	1,200	1,200	0	0	0.4	0
State B	950	1,200	−250	62,500	0.3	18,750
State C	1,450	1,200	+250	62,500	0.3	18,750
					Variance $(\sigma^2) = \Sigma =$	37,500
Standard deviation = $\sqrt{37,500}$ = £193.65						
Portfolio 2						
State A	1,200	1,200	0	0	0.4	0
State B	1,400	1,200	+200	40,000	0.3	12,000
State C	1,000	1,200	−200	40,000	0.3	12,000
					Variance $(\sigma^2) = \Sigma =$	24,000
Standard deviation = $\sqrt{24,000}$ = £154.92						
Portfolio 3						
State A	1,200	1,200	0	0	0.4	0
State B	1,250	1,200	+50	2,500	0.3	750
State C	1,150	1,200	−50	2,500	0.3	750
					Variance $(\sigma^2) = \Sigma =$	1,500
Standard deviation = $\sqrt{1500}$ = £38.73						

may be reduced to £38.73 by investing equally in a combination of companies D and F, i.e. by investment in portfolio 3. The returns from D and F are negatively correlated so that an unusually poor performance by one company is always accompanied by an unusually good one by the other.

We can now return to our statistical formulae to interpret these conclusions more formally. We have previously defined the covariance as being related to the joint risk of two investments. In order to find the degree of joint risk (covariance) it is first necessary to determine the deviation of each investment's outcomes from its expected outcome and to calculate the product of the deviations of each investment under each possible economic state. The answers are then weighted by the probability of each economic state. Table 4.8 shows the calculation of the covariance for each of the three portfolios. The 'deviation' figures for each company's returns are taken from Table 4.5. We now have the figures necessary to determine the correlation coefficients – the degree of co-movement of each combination of projects.

Substituting the covariances from Table 4.8 and the standard deviations from Table 4.5 into the correlation coefficient equation (equation 4.1: $r_{x,y} = \text{covariance}\ (x, y)/\sigma_x \times \sigma_y$), gives the following coefficients:

$$r_{D,E} = \frac{\text{covariance (D, E)}}{\sigma_D \times \sigma_E} = \frac{+24{,}000}{309.84 \times 77.46} = +1$$

$$r_{E,F} = \frac{\text{covariance (E, F)}}{\sigma_E \times \sigma_F} = \frac{-30{,}000}{77.46 \times 387.30} = -1$$

$$r_{D,F} = \frac{\text{covariance (D,F)}}{\sigma_D \times \sigma_F} = \frac{-120{,}000}{309.84 \times 387.30} = -1$$

The combinations of the returns of companies E and F and the returns of companies D and F are perfectly negatively correlated, i.e. they offer the opportunity of eliminating risk completely. At first sight, this seems an odd conclusion in view of the figures in Table 4.7 which showed that investment of equal amounts in E and F (portfolio 2) or in D and F (portfolio 3) resulted in portfolios with positive, rather than zero, standard deviations, i.e. neither portfolio eliminates risk. The explanation for this apparent paradox is that in order to exploit fully the risk reduction properties of investments in two companies it will almost certainly be necessary to invest unequal amounts in each one. A detailed consideration of the procedure for selecting the appropriate proportions is outside the scope of this chapter. However, we may demonstrate the 'truth' of the correlation coefficient by considering investment in companies E and F. In order to eliminate risk completely, it is necessary to invest 83.333% of available funds (i.e. £833.33) in E and 16.667% of available funds (i.e. £166.67) in F. The results of this strategy were shown in Table 4.4 which demonstrates that, whichever state of the world obtains, Mr Filbert will receive a return of £1,200. In other words, the standard deviation of the portfolio in Table 4.4 is zero.

In contrast to investment in either E and F or D and F, investment in D and E offers no opportunity at all for risk reduction by diversification as returns from

Table 4.8 Mr Filbert: covariance calculations

State of the world	*(Deviation* × *Deviation* = *Product)* × *Probability* = *Covariance* $(x_n - E_x)$	$(x_n - E_x)$			
Portfolio 1	*Company D*	*Company E*			
State A	0	0	0	0.4	0
State B	−400	−100	40,000	0.3	+12,000
State C	+400	+100	40,000	0.3	+12,000
				Covariance (D,E)	+24,000
Portfolio 2	*Company E*	*Company F*			
State A	0	0	0	0.4	0
State B	−100	+500	−50,000	0.3	−15,000
State C	+100	−500	−50,000	0.3	−15,000
				Covariance (E,F)	−30,000
Portfolio 3	*Company D*	*Company F*			
State A	0	0	0	0.4	0
State B	−400	+500	−200,000	0.3	−60,000
State C	+400	−500	−200,000	0.3	−60,000
				Covariance (D,F)	−120,000

investment in the two companies are perfectly positively correlated. Investment in E alone offers the same return and a lower variability (standard deviation) than does any combination of investment in E and D. In summary, because Mr Filbert is risk-averse, he should invest his funds either in a combination of shares in E and F or in a combination of shares of D and F.

4.7 Management decisions and risk and uncertainty

Although our explanation of portfolio analysis has been phrased in terms of an individual considering investment in three companies, a similar procedure is appropriate for decisions in which managers are faced with a choice of projects. In practice, the procedure is somewhat more complex than our example suggests (as indeed it is for the investor). The manager must consider not only the returns of and correlations between the returns of new projects but also the correlations of the returns of new projects with the existing activities of the organisation. The task is to find a combination of return and risk which is optimal for the participants of the organisation as a whole. This is further complicated by the need to trade off the risk of a project against its expected return. Many investments provide the possibility of greater returns only if a greater level of risk is accepted.

We have introduced in this chapter two methods which explicitly incorporate risk and uncertainty into decision making – the basic expected value method and the more sophisticated portfolio analysis approach. We have chosen to look at expected values because they involve the use of probabilities and portfolio analysis because it seems to us to be the most relevant and potentially useful means of dealing with risk and uncertainty in practice. However, it will sometimes be the case that the cost and difficulty of applying a method based on the use of probabilities mean that another method of dealing with uncertainty may be more appropriate. One of the most useful approaches not involving a strict application of probability theory is *sensitivity analysis*. This involves calculating the expected pay-off from a project on the basis of most likely outcomes and subsequently investigating the implications of various deviations of actual outcomes from forecast. For example, the value that a particular variable will take if the profit expected from the project is to be reduced to zero may be ascertained and the difference in value expressed as a percentage of its most likely value. This provides an indication of the sensitivity of the project's expected profit to changes in the value of individual variables and points to those estimates in which a small deviation may be critical for the success or failure of the project. These estimates should be examined most carefully before a decision is made on the project. The advent of micro-computers and spreadsheet packages has made the use of sensitivity analysis rapid and inexpensive. We look in more detail at sensitivity analysis in Chapter 11.

We will return only in passing to expected value and portfolio analysis calculations in future chapters. That, however, does not mean that the reader should promptly forget what has just been discussed. This chapter is one of the most important in the entire book. In everything that follows – in most of the examples, illustrations, explanations and problems which we shall use – it should be borne in mind that underlying all our words and figures is the existence of uncertainty.

Discussion topics

1 Discuss the distinction between decisions and predictions. Do you accept the assertion in the chapter that every decision entails making a prediction?

2 Discuss some possible methods by which decision makers could attempt to attach probabilities to outcomes. What factors in practice determine the choice of method?

3 Discuss the advantages and disadvantages of the expected value technique for good decision making.

4 Why is it important to incorporate the notion of risk into decision making procedures? Whose risk should be reflected in decision making?

5 What are the advantages of the portfolio analysis technique of dealing with risk? Have you ever used this technique in your own decision making? If so, how?

6 Explain the distinguishing characteristics of portfolio analysis, and in particular, discuss the concepts of variance, covariance and correlation coefficient.

Exercises

4.1 The plant manager of Mahler Ltd, confronted with a need to replace a machine, has a choice between machine A and machine B, either of which is satisfactory. Each machine has an estimated life of three years, but machine A will cost £4,000, and machine B £10,000. An analysis of the operating costs associated with each of the machines reveals that the cost per unit with machine A is £1 and with machine B is £0.50, excluding depreciation. The product's selling price is £3.

The manager feels that the number of units required for each of the next three years may be 2,000, 3,000 or 5,000 units. An annual requirement of 3,000 units is the most probable. The following table shows the probabilities:

Annual requirements (units)	*Probability*
2,000	0.2
3,000	0.6
5,000	0.2

(a) Calculate the net present value for each of the three activity levels for machines A and B using a discount rate of 6%.

(b) Calculate the expected net present value for each machine. Which machine would you recommend to the manager?

(c) Discuss briefly the limitations of the expected value technique.

4.2 Watteau Ltd, a novelty toy company, is considering whether to produce a new toy called 'Spyman', modelled on the hero of a currently popular television series. A special machine, having no other use, would be required. It would cost £20,000. The company's cost of capital is 5%. The direct cost of a Spyman is expected to be £10, and whatever the number sold the price will be £20. The demand for the toy is not thought likely to last more than three years. The sales in each year are highly uncertain.

The directors have estimated the various possible levels of demand in each year, and forecast the likelihood of the occurrence of each of these demands as in the table below. Because of the nature of the product, the level of demand achieved in any one year is independent of that obtained in any other year.

Year 1		*Year 2*		*Year 3*	
Probability	*Sales* (units)	*Probability*	*Sales* (units)	*Probability*	*Sales* (units)
0.2	500	0.2	250	0.2	100
0.2	1,000	0.3	500	0.2	250
0.4	2,000	0.3	750	0.3	500
0.1	2,500	0.1	1,000	0.3	750
0.1	3,000	0.1	2,000	—	—

The preliminary design studies for the 'Spyman' have already been completed, at a cost of £1,000. If the project is rejected, they could be sold for £2,500.

(a) Calculate the project's expected net present value.

(b) Would you necessarily recommend acceptance if this value were positive? Specifically, how would your conclusion be affected if the company was:
  (i) a one-person firm with no other project available, and the £20,000 required to finance the project was the entrepreneur's lifetime savings?
  (ii) a very large company undertaking many similar projects?

4.3 Poussin Ltd can purchase the patent and the manufacturing rights of any one of three products. The costs of the rights are:

Product A £130,000
Product B £190,000
Product C £200,000

At a meeting with three of Poussin's directors, the management accountant stated: 'We are all agreed on the facts. Each venture is a very short-term project. The fixed manufacturing and advertising costs of each venture will be:

	A (£000)	*B* (£000)	*C* (£000)
Fixed manufacturing costs	120	20	20
Advertising costs	50	30	20

Sales and production will, once known, dovetail and there will therefore be no stock build up. The sales prices and variable costs per unit are:

	A	*B*	*C*
Sales price per unit	£340	£190	£130
Variable cost per unit	£140	£110	£70

However, the sales volume is the crunch question. We do not know what the sales level will be but we do know the various possibilities of what the sales levels could be. Product A could be a complete flop, it could sell well, or it might sell very well. B is also quite variable, whereas with C the range of outcomes is quite small. The various possible sales volumes and their associated probabilities are:

A		*B*		*C*	
Sales volume (units)	*Probability*	*Sales volume* (units)	*Probability*	*Sales volume* (units)	*Probability*
0	0.1	3,000	0.1	7,000	0.8
2,500	0.4	4,000	0.3	8,000	0.1
4,000	0.5	6,000	0.3	9,000	0.1
		8,000	0.3		

Based on the assumption that the above facts are all completely accurate, and we agree with this, all we need do is make the decisions as to which one product to undertake. What are your views, ladies and gentlemen?'

(a) Calculate the expected money value of each product and on the basis of this advise Poussin of the best course of action.

(b) List and briefly comment on three other factors which may be relevant in a practical situation to the final choice between the three available courses of action.

(**c**) *Consider only product A for this section*. The marketing manager agrees that the subjective probabilities assigned to sales levels given are as accurate as it is practical to assess; however it is suggested that if a market research study were undertaken then it would be possible to ascertain with complete accuracy exactly which of the sales levels specified would be effective, i.e. it would indicate whether the sales would be zero, 2,500 or 4,000 units. This market research would cost £20,000 and could be undertaken before deciding whether to purchase the patent and manufacturing rights. Assuming the fixed manufacturing costs are all avoidable if no production takes place then is it worthwhile to undertake the market research? (*Hint*: Re-read section 2.2 of Chapter 2 before answering this part of the question.)

4.4 Once each year, Puccini plc buys a quantity of a perishable commodity. It processes and packages the commodity immediately and holds the cartons for sale one year later. Purchases have to be made in units of 100 kg – the current buying price is £30 per 100 kg. Each 100 kg yields sufficient output for a batch of 100 cartons and the processing and packaging of each batch costs £70. Storage costs, excluding interest, amount to £25 per 100 cartons p.a., payable at the end of the year. Puccini incurs fixed operating costs – i.e. costs which arise independently of the output level – of £70,000 p.a., payable at the end of the year.

Market conditions are such that Puccini takes its selling price as fixed by competitive considerations. Sales are made in cases of 100 cartons. The selling price, next year, for current output is estimated at £200 per 100 cartons. The probability of different volumes of sales has been estimated as follows:

Cases of 100 cartons	*Probability*
2,000	0.2
2,500	0.5
3,000	0.3
	1.0

The directors are considering what quantity of the commodity should now be purchased and processed for sale next year. Assume that the quantity to be purchased will be 200,000 kg, 250,000 kg or 300,000 kg. Any output that is not sold next year will have to be scrapped and will have no scrap value. The cost of capital is 25% p.a.

(**a**) Calculate the quantity which should be purchased in order to maximise the expected value of cash flows from the year's operations.

(**b**) Comment on the limitations of the criterion that the expected value of cash flows from operations should be maximised.

4.5 Pollock Ltd is considering the establishment of a new production centre to manufacture a new product, the fldget. For strategic reasons, the selling price would be set at £50 per unit. However, Pollock is uncertain about the scale of demand at that price. It estimates that two states of demand are equally likely: state A representing relative failure in competing with established products, state B representing relative success in that competition. Once the state has been identified, there remains some uncertainty about the actual level of demand because of uncertainty about general economic conditions:

State A		*State B*	
Volume per annum (units)	*Probability*	*Volume per annum* (units)	*Probability*
8,000	0.2	12,000	0.2
11,000	0.6	15,000	0.6
15,000	0.2	19,000	0.2

It would be possible to commission a market research survey to discover with virtual certainty whether state A or state B prevails.

The manufacture of flidgets would require the purchase of a machine. Two models are available, one which costs £400,000 and has a capacity of 12,000 units per annum and one which costs £600,000 and has a capacity of 20,000 units per annum. Both models would have lives of five years and no scrap value at the end of that time. In addition to the costs of a machine, the manufacture of flidgets would involve variable costs of £25 per unit and an increase of £100,000 per annum in the fixed costs of the firm.

The cost of capital of Pollock is 15% p.a. Levels of demand, prices and costs may be assumed to remain constant for the lives of the machines. Sales may be assumed to take place and production costs to be incurred on the last day of each year.

(a) Calculate the expected net present value of purchasing each model of the machine and hence recommend which should be purchased, assuming that no market research is undertaken.

(b) Calculate the maximum sum which Pollock should be willing to pay for the market research survey, assuming that the decision would be based on a calculation of expected net present values. (*Hint*: Re-read section 2.2 of Chapter 2 before answering this part of the question.)

(c) Discuss shortly the limitations of calculations of expected net present values as a basis for investment decisions.

4.6 The following mean returns and standard deviations have been calculated for the three following securities:

	Mean	*Standard deviation*
Walton	0.07	0.093
Williamson	0.10	0.070
Walter	0.12	0.085

The correlation coefficients between these three securities are:

	Walton	*Williamson*	*Walter*
Walton	+1.000	+0.137	+0.476
Williamson		+1.000	+0.422
Walter			+1.000

(a) Compute the expected return and variance of equally weighted portfolios of the following stocks:
  (i) Walton and Williamson
  (ii) Walton and Walter
  (iii) Williamson and Walter
  Why is the variance for portfolio (ii) greater than that for (i)?

(b) Examine the effect on the variance of an equally weighted portfolio of Williamson and Walter where the standard deviations are as given in the question, but where the correlation coefficient between Williamson and Walter is:
  (i) +1
  (ii) 0
  (iii) −1
  Comment on the results. If the correlation coefficient is −1 what portfolio weights would lead to a portfolio with zero variance?

(c) Which security or portfolio would a 'risk-neutral' wealth maximising decision maker prefer?

4.7 Chattox Ltd makes low quality clothes on a mass production basis. At present there is idle capacity in the plant and an American importer has approached Chattox, requesting it to supply stylish men's shirts at a contract price of £125 per dozen. Management at Chattox is uncertain as to whether the order should be accepted because demand can vary, as shown below, depending on the success of the US advertising campaign.

Demand (dozens)	*Probability*
3,000	0.3
4,500	0.6
6,000	0.1

The shirts can also vary in quality because of the use of two different types of material, depending on the ultimate customer's preference. The variable cost per dozen can thus be either £100 or £82.5, but the selling price for Chattox remains constant at £125 per dozen. The market research department of the American importer, who supplied the above demand probabilities, has also estimated that 75% of customers will prefer the more expensive material, while the remaining 25% will prefer the cheaper kind. Consumer preference probabilities are independent of sales demand probabilities. It is estimated that the incremental fixed costs, if the order is accepted, will amount to £120,000.

(a) Calculate the incremental profit or loss in the *six* states of nature that can occur.

(b) Compute the probability of the occurrence of each of the six states.

(c) Determine the probability that the project will be profitable.

(d) Calculate the expected value if the order is accepted.

(e) Discuss whether the order should be accepted.

Further reading

Ball, R. and Brown, P., 'Portfolio theory and accounting', *Journal of Accounting Research*, Autumn 1969.

Borch, K., *The Economics of Uncertainty*, Princeton University Press, 1968.

Carsberg, B. V., *Economics of Business Decisions*, Chapters 13 and 14, Penguin, 1975 and Pitman, 1979.

Hertz, D. B., 'Risk analysis in capital investment', *Harvard Business Review*, January/February 1964.

Hillier, F. S., 'The derivation of probabilistic information for the evaluation of risky investments', *Management Science*, April 1963.

Markowitz, H., 'Portfolio selection', *The Journal of Finance*, March 1952.

Modigliani, F. and Pogue, G. A., 'An introduction to risk and return', *Financial Analysts Journal*, March/April 1974.

Sharpe, W. F., *Portfolio Theory and Capital Markets*, McGraw-Hill, 1970.

Chapter 5

Costs and benefits for decisions

Managerial decisions are basically of two kinds: *accept or reject* decisions and *ranking* decisions. Accept or reject decisions arise when an organisation is considering a particular opportunity, acceptance of which will not affect its ability to accept any other opportunities that are expected to become available. In such a case a decision may be taken about the worthwhileness of the opportunity under consideration without having to compare it with other opportunities. The remainder of this chapter deals with such decisions.

Ranking decisions involve the choice between two or more competing opportunities. The need to rank the opportunities arises because circumstances exist that prevent the organisation from accepting all opportunities that appear to increase the present value of its cash flows. Such circumstances generally involve either a shortage (scarcity) of resources or mutual exclusivity between opportunities. *Scarce resources* are said to exist when a firm has insufficient supplies of one or more of its resources (e.g. labour, materials, factory space etc.) to accept all available opportunities that appear to be favourable. In this situation, the firm must endeavour to apply its scarce resources in the most profitable way. How it might do so is considered in more detail in Chapters 9 and 10. Two or more opportunities are said to be *mutually exclusive* when acceptance of one of them precludes acceptance of the others, for reasons other than scarcity of resources. Mutual exclusivity normally arises when different means of achieving the same or similar ends are being considered, for example alternative production methods having the same output capacity, or alternative locations for a new factory.

5.1 Principles of relevant cost and revenue determination

A central problem facing organisations is how to identify and evaluate the relevant costs and benefits resulting from the various available alternatives. The principles involved will be explained with particular reference to costs. Similar principles should be applied to benefits, however.

The principles to be applied in determining costs and benefits depend upon the decision maker's objectives. For all decision models, the costs and benefits that are relevant are those which can be affected by the decision. Clearly, if a particular cost or benefit is independent of the decision it should not be allowed to influence it. Recognition of this fact leads immediately to our first two principles of cost evaluation. The first is that *only future costs are relevant*. Decisions can be taken only about alternatives that affect the future. No one can take decisions that will alter the past, except perhaps to the extent that it might be possible to show the past in a different light. Costs that have been incurred include costs that have already been paid and also costs that are the subject of legally binding contracts, even if payments due under the contract have yet to be made. This latter category are called *committed costs*. Although past costs are not of themselves relevant to decisions, they may be useful aids for predicting future costs (see Chapter 7).

This notion of the irrelevance of past costs to decision making seems intuitively appealing and sensible, but it is a very difficult one for many decision makers to implement. Perhaps this is because it may contradict the workings of human nature. People often have an inbuilt desire to 'recover' their past outlays in particular situations. Human nature is not always rational or forward looking. Many examples come to mind. If we are contemplating the sale of a ticket which we hold to a football match, or if we are deciding on a price for the sale of a car, it is often difficult to rid ourselves of the notion that we would like to receive at least as much as we originally paid. Yet in decision making we should ignore these past costs and choose the alternative with the greatest incremental effect on future cash flows, regardless of whether it permits the recovery of past outlays.

The second relevant cost principle that follows from recognition of the fact that costs which are independent of a decision should not be allowed to influence it, is that *only those costs which will differ under some or all of the available alternatives are relevant*, i.e. only differential (or incremental) costs should be included in the analysis.

For example, take the case of an accountant considering the two alternatives of whether to travel to the office by train on five or six occasions during the coming week. Whether travelling five or six times it is cheaper to purchase a weekly season ticket than to pay fares daily. The cost of the season ticket is the same whether five or six journeys are made and thus is not relevant to the choice between the two alternatives. It follows that any apportionment of the cost of the season ticket (say on an 'average cost per journey' basis) is also irrelevant to the decision on whether to go to the office on five or six occasions during the week. The cost would be relevant, however, if a third alternative were to be considered: the possibility of not travelling to the office at all in the coming week. In this situation there would be no need to purchase the season ticket, the cost of which should then be considered as differential and relevant to the decision.

We have argued so far that only future differential costs (and revenues) are relevant for decision purposes. There remains one outstanding problem – the choice of a basis for measuring costs and revenues. Like the first two principles, this choice depends upon the decision maker's objectives and upon the decision model. In previous chapters we have argued for a decision objective which involves maximising the present value of future cash flows. Thus the third, and final, principle of relevant cost estimation is that *only cash costs are to be included*, suitably adjusted for differences in their timing if appropriate.

Our choice of cash as a measurement basis is perhaps less obvious than the first two principles of relevant cost determination. For example, it may not be appropriate for all individuals and firms or for the public sector (central government, local authorities, nationalised industries, etc.). If decision alternatives involve costs that are not easily expressed in cash terms (e.g. the possibility of a strike if production methods are changed) an attempt may be made to express such costs as cash flows. If this proves impracticable or inappropriate the decision maker will have to make a value judgement as to whether net cash benefits are large enough to justify incurring 'non-cash' costs, or vice versa.

The three basic principles discussed above may be summarised as follows: *for making decisions, only differential future cash flows should be considered.* All changes to cash flows resulting from a decision should be taken into account and not just those easily identified with a particular project. So if a decision to be taken in one department of an organisation would cause an increase in cash costs in another department, the increase should be taken into account in assessing the worthwhileness of the decision to be taken in the first department, assuming our objective is to maximise the cash flows of the organisation as a whole.

5.2 The role of alternative budgets

Alternative budgets can play an important part in the determination of relevant costs and revenues. Where a number of opportunities have to be ranked, because they are mutually exclusive or because some resources are scarce, it may be helpful to prepare a series of budgets showing the worthwhileness of each opportunity. Even where only one opportunity is under consideration two alternatives are implied: acceptance of the opportunity or rejection. In order to assess the desirability of the opportunity, future incremental cash flows associated with both acceptance and rejection must be considered. One way of doing this would be to prepare (cash flow) budgets for each alternative. In practice it is unusual (and therefore probably confusing to the decision maker) to present two budgets as an aid to making a decision about a single opportunity. In consequence, the figures in the two budgets are normally combined in a single column cash flow statement. It is crucial to remember, however, that each figure in the statement represents the cash flow if the opportunity is accepted *compared with* the cash flow if it is rejected – the latter is always the implied alternative to acceptance.

In this section, we concentrate on the determination of costs and revenues for inclusion in a single budget to evaluate an opportunity, acceptance of which will not impair a firm's ability to accept other opportunities. The extension of this procedure to ranking decisions is considered in Chapters 9 and 10. An important characteristic of the cash flow budget is that its 'bottom line' (i.e. the 'surplus' if the opportunity is accepted) should be easily interpreted. The most simple form of interpretation is presumably that if the surplus is positive the opportunity should be accepted, and if it is negative the opportunity should be rejected. A (positive) surplus indicates that acceptance of the opportunity would add more to cash resources than would alternative applications of the resources required for acceptance. Such alternative applications of resources already owned include their possible resale. Perhaps the most obvious alternative for resources not yet owned is not to purchase them!

We consider now the general procedures to be followed in determining relevant costs. The procedures are illustrated in the numerical example which follows. The relevant cost of using a particular resource on a project may be found by calculating the difference between cash flows expected if the resource is applied to the project and those if it is not. This is the differential cash flow approach to decision making. In order to calculate the expected cash flow relating to a resource if the opportunity under consideration is rejected, it is necessary to establish the best alternative use to which the resource could be put in the event of rejection. Thus the procedure for calculating the relevant cost of using a resource is in two steps.

1. Estimate cash flows expected if the resource is put to its best alternative use.
2. Compare these cash flows with those expected if the resource is applied to the project under consideration.

If the cash outflow resulting from applying the resource is greater than the cash outflow resulting from the best alternative use, the difference is called a cost. If cash inflows are involved, rather than outflows, a cost arises if the cash inflow expected from the best alternative use is greater than the cash inflow expected from application to the project. A mixture of cash inflows and outflows may be handled using the same principles.

Let us take an example. Nicholson Ltd manufactures a wide range of fashion products. The directors are considering whether to add a further product, the spur, to the range. A market research survey, recently undertaken at a cost of £5,000, suggests that demand for the spur would last for only one year, during which 50,000 units could be sold at £18 per unit. Production and sale of spurs would take place evenly throughout the year. The following information is available regarding the costs of manufacturing spurs.

Raw materials

Each spur would require three types of raw material: white, hart and lane. Quantities required, current stock levels and costs of each raw material are shown in Table 5.1. White is used regularly by the company and stocks are replaced as they are used. The current stock of harts is the result of over-buying for an earlier contract. The material is not used regularly by Nicholson Ltd and the best use of any stock that was not used to manufacture spurs would be to sell it. The company does not carry a stock of lanes and the units required would be specially purchased.

Labour

Production of each spur would require $\frac{1}{8}$ hour of skilled labour and 1 hour of unskilled labour. Wage rates are £6 per hour for skilled labour and £4 per hour for

Table 5.1 Raw material information

Raw material	*Amount required per spur*	*Current stock level*	*'Costs' per metre of raw material*		
			Original cost	*Current replacement cost*	*Current resale value*
	(metres)	(metres)	(£)	(£)	(£)
White	1.0	100,000	2.10	2.50	1.80
Hart	2.0	60,000	3.30	2.80	1.10
Lane	0.5	0	—	5.50	5.00

unskilled labour. In addition one supervisor would be required to devote all his working time for one year to supervision of the production of spurs. The supervisor is paid an annual wage of £10,000. Nicholson Ltd does not currently employ any skilled labour and must recruit specifically for the new product. If spurs are not manufactured, Nicholson Ltd expects to have available 100,000 surplus unskilled labour hours during the coming year. Because they intend to expand their activities in the future, and because of the high cost of making staff redundant, the directors have decided not to dismiss any unskilled workers in the foreseeable future. The supervisor is due to retire immediately on an annual pension, payable by the company, of £4,000. He has agreed to stay on for a further year if necessary, and to waive his pension for one year in return for a year's wage. Subsequent pension rights would not be affected.

Machinery

Two machines would be required to manufacture spurs, a marchi and a medwin. Some details of each machine are given in Table 5.2. Depreciation has been charged on each machine for each year of its life using the formula: $D = (C - S) \div L$, where D is the annual depreciation charge, C is the original cost of the machine, S is the expected resale value at the end of the machine's useful life, and L is the useful life in years, estimated when the machine was purchased. This is known as the straight line method, and is one of a number of depreciation methods commonly used by

Table 5.2 Details of machinery

	Marchi	*Medwin*
Original cost (£)	70,000	50,000
Accumulated depreciation (straight line) (£)	30,000	36,000
Written down value (£)	40,000	14,000
Age (years)	5	6
Expected remaining useful life (years)	5	1
Expected resale value at end of useful life (£)	10,000	8,000

Table 5.3 Values of machines

		Start of year (£)	*End of year* (£)
Marchi:	Replacement cost	80,000	65,000
	Resale value	60,000	47,000
	Discounted present value*	90,000	73,000
Medwin:	Replacement cost	13,000	9,000
	Resale value	11,000	8,000
	Discounted present value*	0	0

* Discounted present value of expected net receipts from continuing to operate the machine in its present use.

accountants. Table 5.3 contains details of various values of the two machines at the start and end of the year during which spurs would be manufactured. Nicholson Ltd owns a number of marchi machines which are used regularly on various products. Each marchi is replaced as soon as it reaches the end of its useful life. Medwin machines are no longer used, and the one which would be used for spurs is the only one the company now has. If it was not used to produce spurs it would be sold immediately.

Overheads

In addition to machinery costs, Nicholson Ltd incurs various other production overheads. Some, for example rent and rates, are fixed in total regardless of output levels and of the mix of products manufactured. Others, for example lighting and heating, have a fixed element and a variable element, the latter depending upon the volume of activity. For costing purposes, fixed overheads (including costs which are fixed in total and the fixed elements of other costs, but excluding depreciation) are allocated by the company to products on the basis of total labour hours required. The allocation for the coming year is £3.50 per labour hour. Variable overhead costs for spurs are estimated at £1.20 per unit produced.

We now consider the relevant cost to Nicholson Ltd of using each resource required for the production of spurs, applying the procedure outlined earlier, i.e. in each case we compare the cash flows associated with manufacture with those associated with non-manufacture. The difference between the two represents the incremental cost (or benefit) of each item. It should be noted that these figures may differ from those obtained by applying conventional cost accounting methods. The two approaches are compared in the next section.

Raw materials

Cash flows are as follows:[12]

[12] A minus sign signifies a cash outflow and a plus sign a cash inflow.

	Manufacture – (£)	*Non-manufacture* = (£)	*Difference* (£)
White	– 125,000	0	– 125,000
Hart: Sale of surplus	0	+ 66,000	
Purchase of additional units	– 112,000	0	– 178,000
Lane	– 137,500	0	– 137,500
			– 440,500

Fifty thousand metres of white would be required (50,000 spurs each requiring one metre). As white is used regularly by the company and stocks are replaced as used, the 50,000 metres required would be replaced for use on other jobs at the current replacement cost of £2.50 per metre, a total cash outflow of £125,000. This cash outflow would not be incurred if spurs were not produced. 100,000 metres of hart would be required (50,000 spurs each requiring two metres). If spurs were manufactured, Nicholson Ltd would use the 60,000 metres it has in stock, which have already been paid for, and would buy a further 40,000 metres at £2.80 per metre, a total cash outflow of £112,000. If spurs were not produced the company would sell its current stock of harts for £1.10 per metre, a total cash inflow of £66,000. Twenty-five thousand metres of lane would be needed (50,000 spurs each requiring 0.5 metres), and these would be specially purchased at £5.50 per metre, a total cash outflow of £137,500. There would be no cash flows associated with lane if spurs were not produced. To summarise, the relevant cost of raw materials is generally given by their current replacement cost, unless the materials are already owned and would not be replaced if used, in which case the relevant cost of using them is their current resale value or their value if applied to another product if this is greater than the current resale value.

Labour

Cash flows are as follows:

	Manufacture – (£)	*Non-manufacture* = (£)	*Difference* (£)
Skilled: Wages	– 37,500	0	– 37,500
Unskilled: Wages	– 200,000	– 200,000	0
Supervisor: Wages	– 10,000	0	
Pension	0	– 4,000	– 6,000
			– 43,500

Manufacture of spurs would involve 6,250 skilled labour hours (50,000 spurs each requiring $\frac{1}{8}$ hour) and 50,000 unskilled labour hours (50,000 spurs each requiring 1 hour). The additional wage payments for skilled labour will be £37,500

(6,250 hours × £6 = £37,500). Unskilled labour of £200,000 (50,000 × £4 = £200,000) will be the same whether or not spurs are produced. Thus unskilled labour wages are not relevant costs. The relevant cost of the supervisor is the difference between the wages paid and the pension cost that would be avoided.

Machinery

The likely effect of using a marchi machine is to bring closer the time at which it will have to be replaced. In order to estimate the relevant cost of using the marchi machine we need strictly to estimate all future cash flows associated with marchi machines on the alternative assumptions that spurs are and are not manufactured, and to discount them to present values to give measures of relevant cash flows. In practice, where a machine is used regularly, it may be sufficient to use the fall in its replacement cost value as an approximation to the relevant cost of using it. By following this procedure we are, in effect, implying that the firm is willing to expand its general machine capacity by buying a machine of equivalent age to the one to be used either immediately (if the manufacture proceeds) or at the end of the production period (if it does not). A rigorous analysis of the relevant cost of using fixed assets is beyond the scope of an introductory text.[13] Determination of the cash flows associated with the medwin machine is straightforward; it will be sold either immediately (if spurs are not manufactured) or after one year (if they are), at the prices given in Table 5.3. On the assumption that a second hand marchi machine will be purchased, the cash flows associated with machinery are:

	Manufacture – (£)	*Non-manufacture* = (£)	*Difference* (£)
Marchi: Replacement cost	– 80,000	– 65,000	– 15,000
Medwin: Resale value	+ 8,000	+ 11,000	– 3,000
			– 18,000

Overheads

Cash flows are as follows:

	Manufacture – (£)	*Non-manufacture* = (£)	*Difference* (£)
Variable overheads	– 60,000	0	– 60,000
Fixed overheads	– X	– X	0
			– 60,000

[13] Readers who wish to pursue this problem further might refer to Baxter, W. T., *Depreciation*, Sweet & Maxwell, 1971, or to Carsberg, B. V., 'On the linear programming approach to asset valuation', *Journal of Accounting Research*, Autumn 1969.

Variable costs (i.e. costs which vary with the level of activity) are £1.20 per spur produced, a total cash outflow of £60,000 (50,000 × £1.20) incurred only if manufacture takes place. All other overhead costs are fixed, i.e. the same in total whether or not spurs are produced. Whatever their level (we have assumed £X in total) it will be the same for manufacture and non-manufacture. This illustrates the important rule that, for decision purposes, only costs that will vary as a result of the decision being taken are relevant.

Sales revenue

If we apply to revenue the differential cash flow analysis used for costs we find, not surprisingly, that relevant revenue equals unit sales price (£18) multiplied by the number of units expected to be sold (50,000):

	Manufacture – (£)	*Non-manufacture* = (£)	*Difference* (£)
Sales revenue	+900,000	0	+900,000

For presentation to management, the results of the above analysis (i.e. the figures in the 'Difference' column) may be summarised in a single statement. A possible form of such a statement is given in Table 5.4. Supplementary information should be provided concerning the basis of calculation of the figures in the statement, along the lines discussed previously in this section, dealing particularly with points of possible contention such as the cost of using the marchi machine. The surplus figure of £338,000 is the expected increase in the company's cash resources which will arise as a result of manufacturing spurs rather than applying the resources

Table 5.4 Relevant costs and revenues expected from the manufacture of spurs

	£	£
Raw materials: White	125,000	
Hart	178,000	
Lane	137,500	440,500
Labour: Skilled	37,500	
Unskilled	0	
Supervisor	6,000	43,500
Machinery: Marchi	15,000	
Medwin	3,000	18,000
Variable overheads		60,000
		562,000
Sales revenue		900,000
Surplus from manufacture		338,000

required to their best alternative uses. Thus, on the basis of the figures in Table 5.4, production and sale of spurs is worthwhile.

The figures presented in Table 5.4 may not represent the complete picture, however. As we noted earlier, the direct cash consequences of a decision may not be the only factors of interest to the decision maker. In our example, production of spurs may have implications beyond those we have considered. For example, the new product may complement or compete with existing products; it may entice new customers to the company's whole range of products; it may change the risk associated with the company's overall activities; and so on. These, and other similar factors should be quantified and incorporated into the analysis as far as possible. At the very least they should be mentioned in notes appended to the decision budget so that decision makers can use their own value judgements to balance them against the cash items included in the budget.

We have made no attempt in our statement to adjust for differences in timing between cash flows. In practice, where cash flows arise at significantly different times (for example, if all costs are payable at the start of a year and all revenues receivable at the end) it will be necessary to apply an interest adjustment to ensure that distortions created by the timing differences are removed.

One important conclusion to emerge from the analysis in this section is that for no resource was the cost already incurred (i.e. historical cost) the appropriate measure of its relevant cost. This conclusion is unfortunate because accounting records have conventionally been, and to a large extent still are, based on the measurement, recording and matching of historical costs (also called original, past or sunk costs). We now turn to a more detailed consideration of this problem.

5.3 A comparison with conventional cost accounting

The figures in Table 5.4 differ from those we would have obtained by applying conventional cost accounting to the problem of Nicholson Ltd. Conventional cost accounting often involves the use of *standard costs* for measuring the costs of using resources. Standard costs are discussed in detail in Chapters 13–15. Each resource is assigned a standard cost which may be based on its historical cost, its current cost (the cost at today's prices) or its expected cost (the cost expected at the time the resource will be used). The use of standard costs has the advantage that it avoids the need to calculate the cost of each resource on each occasion that a new opportunity is being evaluated. On the other hand, it sometimes means that the idiosyncrasies of a particular decision are overlooked. Broadly speaking, the conventional cost accounting approach involves matching the historical, current or expected costs of the resources actually used on a project against its revenues. These costs sometimes include fixed costs which are allocated on one (or more) of a number of bases. Even if current or expected costs are used, the conventional approach may over- or under-estimate the worthwhileness of particular opportunities. The dangers involved in allocating fixed costs, and effectively treating them as if they are variable, are illustrated more fully in Chapter 16 (pp. 361–5).

Consider the statement in Table 5.5, which includes costs measured according to

Table 5.5 Conventional accounting 'profitability' of manufacturing spurs

	£	£
Cost of market research survey		5,000
Raw materials:		
White (50,000 metres at £2.10)	105,000	
Hart (60,000 metres at £3.30 + 40,000 metres at £2.80)	310,000	
Lane (25,000 metres at £5.50)	137,500	552,500
Labour:		
Skilled (6,250 hours at £6.00)	37,500	
Unskilled (50,000 hours at £4.00)	200,000	
Supervisor	10,000	247,500
Depreciation of machinery:		
Marchi ([40,000 – 10,000] ÷ 5)	6,000	
Medwin ([14,000 – 8,000] ÷ 1)	6,000	12,000
Overheads:		
Fixed (112,500 × £3.50)	393,750	
Variable (50,000 × £1.20)	60,000	453,750
		1,270,750
Sales revenue		900,000
Loss from manufacturing spurs		370,750

the historical costs of resources required, and compare the figures with those in Table 5.4. The first difference concerns the treatment of historical costs. This application of conventional cost accounting practice involves charging resources to particular projects at their original cost as, for example, with the market research survey, raw material white and the first 60,000 metres of raw material hart. In support of this procedure, it might be argued that if the value of a resource has fallen (or risen) since purchase, the loss (or profit) should be taken into account; but if the value has changed the consequent loss (or profit) has already occurred regardless of any decision to be made now and should not be added to (or subtracted from) the costs of the opportunity under consideration. The crucial question is which cash flows will be affected by the decision? The answer to this question depends on the currently available alternative uses of the resource, and will be equal to its historical cost only by accident.

The second difference is the treatment of depreciation of assets. The straight line method of depreciation has already been mentioned. It is widely used in the reporting of financial information, and in common with other conventional methods of depreciation has the characteristic that the annual depreciation charge is based on an allocation of the original cost of the asset less its expected ultimate resale value. The treatment of depreciation is thus an extension of the conventional practice of matching or recovering past costs. For decision purposes we need to know the sacrifice involved in using the asset on the particular project under consideration. There is no obvious reason why this should correspond to the writing off of original cost that typifies the conventional accounting concept of depreciation.

A third area of difference concerns fixed costs. Costs that are fixed regardless of the decision under consideration (for example, unskilled labour wages and fixed overhead costs in the case of Nicholson Ltd) are not relevant costs of that decision for they cannot be affected by it. Nevertheless, in conventional accounting practice, fixed costs are often allocated to available opportunities. Later chapters explore cost allocation problems in more detail.

A final main area of difference relates to the impact of a project on a firm's other activities (for example, the deferral of the supervisor's pension in the case of Nicholson Ltd). Under conventional practice, only the amount paid for the resource is treated as a cost; cash flow changes elsewhere in the organisation are not usually considered even though they are a direct consequence of the decision being taken.

The differences between conventional practice and differential cash flow analysis may lead to startling differences in 'profitability'. In our example a conventional 'loss' of £370,750 is in fact an incremental cash surplus of £338,000. In general, when prices are rising, the application of conventional historical cost accounting results in the under-statement of the current relevant cost of using resources such as stock and fixed assets and a consequent over-statement of profitability. On the other hand, inclusion of allocated fixed costs overstates relevant costs and leads to an under-statement of profitability. Such differences may lead to incorrect advice, as in the case of Nicholson Ltd.

Some of the differences outlined above may be reduced if current or expected costs are used instead of historical costs in conventional cost accounting statements. Two main adjustments are required to historical cost figures for the purpose of determining current costs. The first is to increase the cost of stock used (e.g. of raw materials) from its historical cost to its current cost. The second is to base the depreciation charge for fixed assets (e.g. machines) on the current cost rather than the historical cost of the assets concerned.

The adoption of current costs rather than historical costs would have some effect on the statement in Table 5.5. The precise changes would depend upon which of a number of possible methods for measuring current costs was chosen. The cost of raw materials and depreciation would probably be adjusted to figures very similar to those in the relevant cost statement in Table 5.4. In other respects (inclusion of the cost of the market research survey, unskilled labour wages and fixed overheads, and the omission of the saving on the supervisor's pension) the use of current costs instead of historical costs fails to remove problems created by the application of conventional accounting procedures.

The approach to the determination of relevant costs and revenues for decisions which we have recommended in this chapter recognises that the cost of using a resource depends upon the alternative uses to which it could be put. We conclude the chapter by noting that such an interpretation of cost is consistent with the economist's concept of *opportunity cost*, which is normally defined in terms of the value of the best opportunity forgone by not applying a resource to an alternative use. Agreement between definitions of cost used by accountants and economists would have many benefits, particularly where accounting data are being used as input to economic models. Unfortunately, there is still some way to go before such agreement is achieved.

Discussion topics

1. Explain the difference between accept or reject and ranking decisions and discuss the importance of the distinction.
2. What are the main principles of relevant cost and revenue determination? Illustrate your answer with applications of each principle.
3. 'Past costs are irrelevant to *all* decisions.' Do you agree? Can you think of any decisions in which past costs might play a part? Are committed costs the same as past costs?
4. 'The economist's notion of opportunity cost is a valuable contribution to managerial decision making.' Discuss.
5. Explain the distinction between fixed costs and variable costs, and discuss its importance to the determination of relevant costs for decision making.
6. To what extent do current cost adjustments increase the usefulness of historical cost accounting numbers for managerial decision making?

Exercises

5.1 Memlinc Ltd manufactures scientific instruments. It is considering whether or not to accept a contract to manufacture a batch of oscilloscopes. The contract would last for 52 weeks. The company's cost accountant prepares the following statement on the basis of which it is recommended that the contract should not be accepted.

	£	£
Materials: A – already in stock (original cost)	3,750	
B – ordered (original contract price)	4,500	8,250
Labour		17,500
Machinery: Leased at £250 per week	13,000	
Already owned – depreciation	10,000	23,000
General overheads: 100% on labour		17,500
		66,250
Contract price offered		60,000
Loss on contract		6,250

The cost accountant supplies the following additional information:

1. Material A was purchased two years ago. If sold now it would realise £2,500. Alternatively it could be adapted and used on another job as a substitute for material presently costing £4,000. It would cost £750 to make the necessary adaptation. Material B was ordered six months ago. Delivery has been delayed by a strike at the supplier's factory and agreement has been reached between the supplier and Memlinc Ltd that a discount of £1,000 be allowed against the original contract price to compensate for the delay. If material B is not

used on the job under consideration the only alternative is to sell it for £2,250.

2. The accountant's estimate includes £5,000 in respect of a supervisor's wages. Unlike the rest of the labour used on the job the supervisor will be employed whether or not the contract is accepted. However if the supervisor does have to work on the job under consideration the company will have to employ someone else at £75 per week to do the work he or she could otherwise have done.
3. Two machines will be used on the job. One is a machine the company leases for £250 per week. This is at present being used in another department and if transferred for use on the job being considered another machine will have to be leased for £140 per week and additional labour costing £150 per week hired to maintain production in the other department. The second machine was purchased by the company three years ago for £50,000. Its estimated life was then five years and hence depreciation at the rate of £10,000 per annum is being written off. If not used on the job, the machine would be sold now for £12,500; otherwise it will be sold after completion of the contract for an estimated price of £6,000.
4. As in past years, general overheads, which include such items as rent, rates and other administrative expenses, are recovered at the rate of 100% on direct labour. All expenses included under this heading will remain unchanged whether or not the contract is accepted.
5. The storage space necessary if the job is undertaken can be provided only if the construction of a new works canteen is delayed for one year.

(a) If you think it necessary, redraft the cost accountant's statement. Explain any alterations you make.

(b) Advise Memlinc Ltd whether or not to accept the contract.

5.2 The Van Dyck Motor plc has recently suffered a strike which lasted for two weeks. During that time no cars were produced. The company issued a press statement to the effect that the cost of the strike was £5 million. This figure was arrived at by the managing director who estimated that production lost was 1,000 cars, each of which could have been sold for £5,000 giving a total loss of turnover of £5,000,000. The company's cost accountant feels that the managing director was over-stating the cost of the strike and provides the following statement to support his view.

	£000
Expenses avoided	
Materials (£1,000 per car)	1,000
Production labour (£500 per car)	500
Depreciation of machinery	1,750
Overheads: 200% on labour	1,000
	4,250
Loss of sales revenue	5,000
Cost of strike	750

The following additional information is available:

1. Depreciation of machinery is based on the conventional straight line method of calculation. The plant manager estimates that the machinery will fall in

value by £200,000 each week regardless of the level of production. In addition, it is felt that its value will fall by £150,000 for every 100 cars that are produced.

2. Overhead expenses are recovered at the rate of 200% on production labour. Most of the overhead expenses are unaffected by the level of production, e.g. rent, rates, maintenance, staff wages, but some, such as power and lighting, vary directly with production. The general manager estimates that the latter type of overhead expense, varying directly with the level of production, amounts to £10,000 for every 100 cars produced.
3. During the period of the strike the maintenance staff, whose wages are included in the fixed overhead expense, carried out a major overhaul on one of the company's machines using materials costing £10,000. This overhaul would normally have been performed by an outside contractor at a price, including materials, of £100,000.
4. The sales manager feels that about one-half of the production lost could be made up and sold in the next month by the production labour working overtime. Labour is paid at the rate of time-and-a-half for overtime working.

Prepare a statement clearly showing the cost to the company of the strike. State any assumptions which you make and explain any differences between your figures and those of the cost accountant.

5.3 Ketchum Ltd is considering the manufacture of certain components, incorporated in its range of final products, which have previously been purchased from outside suppliers. This additional manufacturing operation would cover only the next twelve months, since capacity which is presently unused will then, it is expected, be required to fill rising demand for the final products themselves. The following information has been assembled:

1. 90,000 units of the component would be required over the year.
2. One kg of raw material type A is required for each unit of the component. The current cost of such material is £1.60 per kg, but an alternative material, with a current replacement cost of £1.80 per kg and a realisable value of £1.00, could be used. The company has in stock 30,000 kg of the alternative material which would be sold if not used to manufacture the component.
3. One kg of raw material type B is required for each unit of the component; 125,000 kg which cost £200,000 are currently in stock. So far as not used for the manufacture of the components, this material might be transferred to another department where it can be used in place of material currently costing £1.50 per kg. Alternatively, it might be sold for £1.25 per kg.
4. Additional labour will be required at the rate of one half-hour of skilled labour and two hours of unskilled labour per unit. Hourly wage rates are currently £3.00 for skilled labour and £1.50 for unskilled labour. Further supervisors would be required at a minimum annual cost of £14,000; this would increase by £7,000 for each 15,000 units, or part thereof, of the component manufactured in excess of 60,000 units.
5. A training programme for the skilled labour force, costing £28,000, has already been carried out in anticipation of a decision to manufacture the components. A further expenditure of £14,000 will be required if units to be manufactured exceed 60,000.

6. It is estimated that existing machinery can be used for the manufacture of 45,000 units with the result that its future scrap value will be reduced by £20,000. (The present value of this reduction is estimated at £12,000.) For every 15,000 units in excess of that production level, a machine must be hired for £6,000.
7. Variable overheads are estimated at £0.80 per hour of direct labour and the application of the company's normal costing techniques would involve a charge of £1.20 per direct labour hour in respect of fixed overheads other than depreciation.
8. The cost of one unit of the component from outside suppliers is expected to be £11.00.

(a) Produce a statement showing the total cost of the 90,000 units if the company chose to manufacture at each of the following levels and purchase the balance from the outside supplier:

30,000 units
45,000 units
60,000 units
75,000 units

(b) Comment on any matters, not quantified in the statement produced in answer to (a), which you feel would be relevant in arriving at a final decision.

5.4 Because of a fall in demand for its products, the production manager of Beltrami Ltd has proposed that over the next six months idle capacity and labour should be used for the manufacture of a component normally purchased from outside suppliers. The following statement is used to support this case:

Cost of manufacturing 200,000 units required	£
Materials:	
Type A, 100,000 kg at actual cost of £0.40 per kg	40,000
Type B, 5,000 kg at actual cost of £7.00 per kg	35,000
Type C, 10,000 kg at estimated cost of £3.00 per kg	30,000
Labour:	
Grade 1, 16,000 hours at £3.25 per hour	52,000
Grade 2, 4,000 hours at £2.50 per hour	10,000
Grade 3, 10,000 hours at £2.00 per hour	20,000
Overheads	
Depreciation of existing machines, 8,000 hours of machine time at £1 per hour	8,000
Depreciation of additional machines, £60,000 at 10% for six months	3,000
Other overheads, 10,000 machine hours at £3.20 per hour	32,000
Total cost	230,000
Cost per unit	1.15

The following information is also available:

1. Type A material is regularly used by the company; large stocks are currently held because of substantial purchases made before a recent price increase to £0.60 per kg.

2. 3,000 kg of Type B material have been in storage since excess stocks were purchased for a special order last year. The company has been looking for an opportunity to recover the cost, since the resale value of the material is only £5 per kg. The cost of purchasing Type B material at the present time would be £7 per kg.
3. Grade 1 labour is normally in short supply in the area, so no lay-offs are contemplated, although 16,000 hours of labour of this type will be idle if not employed in the manufacture of the components. If the labour involved is so used, the trade union has insisted on an extra payment of £0.50 per hour in excess of the normal hourly rate of £2.75 because of the unfamiliar work.
4. One hour of either Grade 1 or Grade 2 labour is needed for every 10 units of production. The production manager suggests that Grade 2 labour be employed only to supplement instead of to replace Grade 1 labour, despite the lower hourly rate, because of the problems of recruiting a substantial amount of Grade 2 labour for the short term.
5. Grade 3 labour can be hired as needed.
6. Production plans for the company's normal activities indicate that 8,000 hours of machine time (sufficient for 160,000 units) will be available during the six month period. The depreciation charge included is based on the company's usual costing policies; however, it is not anticipated that the use of the machines will have the effect of reducing measurably their scrap value when they are replaced next year on the company's planned move to a new factory.
7. Two additional machines would be required to raise production of the component to the level of 200,000 units. These would be purchased for £60,000 or leased for six months for £4,000 each. If purchased, they would be stored after use in the manufacture of the components, for eventual installation in the new factory next year.
8. The charge for other overheads is based on the company's usual costing system and includes £1.20 per machine hour for fixed costs and £2 for variable costs. It is not anticipated that the manufacture of the components would involve the incurring of any additional fixed costs, and it is expected that the amount of variable overheads will conform with the company's usual experience.
9. The cost of each component bought from the existing supplier is £1.20.

(a) Prepare a recommendation supported by appropriate calculations as to what policy should be pursued by the company, on financial grounds alone, assuming that the additional machines referred to in paragraph 7 will be leased and stating any other assumption which you make.

(b) Discuss any factors other than those quantified in your answer to (a) which you feel might be relevant in arriving at the final decision.

Further reading

Amey, L. R., 'On opportunity costs and decision making', *Accountancy*, July 1968.

Buchanan, J. M., *Cost and Choice: An Inquiry in Economic Theory*, Markham, 1969.

Buchanan, J. M. and Thirlby, G. F. (eds.), *LSE Essays on Cost*, London School of Economics and Political Science/Weidenfeld & Nicolson, 1973.

Coase, R. H., 'The nature of costs', in Solomons, D. (ed.), *Studies in Cost Analysis*, 2nd edn., Sweet & Maxwell, 1968.

Edwards, R. S., 'The rationale of cost accounting', in Solomons, D. (ed.), *Studies in Costing*, Sweet & Maxwell, 1952.

Gould, J. R., 'The economist's cost concept and business problems', in Baxter, W. T. and Davidson, S. (eds.), *Studies in Accounting*, Institute of Chartered Accountants in England and Wales, 1977.

Part 2

Applications

Chapter 6

Cost behaviour and cost–volume–profit analysis

The use of incremental analysis explained in the previous chapter requires the identification of those costs which are relevant to decision making. In particular, incremental analysis demands a knowledge of which costs change, and which costs do not change, as a consequence of a particular decision. Identification of the ways in which the enterprise's costs behave in response to changes in the level of its activities is, therefore, an important first step in helping to estimate the effects of particular decisions on future cash flows. The responses of costs to changes in circumstances (including changes in activity levels) are known collectively as *cost behaviour*. We might be better able to understand the importance of cost behaviour as follows. As one important objective of a firm's managers is to generate from operations the maximum possible amount of cash, managers must strive to attain the output level which is expected to maximise cash resources. Therefore, information on how costs behave in relation to changes in output levels is vital for optimal planning and decision making.

So far we have deliberately avoided attaching labels to particular costs. We have simply stated that a cost is relevant to a decision if it involves an incremental future cash flow to the organisation. In practice, however, it is usual and useful to classify costs in certain basic ways, and to group together those costs which behave in the same way. For example, cost classifications and groupings help to identify relevant and irrelevant costs, and are important for the forms of cost–volume–profit analysis considered later in this chapter. The next section looks at some of these cost classifications, with particular reference to the behaviour of costs in response to changes in output levels.

6.1 Patterns of cost behaviour

Variable costs

A cost is variable if it is expected to vary as a function of the level of output or the level of sales. Raw materials and labour paid on an hourly basis are good examples

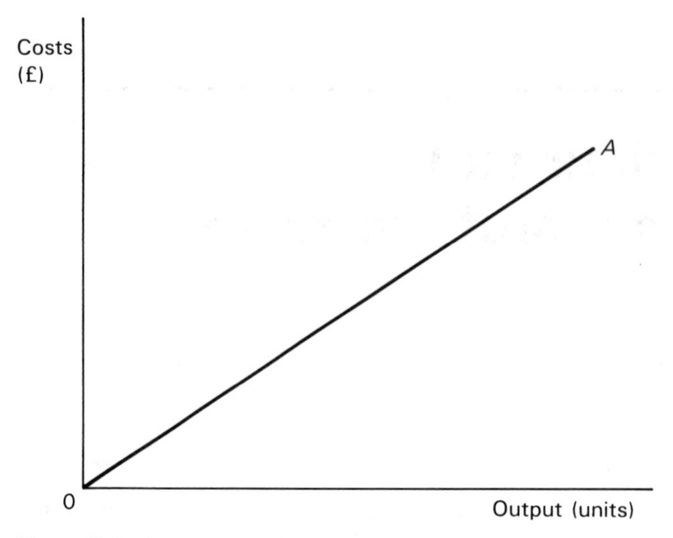

Figure 6.1 Variable cost function.

of costs which vary with the level of output; sales commission is an example of a cost which varies with the level of sales. Accountants often assume that variable costs are linear (i.e. the functional relationship between costs and output is expressed as a straight line, such as the line $0A$ in Figure 6.1). This assumed linear relationship means that the cost per unit of output is presumed to be constant at all levels of output. The relationship can be expressed by the equation:

$$y = bx$$

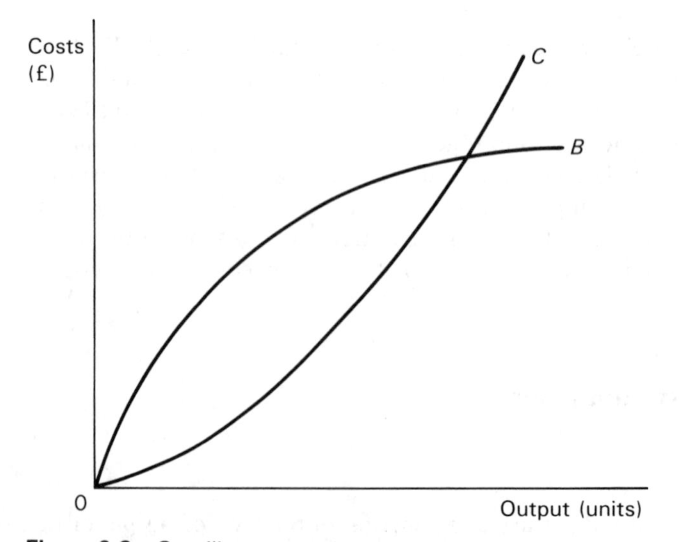

Figure 6.2 Curvilinear cost functions.

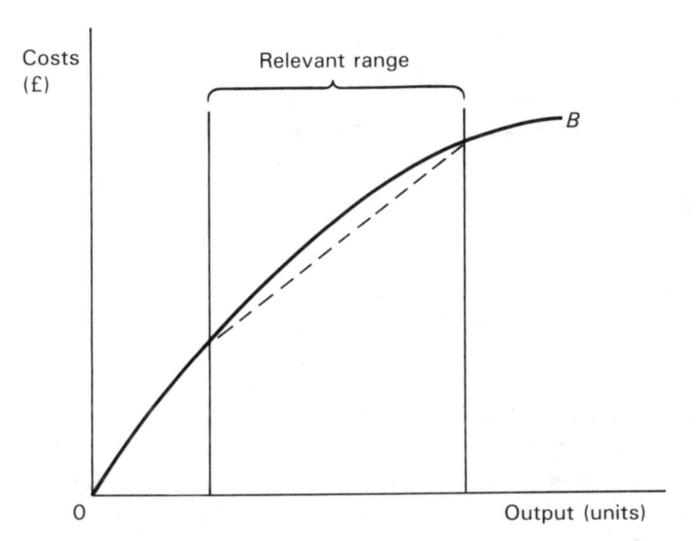

Figure 6.3 The relevant range and linear approximation.

where y = expected cost, x = expected level of output and b = constant cost per unit. (This relationship is an example of a cost 'model'. Models were first introduced in Chapter 3.)

For instance, if labour is a variable cost, and each unit of output requires two hours of labour at £3 per hour, then 100 units of output should require a total labour cost of £6 × 100 = £600 (i.e. y = £600 where b = £6 per unit and x = 100 units). Knowing that labour is a variable cost will help the firm to plan for future decisions which involve the use of labour.

However, for reasons discussed in the next section, the simple linear relationship between costs and output may not always hold, and a curvilinear function may be a better representation of actual cost behaviour, as shown in Figure 6.2. For curve $0B$, an extra unit of output causes a *less* than proportional increase in cost (e.g. it takes less than two labour hours to produce an additional unit at high output levels, due perhaps to the workers becoming more efficient); for curve $0C$, an extra unit of output causes a *more* than proportional cost increase (e.g. it costs more to produce an additional unit at high output levels, perhaps because it is necessary to work overtime and hence incur additional costs).

If the variable cost function is curvilinear, appropriate cost calculations can become very complicated. For this reason, linear functions are often used as approximations within certain relevant output ranges which the firm has experienced in the past. Figure 6.3 provides an illustration of a linear approximation (the dashed line). The importance of the relevant range is discussed further in section 6.3.

Fixed costs

Fixed costs are those costs which are likely to remain unchanged regardless of the level of output or the particular decision under consideration. Rent, rates and directors' salaries are examples of costs which are often fixed for a particular decision. Note that the term 'fixed' relates primarily to short-term decisions. In the long term very few costs are irrevocably fixed. Indeed the long run is frequently defined in economics textbooks as a period over which all costs are avoidable. A graphical description of a linear fixed cost function (AB) is shown in Figure 6.4. The function can be expressed by the equation:

$$y = a$$

where y = expected cost and a = constant amount.

It should be clearly understood that the decision variable x (the level of output) does not affect the level of fixed costs (i.e. it does not enter the cost equation). For instance, if a firm expects to pay £1,000 for the rent of a factory during the forthcoming year, then, provided that the level of production does not require the use of another factory, the number of units produced will not affect the amount to be paid for factory rent. It will remain constant at £1,000, and will be independent of the level of output. Such a fixed cost is not relevant for short-run decisions, as explained in the previous chapter.

The presumption in Figure 6.4 is that the item of fixed cost under consideration will remain constant at all output levels, including zero output. It may be more realistic to assume that there are some fixed expenses which are avoidable at zero output, but are constant at all other output levels. (For example, if the firm referred to above decides to produce nothing, it may be able to avoid payment of rent on the factory.) If so, a function similar to that shown in Figure 6.5 may be more representative. In Figure 6.5, the fixed cost line does not begin at point A on the vertical axis, but rather at point A_1, which corresponds to the output level 0_1, the point at which the cost is incurred.

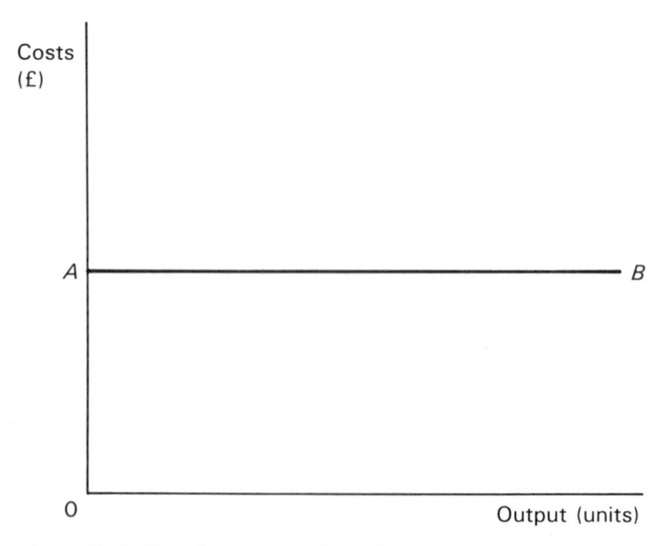

Figure 6.4 Fixed cost function (1).

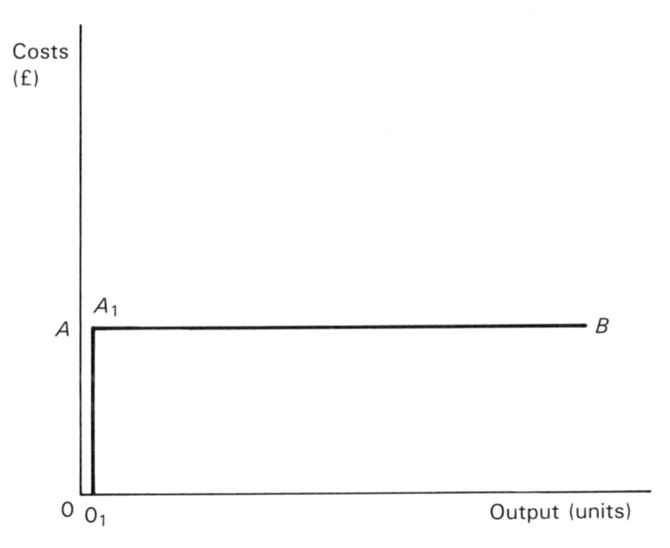

Figure 6.5 Fixed cost function (2).

Step costs

Step costs result from input factors which cannot be increased in very small amounts. They can be increased only in discrete 'steps'. Strictly speaking, nearly all variable costs fall into this category. Examples of such costs might be certain items of small equipment, secretarial salaries and supervisory labour. For instance, for output levels of 0–1,000 units, the firm may need only one supervisor, for levels of 1,001–2,000 units, two supervisors may be needed, for levels of 2,001–3,000 units, three supervisors may be needed. Thus a pattern develops similar to that shown in Figure 6.6.

Figure 6.6 shows that the cost item remains constant at an amount of £A for output levels between 0 and s. When output increases beyond s, the cost increases to £B and remains at this amount up to output level t, when it increases to £C, and so on.

Step costs cannot be described by a simple algebraic function and, for simplicity, such costs are often dealt with in one of the following ways:

1. If the steps are sufficiently shallow and frequent, a continuous function of the form $y = bx$ may be used as an approximation, as shown by the straight line in Figure 6.6.

2. If the likely output range lies completely within one step, for example between s and t, or between t and u, the step cost may be treated as a fixed cost.

3. If neither of the above conditions is satisfied, and step costs cannot be treated as being variable or fixed, more elaborate analysis is needed. The form of this analysis is explained later in this chapter.

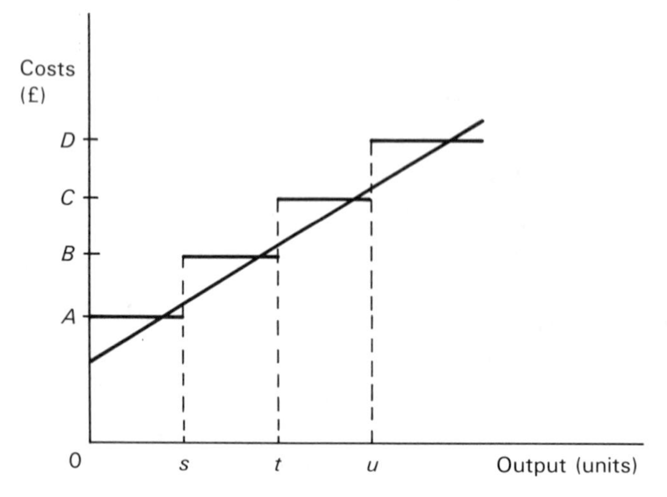

Figure 6.6 Step cost function.

Semi-variable costs

Costs which possess both a fixed and a variable component are called 'semi-variable' or 'mixed' costs. A good example of such a cost is an electricity cost, which includes a basic fixed charge irrespective of use, and a cost element which depends solely upon use; or a telephone cost which is in the nature of a fixed rental together with an additional charge for each call made. The variable element of a semi-variable cost function may be either linear or curvilinear, as explained earlier. For simplicity, we show the semi-variable function as a linear function as in Figure 6.7.

The line *BC* shows the total cost, which cuts the vertical line at point *B*, representing the constant level of fixed cost. The semi-variable cost function can be

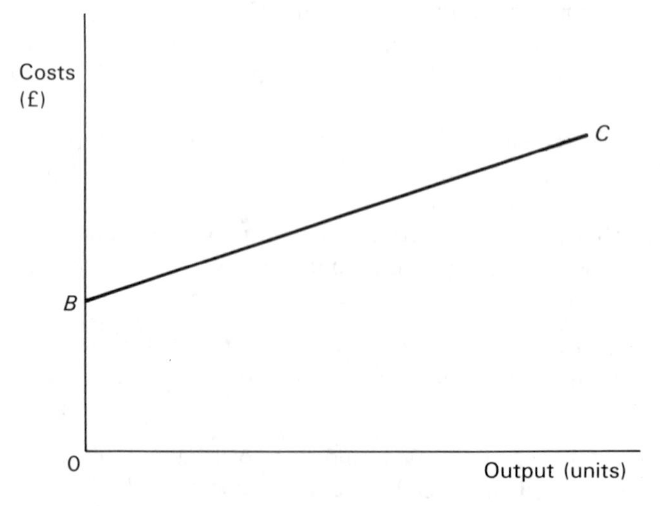

Figure 6.7 Semi-variable cost function.

expressed by the equation:

$$y = a + bx$$

where y = expected cost, a = constant amount (i.e. the fixed element of the cost), b = variable cost per unit of output and x = level of output.

This, as we shall see, is a very important cost function, because it mirrors the organisation's *total cost* function (i.e. it involves the estimation of both fixed and variable costs). The estimation of the total cost function, which is often fundamental to business planning, is the subject of the following chapter.

The four patterns of cost behaviour described here are not the only patterns which can be observed. Rather, they are guidelines to be used in the determination and construction of the cost functions necessary to analyse and evaluate business decisions. In particular, two points concerning the behaviour of costs should be clearly recognised: the linearity assumption and the use of the relevant range.

6.2 The linearity assumption

Much cost behaviour can be described accurately only by non-linear functions. In practice, linear approximations are often used to simplify the calculations involved in the analysis of cost behaviour. This is not unreasonable as statistical studies have presented evidence which suggests that within specified output limits, organisations do have cost functions which are approximately linear.[14]

6.3 The relevant range

The assumption of linearity may be unrealistic if taken to extremes. As there are usually upper and lower limits to the levels of an organisation's attainable output, there will equally be upper and lower limits to the firm's cost functions. For each organisation there will be a relevant range of output levels within which it is likely to incur costs. One dimension of this is the range of time periods over which the cost functions are valid (the period during which the nature of demand for the firm's output can be reasonably predicted is usually fairly short). Furthermore, it may be unwise to extrapolate a cost function indiscriminately to estimate costs for an output level outside the range for which the function was originally calculated – the behaviour of the function may well have changed by then. It is, therefore, imprudent to be categorical about the appropriate classification of certain costs. Very few costs are *always* variable and fewer still are *always* fixed. *A cost which is fixed for one decision or one time period may well be variable for a different decision, or in another time period.* Each situation must be assessed individually and treated on its own merits.

[14] See e.g. Johnston, J., *Statistical Cost Analysis*, McGraw-Hill, 1960 (especially Chapters 4 and 5).

6.4 Cost–volume–profit relationships

Decision making and planning by management do not involve only the determination of relevant cost behaviour; we have assumed that a major objective of managers is the generation of cash. Planning and decision making involve a consideration of the combined effect on *both* cost and revenue functions of changes in the level of activity. This is achieved by an examination of the often intricate relationship of costs, volume and revenues which in turn gives insights into the incremental impact on cash flows of the various choices open to management. The technique used in this examination is usually termed 'cost–volume–profit' (CVP) analysis, although the term 'cost–volume–surplus cash flow' would be a more appropriate, but more cumbersome, description of the relationships to be analysed.

Cost–volume–profit analysis is based on the following relationship:

Profit = Revenues − Total costs

If we use the term π to denote profit for the period, P to denote the selling price per unit, x to denote the level of output produced and sold during the period, a to denote the level of fixed costs for the period, and b to denote the variable cost per unit produced and sold, we can then derive the expanded CVP equation as follows:

$$\pi = Px - (a + bx)$$

CVP analysis thus assumes that the firm's total costs can be separated into their fixed and variable components. However, as we shall see in the following chapter, it is seldom immediately obvious which costs are fixed and which are variable, and quite sophisticated statistical techniques may be necessary in order to segregate costs into appropriate categories for decision making purposes.

Using the data for Burnden Ltd given in Table 6.1, we can see how the cost–volume–profit equation might be used to answer certain questions relevant to managerial decision making, such as:

1. What is the output level in units at which Burnden Ltd breaks even (i.e. makes neither a profit nor a loss, or, put another way, exactly covers its total costs)?

2. How many units must be sold to show a profit of £5,000?

3. What selling price would have to be charged to show a profit of £6,000 on sales of 10,000 units?

1. *Break-even point in units*

$$\pi = Px - (a + bx)$$

Then Burnden Ltd breaks even at a level of output (x) where:

$$a + bx = Px$$

Table 6.1 Burnden Ltd (cost–volume–profit data)

Selling price (£)	5
Fixed costs per annum (£)	30,000
Semi-variable costs:	
Fixed element (£)	10,000
Variable element (£ per unit)	1
Variable costs (£ per unit)	2
Relevant range of output (units)	6,000–24,000

Substituting in the above we have:

$$40{,}000 + 3x = 5x$$

$$\therefore \quad x = 20{,}000 \text{ units}$$

2. *Units to be sold to show a profit of £5,000*
Substituting in the CVP equation we have:

$$5{,}000 = 5x - (40{,}000 + 3x)$$

$$2x = 45{,}000$$

$$\therefore \quad x = 22{,}500 \text{ units}$$

3. *Selling price to be charged to show a profit of £6,000 on sales of 10,000 units*
Substituting in the CVP equation we have:

$$6{,}000 = P(10{,}000) - (40{,}000 + 3(10{,}000))$$

$$\therefore \quad 6{,}000 = 10{,}000P - 70{,}000$$

$$\therefore \quad 10{,}000P = 76{,}000$$

$$\therefore \quad P = £7.60 \text{ (i.e. an increase of £2.60 per unit).}$$

The above equations are *one* means of presenting CVP information. An alternative form of presentation, which may serve to clarify the underlying cost and revenue relationship assumed, is the use of graphs. Two graphs in particular are used to portray CVP relationships, the break-even chart and the profit–volume chart.

6.5 The break-even chart

The break-even chart, used frequently by accountants, serves a variety of functions. The initial purpose of the chart may have been simply to inform management of the level of output at which total revenue just covers total cost. Nowadays, in conjunction with the relevant range notion, the chart can be used to give an estimate of profit at different output levels (i.e. the break-even chart can be viewed as representing a series of summarised income statements).

Using the data for Burnden Ltd taken from Table 6.1, we can construct a break-even chart by summing the various cost categories. The chart is shown in

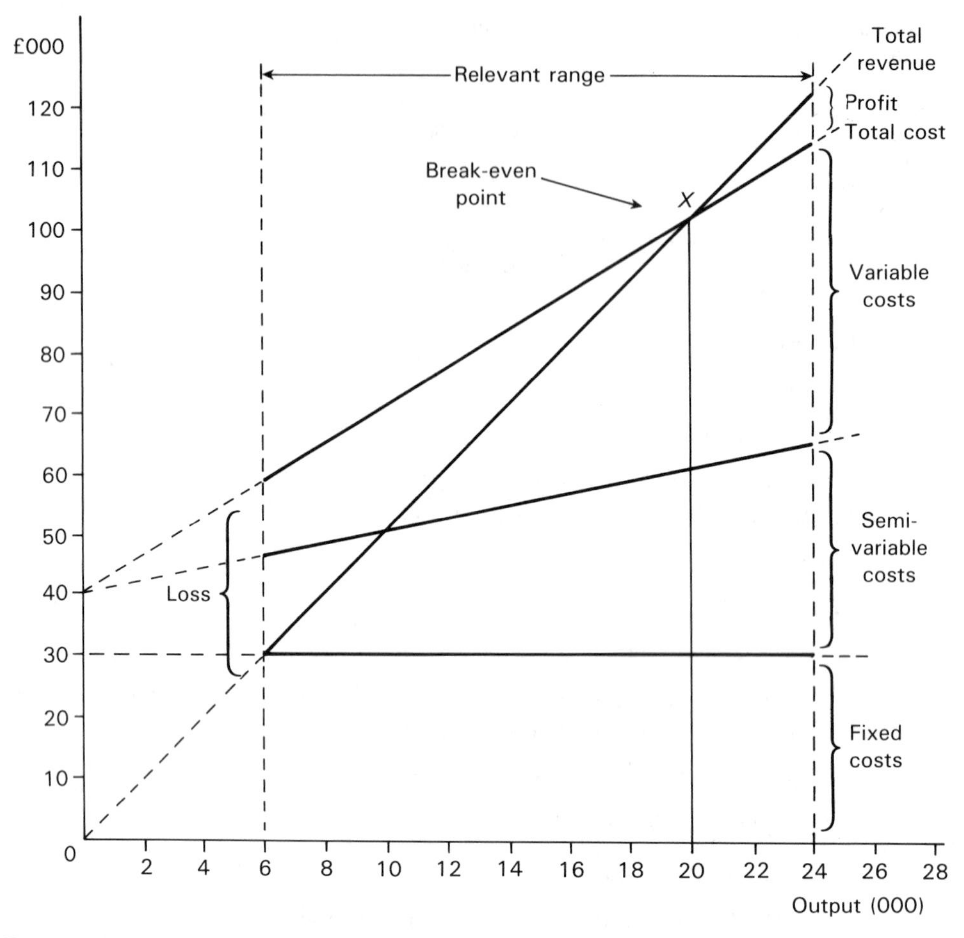

Figure 6.8 Break-even chart.

Figures 6.8. There is no 'best' order of aggregating vertically the costs. However, it is most usual to begin with fixed costs, then to add the semi-variable costs and finally to add the variable costs. We shall deal with the problem of step costs later in this chapter. The two most important linear functions in Figure 6.8 are the total revenue function and the total cost function.

The point (X) at which the total revenue line cuts the total cost line is the point where Burnden Ltd makes neither a profit nor a loss. This is the *break-even point* which lends its name to the chart. Visual inspection of the graph shows the break-even point to be 20,000 units, the amount arrived at by application of the basic CVP equation.

This break-even output information may be useful to the firm in assessing the probability of making a profit in the coming year. After calculating the break-even point, managers may assess how likely it is that an output of at least 20,000 units will be produced and sold. It will be less useful in guiding the firm to an optimal output decision (what output level will produce the highest profit?). Within the limits imposed by the relevant range, it is apparent from the chart that the maximum output (24,000 units) will produce the highest profit. It also seems that, without the upper limit imposed by the relevant range, any increase in output above 24,000 units will increase profit. In theory, the optimal level is infinity. This conclusion follows from the assumed linearity of the cost and revenue functions, and is one of the weaknesses of the method.

6.6 Break-even analysis and the contribution margin

We can see from the break-even chart in Figure 6.8 that at output levels below 20,000 units, Burnden Ltd makes a loss equal to the distance between the total cost line and the sales revenue line; above 20,000 units, Burnden Ltd makes a profit equal to the distance between the sales revenue line and the total cost line.

Suppose now that Burnden Ltd sells only 19,999 units, one unit *below* the break-even point. What will be the amount of the loss? Recall that the cost–volume–profit equation is:

$$\pi = Px - (a + bx)$$

$$\therefore \quad \pi = 19{,}999(5) - (40{,}000 + 19{,}999(3))$$

$$\therefore \quad \pi = -\pounds 2 \text{ (i.e. a loss of £2)}$$

Now suppose that Burnden Ltd sells 20,001 units, one unit *above* the break-even point. What will now be the profit for the year?

Substituting in the basic CVP equation we have:

$$\pi = 20{,}001(5) - (40{,}000 + 20{,}001(3))$$

$$\therefore \quad \pi = \pounds 2 \text{ (i.e. a profit of £2)}$$

What is the significance of these figures of £2 loss and £2 profit respectively? Is it a coincidence that the answer is £2 in each case? The significance lies in the fact that each additional unit produced and sold is generating an incremental profit of £2, as represented by the difference between the selling price per unit of £5 and the variable cost per unit of £3. This incremental profit is known as the *contribution margin* or *contribution* on each unit sold, and as we shall see throughout later chapters, this is a widely used and important concept in managerial decision making. Its use may be seen more immediately by an examination of the second graphical representation of the data for Burnden Ltd, the *profit–volume chart*, shown in Figure 6.9.

While the break-even graph is obviously useful for estimating the break-even point, it is less useful as a means of highlighting the profit or loss at different volume levels (i.e. to find profit figures from the break-even chart it is necessary to determine the difference between two sloping lines). A more convenient method of showing the impact of changes in volume on profit is the profit–volume chart. The horizontal axis of the profit–volume chart denotes the various levels of sales volume; the vertical axis shows the amount of profit or loss for the period. In our example, if

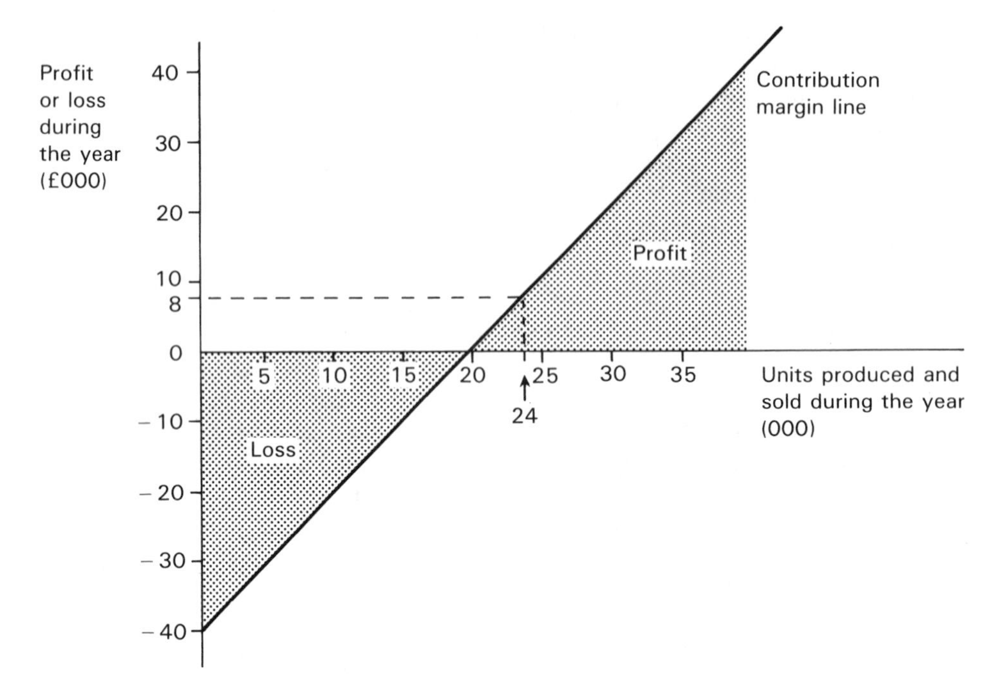

Figure 6.9 The profit–volume chart.

Burnden Ltd sells zero output, the maximum loss it will incur is the fixed costs of £40,000. It cannot lose more than its outlay on fixed costs. With each additional unit sold, a contribution of £2 is being made to total fixed costs, until Burnden Ltd reaches a sales volume level of 20,000 units (the break-even point), at which point the contribution generated of £40,000 (20,000 × £2) exactly covers the fixed costs. This is the point at which the sloping line cuts the horizontal axis. With each successive unit sold above 20,000 units, Burnden Ltd generates a surplus of £2. If, for instance, Burnden Ltd sells 24,000 units (as shown by the broken line on Figure 6.9) it will show a profit of £8,000, represented by the contribution margin of 24,000 units at £2 per unit = £48,000, minus fixed costs of £40,000. This excess of actual sales over the break-even sales level is often referred to as the *margin of safety*. The magnitude of the margin of safety indicates the possible reduction in sales which the firm can withstand before it incurs any loss. Thus the slope of the profit line in the profit–volume graph is always determined by the contribution margin, which in this case is £2 per unit or 40% of selling price.

Many of the problems posed by CVP analysis can be addressed more directly by the application of the concept of the contribution margin. The contribution margin per unit is simply the difference between the selling price per unit P and the variable cost per unit b. Our cost–volume–profit equation is of the form:

$$\pi = Px - (a + bx)$$

Rearranging the terms in the equation to accommodate the notion of contribution margin, we now have:

$$\pi = (P - b)x - a$$

where profit equals the contribution margin per unit $(P - b)$ multiplied by the number of units sold (x) less the fixed costs for the period (a). This is the relationship which is shown by the profit–volume chart. If we further rearrange the profit equation as follows:

$$\pi + a = (P - b)x$$

we can see the real meaning of contribution margin. The term is not used in isolation; the units sold by the firm make a contribution to *two* items; profit (π) and fixed costs (a). Phrased differently, we might say that before the firm can earn profits it must cover its fixed costs; this it does by selling sufficient units which yield a positive contribution.

Using the idea of contribution margin, we can now answer some possible questions raised by the example of Burnden Ltd.

1. *What is Burnden Ltd's break-even point in units?*
   For profit to equal zero: $a = (P - b)x$

$$x = \frac{a}{(P - b)}$$

$$\text{Break-even point in units} = \frac{\text{Fixed costs}}{\text{Contribution margin per unit}}$$

$$= \frac{£40{,}000}{£2}$$

$$= 20{,}000 \text{ units}$$

2. *What is Burnden Ltd's break-even point in sales revenue?*

   For profit to equal zero: $x = \dfrac{a}{(P - b)}$

   Multiplying both sides by P gives: $Px = \dfrac{a}{(P - b)} \times P$

   Break-even point in sales revenue

$$= \frac{\text{Fixed costs}}{\text{Contribution margin per unit}} \times \text{Sales price}$$

$$= \frac{£40{,}000}{£2} \times £5$$

$$= £100{,}000$$

3. *How many units must Burnden Ltd sell to show a profit of £5,000?*
   To cover fixed costs and generate profit: $\pi + a = (P - b)x$

   Rearranging for x gives: $x = \dfrac{a + \pi}{(P - b)}$

   $$\text{Level of sales required} = \frac{\text{Fixed costs} + \text{Required profit}}{\text{Contribution margin per unit}}$$

   $$= \frac{£40{,}000 + £5{,}000}{£2}$$

   $$= £22{,}500 \text{ units}$$

4. *What is the level of sales revenue which results in a profit of £5,000?*

   To determine the units necessary for a given level of profit: $x = \dfrac{a + \pi}{(P - b)}$

   Multiplying both sides by P gives: $Px = \dfrac{a + \pi}{(P - b)} \times P$

   $$\text{Level of sales} = \frac{\text{Fixed costs} + \text{Required profit}}{\text{Contribution margin per unit}} \times \text{Sales price}$$

   $$= \frac{£40{,}000 + £5{,}000}{£2} \times £5$$

   $$= £112{,}500$$

6.7 Break-even analysis and flexible budgeting

In practice, organisations will probably incur fixed costs in large indivisible lumps (e.g. the purchase of new factories or machines) and the total 'fixed' cost function will be analogous in form to the step variable functions discussed earlier in this chapter. Suppose that Burnden Ltd has a total cost function whose variable element remains £3 per unit. But now assume that the relevant range restriction is relaxed and that the 'fixed' element of total costs increases in lumps at various output levels as follows:

Output range	*Total fixed cost* (£)
0– 5,000	10,000
5,001–10,000	15,000
10,001–15,000	20,000
15,001–20,000	25,000
20,001–25,000	35,000
Above 25,000	Increases by £15,000 for each additional 5,000 units

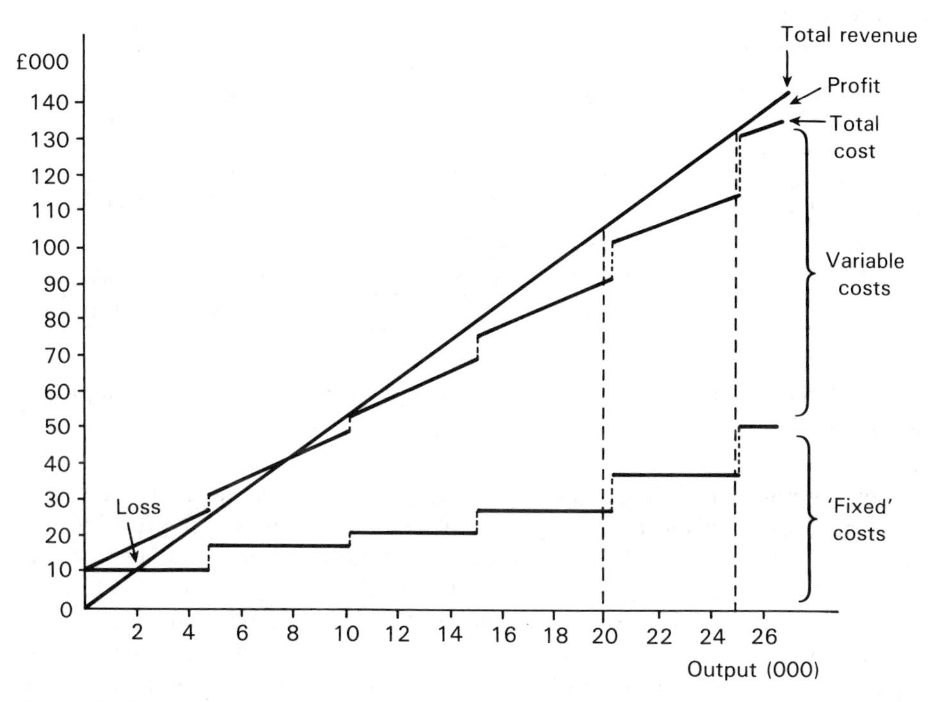

Figure 6.10 Break-even chart with step costs.

It is not worthwhile producing above 25,000 units, for each additional 5,000 units above that level yield a contribution to fixed costs of £10,000 (£[5 – 3] × 5,000), which is less than the increase in fixed costs of £15,000.

The break-even chart reflecting the revised cost figures is shown in Figure 6.10. It is apparent from this chart that maximum profit is attained at output levels of either 20,000 or 25,000 units. At both these points, the difference between total revenue and total cost is £15,000. As the total cost function is not a smooth curve there is no simple algebraic formula that will yield either the break-even points or the level of output that maximises profit. The break-even point (or points) is normally determined most easily from a graph. The output level (or levels) leading to maximum profit may also be observed from the chart. Alternatively, we may calculate the profit at various feasible levels of output, choosing the one that yields the highest profit. This is the basis of the procedure known as *flexible budgeting*.

Where step costs are involved, the optimal output level will often lie at one of the points just before a new injection of fixed costs becomes necessary. We may, therefore, decide that we shall obtain a satisfactory approximation to the optimal plan if we prepare flexible budgets for output levels of 5,000, 10,000, 15,000, 20,000 and 25,000 units. The calculations are shown in Table 6.2 and confirm the results obtained by examining the break-even chart. The optimal output levels are 20,000 and 25,000 units. To reinforce the earlier claim that an increase in output above 25,000 units is not worthwhile consider the profit at, say, 30,000 units; it is

Table 6.2 Flexible budgets

	Output level (units)				
	5,000 (£)	*10,000* (£)	*15,000* (£)	*20,000* (£)	*25,000* (£)
Variable costs (£3 per unit)	15,000	30,000	45,000	60,000	75,000
Step fixed costs	10,000	15,000	20,000	25,000	35,000
Total costs	25,000	45,000	65,000	85,000	110,000
Sales revenue (£5 per unit)	25,000	50,000	75,000	100,000	125,000
Profit	—	5,000	10,000	15,000	15,000

£10,000.[15] This is less than the profit expected at 20,000 or 25,000 units and consequently an inferior output level in terms of the firm's assumed objective of maximising cash resources.

Both graphical analysis and flexible budgets lead us to the same answer. Which is superior? The flexible budgeting approach boasts a numerical precision that graphical analysis may not always be able to match. On the other hand, a break-even chart illustrates graphically the relationship between cost and profit for all output levels. It may be a simpler means of conveying the often complicated nature of this relationship to management. In addition, the break-even chart shows the range of output levels at which profits are expected to be made. In our example, the firm expects to make a profit at all output levels between 7,500 and 25,000 units. Had we extended the graph to cover higher volumes we should have seen that output levels between 25,000 and 30,000 units and between 32,500 and 35,000 units were also expected to be profitable. This indication of the profitable ranges might prove useful to the firm in assessing the *sensitivity* of profit to deviations from the planned level of output. Sensitivity analysis is discussed in more detail in Chapter 11.

Both break-even charts and flexible budgets have their advantages. It seems probable that a combination of the two techniques will lead to better decisions being made than if either method is used in isolation. Graphical analysis could be used to establish the general ranges within which production is at its most profitable and flexible budgeting could be applied to 'sharpen up' the figures.

6.8 An alternative approach to cost–volume–profit analysis

In our discussion of the construction and interpretation of break-even charts, we

[15]

	£
Variable costs	90,000
Step fixed costs	50,000
Total costs	140,000
Sales revenue	150,000
Profit	10,000

have stressed the critical assumption of linearity, in relation to both variable costs and fixed costs. The break-even and profit–volume graphs presented in this chapter not only make the same linearity assumption about costs but also assume that selling prices remain unchanged whatever the output level.

How realistic are these assumptions? It may be argued that, if taken to extremes, they conflict with economic reasoning. For instance, an economist might argue that the firm would have to reduce its unit selling price in order to increase its level of sales volume. Consider the graphical presentation of the alternative CVP chart shown in Figure 6.11.

This chart does *not* assume linearity of costs and revenues, but rather assumes that both costs and revenues are curvilinear. The total revenue curve begins to slope upwards less steeply as price reductions become necessary, and then slopes downwards as the adverse effect of price reductions outweighs the beneficial effects of increased sales volume in terms of total revenue; the total cost curve is curvilinear because costs rise at a slower rate as efficiency increases and then more rapidly as diminishing returns occur. Note that this chart shows two break-even points X and Y. (Because of the curvilinear cost and revenue functions it is possible to have more than two break-even points.)

If we now superimpose the conventional (linear) break-even chart on the alternative (curvilinear) graph, as in Figure 6.12, we can see more clearly the possible similarities and differences between the two approaches.

Within the relevant range of output levels, the two graphs show a similar relationship. Outside this range, it would be dangerous to assume such a relationship. The conventional graph implies that profit will grow to infinity, or at least to the constraining point of maximum capacity, whereas the alternative graph is based on what is perhaps the more realistic assumption that profit will be influenced by the effect of cumulative price reductions and the diminishing returns of cost factors.

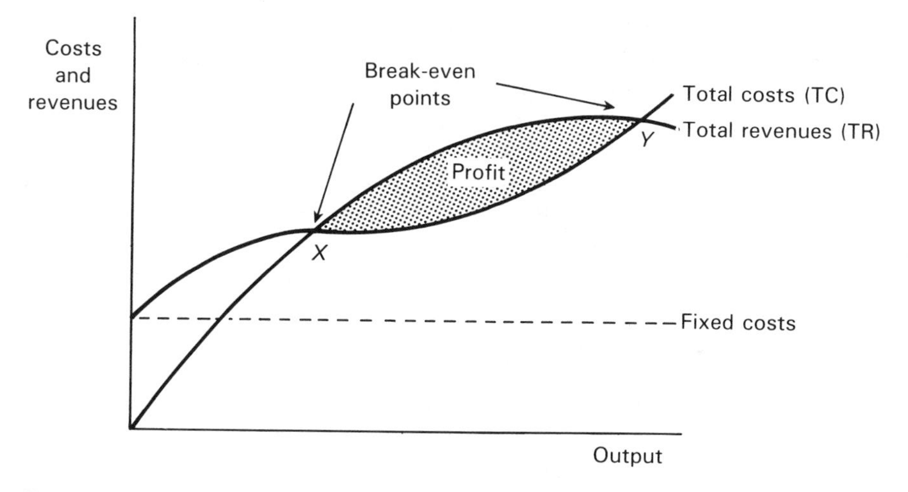

Figure 6.11 Alternative CVP chart.

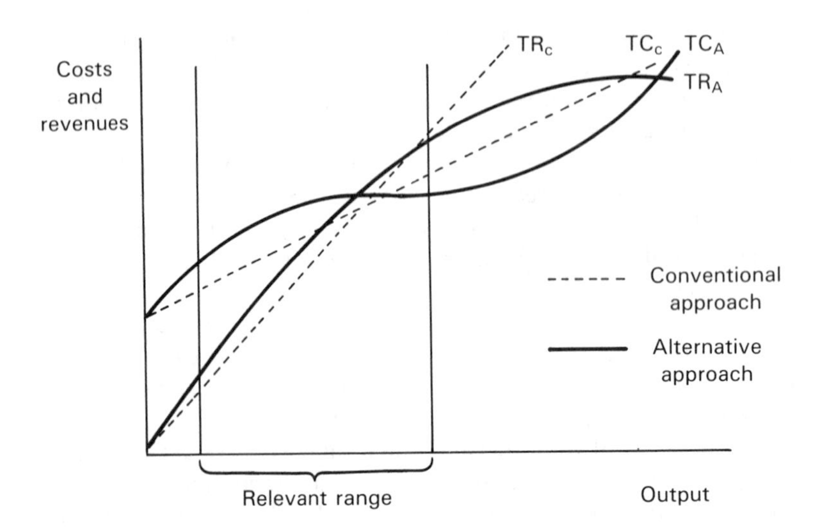

Figure 6.12 Comparison of alternative CVP graphs.

6.9 Multi-product firms

Before leaving our analysis of cost–volume–profit relationships we shall examine briefly the effects of relaxing one of the simplifying assumptions made throughout this chapter, namely, that the firm produces only one product. Are the techniques of break-even analysis and flexible budgeting as useful and simple to apply to multi-product firms as to those manufacturing a single product? Provided that none of the firm's input factors is in short supply there seems to be no reason why the techniques should not be equally useful and straightforward. All that is required is a separate break-even or flexible budgeting analysis of each product.

Two particular problems may arise if this approach is followed. First, there may be interdependences between the production or demand functions of two or more of the firm's products, i.e. the demand for, or cost of manufacturing, a product may be affected by the demand for or level of production of some other product. If this is the case, it will be necessary to consider the interdependent products together. This should present no particular problems if the output mix of the products is determined by the nature of the interdependence. The combination of interdependent products may be dealt with as though it were a single product. If the product mix is not determined independently it will be difficult to deal satisfactorily with different products on one graph.

Second, there is the question of how the fixed costs of the firm should be dealt with. Should these be allocated on some basis between the various products for inclusion in the individual break-even charts and flexible budgets? Following the principles developed in this and the previous chapter for dealing with fixed costs, the answer will depend upon their nature. If the costs clearly relate to a particular product and would not be incurred if that product were not to be manufactured, then they should be regarded as fixed costs of the product and included in the analysis relating to it. If, on the other hand, the costs are in the nature of general overheads, created by the existence of the firm itself rather than of any particular product, then to allocate them to individual products will be misleading and may lead to incorrect output decisions. Initial output decisions should be made for each product, regardless of general fixed costs. Then a budget should be prepared for the firm as a whole, based on the optimal output levels for each product and incorporating the general fixed costs of the firm, to ensure that the predicted contributions from the individual products are sufficient to cover the non-allocable fixed costs. The construction of a break-even chart for the firm *as a whole* seems unnecessary in these circumstances and may be confusing as it depends upon a prior management decision on optimal output mix which management may not be able to make rationally without a cost–volume–profit analysis.

Discussion topics

1 'In the long term there are no fixed costs.' Discuss what is meant by this statement.

2 'Fixed costs are always irrelevant to rational economic decisions.' Discuss.

3 'The assumption of linearity of costs negates much of the usefulness of the accountant's work in the area of cost–volume–profit analysis.' Discuss.

4 Explain the following concepts used in this chapter:

   Relevant range
   Curvilinear functions
   Contribution margin
   Margin of safety

5 'Cost classifications such as "variable" and "fixed" are misleading. Only *differential* costs are important for managerial decision making.' Discuss.

6 Compare and contrast the break-even chart and the profit–volume chart as providers of useful information to management.

7 Discuss the economist's contribution to cost–volume–profit analysis.

8 Discuss the practical problems involved in using break-even charts and profit–volume charts for multi-product firms.

Exercises

6.1 The following graphs reflect the pattern of certain overhead cost items in a manufacturing company for a year.

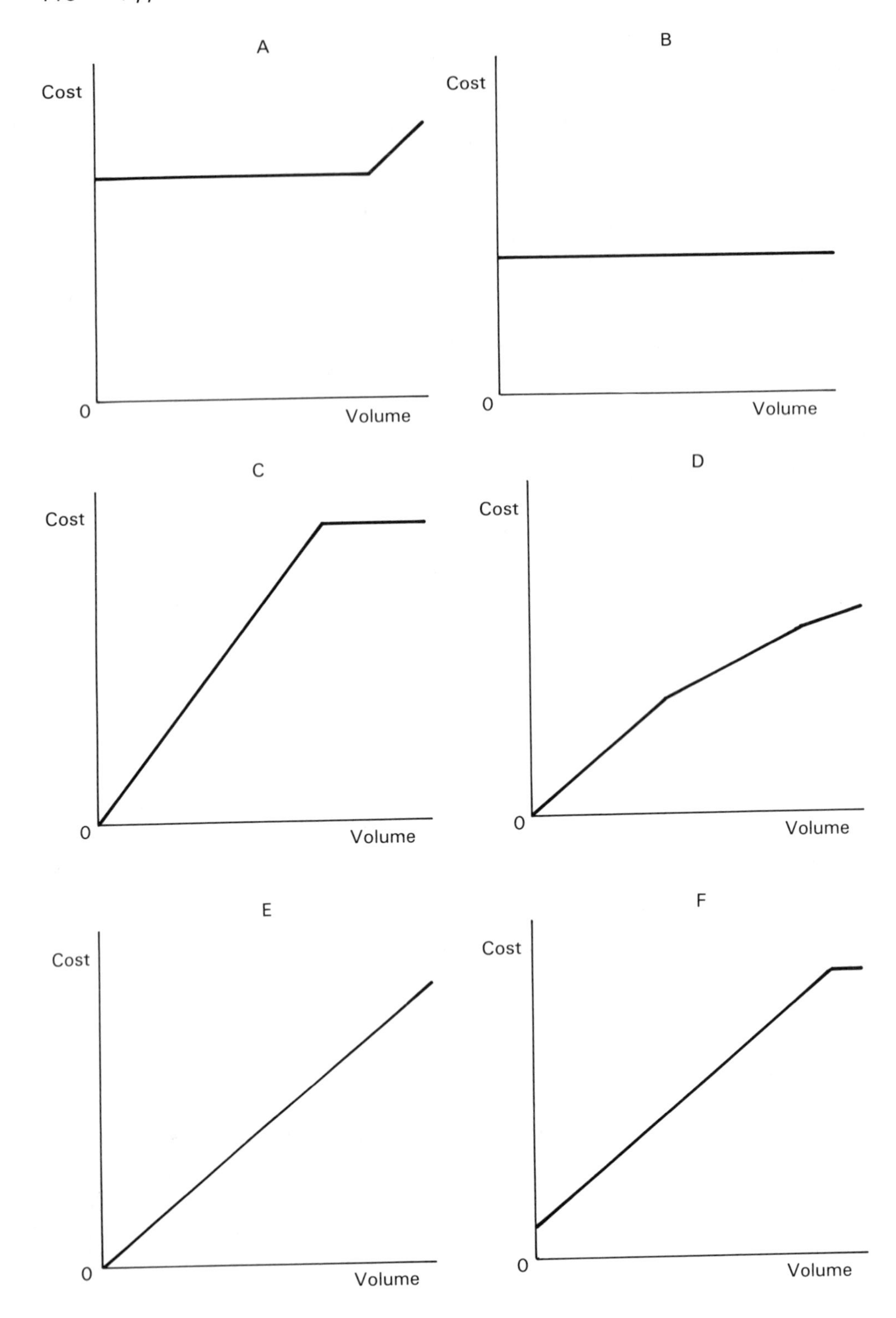
A
Cost
0
Volume
B
Cost
0
Volume
C
Cost
0
Volume
D
Cost
0
Volume
E
Cost
0
Volume
F
Cost
0
Volume

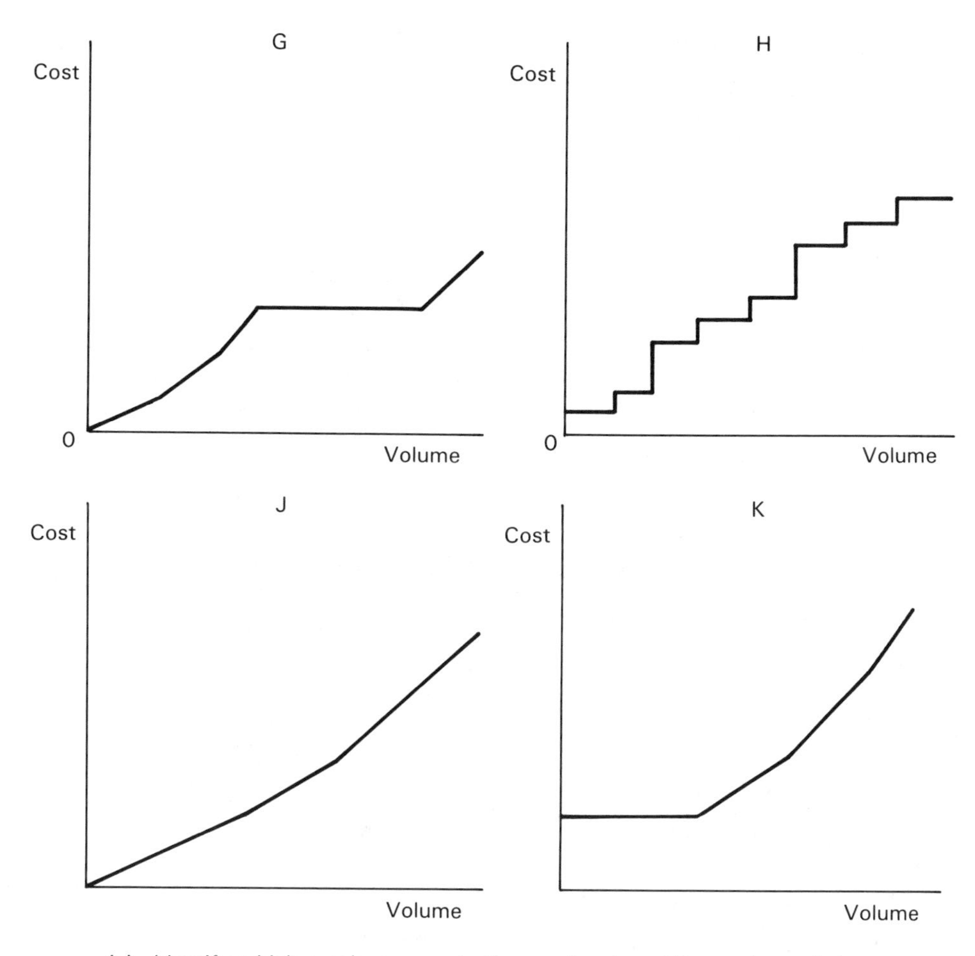

(a) Identify which graph represents the overhead cost items shown below: (a graph may be used more than once).

Brief description	*Details of cost behaviour*
(i) Depreciation of equipment	When charged on straight line basis
(ii) Cost of a service	£50 annual charge for subscription: £2 charge for each unit taken, with a maximum total charge of £350 p.a.
(iii) Royalty	£0.10 per unit produced, with a maximum charge of £5,000 p.a.
(iv) Supervision cost	When there is one charge hand for every eight workers or less, and one supervisor for every three charge hands, and when each person represents 40 hours of production, thus:

Hours	
Under 320	one charge hand
321–640	two charge hands
641–960	three charge hands,
etc.	plus one supervisor

(v) Depreciation of equipment	When charged on a machine-hour rate
(vi) Cost of a service	Flat charge of £400 to cover the first 5,000 units:
	Per unit
	£0.10 for the next 3,000 units
	£0.12 for the next 3,000 units
	£0.14 for all subsequent units
(vii) Storage/carriage service	*Per ton*
	£15 for the first 20 tons
	£30 for the next 20 tons
	£45 for the next 20 tons
	No extra charge until the service reaches 100 tons; then £45 per ton for all subsequent tonnage.
(viii) Outside finishing service	*Per unit*
	£0.75 for the first 2,000 units
	£0.55 for the next 2,000 units
	£0.35 for all subsequent units

(b) Give an example of an overhead cost item that could represent those graphs to which you do not refer in your answer to (a).

(c) Draw one graph of a pattern of an overhead item not shown and give an example of an overhead cost item that it would represent.

6.2 Monet Ltd can achieve a production of 5,000 units with its existing plant and premises. The current fixed overheads are at the rate of £100,000 p.a. whilst variable costs are £60 per unit and the selling price per unit is £100. The company's bankers are prepared to finance further expansion and the directors estimate that the following *increases* in fixed overheads will occur if production is increased:

Production between 5,000 and 10,000 units	a further £200,000 p.a.
Production in excess of 10,000 units	a further £200,000 p.a.

Incorporate the above information in a break-even chart and state the break-even points.

6.3 Rothko Ltd produces a single product for distribution to wholesalers. The product has a list selling price of £10 per unit. Variable costs of production are £5 per unit, and fixed costs of production are £50,000 p.a. The distribution of the product results in additional costs of 90p per unit (variable) and £11,500 p.a. (fixed).

(a) Calculate the expected break-even point.

(b) Assuming Rothko Ltd predicts sales of £200,000 for the year, calculate the expected profit (assuming sales and production are equal).

(c) The company does have some idea about the effects on demand of changes in prices, advertising, competitors' actions, etc. Assume that a 5% decrease in price will increase total volume by 15% (in units), that an additional expenditure of £7,500 on advertising will further increase the original volume by 5%, but that the increased production will result in an increase in variable costs of production by 10p per unit in excess of 21,000 units. Maximum practical capacity is 25,000 units. What effect will these changes have on net profit?

(d) As an alternative, Rothko Ltd can also expand its sales by 20% (volume) by offering its wholesalers a rebate of 1% on all the units they purchase, and by incurring advertising expenditure of £20,000. Is this a better alternative than (c)? Support your reasoning with calculations.

6.4 Wagner plc manufactures an instrument which has a variable cost structure as follows:

	£
Materials	30.00
Labour	7.50
Variable overhead	3.00
	40.50

The instruments sell at £67.50 each and the company expects a sales revenue from this product in the current year of £1,012,500. Fixed overhead expense attributable to this product is budgeted at £105,000. A wage agreement with the employees states that a 10% increase will be paid to labour in the forthcoming year, whilst the managing director believes that material prices will rise by $7\frac{1}{2}$%, variable overhead by 5%, and fixed overhead by 3%, from the beginning of the new financial year.

(a) Calculate the new selling price if the contribution ratio is to be maintained.

(b) Calculate the sales volume required in the forthcoming year if price remains the same and profit is to be maintained.

6.5 Power Ltd's condensed income for 19X2 is as follows:

		£
Sales (100,000 units)		1,000,000
Cost of goods sold		600,000
Gross margin		400,000
Selling expenses	150,000	
Administrative expenses	100,000	250,000
Net profit (before income taxes)		150,000

The budget committee has estimated the following changes for 19X3:

30% increase in number of units sold
20% increase in material unit cost
15% increase in direct labour cost per unit
10% increase in variable indirect cost per unit
5% increase in indirect fixed costs
8% increase in selling expenses, arising solely from increased volume
6% increase in administrative expenses, reflecting anticipated higher wage and supply price levels (any changes in administrative expenses caused solely by increased sales volume are considered immaterial)

As inventory quantities remain fairly constant, the committee considered that, for budget purposes, any change in inventory valuation can be ignored. The composition of the cost of a unit of finished product during 19X2 for materials, direct labour, and production overhead, respectively, was in the ratio of 3 to 2 to 1. In 19X2, £40,000 of the overhead was for fixed costs. No changes in production methods or credit policies were contemplated for 19X3.

(a) From the data above compute the *unit sales price* at which Power Ltd must sell its only product in 19X3 in order to earn a budgeted profit (before income tax) of £200,000.

(b) The sales manager is unhappy about the prospect of an increase in selling price and wants to know how many units must be sold at the old price to earn the £200,000.

(c) One of the company directors believes the estimated increase in sales is over-optimistic and wants to know what annual profit will be if the selling price determined in (a) is adopted but the increase in sales volume is only 10%.

6.6 Mr Weber's trading operations for the years ending 31 May 19X0 and 19X1 respectively are summarised below:

	19X0 (£)	*19X1* (£)
Sales	200,000	231,000
Cost of goods sold	160,000	189,000
Gross profit	40,000	42,000
Operating expenses	10,000	9,500
Net profit	30,000	32,500

Weber is very disappointed with the recent year's results, particularly as his selling prices were 10% higher than in the previous year and his operating expenses £500 lower. He has asked you to explain why 'a 15% increase in turnover has produced only an 8% increase in net profit', and to offer such advice as you consider appropriate.

Prepare an appropriate analysis of the figures, and write a brief report for Weber, explaining the figures and advising on future action.

6.7 Picasso Ltd's head office is located in London. The company leases factory buildings in areas A, B and C. The same single product is manufactured in all factories. The following information is available for 19X0 operations:

	Total (£)	*A* (£)	*B* (£)	*C* (£)
Sales	900,000	200,000	400,000	300,000
Variable costs	500,000	100,000	220,000	180,000
Fixed costs:				
Factory	180,000	50,000	55,000	75,000
Administration	59,000	16,000	21,000	22,000
Allocated head office expenses	63,000	14,000	28,000	21,000
Total	802,000	180,000	324,000	298,000
Net profit from operations	98,000	20,000	76,000	2,000

Head office expenses are allocated on the basis of units sold. The selling price is £10.

Management is undecided whether to renew the lease of the C factory which expires on 31 December 19X1, and will require an increase in rent of £15,000 per year if renewed. If the factory is shut down, the amount expected to be realised from the sale of the equipment is greater than its book value and would just cover all termination expenses. If the C factory is shut down, the company can continue to serve customers of the C factory by either expanding the A factory, which would increase present fixed costs by 15% (additional shipping expense of £2 per unit would be incurred on the increased production) or entering into a long-term contract with a competitor, who will serve the C factory customers, and who will pay Picasso Ltd a commission of £1.60 per unit.

The company is also planning to establish a subsidiary company in Ireland to produce the same product. Based on estimated annual Irish sales of 40,000 units, cost studies produced these estimates for the Irish subsidiary:

	Annual cost	
	Total (£)	*Variable* (%)
Direct materials	193,600	100
Direct labour	90,000	70
Factory overhead	80,000	64
Administrative expenses	30,000	30

The Irish production will be sold by manufacturer's representatives who will receive a commission of 8% of the sales price. No proportion of the UK head office expense will be allocated to the Irish subsidiary.

(a) Prepare a schedule computing Picasso Ltd's estimated net profit from UK operations under each of the following procedures:
(i) expansion of the A factory;
(ii) negotiation of a long-term contract on a commission basis.

(b) Calculate the sales price per unit necessary to give management a 10% profit on its Irish production.

(c) Calculate the break-even point in £s if the Irish product sells at £11 per unit.

6.8 The Velasquez Engineering Co. plc manufactures a range of products. Whilst compiling the budget for the next financial year, the management realises that a decision has to be made concerning the method of manufacture of one product, a precision made hand razor. This product is designed to sell for £1. A choice must be made between three alternative production processes A, B and C, and the management seek to find the most profitable method.

	A	*B*	*C*
Variable cost per product (p)	80	85	90
Fixed costs of process (£)	95,000	60,000	37,500

Maximum production in any process is 1 million razors.

(a) Present the information in the form of a profit–volume graph to highlight factors significant to this decision, commenting on the information in the light of the problem under consideration.

(b) List other matters which you would take into account before deciding which process to use.

6.9 Michelangelo Ltd manufactures a single product which sells at £1.20 per unit. The variable cost of this product is 60p per unit. At present the fixed expenses of the organisation are £30,000 p.a. Michelangelo is currently selling its full productive capacity of 100,000 units p.a. at what the company's directors believe is the optimum price–volume relationship for the product. However, they are considering selling the product under an additional brand name. While being virtually identical from the manufacturing point of view, brands will be differentiated by the packaging and the marketing approaches adopted. Sales of the existing and the new brand when both are priced at 90p per unit are expected to total 300,000 units.

The introduction of the additional brand will require the firm to increase its productive capacity. To do this will increase Michelangelo's fixed costs to £60,000 p.a. However, as this will involve some re-equipment, there will be economies of operation arising which will reduce variable costs to 50p per unit.

(a) Present the above information graphically.

(b) For both the existing situation and the proposed scheme calculate: (i) the break-even point; (ii) the profit; (iii) the margin of safety in units, and (iv) the sales required under the proposed scheme to maintain the present profit position. In relation to these situations, discuss whether the proposed scheme will improve the company's position.

(c) Briefly discuss the criticisms that might be made of the conventional linear break-even graph. Do these criticisms invalidate its use in practical situations?

6.10 Schubert Ltd manufactures two products. Analysed profit and loss accounts for the last two years run as follows:

		19X0			*19X1*	
	Total	*Product A*	*Product B*	*Total*	*Product A*	*Product B*
Sales: Units	5,685	3,790	1,895	7,485	4,990	2,495
	(£)	(£)	(£)	(£)	(£)	(£)
Value	151,600	75,800	75,800	199,600	99,800	99,800
Materials	34,155	15,080	19,075	47,355	20,940	26,415
Direct labour	34,100	18,840	15,260	49,520	27,450	22,070
Supervisory factory labour	7,500	3,750	3,750	8,250	4,125	4,125
Factory rent	10,000	6,000	4,000	10,000	6,000	4,000
Fuel and power	16,280	9,550	6,730	20,475	11,960	8,515
Depreciation of machinery	15,900	7,500	8,400	15,900	7,500	8,400
General administration costs	16,350	8,175	8,175	17,420	8,710	8,710
Total costs	134,285	68,895	65,390	168,920	86,685	82,235
Net profit	17,315	6,905	10,410	30,680	13,115	17,565

At the start of 19X1 materials prices were increased by an average of 5% and there was a general factory wage increase of 10%; there were no wage increases for administration employees and no other price changes during the period. There were also no changes in methods of production or efficiency of operation during the period. Normally, the units sold of product A and product B are in the ratio of 2:1.

Overhead costs are divided between products in the following way. Depreciation is expressed as a rate per machine hour and divided between products on a time basis; fuel and power are measured separately for each machine and divided similarly. Factory rent is divided in proportion to the floor space used by each machine and then on a machine hour rate; and other overheads are divided equally between the products because sales value is normally about the same for each and there is no more obvious basis.

(a) Draw a break-even chart for Schubert Ltd showing total sales value on the horizontal axis and calculate the appropriate turnover necessary if a profit of £25,000 is to be made. Make and specify any reasonable assumptions which are necessary for your answer.

(b) Describe shortly the main limitations of break-even analysis for business decision taking.

6.11 It is 19X6. Mr Normanton, the managing director of Normanton Manufacturing Ltd is concerned that while there has been a rapid increase in demand in the company's rather unstable industry in recent years, Normanton has not been able to match the growth of its main rival Cairns Ltd. He is also worried because raw materials, which currently account for half of the variable manufacturing costs for both companies, are about to be increased in price by 10%, and he is aware that the manufacturing process employed by Cairns Ltd uses less raw materials.

The managing director has been able to obtain the following actual or estimated figures for the two companies.

	Normanton	*Cairns*
19X3 sales (units)	60,000	58,000
19X4 sales (units)	80,000	90,000
19X5 sales (units)	100,000	118,000
Fixed manufacturing overheads (£)	385,000	490,000
Variable manufacturing costs per unit (£)	3.60	2.40
Fixed selling and administrative expenses (£)	165,000	160,000
Variable selling costs per unit (£)	1.20	1.40

All administrative costs are fixed for both companies. The selling price has remained constant at £12 per unit since January 19X3, but both companies are planning to increase it to £12.50 following the price increase in raw materials. Neither company carries significant levels of stocks or work-in-progress.

(a) Write a note to the managing director commenting on the effect on the break-even point and the profitability of different levels of sales of the differences in the manufacturing processes adopted by Normanton Manufacturing Ltd and Cairns Ltd.

(b) Calculate the break-even point in units and the number of units which must be sold to achieve profits of £150,000, for both companies *after* the increase in raw materials and selling prices.

(c) Outline briefly the main limitations of cost–volume–profit analysis.

6.12 Inishbofin Airways Ltd provides a daily service to and from the island from its airstrip at Cleggan. Its budgeted profit and loss account for 19X2, based on the level of operations achieved in 19X1, is as follows:

	£	£
Revenue (3,650 passenger flights)		73,000
Aircraft depreciation	14,000	
Aircraft maintenance	8,000	
Fuel and other operating costs	9,000	
Management and administration	10,000	
Pilot's salary	13,000	
		54,000
Profit		19,000

The company is considering two schemes to increase profits in 19X2. The first would involve the introduction of two daily return flights between May and August inclusive; the price per flight would be reduced from £20 to £16 during this period and the effect on the number of passenger flights is estimated to be as follows:

	19X1	*19X2*
May	300	420
June	500	760
July	700	1,140
August	700	1,280

The change in flight frequency would increase annual fuel and other operating costs by one-third; maintenance costs would go up by £1,000 and the pilot would be paid an extra £400 per month for each month affected.

The second scheme would involve the hiring out of the plane on an hourly basis for special trips between May and August. The plane would be hired out for £250 per hour, fuel and other operating costs would be £100 per hour, and the need to have the plane available would involve the same maintenance costs and extra payments to the pilot as the first scheme.

The company is very uncertain about the demand for this service. Management has estimated that the demand will be somewhere between 40 and 100 hours, with the following probability distribution:

40 hours	25% chance
70 hours	50% chance
100 hours	25% chance

(a) Calculate the estimated additional profit from operating the first scheme.

(b) Calculate the number of hours for which the plane would have to be hired under the second scheme to produce an estimated additional profit equal to that of the first scheme.

(c) Discuss how the company might decide between the two alternative schemes, given the probability distribution provided for the second scheme and assuming that the estimates made under the first scheme were almost certain to be correct.

6.13 Cong Printers Ltd publishes a weekly newspaper. Its profit and loss account for the year ended 31 August 19X3 was as follows:

	£	£
Sales revenue (50 issues)		200,000
Advertising revenue		200,000
		400,000
Paper	150,000	
Payments to journalists	100,000	
Depreciation	40,000	
Distribution costs	30,000	
Other expenses	30,000	
		350,000
Profit		50,000

The board is considering two means of increasing profitability for the year ended 31 August 19X4. The first plan would involve the publication of 50 issues of a midweek edition. Market research suggests that this would achieve 80% of the 10,000 circulation of the existing weekend paper, and have to sell at only 35p. In order to maintain sales of the existing paper at present levels, its price would be held stable at 40p. In the absence of the midweek edition, this would be raised to 44p to help offset the anticipated increase for the coming year of 20% in the cost of paper and 15% in the rate of pay for journalists.

Advertising would cover eight pages in the midweek edition, as opposed to ten in the existing paper, though the total number of pages would remain the same. Advertising rates would average £350 per page. The average rate of £400 per page for the existing edition would be maintained, though if the midweek edition were not introduced, this would be increased to £450.

If the midweek paper is published, paper costs will be increased in proportion to the extra volume of pages printed, and journalists' pay will be increased by £45,000. Half of the distribution costs and other expenses will be increased in proportion to the increased volume of pages published; the balance of these costs, and depreciation, will not be increased, either through price changes or because of the increase in the level of activity.

The alternative scheme involves offering the facilities of the company for printing programmes, advertising handouts and other miscellaneous work. This work would require the hiring of a manager at £12,000 per year, and paper and other operating costs would be, on average, 50% of revenue from printing. Revenue from this activity is very uncertain, and the board has estimated the following probability distribution:

15% chance	£36,000
50% chance	£64,000
35% chance	£80,000

(a) Calculate the estimated additional profit from publishing the midweek edition.

(b) Calculate the level of revenue needed under the second scheme to produce an estimated additional profit equal to that from publishing the midweek edition.

(c) Discuss how the board might decide between the two alternative schemes, given the probability distribution provided for the second scheme and assuming that the estimates made under the first scheme were almost certain to be correct.

Further reading

Ajinkya, B., Atiase, R. and Bamber, L. S., 'Absorption versus direct costing; income reconciliation and cost–volume–profit analysis', *Issues in Accounting Education*, Fall 1986.

Bell, A. L., 'Break-even charts versus marginal graphs', *Management Accounting*, February 1969.

Dean, J., 'Methods and potentialities of break-even analysis', *The Australian Accountant* (October/November 1951), reprinted in Solomons, D. (edn.), *Studies in Cost Analysis*, 2nd edn., Sweet & Maxwell, 1968.

Goggans, T., 'Break-even analysis with curvilinear functions', *The Accounting Review*, October 1965.

Jaedicke, R. K. and Robichek, A. A., 'Cost–volume–profit analysis under uncertainty', *The Accounting Review*, October 1964.

Jenkins, D. O., 'Cost–volume–profit analysis', *Management Services*, March/April 1970.

Koehler, R. and Neyhart, C. A., 'Difficulties in flexible budgeting', *Management Planning*, May/June 1972.

Vickers, D., 'On the economics of break-even', *The Accounting Review*, July 1960.

Chapter 7

Cost estimation

Previous chapters have demonstrated the essentials of good management decision making, stressing that managers must try to identify the relevant cash flows associated with individual decisions and explaining that this can be done most easily if they have some knowledge of how costs and revenues behave over particular activity levels. Management's knowledge of how a firm's costs actually behave is, however, necessarily limited to an analysis of the results of *past* decisions, whereas planning requires estimates of *future* costs.

For purposes of decision making, managers will wish to know which costs are likely to change with particular activity levels (and hence affect the firm's cash outflows) and which costs are likely to remain unchanged (and have no incremental impact on cash resources). In most cases this knowledge is not easy to acquire. Although costs cannot usually be predicted with absolute accuracy, it may be possible to identify a cost function which can be used to *estimate* the costs which the firm is likely to incur. For example, if it can be shown that costs are related to some independent variable such as machine hours or units of output, it may be possible to estimate the levels of future costs associated with different levels of this independent variable by using a relationship based on past cost levels. In this chapter we consider methods of cost prediction based on past data.

7.1 The prediction of costs

The basic idea underlying cost prediction is to estimate the variable and fixed component of different types of costs. Some costs, such as raw materials, will have only a variable element; some, such as rent, rates and insurance will have only a fixed element, at least in the short term; others, such as telephone and electricity costs, will have both a fixed and a variable element. The most frequently used form of a simple cost function to be used for estimation purposes may be written as:

$$y = a + bx$$

where y is the total cost, and is known as the *dependent* variable, because its amount depends upon some other factor. In this case that other factor is denoted by the *independent* variable x, which may be the quantity of output produced, or the number of orders processed, or any other measure of the units of activity which is thought to influence the level of total costs. The parameters, a and b, the total fixed cost and the variable cost per unit of activity respectively, attempt to explain and predict the relationship between the dependent variable y and the independent variable x. For example, suppose that the total cost of using electricity per month is estimated to be £500 plus £0.3 per kilowatt-hour used. Kilowatt-hour is the independent variable. If usage for the following month is expected to be 3,000 kilowatt-hours, the total cost of using electricity will be

$$\begin{aligned} y &= £500 + £0.3\ (3{,}000) \\ &= £1{,}400 \end{aligned}$$

It is important to ask whether such a simple cost function can adequately solve the problem at hand. Particularly, is it realistic to assume that total cost is influenced by only one independent, explanatory variable? If it is obviously unrealistic to make this assumption, a more sophisticated multiple cost function is required. The representation of such a function might be of the form:

$$y = a + bx_1 + cx_2$$

where x_1, the first explanatory variable, might be the labour hours used in production, and x_2, the machine hours used. Future cost levels may also be influenced by changes in the prices of inputs and by changes in efficiency. We consider later in the chapter how expected changes in prices and efficiency might be incorporated into an analysis of future cost behaviour. In order to simplify the analysis and to highlight the important features of alternative methods in our discussion of cost estimation procedures we shall assume the existence of only one explanatory variable in addition to expected price and efficiency changes. This explanatory variable will usually be the level of output.

We must also add that an analysis of past costs, however sophisticated the technique used, is appropriate for managerial decision making only if management is contemplating undertaking similar activities in the future to those previously undertaken. If no similar activities have been undertaken in the past, then there will be an absence of comparable data to be used as a basis for analysis, and so alternative methods of cost estimation will be needed. One method which anticipates how future operations should be carried out is known as the engineering method.

7.2 The engineering method of cost estimation

Suppose that a firm is considering the production of a product never previously manufactured as part of its normal business activities. The product could be as physically large and expensive as an oilrig, or as small and cheap as a toothbrush. How might the firm estimate the costs to be incurred by the new product? The firm's managers have no previous experience of this type of production and have no data base from which to make projections. One possible method might be to estimate directly the required production inputs needed to yield a certain output. These estimates of production inputs will usually be carried out by the firm's engineers, hence the name given to this method.

The engineers will calculate the raw material inputs based on the estimated material content of the product specification; labour inputs may be based on 'time and motion' studies; and an estimate of the capital equipment needed for production will provide the basis for a calculation of the relevant cost of using such equipment. Expected prices for each input factor can then be used to estimate the direct production costs. It is important to note that material, labour and equipment represent physical factors of production, and if these physical factors are relatively easy to identify with units of output, including the impact of any economies or diseconomies of scale, then cost estimation may be straightforward. However, problems arise immediately when the engineers attempt to calculate costs which are not so easily identifiable with units of output, for example, indirect production costs such as maintenance, insurance and power. Nevertheless, the observation and measurement by expert engineers of relationships between inputs and outputs can lead to very accurate predictions of future costs, and may yield results which benefit the overall planning system of the firm. For example, observation of the efficiency with which the labour force carries out its work on particular contracts may give useful information on how to set appropriate standards for work undertaken elsewhere within the firm by the labour force. In addition, if the new product has been manufactured previously by other firms (e.g. the oilrig or toothbrush mentioned earlier) information may be available about the production cost functions of those firms.

The biggest disadvantage of the engineering approach, which may limit its general use, is its costliness. If the production process is complex, the preparation of a full specification of inputs will require much expert work, entailing a large cost, which will be worthwhile only if the additional net benefits it creates are greater than the costs involved. However, the engineering method, or at least some variation of it, may have to be used if there are no past costs on which to base an analysis.

7.3 Historical cost-based methods of cost estimation

Few firms change the nature of their activities to the extent that cost estimation based on past activities is useless, but before we examine some of the methods used to predict future costs based on past data, a word of explanation is necessary. The use of past costs as aids to decision making does not violate anything we have previously said concerning the irrelevance of past costs as direct inputs to rational decisions. In the particular area of cost prediction it is not the past, historical costs *per se* which are useful for decision making, but rather the probability that they may offer some clues as to the likely levels of future costs, the real decision variables.

Where it is believed that past costs can be useful for information purposes, three preparatory steps should be undertaken to ensure that the greatest possible benefit is gained from using the data: choice of independent variable, selection of time period and examination of accounting data.

Choice of independent variable

The choice of an appropriate independent variable (basis of activity) is of vital importance in cost estimation. It may not always be obvious which basis should be used, particularly when the firm produces many different products. For example, in a manufacturing firm the total cost for any item might well vary with the level of output, the number of labour hours worked, the actual wages paid to labour, the number of machine hours used, and so on. The art lies in choosing the activity measure whose variations are most closely associated with fluctuations in the cost item which is being estimated. If more than one measure shows a very high correlation with changes in total cost, then management may well choose the one which entails the least expense in gathering the data. As most important managerial decisions in a manufacturing firm are concerned, in some way, with the level of output produced, it is usual to express costs as a function of output levels. This explains why we use units of output as the measure of activity level throughout the remainder of this chapter.

Selection of time period

The time period covered by past observations should not be chosen arbitrarily. It should be long enough to allow periodic costs to be included, and yet should attempt to allow for fluctuations in activity levels. In particular, the chosen time period should be one in which the firm's production process has remained reasonably constant. For example, if there have been changes in technology or changes in the make-up of the skilled labour force, or, indeed, changes in the prices of input factors, costs and activity levels may not be comparable. Where such environmental changes are significant it may be unwise to use observations for time periods before the changes took place. This poses a major problem for the cost estimator. On the one hand, he or she would like to include as many observations as possible in order to increase the accuracy of the estimates; on the other hand the estimator wants to use a time period during which there have been few changes in the production process. Resolution of the problem must always be on an individual basis. Trade-offs between using sufficient observations to impart a high level of statistical significance to the results and including only reasonably up-to-date information are inevitable.

Examination of accounting data

The accounting policies used by the firm may determine the ways in which data are accumulated in the financial records. For instance, the wages paid in one period may be calculated by reference to output in the previous period. Suppose for example, that the firm's labour costs, the dependent variable y, and the output level, the independent variable x, are derived as follows for three successive weeks of the year:

	y (£)	x (units)
Week 1	10,000	4,500
Week 2	9,000	6,200
Week 3	12,000	7,000

If the firm follows the policy of paying its labour force in the succeeding week for output reached in the previous week, then it would not be a valid basis for estimation to attempt to correlate the £10,000 for wages paid in week 1 with the 4,500 units of output of week 1. The wages paid in week 2 of £9,000 relate to the output of week 1, and those paid in week 3 (£12,000) relate to the output of week 2. Adjustments must be made to correct the inherent bias in the data. The wages figure should also be examined closely to eliminate any possible bias arising from changes in labour rates during the period.

For cost prediction purposes it is necessary to ensure that all costs have been adjusted to current price levels; unadjusted data may produce misleading estimates of future costs. For example, suppose that management is attempting to correlate wages paid to the labour force over a period of five years with output produced during those years in order to predict the level of wages dependent upon output for 19X5. The unadjusted data for the five year period are as follows:

	Wages paid (£)
Year 19X0	10,000
19X1	13,000
19X2	16,000
19X3	18,000
19X4	27,000

Suppose information is given that the labour force was given a wage increase of 20% at the beginning of 19X1 and a further increase of 15% at the beginning of 19X2. In order to ensure that the amounts for wages paid will produce consistent estimates of future costs, it is necessary to adjust those yearly payments which do *not* incorporate the increases of 20% and 15%. Thus the payments for 19X0 and 19X1 should be indexed by a factor reflecting the change in rate. There is no need to change the figures for the final three years, as these already incorporate the increased rates. Adjusted figures for the two years then become:

19X0 £10,000 (1.2) (1.15) = £13,800
19X1 £13,000 (1.15) = £14,950

The factors of 1.2 and 1.15 represent the adjustments necessary to reflect increases of 20% and 15%. Note that both factors are applied to the 19X0 payments, as two years' adjustments are necessary to update the 19X0 figures to 19X5 levels.

Having chosen the appropriate independent variable, selected the time period and adjusted for any bias in the accounting data, we now examine some of the possible methods of estimating future costs. First let us pause to remind ourselves exactly what it is we are trying to achieve. Suppose that a firm's production manager has been informed that during the last month the firm produced 1,000 units and incurred total costs (cash outflows) in so doing of £50,000. There is obviously some information contained in this message – the manager now knows both the level of production and the total cost of production. But in planning for the future more information would be desirable. The manager will be particularly interested in the breakdown of the total cost figure and will wish to know what proportion of the cash flow of £50,000 is fixed over different levels of production and what proportion is variable. It is this segregation of total costs into fixed and variable elements which the analysis of past costs attempts to achieve.

We might equally state that the analysis of past costs is intended to determine both the intercept (the level of fixed costs, a) and the slope (the variable cost per unit of activity, b) of the total cost function. The graph below presents the familiar cost function to be estimated:

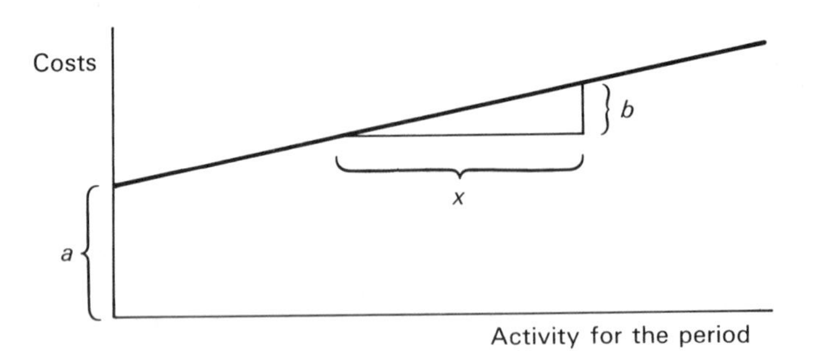

Our estimation of the likely cost relationship is preceded by two actions: derivation of the relevant past data and plotting the data.

We will use the following data for all our illustrations in this chapter. These data show the total manufacturing costs *adjusted to current price levels* and total units of output produced, our chosen activity base, in respect of Goodison Ltd for the first six months of the year; we wish to predict the cost–volume relationship for July.

	Output (units)	*Total manufacturing costs* (£)
January	80	10,200
February	90	10,900
March	100	12,100
April	80	10,800
May	120	13,700
June	110	12,500

We can now plot the data as in Figure 7.1. Each cross represents a relationship between costs and output. The pattern revealed by Figure 7.1 shows no very unusual

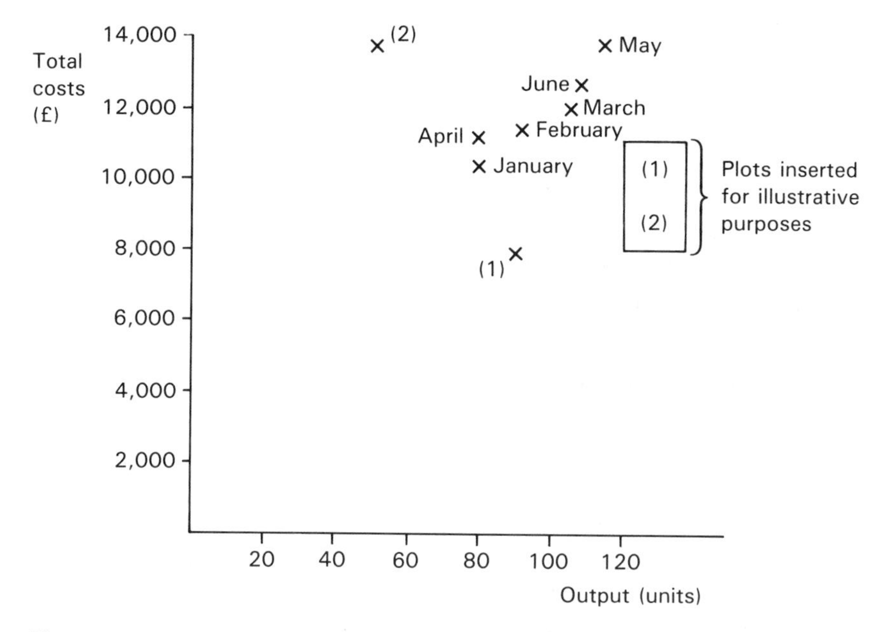

Figure 7.1 Scatter plotting of total manufacturing costs per month.

or abnormal relationships (i.e. the plots are reasonably closely clustered and total cost increases with units of output). But if, for example, one or more of the observations fell obviously outside the general relationship, as with plots (1) and (2), it would be necessary to find the reasons for these unusual observations, and, if they were considered to be abnormal and unrepresentative, to discard them.

We are now in a position to look closely at three approaches to the estimation of the firm's total cost function, or expressed differently, we will examine three ways of predicting the level of fixed costs, a, and the variable cost per unit, b, in the total cost equation. The methods chosen for estimation are not the only ones used by management in predicting costs, but they are probably the most widely used in practice. Note that in practice many managers make use of computer programs that apply these and other more refined methods.

7.4 The 'high-low' or 'range' method

The high–low method is the cheapest and easiest to use of the three methods. It attempts to segregate total past costs by examining only two observations, those representing the highest and lowest costs or, alternatively, the highest and lowest levels of past activity, over the range of observations. The slope of the line which connects these two points is then taken to represent the variable cost per unit of activity for *all* levels of activity. Using the data for Goodison Ltd we can use the high–low method as follows:

Total cost function	$\text{TC} = a + bx$
(1) Highest cost level (May) gives	$£13{,}700 = a + b\ (120 \text{ units})$
(2) Lowest cost level (January) gives	$£10{,}200 = a + b\ (80 \text{ units})$
(1) minus (2) gives	$£\ 3{,}500 = 0 + b\ (40 \text{ units})$

$$\therefore \quad b = \frac{£3{,}500}{40 \text{ units}} = £87.5 \text{ per unit}$$

Substituting for b in equation (1) gives

$$£13{,}700 = a + £87.5\ (120)$$

$$£13{,}700 = a + £10{,}500$$

$$\therefore \quad a = £(13{,}700 - 10{,}500) = £3{,}200$$

The estimated total cost function is $£3{,}200 + 87.5x$

A graphical representation of the total cost function estimated by the high–low method is given by Figure 7.2. The total cost line does not in fact exactly bisect any of the other four observations (i.e. those for February, March, April or June), but equally, the vertical differences (deviations) between these four plots and the estimated total cost function are quite small. If there were in fact no deviations from the line, we would say that we had very high confidence in the particular method

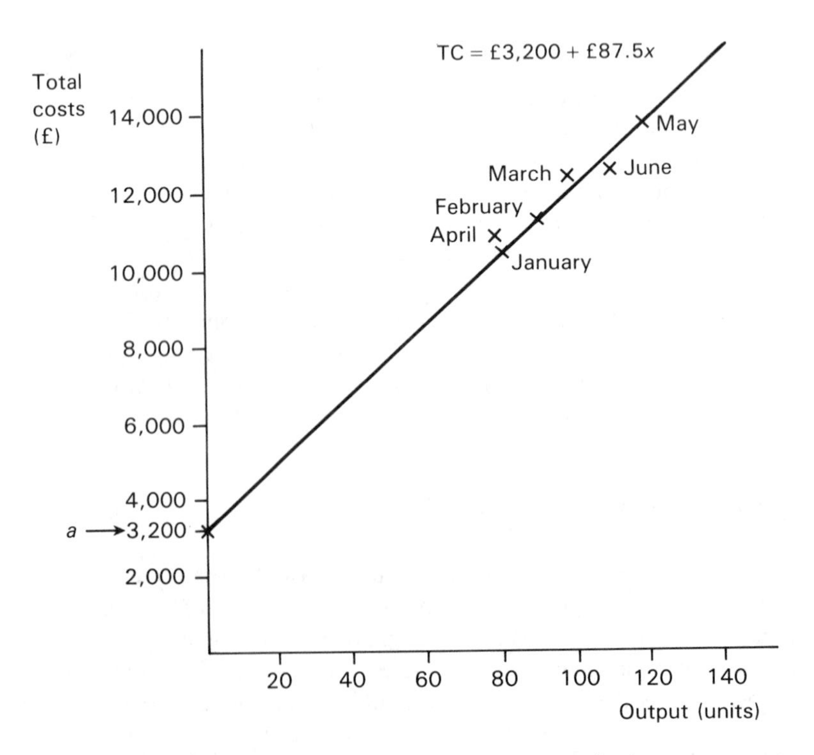

Figure 7.2 Total cost function using high–low method.

chosen. In the case of Goodison Ltd, the high–low method appears to offer some promise for cost estimation, but the method does have some important shortcomings. The most critical of these lies in the very name given to the method; because only the highest and the lowest observations are chosen for study, all other observations lying between the two extremes are ignored. Thus the reliability of the estimates generated for a and b depends upon how typical of the whole range of data the highest and lowest points are. It may well be that it is undesirable to use extreme values simply because they are untypical of the relationship between costs and activity.

7.5 The visual inspection method

The visual inspection method entails plotting all the relevant observations on a scattergraph, and then fitting a line to the data by visual inspection. Figure 7.3 shows a freehand line drawn to fit the data for Goodison Ltd. The line intercepts the vertical axis at approximately £3,400, the estimated level of fixed costs. Thus the total cost function can be estimated by calculating the total costs at any particular activity level and subtracting £3,400 so as to give the variable cost element of total costs. For example, at a level of 120 units, the total cost freehand line shows

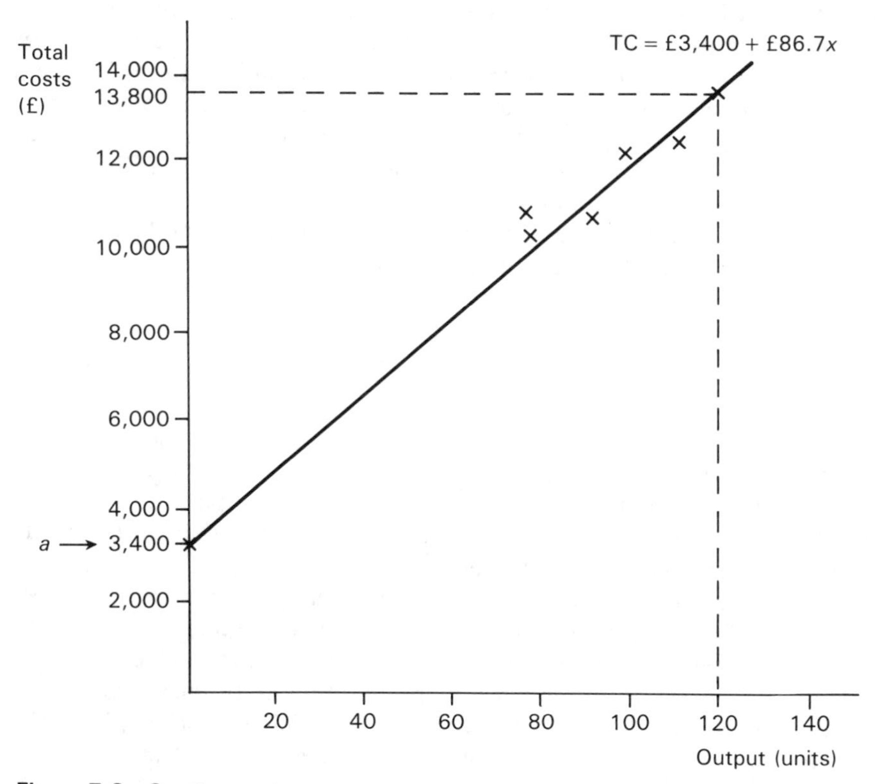

Figure 7.3 Scattergraph.

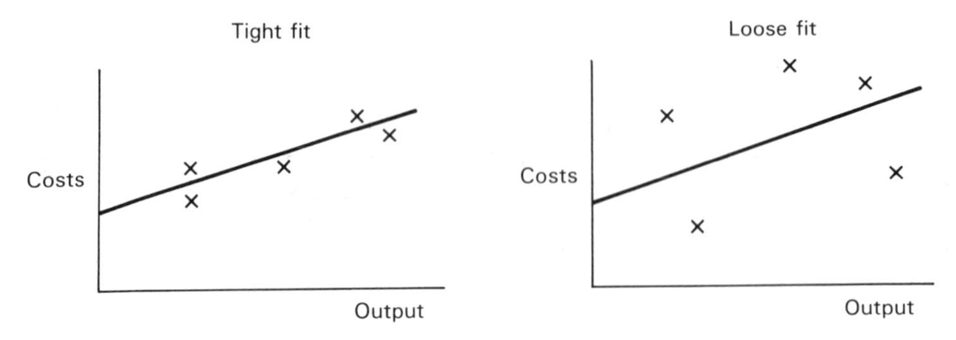

Figure 7.4 Different degrees of fit.

£13,800. Therefore total variable costs are £13,800 – £3,400 = £10,400, and the variable cost per unit is £10,400/120 = £86.7. The estimated TC function becomes £3,400 + £86.7x.

As with the high–low method, visual inspection has its disadvantages. Although it uses all the data, and not merely the two extreme points, it is very subjective. It is unlikely that everybody would construct the same freehand line, and different estimates could easily be derived for the total cost function; but perhaps most important of all, neither the high–low method nor the visual inspection method give any clue as to how inaccurate the estimates derived from the methods can be. For example, a mistake in drawing the line may result in a substantial error which could directly affect the quality of management planning. In addition, even though the line may be 'well' drawn, it may represent a tight fit for some data sets, and a loose fit for others, as shown in Figure 7.4. Thus there is no indication of how much reliance can be placed on estimates made from the line.

The defects of these comparatively unsophisticated methods can be overcome by the use of the statistical technique known as linear regression analysis.

7.6 Linear regression analysis

Linear regression analysis refers to the measurement of the average amount of change in one variable (e.g. manufacturing costs) which is associated with unit increases in the amounts of one or more other variables (e.g. output). It is a method of regressing y (the dependent variable) on x (the independent variable). It is widely used where computing facilities are available.

Regression analysis has two purposes. First, it fits a line to the observed relationships between costs and volume which is known as the *line of best fit*, and second, it tells the user how much confidence can be placed in the goodness of the fit of the regression line. Neither of these two purposes is fulfilled by the approaches of the high–low method or the visual inspection graph. This section considers the procedure for determining the line of best fit; how the goodness of fit of the line might be measured is explained in the next section.

Regression analysis fits a line to the data so as to minimise the sum of the squares of the vertical distances from the regression line to the plots of the actual observations, i.e. so that the sum of the squares of these deviations is less than the sum of the squared deviations from any other line. Thus it is a method of line fitting which is free from subjectivity. The mathematical technique which gives this assurance is called the *least-squares* method. Squared figures are used because, as a squared number is always positive, values for each observation can be added to arrive at a measure of overall difference. If unsquared figures were used, large positive and negative amounts might cancel out, with the result that misleadingly close relationships might appear.

The least-squares method entails the use of two mathematical equations known as *normal equations* which must be solved simultaneously to derive values for a and b for inclusion in the total cost function. These equations are of the form:[16]

(1) $\Sigma y = na + b\Sigma x$

(2) $\Sigma xy = \alpha\Sigma x + b\Sigma x^2$

where n = the number of observations; Σx = the sum of the observations of the independent variable (e.g. x = level of output); Σy = the sum of the observations of the dependent variable (e.g. y = total costs); Σx^2 = the sum of the squares of the x observations; Σxy = the sum of the product of each pair of observation; a = total fixed costs; b = variable cost per unit of output.

Before we use the available data to calculate the regression line for Goodison Ltd, we briefly mention some of the assumptions which underlie linear regression analysis. The use of sophisticated mathematical models can often blind us to the fact that they may be based on simplifying assumptions which, if they do not hold up, can cast doubts on the results of the model. The results of applying regression analysis are only as good as the input data fed into the model.

There are at least three important assumptions underlying linear regression analysis. First, linearity of the relationships between costs and volume is assumed (we return to this aspect later); second, it is assumed that there is a uniform dispersion of actual costs about the regression line, and third it is assumed that successive cost measurements do not depend on each other. These latter two assumptions relate to technical problems of statistical analysis, which will not be explored further. We now use linear regression analysis to determine the total cost function of Goodison Ltd.

Substituting the appropriate figures from Table 7.1 into the simultaneous equations gives:

(1) $70{,}200 = 6a + 580b$

(2) $6{,}890{,}000 = 580a + 57{,}400b$

[16] It is beyond the scope of this text to explain how these simultaneous equations are derived. Interested students should refer to an introductory statistics book. For our purposes we shall accept the mathematical validity of the simultaneous equations.

Table 7.1 Regression analysis data

Month	Output x	Total manufacturing costs y	xy	x^2	y^2
January	80	10,200	816,000	6,400	104,040,000
February	90	10,900	981,000	8,100	118,810,000
March	100	12,100	1,210,000	10,000	146,410,000
April	80	10,800	864,000	6,400	116,640,000
May	120	13,700	1,644,000	14,400	187,690,000
June	110	12,500	1,375,000	12,100	156,250,000
Totals	$\Sigma x = 580$	$\Sigma y = 70,200$	$\Sigma xy = 6,890,000$	$\Sigma x^2 = 57,400$	$\Sigma y^2 = 829,840,000$

Multiplying equation (1) by 580, and equation (2) by 6 we have:

$$(1)\quad 40,716,000 = 3,480a + 336,400b$$

$$(2)\quad 41,340,000 = 3,480a + 344,400b$$

Subtracting (1) from (2) gives:

$$624,000 = 8,000b$$

$$\therefore \quad b = 78$$

Substituting 78 for b in (1) gives:

$$70,200 = 6a + 45,240$$

$$\therefore \quad a = 4,160$$

With these two calculated values of a and b we now write our straight line equation of

$$y = 4,160 + 78x$$

It is estimated that the manufacturing costs for Goodison Ltd comprise a fixed element of £4,160 and a (linear) variable element of £78 per unit of output.

7.7 The coefficient of correlation

We have now derived an expression which may be used to predict the future level of total costs for Goodison Ltd. As yet, however, we do not have any indication as to how accurate the predictions from the regression model are likely to be. The statistic which is normally used to assess the goodness of fit of a regression line is known as the coefficient of correlation (first introduced in the discussion of the portfolio approach to risk measurement in Chapter 4). The correlation coefficient can be measured from the following mathematical formula:[17]

$$r = \frac{n(\Sigma xy) - (\Sigma x)(\Sigma y)}{\sqrt{[(n(\Sigma x^2) - (\Sigma x)^2]}\sqrt{[n(\Sigma y^2) - (\Sigma y)^2]}}$$

The correlation coefficient squared, r^2 (known as the *coefficient of determination*) is a widely used statistic. It indicates the percentage of the variation in total costs that is accounted for by the changes in the observed values of output

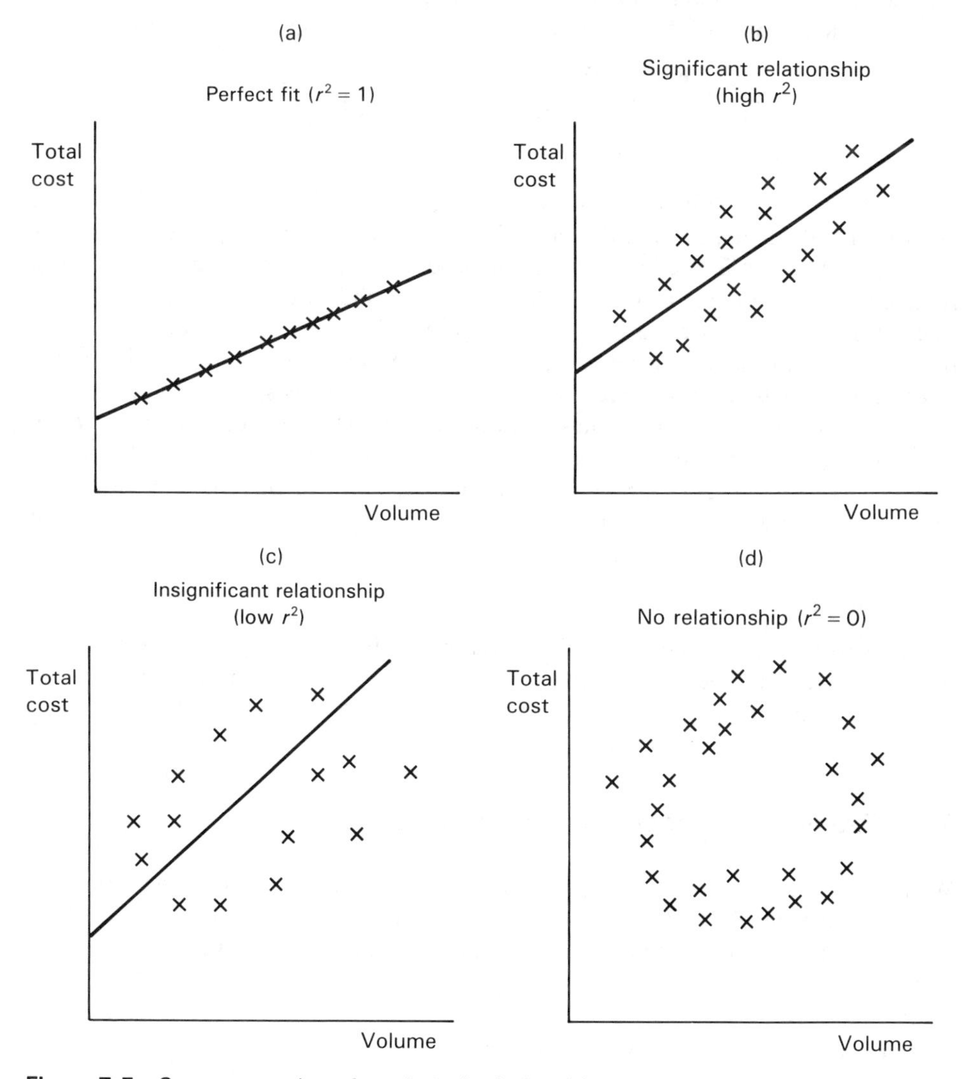

Figure 7.5 Some examples of statistical relationships.

[17] For a detailed explanation of the derivation of this formula, interested students should consult an introductory statistics book.

levels. It denotes the predictive value of the model. Its value will always lie between 0 and 1. For instance, if all the plotted observations fell on a straight line, then the r^2 statistic would be exactly +1, and we could say that costs and output were perfectly correlated. If, however, the plots appeared in the form of a circle around the regression line, then r^2 would approximate to zero. This would indicate that no single line was better than any other in explaining the cost/output relationship. Thus r^2 gives information as to how confident management can be in the explanatory and predictive power of the model. Figure 7.5 gives some examples of graphical representations of different possible relationships.

The calculations of r^2 for Goodison Ltd can be determined as follows:

$$r = \frac{6(6{,}890{,}000) - 580(70{,}200)}{\sqrt{6(57{,}400) - 580^2}\sqrt{6(829{,}840{,}000) - 70{,}200^2}} = 0.977$$

$$\therefore \quad r^2 = 0.954 \text{ (or 95.4\%)}$$

This indicates that 95.4% of the variation in the total manufacturing costs of Goodison Ltd for the six month period is accounted for, although not necessarily caused, by changes in the level of output produced during that same period. The remaining 4.6% is explained by random variation and also by the effect of other interacting, but unknown, variables. In the case of Goodison Ltd, management can be very confident that a single independent variable, the level of output, will provide a reasonable predictor of changes in total manufacturing costs. In a situation where a low r^2 is obtained, consideration should be given to whether a cost function which uses a single independent variable provides an adequate estimate of total costs. It may be necessary to add further explanatory variables to the cost function. For instance, as suggested earlier in this chapter, an appropriate form of the cost function may be:

$$y = a + bx_1 + cx_2 + dx_3 + \cdots + nx_n$$

This form of cost function can be solved by the use of *multiple linear regression* techniques. These measure the changes in the cost for each of the explanatory variables, while keeping the others constant.

7.8 Evaluation of cost estimation methods

We have looked now at three separate methods of cost estimation, and seen how each one has yielded a different total cost function. The cost functions for the three methods, each of which used exactly the same data, are as follows:

Method	*Cost function* $(a + bx)$
High–low	£3,200 + £87.5x
Visual inspection	£3,400 + £86.7x
Regression analysis	£4,160 + £78.0x

As we move through various stages of sophistication we can see, in this instance, the counterbalancing effects of the three methods; the fixed element of total costs increases and the variable cost per unit falls. These conclusions would not, of course, necessarily hold true for any firm other than Goodison Ltd. The importance of the different functions lies in how they are used. Management will wish to use the data to predict future costs, and therefore to plan future operations for the firm. Suppose, for example, management expects to produce 130 units in July. If it uses regression analysis to predict total costs at this level of output, it will expect to incur £4,160 + £78(130) = £14,300; using the high–low method, total costs will be expected to be £3,200 + £87.5(130) = £14,575. The differences in predicted total costs are small, but the differences between the two elements of cost are substantial. We have earlier stressed the relevance of incremental costs in decision making. The high–low method predicts a variable cost for each additional unit produced of £87.5; regression analysis, at a very high level of confidence, predicts a variable cost per unit of £78. If it transpires that Goodison Ltd's fixed costs are indeed constant over wide ranges of output, so that the incremental costs relevant for decision making correspond to the variable costs, then the planning of costs for decision making may take on very different perspectives, depending upon which cost function is accepted.

7.9 The learning curve

There is one particular respect in which the uncritical use of past data to predict future costs may result in errors in estimation. When a new product is to be manufactured or a new production process started, it is frequently the case that employees will take longer to produce the first units of the product than to produce subsequent units, because there is a learning process involved. As the employees become more familiar with the production process, they produce an increasing number of units in a given period of time. The rate at which their efficiency increases is called the *learning rate* and is usually estimated by a *learning curve*. In estimating future costs, it is important that the management should take account of this learning effect, which will influence not only the labour cost but also the cost of other resources, the use of which varies with labour time, for example, power costs. The learning curve is essentially an empirical phenomenon, i.e. it has been observed to occur on certain kinds of production processes, particularly those which are labour intensive and in which the workforce performs repetitive tasks which they can learn to carry out more efficiently.

Let us consider a simple example to explain the meaning of the learning rate. Suppose that a company has received an order to produce eight oilrigs. It estimates that the first rig will take 200 days to manufacture and that the learning rate, on the basis of past experience, will be 90%. What this means is that when the cumulative number of units produced doubles, the average time per unit taken to produce *all* units will be 90% of the average time per unit taken to produce the previous (cumulative) units. The calculations of the oil rigs are shown in Table 7.2. The cumulative average time for the first two rigs (180 days per rig) is 90% of the time

Table 7.2 Learning curve effect (90% learning rate)

Cumulative units	*Cumulative average time per unit* (days)	*Total time for cumulative units* (days)	*Marginal time per unit for additional units* (days)
1	200	200	200
2	90% × 200 = 180	180 × 2 = 360	360 − 200 = 160
4	90% × 180 = 162	162 × 4 = 648	$\frac{648 - 360}{2} = 144$
8	90% × 162 = 145.8	145.8 × 8 = 1,166.4	$\frac{1{,}116.4 - 648}{4} = 129.6$

taken to produce the first rig (200 days). So the total time taken to produce two rigs is 360 days (180 days × 2 rigs) and the marginal time taken to produce the second rig is 160 days (360 days − 200 days). Similar calculations are undertaken for each successive doubling of output.[18]

The rather cumbersome nature of the calculations arises because the learning curve is based on real world observations – the relationships described are empirical. For repetitive, labour intensive tasks, the learning rate appears to vary between 65% and 90% in the early stages of production. It eventually reaches a steady state in which no further efficiency gains from learning are achieved. Whenever an estimate of the costs of a new production process is being made, the predicted effects of learning, based on past experience, should be included. However, it should be borne in mind that the effects will not continue indefinitely and may not exist at all for some non-repetitive, non-labour intensive processes.

7.10 The relevant range

We cannot leave the subject of cost estimation without returning to the problem of linearity. In our example of Goodison Ltd we examined only output levels in a range from 80 to 120 units, and yet from this limited range of observations we developed a cost function which could be used to predict costs at all output levels. Or could it? Figure 7.6 (which is unrelated to the example of Goodison Ltd) points out some possible difficulties in making any sweeping generalisations from particular observations.

[18] The following formula is available to calculate the cumulative average time per unit:

$$y = ax^{-b}$$

where y = cumulative average time per unit (or batch)
a = time taken to produce the first unit (or batch)
x = number of units (or batches) produced in total

$$-b = \frac{\text{log or } r}{\text{log of } 2}$$

r = learning rate

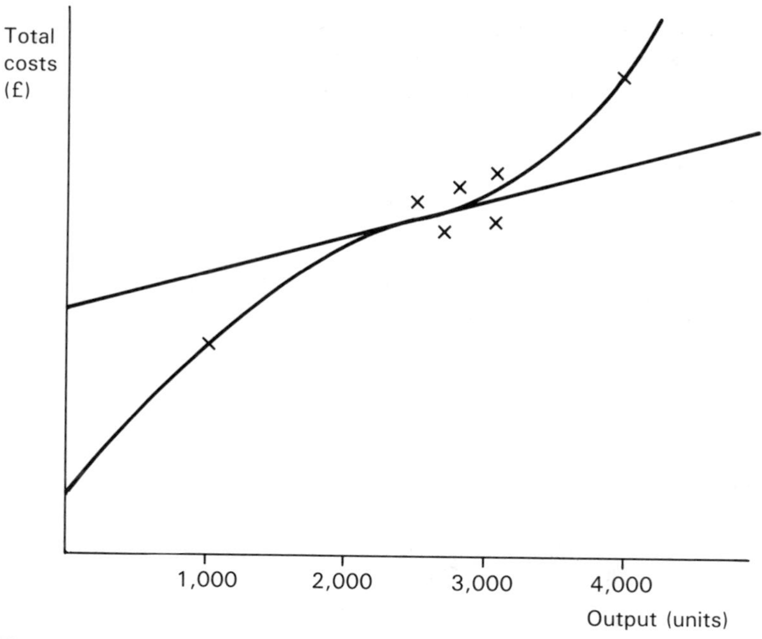

Figure 7.6 The relevant range.

The middle five plots represent actual observations in the range from 2,500 to 3,000 units of output, the firm's regularly achieved level in any particular period. The straight line represents the total cost function as estimated by regression analysis. It may well explain most of the variations in total cost, but the actual cost function may be of the curvilinear form shown on the graph, and the plots on the curved line may better estimate levels of total cost at the more extreme ranges of 1,000 units and 4,000 units respectively. If this is so, then management would indeed make large errors in cost prediction if, say, only 1,000 units were produced during any period.

The moral of this exercise is important. Regression analysis may give a high value for the r^2, but this value may only hold for the relevant range of observations; the more extreme are the output levels beyond the observed range, the less will be our confidence in the prediction of future costs.

Discussion topics

1. Discuss some of the factors which should be considered when choosing an appropriate activity base for cost prediction.
2. 'The "engineering method" is the most useful but the least practicable method of cost estimation.' Discuss.
3. 'The use of past data for cost estimation necessarily possesses many disadvantages. Suggest what some of these disadvantages might be, and how they might be overcome.

4 'The derivation of the statistical regression line depends on the validity of certain assumptions.' Discuss the importance of these assumptions.

5 Discuss some possible advantages and disadvantages of using the high–low method for cost estimation.

6 Discuss the significance of the r^2 statistic in regression analysis.

7 Why may statistical analysis offer more insight into cost prediction than the use of simpler arithmetic manipulations?

8 'Simple regression analysis is inappropriate to most real world situations. Most managers know that a single independent variable does not offer a reasonable explanation of changes in costs.' Discuss.

Exercises

7.1 The following table shows turnover and advertising expenditure for ten similar small manufacturing companies.

Company	*Advertising expenditure* (£000)	*Turnover* (£000)
A	2.6	138
B	3.1	163
C	3.5	166
D	3.7	153
E	4.1	177
F	4.4	201
G	4.6	216
H	4.9	208
I	5.3	226
J	5.8	238

(a) Which is the dependent and which is the independent variable?

(b) Calculate a regression equation linking advertising expenditure and turnover by the least-squares method.

(c) (i) What turnover is expected for nil advertising expenditure?
(ii) What turnover would £12,000 advertising expenditure be expected to produce?
(iii) Comment on (c)(i) and (ii).

7.2 The following information relates to the patterns of cost behaviour of indirect labour in relation to units produced.

Units produced	*Cost of indirect labour* (£)
20	10,800
40	15,000
100	26,600
160	40,000
120	30,800
20	11,200
60	18,600
100	28,000
120	31,000

(a) Using linear regression, calculate total fixed costs and the variable cost per unit.

(b) Calculate and comment on the r^2 value of the estimate.

(c) Compare and contrast the estimates derived from the linear regression method with those derived from the high–low method.

7.3 A division of Munch Ltd processes a single type of chemical. Processing costs and output for the last thirteen accounting periods (of four weeks each) have been as follows:

							Period						
	1	*2*	*3*	*4*	*5*	*6*	*7*	*8*	*9*	*10*	*11*	*12*	*13*
Costs (£):													
Materials	1260	1480	1610	1740	1990	1930	2160	2140	2010	1780	1570	1660	1590
Direct labour	1870	2140	2160	2260	2540	2340	2520	2550	2400	2690	2500	2560	2480
Overheads	770	820	810	830	960	900	940	950	940	870	800	820	790
Total costs	3900	4440	4580	4830	5490	5170	5620	5640	5350	5340	4870	5040	4860
Output (tons)	120	150	160	170	200	170	200	200	180	160	140	150	140

The price of materials was increased by 10% at the end of period 5; a wage increase of 20% was given to all employees classified as 'direct' at the end of period 9. There have been no other increases in processing costs during the past year.

You have been requested to prepare a flexible budget for the coming year.

(a) Describe what calculations you would undertake, using the above information, as a basis for your budget.

(b) Explain how you would establish the reliability of the budgetary estimates derived from the calculations.

(c) Discuss the limitations of your method of calculation.

7.4 The results of the Russian division of Rimsky Ltd over the last five years are summarised as follows:

			Year		
	1	*2*	*3*	*4*	*5*
Sales (£000)	70	93	119	118	152
Costs (£000):					
Materials	20	28	42	37	48
Labour	27	36	39	48	54
Overheads	24	24	28	33	32
	71	88	109	118	134
Net profit (£000)	(1)	5	10	0	18
Sales (units)	2,100	2,800	3,400	3,100	4,000

The Russian division manufactures a single product. Stocks have been negligible at all relevant times. Price changes have been rare in Rimsky's business. During the last five years, the only changes in the prices of resources used have been an increase in the price of materials of 25% three years ago (at the end of year 2), and an increase in wage rates of $33\frac{1}{3}$% two years ago (at the end of year 3); overhead costs have not been affected by price changes.

Plans for the coming year (year 6) are now being prepared. No further increases in the prices of resources are expected. The sales manager has provided the following estimates of the sales price–volume relationship for the coming year:

Volume	*Price* (£)
4,500	37
4,000	40
3,400	42

(a) Estimate the optimal selling price from amongst the three possible prices £37, £40 or £42 using linear regression analysis to estimate the cost–volume relationship.

(b) Discuss the advantages and limitations of linear regression analysis for the estimation of cost–volume relationships.

7.5 Webern Ltd manufactures chariots. Summarised income statements are shown below. Wage rates were increased by 10% on 1 January 19X4 and a further award of 30% is expected at the end of 19X7. The cost items marked with an asterisk have tended to increase at 5% p.a. in step with the index of retail prices; the price index at the mid-point of 19X8 is expected to stand 20% above its level at the corresponding point of 19X6.

	Year ended 31 December			
	19X3	*19X4*	*19X5*	*19X6*
	£	£	£	£
Costs				
Materials*	70,000	103,000	104,000	120,000
Wages and salaries	98,000	168,000	168,000	189,000
Factory rent	20,000	20,000	20,000	20,000
Depreciation of machinery	50,000	80,000	80,000	80,000
Sundry overheads*	48,000	50,000	53,000	56,000
	286,000	421,000	425,000	465,000
Sales	308,000	540,000	510,000	736,000
Profit	22,000	119,000	85,000	271,000
Number of chariots manufactured and sold	1,100	1,800	1,900	2,300

(a) Calculate, using regression analysis, estimated costs in 19X8 for an output of 500, 2,000 and 2,500 chariots.

(b) Calculate the number of chariots that Webern must make and sell for £300 each in 19X8 just to cover costs.

(c) Comment on the limitations of your method of cost estimation.

7.6 At the end of last year Mr Hutton, a manufacturer of wooden furniture, accepted a contract to produce 200 cricket bats. The details of the contract were:

	£
Materials: Wood	1,000
Rubber	400
Labour (400 hours @ £4/hr)	1,600
Variable overheads	600
	3,600
Profit	400
Sales value	4,000

Hutton was slightly concerned over how long his staff would take getting used to the new manufacturing methods and noticed that the first 100 bats took 250 hours to produce and the second 100 only 150 hours. The staff feel that they have not fully adapted to the new product and could do still better. Hutton's estimates for the variable overheads incurred on the contract were £1 per labour hour plus £1 per bat.

Hutton has received three more contracts to supply first 600 bats, secondly 100 bats and finally 300 bats.

Find the marginal cost of each successive contract using:

(a) A tabular approach for the first contract.

(b) For the other contracts the formula:

$$y = ax^{-b}$$

Further reading

Benston, G. J., 'Multiple regression analysis of cost behavior', *The Accounting Review*, October 1966.

Draper, N. R. and Smith, H., *Applied Regression Analysis*, Wiley, 1966.

Hirschmann, W. B., 'Profits from the learning curve', *Harvard Business Review*, January/February 1964.

Johnston, J., *Econometric Methods*, 2nd edn., Chapters 1 & 2, McGraw-Hill, 1972.

Liao, S. S., 'The learning curve: Wright's model vs Crawford's model', *Issues in Accounting Education*, Fall 1988.

Nurnberg, H., 'The ambiguous high–low method', *Issues in Accounting Education*, Spring 1986.

Wood, D. and Fildes, R., *Forecasting for Business: Methods and Applications*, Longman, 1976.

Chapter 8

Pricing decisions

In previous chapters we have developed the notion that the long-run objective of an organisation should be to generate surplus cash from its operations – i.e. the objective of maximising the discounted present value of future net cash inflows. In this context, surplus cash represents the residual after deducting the total cash costs of operations from the total cash revenues from operations. We have also looked in some detail at how we might classify, analyse and predict costs so as to improve decision making – but we have spent little time on an examination of the other part of the equation, namely the determination of total revenues. Yet perhaps the most important operating decisions of all are concerned with the establishment of selling prices for an organisation's goods and services. It is the volume of sales multiplied by the selling price which determines the total cash inflows. In the long run an enterprise's total cash inflows must exceed its total costs if the enterprise is to survive. In this chapter we look at how accounting data might be used by management in making selling price and output level decisions. Our analysis is conducted from two separate viewpoints, depending upon the market for the enterprise's goods. We might identify the two market situations as ones:

(i) where demand for the firm's goods can be reasonably well estimated;
(ii) where it is very difficult to predict demand.

In practice, many companies may have little difficulty in pricing their products. Under certain market conditions a single market price, or at least a relatively narrow range of market prices, will exist for a product and customers will pay that price and no more. Hence the company will simply charge the market price. Such a situation might be found in particular industries where small firms are competing with a few very large companies who exercise effective price control. The small firms have little choice but to accept the prices determined by the pricing policies of the large companies. The oil and chemical industries are examples of industries which are dominated by a few very large companies. A similar situation will exist where there is a highly competitive market for a product. If any one firm attempts to charge more than the market price customers will go to another supplier. Furthermore, the pressures of competition will tend to drive the market price down so that it is likely that all firms will be charging a price close to their long-run marginal production costs. Hence any attempt to charge below the market price is likely to spell financial failure for a firm. Supermarket chains and discount warehouses are examples of highly competitive sectors of the economy.

8.1 Pricing decisions in context

Before we analyse the accountant's contribution to pricing, we consider the organisational context within which pricing decisions are taken. The price to be charged for a product is one element in the organisation's *marketing strategy*. That strategy will be designed to achieve the organisation's goals, which we have assumed to be best represented by cash maximisation. If the organisation produces many different products, it has the problem of deciding which marketing strategy to pursue so that cash is maximised for all products.

The selling price chosen for each product is an important part of the marketing strategy. For instance, certain prices may be lowered to attract customers away from competitors; others may be raised if it is thought that no significant loss of market share will occur. However, the choice of selling price is not the only tactical device available to managers in designing the organisation's marketing strategy. The quantity of a particular product which the organisation will be able to sell will depend also on the promotional strategy adopted, including the extent and nature of advertising, on the design and quality of the product, on the intensity of the selling effort expended and on the selection of distribution channels. Although these are strictly matters for the marketing staff rather than for the accountant, it should be evident that marketing and financial implications are heavily interdependent. For example, the design of the product will affect its manufacturing cost and the intensity of selling effort will affect selling and distribution costs. It is essential that the marketing and accounting staff liaise frequently while the marketing strategy is being developed.

Other factors will also influence the relationship between the selling price charged and the quantity demanded. These will be reflected in the *price elasticity of demand* for the firm's products (i.e the responsiveness of changes in demand to changes in price). If demand for a product is price elastic, relatively small changes in price will result in relatively large changes in demand. If demand is price inelastic, the quantity demanded will be relatively unaffected by changes in selling price. The extent of demand elasticity depends on a variety of factors. For example: How necessary is the product? – the more necessary it is, the more inelastic will be the demand for it. What are current consumer tastes and how are they likely to change over time? – products which are highly susceptible to consumer taste, such as fashion goods, are likely to have elastic demand over time. How readily available are substitute products? – the more readily available are acceptable substitutes, the more elastic will be the demand for the product. How competitive is the market within which the product is sold? – the more competitive the market, the more elastic the demand for the product.

Finally in this section, we consider one situation where it is likely to prove particularly difficult to predict demand; that is, where a *new product* is to be manufactured and sold. The problem is likely to be acute if the new product is dissimilar to any product previously sold by the producing firm or other firms. Such a situation arose at the start of the microchip technology revolution when firms were considering applications of the new technology (digital watches, electronic calculators, personal computers, etc.) which had not been possible, at least at a comparatively low cost, using previously available methods. In such situations, firms will undertake market research. For example, they might engage in *test marketing*, i.e. selling the new product in a number of different (and perhaps quite small) areas, possibly at a different price in each area, in an attempt to collect information concerning the likely demand for the product at various prices. When the new product is eventually launched fully, the selling organisation may also pursue particular *pricing strategies*, designed to maximise cash returns over the life of the product. For example, in the early part of the product life, before other firms have developed the technology necessary to compete, the firm might follow a *skimming* pricing strategy. It will set a high initial price for the product and progressively lower it as the market broadens and competitors emerge. Such a strategy was evident in the early days of personal computer development. Alternatively, if a firm is attempting to enter an already established market, it might pursue a *penetration* pricing strategy, i.e. it will set a low initial price in an attempt to acquire a substantial share of the market and subsequently increase the price as its market position strengthens. Such a strategy has been evident amongst later entrants to the personal computer market, such as Amstrad.

On some occasions with a new product, a firm may be fairly sure of the price at which it will be able to sell the product – for example, because it is to be sold in a mature market – but needs to know the maximum or *target cost* at which manufacture and sale of the product will be profitable. Production of new models of refrigerator or washing machine are examples of such a situation.

The brief discussion above should have made it clear that decisions concerning the pricing of goods and services are not the sole preserve of the accountant. It is beyond the scope of this chapter to investigate marketing and other strategic areas in more detail. Rather, we shall discuss how accounting information might provide one useful input to pricing decisions by looking at both optimal pricing decisions, where firms have a reasonably clear idea of the relationship between selling price and demand, and methods based primarily on cost, which may be of use where the selling price–demand relationship is very uncertain or unknown.

8.2 Optimal price setting

Most firms operate in an environment where the selling prices charged for their products are in some way (intuitively or formally) related to the quantities demanded by customers. Generally speaking, the lower the selling price of the product, the more units of the product that will be taken up by the market. We might term this relationship the firm's *demand schedule* or *demand function*. The precise quantification of this relationship is generally very difficult to determine in practice, particularly as it is likely to be changing over time.

The firm's *supply schedule* refers to the costs incurred in producing and selling the units of output sold. The supply schedule is usually easier to estimate than the demand schedule, primarily because the firm has more control over its costs than it has over the demand for its products and thus can predict costs with more confidence. Nevertheless, if demand and supply schedules can be drawn up, the firm will be in a position to attempt to derive (simultaneously) both its optimal output level and its optimal selling price – information vital in pursuing the goal of cash maximisation. We can derive optimal selling prices by any (or all) of three methods: graphical analysis, flexible budgets, or simple differential calculus.

Suppose that a firm, Ewood Ltd, makes one product. Total fixed costs per annum are £8,000 and a variable cost of £30 is incurred for each additional unit produced and sold over a very large range of outputs. The present selling price for the product is £70, at which price 300 units are demanded annually. The sales manager of Ewood Ltd estimates that each successive £10 increase in price will result in a drop in annual demand of 100 units; similarly each successive £10 reduction in price will cause an increase in demand of 100 units. It is possible to charge intermediary prices within each £10 range with proportionate changes in demand.

To derive the optimal selling price we first calculate total cost and total revenue functions for the product, regardless of which of the three methods we are going to use. The total cost function is a straightforward calculation, based on the level of fixed costs and the variable cost per unit of output:

$$\text{Total cost} = \text{TC} = £8{,}000 + £30x \qquad (8.1)$$

where x is the annual level of demand and output.

Calculation of the total revenue function is more difficult. It must be done in two stages. First, selling price (SP) is expressed as a function of the level of output. At present, selling price is £70 and output is 300 units. Each increase or decrease in price of £10 results in a corresponding decrease or increase in demand of 100 units. If the selling price was increased by £30 (i.e. to £100) demand would be zero. Thereafter, to increase demand by *one* unit, selling price must be reduced by £10/100 units or 10p. Hence the maximum selling price attainable for an output of x units is:

$$\text{Selling price} = \text{SP} = £100 - £0.1x \qquad (8.2)$$

This selling price equation determines the slope of the line of Ewood Ltd's demand schedule, as shown in Figure 8.1. Point A on Figure 8.1 represents the current situation, where, at a selling price of £70, 300 units are demanded.

Second, total revenue is expressed in terms of the selling price equation. This is an easier calculation. As total revenue is the product of the selling price per unit and the number of units sold, the equation for total revenue is:

$$\text{Total revenue} = \text{TR} = \text{SP}x = (£100 - £0.1x)x = £100x - £0.1x^2 \qquad (8.3)$$

We can now calculate the optimal output level and selling price using each of our chosen methods.

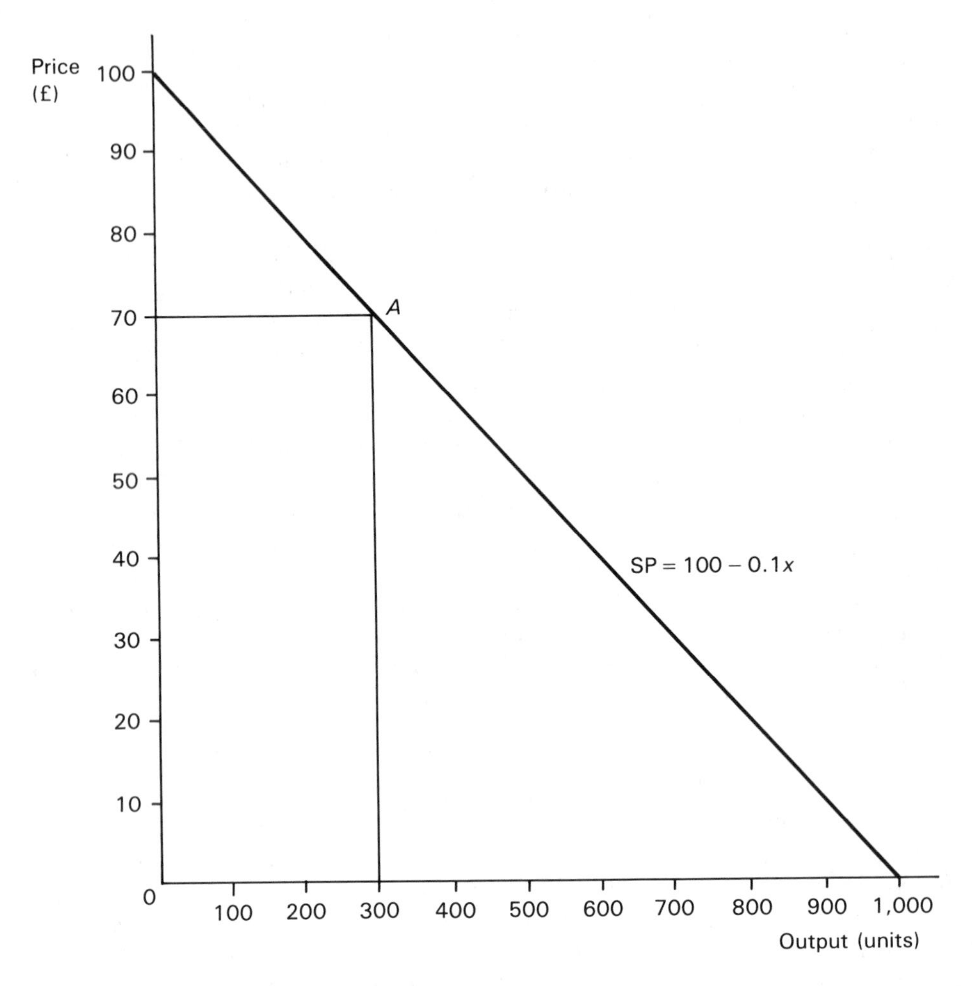

Figure 8.1 Ewood Ltd: demand schedule.

Optimal pricing using graphical analysis

The relationship between selling price, demand and total revenue can be tabulated as shown in Table 8.1. The bell-shape total revenue curve is depicted in Figure 8.2.

We can calculate total costs for Ewood Ltd in the same manner, as in Table 8.2. This is shown graphically in Figure 8.3.

Finally, we can determine the relationship between output and profit for Ewood Ltd as in Table 8.3.

This relationship between revenue, cost and profit can be shown graphically as in Figure 8.4. Figure 8.4 is a form of break-even chart (introduced in Chapter 6) in which the slope of the total revenue line is curvilinear, whereas total costs are assumed to be linear in relation to output.

The optimal output level is the point at which the highest profit is achieved.

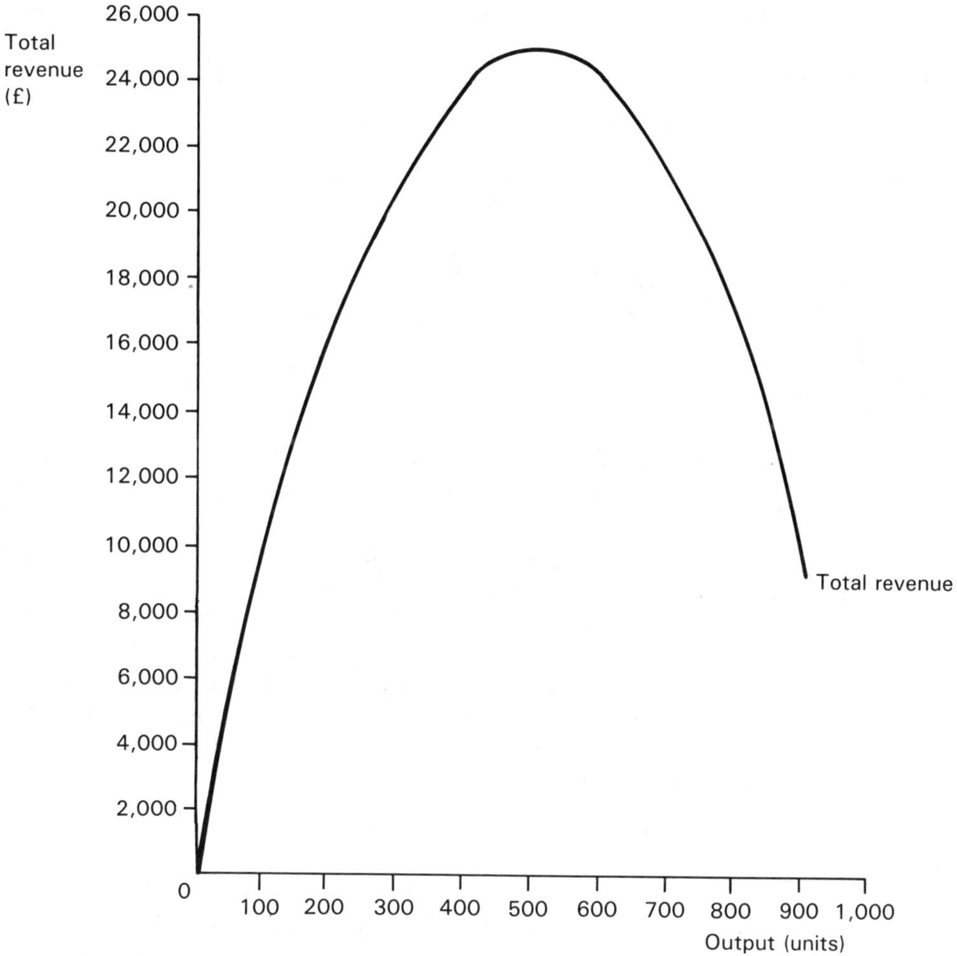

Figure 8.2 Ewood Ltd: total revenue function.

Table 8.1 Ewood Ltd: price, demand and revenue information

Price (£)	*Demand and output* (units)	*Total revenue* (£)
100	0	0
90	100	9,000
80	200	16,000
70	300	21,000
60	400	24,000
50	500	25,000
40	600	24,000
30	700	21,000
20	800	16,000
10	900	9,000

Table 8.2 Ewood Ltd: cost and output information

Units of output	*Variable costs* (£)	*Fixed costs* (£)	*Total cost* (£)
100	3,000	8,000	11,000
200	6,000	8,000	14,000
300	9,000	8,000	17,000
400	12,000	8,000	20,000
500	15,000	8,000	23,000
600	18,000	8,000	26,000
700	21,000	8,000	29,000
800	24,000	8,000	32,000
900	27,000	8,000	35,000

This is shown by point *y* on the graph in Figure 8.4 and it represents the greatest vertical distance between the total revenue and total cost lines at a level of 350 units of output.

An alternative form of presentation is to use a profit–volume graph (also introduced in Chapter 6) to explain the relationships of costs, revenues and profits. Figure 8.5 shows the profit–volume graph for Ewood Ltd. It can be seen from the profit–volume graph that the optimal output level is approximately 350 units.

Having calculated the optimal output level we are now in a position to answer the other part of our original question – what is the optimal selling price for Ewood Ltd? This we can find by substituting the optimal output level (350 units) in the selling price equation (equation (8.2)):

$$SP = £100 - £0.1(350)$$

$$SP = £65$$

The optimal selling price for Ewood Ltd is £65 per unit, the maximum price at which 350 units can be sold.

Table 8.3 Ewood Ltd: revenue, cost and output information

Output (units)	*Total revenue* (£)	*Total cost* (£)	*Profit (loss)* (£)
100	9,000	11,000	(2,000)
200	16,000	14,000	2,000
300	21,000	17,000	4,000
400	24,000	20,000	4,000
500	25,000	23,000	2,000
600	24,000	26,000	(2,000)
700	21,000	29,000	(8,000)
800	16,000	32,000	(16,000)
900	9,000	35,000	(26,000)

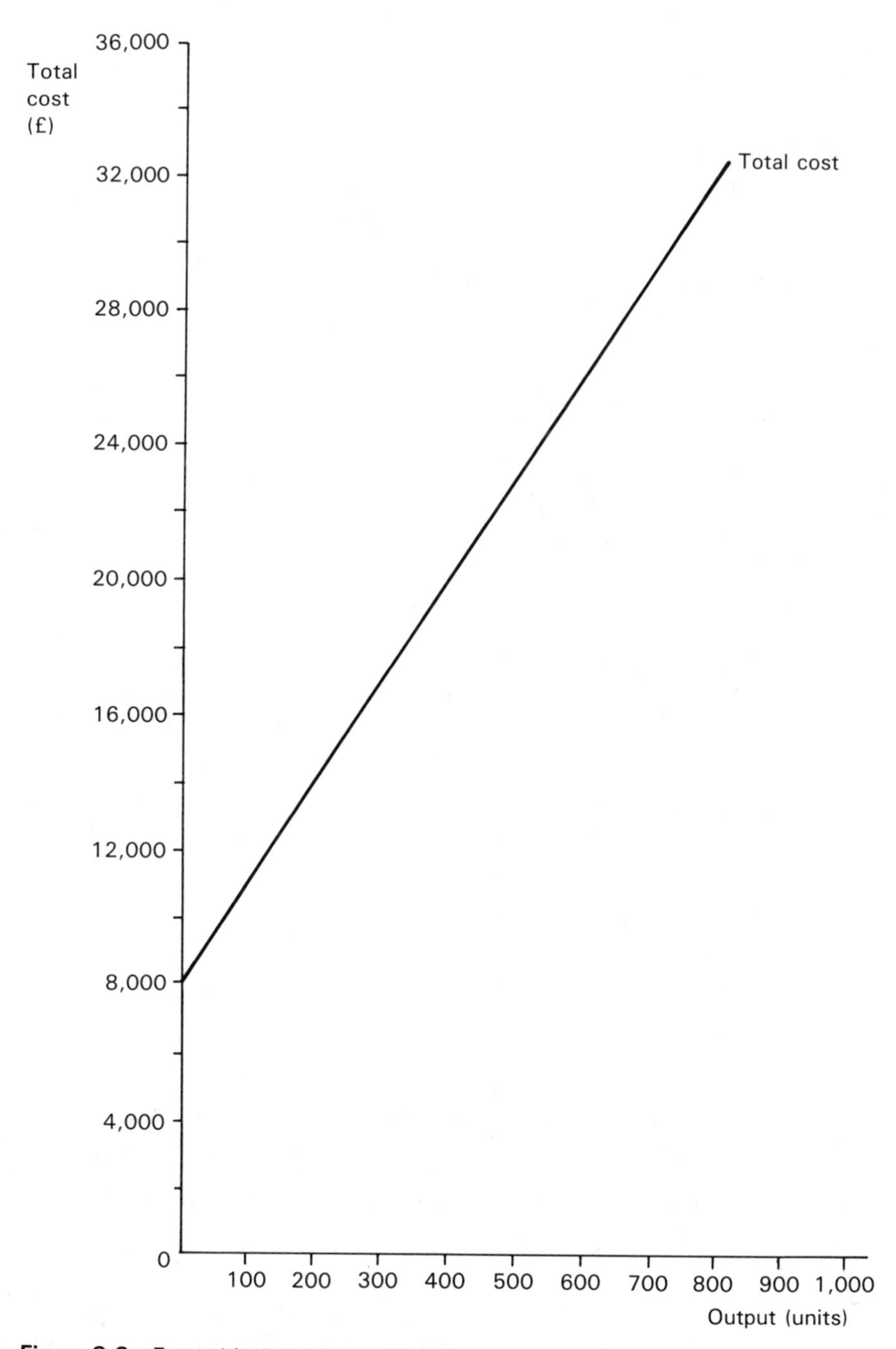

Figure 8.3 Ewood Ltd: total cost function.

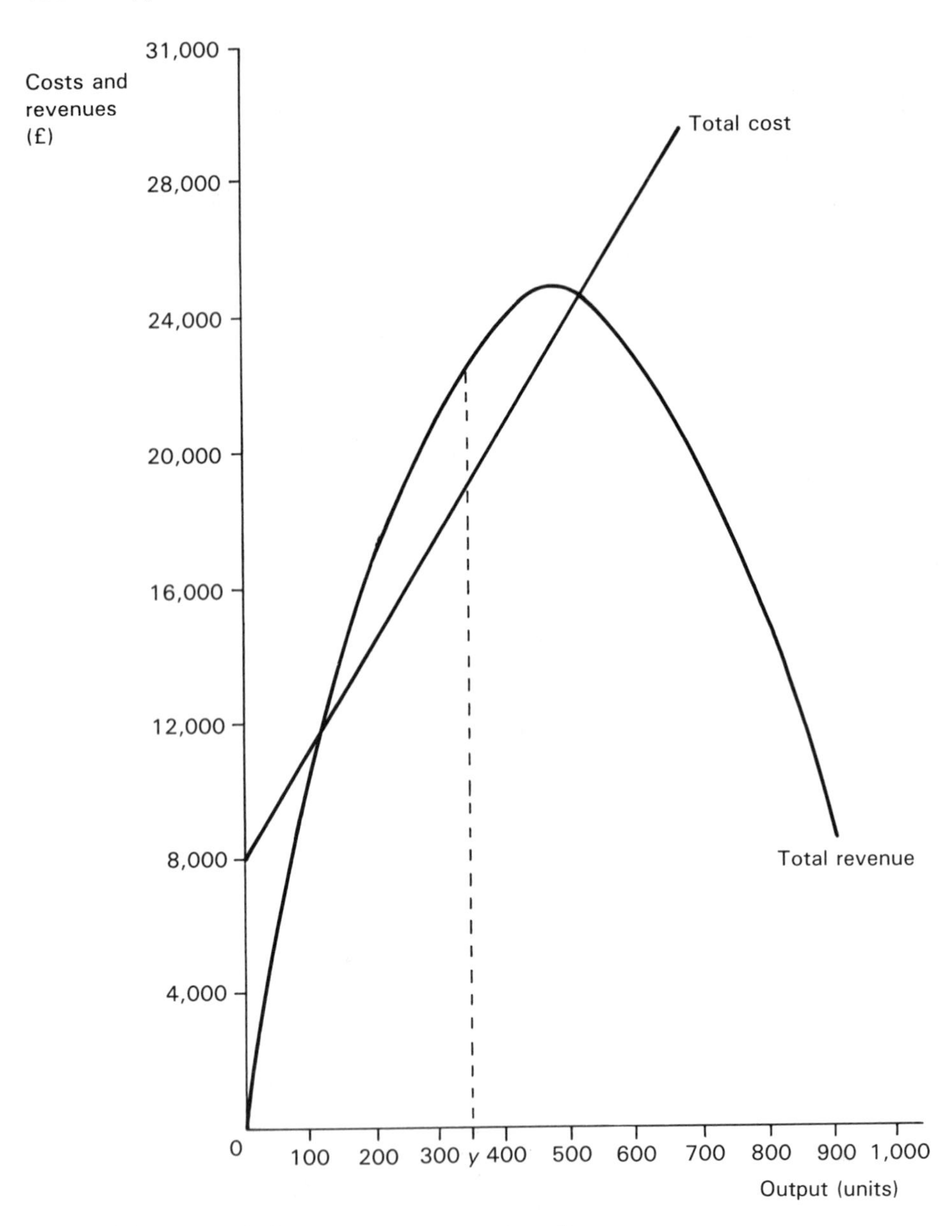

Figure 8.4 Ewood Ltd: costs, revenues and profits.

Flexible budgeting

As an alternative to the use of graphical analysis, the technique of flexible budgeting, introduced in Chapter 6, may be used to determine the optimal selling price and output level. The flexible budgets for Ewood Ltd are prepared on the basis of the estimated total cost function (£8000 + £30x), and the estimated total revenue

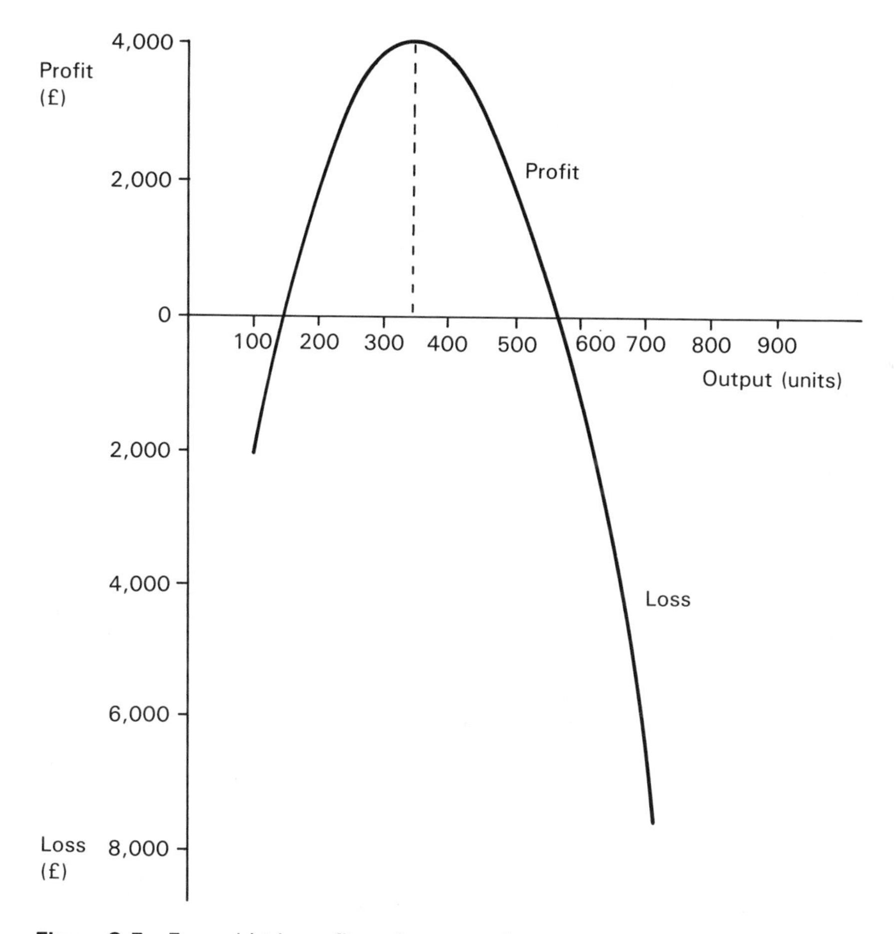

Figure 8.5 Ewood Ltd: profit–volume graph.

function (£100x – £0.1x^2) derived from the demand schedule shown in Figure 8.1. Table 8.4 shows the flexible budgets prepared for different levels of output. The budgeted figures show that the optimal output level is 350 units and the optimal selling price is £65. In order to be sure that the optimal price–output combination has been discovered, it may be necessary to prepare further budgets for output levels just above and just below 350 units to ensure that they produce lower expected profits than does the output of 350 units.

Optimal pricing and simple calculus

The optimal output level is represented by the point at which *marginal cost* (the change in total cost as a result of making one additional unit) is equated to *marginal revenue* (the change in total revenue resulting from the sale of one additional unit). In effect the decision rule is that production should be increased so long as incremental benefits exceed incremental costs. This condition is satisfied until marginal

Table 8.4 Ewood Ltd: flexible budgets

		Output level (units)												
		100 (£)		*200* (£)		*300* (£)		*350* (£)		*400* (£)		*500* (£)		*600* (£)
Variable costs	(£30 per unit)	3,000		6,000		9,000		10,500		12,000		15,000		18,000
Fixed costs		8,000		8,000		8,000		8,000		8,000		8,000		8,000
Total costs		11,000		14,000		17,000		18,500		20,000		23,000		26,000
Sales revenue	(£90 per unit)	9,000	(80)	16,000	(70)	21,000	(65)	22,750	(60)	24,000	(50)	25,000	(40)	24,000
Profit/(loss)		(2,000)		2,000		4,000		4,250		4,000		2,000		(2,000)

cost equals marginal revenue. Beyond this point increases in production will give rise to extra costs greater than the extra benefits, resulting in a fall in total profits, assuming that marginal revenue does not increase again relative to marginal cost.

Marginal cost and marginal revenue equations may be derived using differential calculus and the resulting equations may be solved to determine the optimal output level.

$$\text{Total cost} = £8000 + £30x \tag{8.1}$$

$$\therefore \text{Marginal cost} = \frac{\text{dTC}}{\text{d}x} = £30$$

$$\text{Total revenue} = £100x - £0.1x^2 \tag{8.3}$$

$$\therefore \text{Marginal revenue} = \frac{\text{dTR}}{\text{d}x} = £100 - £0.2x$$

$$\text{At the optimal output level } \frac{\text{dTC}}{\text{d}x} = \frac{\text{dTR}}{\text{d}x}$$

$$\therefore £30 = £100 - £0.2x, \ \therefore x = 350 \text{ units}$$

The optimal output level is 350 units. The highest selling price at which this output can be sold is found, as before, by substituting for x in the selling price equation (equation (8.2)):

$$\text{SP} = £100 - £0.1\ (350)$$

$$\therefore \text{SP} = £65$$

8.3 Evaluation of optimal price setting methods

If the application of calculus can derive the optimal selling price so speedily, why do we need to examine either the graphical analysis or the flexible budgeting methods?

The answer to this question lies with the uses to which the information will be put. While managers will be interested in the optimal selling price and output level derived from the estimated functions, they will be interested equally in the *sensitivity* of profit to changes in output and changes in selling price. For example, Ewood Ltd currently charges a unit price of £70 at which annual demand is 300 units. Both graphical analysis and flexible budgeting reveal that this present policy may be expected to produce a profit of £4,000, only £250 less than that obtainable from the optimal price–output combination. The managers of Ewood Ltd might decide that the costs involved in changing selling price, such as the costs of preparing new price lists for customers, are greater than the additional profit of £250 that may be expected from a change of selling price. Differential calculus does not give this information, whereas the provision of information on the sensitivity of profit to changes in costs and revenues is the essence of both the graphical and flexible budgeting approaches.

In addition, both graphs and flexible budgets can handle more easily cost and revenue functions which are not in a convenient form for algebraic manipulation (e.g. step-variable cost functions), and may present relevant data to management more clearly and comprehensively than do algebraic methods. Indeed, both sorts of representation of most aspects of business activity are very common in practice, presumably because of their clarity of exposition.

In practice a combination of the three methods may prove to be the most helpful way of calculating and explaining optimal output levels and optimal selling prices.

As we noted earlier, there will be considerable uncertainties associated with the estimates; in particular with demand estimates. This will be the case especially where a new product is being analysed. Even with existing products, the analysis may suggest radical changes to selling prices and/or output levels. In such cases it may be wise to implement these gradually, as a means of increasing management's level of confidence in the demand relationship predictions. For example, if the above analysis for Ewood Ltd had suggested halving the current price, it might be prudent to try initially a £5 or £10 reduction to see if the effects on demand are as predicted by the equation.

8.4 Cost-plus pricing

The sort of approaches described in the previous section are based on the notions of supply and demand. In many situations, however, firms may find it extremely difficult, even with the support of their marketing departments, to predict how many units can be sold at particular selling prices, for example where a new product is to be manufactured. In cases such as these, price analysis must be supported by other methods which rely primarily on the determination of appropriate costs. The choice of supporting method will depend upon the situation; whether management is pricing its normal products or whether special non-recurrent orders are being priced.

One of the most common beliefs surrounding pricing decisions seems to be that a substantial number of firms set prices solely by the use of a formula, based entirely on cost. Empirical work has been undertaken to test this supposition but little evidence has been produced to substantiate the view that prices are, in practice, set with no reference to demand conditions. A number of the researchers discovered procedures that took a cost-plus calculation *as the first step* in price determination but which later included a consideration, often informal, of market demand conditions. In the light of these conditions the price initially calculated using the cost-plus formula was amended.[19]

An example of the sort of form a cost-plus calculation might take is given in Table 8.5. The formula might be applied to a single job or to a whole product line. The direct costs of the job or product, i.e. those directly identifiable with the job or product, are estimated and to these is added an amount to recover production

[19] A sample of empirical evidence may be found in Hall, R. L. and Hitch, C. J., 'Price theory and business behaviour', *Oxford Economic Papers*, May 1939, reprinted in Wilson, T. and Andrews, P. W. S. (eds.), *Oxford Studies in the Price Mechanism*, Clarendon Press, 1951; Edwards, R. S., 'The pricing of manufactured products', *Economica*, August 1952; Pearce, I. F., 'A study in price policy', *Economica* May 1956; and Skinner, R. C., 'The determination of selling prices', *Journal of Industrial Economics*, July 1970.

Table 8.5 Example of cost-plus calculation

		£
Direct costs:		
Labour	4,780	
Materials	1,860	
Machine depreciation	2,600	9,240
Production overheads:		
80% on direct cost*		7,392
Total cost		16,632
Profit mark-up:		
20% on total cost		3,326
Price		19,958

*The overhead allocation is normally a predetermined percentage of one or, as in this example, all of the items included as direct costs. It may be based on money values or on some other unit measure, e.g. labour hours.

overheads (sometimes including depreciation), which may include both variable and fixed costs. A mark-up is also added, to cover selling and administrative overheads and profit, often designed to reflect what the decision maker regards as a 'reasonable' level of profit.

The use of such a formula is appealing. It looks objective and accurate and is relatively easy to apply. Furthermore, it enables management to delegate pricing decisions to subordinates. But the formula suffers from a number of defects and to apply it without affording them proper consideration may lead to suboptimal pricing decisions.

First, the inclusion of direct costs in the formula may be criticised. Frequently, they are interpreted as costs that are easily traceable to a specific job or product. They are not necessarily the same as variable costs and may not correspond to changes in the firm's cash flows.

If the overhead costs in the formula are fixed they will have to be paid whether or not the job being priced is undertaken. They are not avoidable costs but allocation may lead to their being treated as if they were. A firm may quote a cost-plus price for a contract that results in the contract going elsewhere even though the firm would have been justified in quoting a lower price, sufficient to cover total incremental cost, thereby winning the contract. For long-term pricing decisions, overhead costs (which are fixed in the short run) may be relevant because in the long run all costs are avoidable. It does not follow that the sort of crude allocation method normally employed in the cost-plus formula is the best way of taking account of such costs.

There are other reasons for doubting the wisdom of overhead allocation. To allocate, it is necessary to choose both a basis for the allocation and a percentage to be applied to the base. The basis would represent some measure of the resources to be used. In practice, the choice varies according to the nature of the firm's business;

the choice of a monetary base (often adopted) may not be a satisfactory measure of capacity utilisation.

The percentage applied to the base is frequently calculated by reference to historical data. Whether these are a good representation of the present and future is a matter for investigation.

The practice of overhead recovery as a percentage of direct cost may lead to the magnification of errors in estimating direct cost. As an extreme example take the case of the Ferranti contracts to manufacture Bloodhound missiles for the government. Price was fixed by a cost-plus formula. Direct labour was over-estimated by £732,000. This caused an error of just under £5 million in total cost estimation when the overhead percentage of 564% was applied.[20]

The profit mark-up seems to imply an attempt to ensure that the firm makes a 'reasonable profit'. It is unlikely that this will accord with the objective assumed in this text of maximising the cash resources of the organisation. This latter goal is most likely to be achieved if all projects showing an expected surplus of revenue over incremental costs are accepted.

The final defect to be noted here reflects a direct contrast with the economist's approach to pricing. Because the cost-plus formula pays no regard to demand conditions, the formula will produce the same answer whether the firm is operating in a highly competitive market or in a near monopolistic position. A seller cannot set both price and sales volume without reference to the demand function for the particular product. The sales volume will normally depend, at least in part, upon the price set and the relationship between selling price and demand will depend, amongst other things, upon the type of market in which the firm operates.

In many cases the difficulty encountered in estimating a firm's demand curve inhibits the use of the type of analysis for setting prices which we discussed in the previous section. The cost-plus solution to this problem is simple: ignore it. However, this approach contravenes a basic principle of good decision making: it is preferable to obtain an answer that is approximately right than one that is precisely wrong. Most decisions are beset with difficulties and to ignore them will almost inevitably lead to suboptimal courses of action being pursued.

In the context of pricing decisions, we should recognise that difficulties exist in forecasting demand conditions. Management experience and intuition may well make an important contribution to the decision. However, that is no reason to ignore the other information needed to set prices: the relevant cost of particular courses of action and the associated rules for ascertaining the minimum price that should be set if a product is to be offered for sale. This information will at least provide some assistance to the price setter in determining pricing policies.

8.5 Contribution margin pricing

Many of the deficiencies of cost-plus pricing can be overcome by the use of contribution margin pricing. This is especially the case in relation to short-term

[20] See Flower J. F., 'The case of the profitable Bloodhound', *Journal of Accounting Research*, Spring 1966.

pricing decisions. In essence, this approach tries to establish a price that is at least great enough to cover all incremental costs associated with the production and sale of a product.

Contribution margin pricing enjoys at least two advantages over full cost-plus pricing. First, no allocation of fixed costs to products is necessary and second, the contribution approach provides information about cost–volume–profit relationships, thereby making it easier to develop pricing formulae. As an example of contribution margin pricing, consider the following data for Deepdale Ltd presented in a 'conventional' form in Table 8.6 as a first step in determining selling prices.

The total cost for each of the three products, £16, £15.50, and £22 respectively, is an average total cost, which entails the allocation of fixed overheads. To this total cost has been added a profit margin determined by management. If business activity is poor, it may well prove to be in Deepdale Ltd's interest to sell its three products at prices lower than those determined by average costs. How much lower can be shown by applying the contribution margin approach. By rearranging the data we can first identify the incremental costs, in this case presumed to be the total direct and variable costs, associated with each of the three products, as shown in the table at the top of the next page.

It can be readily seen that if the company cannot sell its three products at their cost-plus prices, it will still make a *contribution* towards fixed costs and profit if it sells product A at any price in excess of £8, product B at any price in excess of £8.50, and product C at any price in excess of £10.75. These three amounts, £8, £8.50 and £10.75 respectively, might be referred to as *minimum* acceptable prices for the products as they just cover all the incremental costs. They would not, of course, represent the actual prices charged in normal conditions for the firm's regular

Table 8.6 Deepdale Ltd: product selling price data (1)

	Product A (£)	*Product B* (£)	*Product C* (£)
Direct material	3.00	4.00	5.00
Direct labour	2.50	2.00	3.50
Total direct cost	5.50	6.00	8.50
Production overheads:			
Variable	1.50	2.00	1.50
Fixed	5.00	4.00	7.00
Total cost of production	12.00	12.00	17.00
Selling costs:			
Variable	1.00	0.50	0.75
Fixed	1.20	1.20	1.70
Fixed administrative cost	1.80	1.80	2.55
Total cost	16.00	15.50	22.00
Profit margin (%)	2.40 (15)	1.55 (10)	4.40 (20)
Cost-plus selling price	18.40	17.05	26.40

	Product A (£)	*Product B* (£)	*Product C* (£)
Direct material	3.00	4.00	5.00
Direct labour	2.50	2.00	3.50
Variable production overheads	1.50	2.00	1.50
Variable selling costs	1.00	0.50	0.75
Incremental costs	8.00	8.50	10.75

products. Such a pricing policy would quickly lead to bankruptcy, as there would be no contribution to fixed costs or profit. The actual prices to be charged for the products will be higher than the minimum prices, and must take into account other factors such as the degree of competition and the level of demand, insofar as these can be estimated.

Let us pursue this argument a little further. Suppose, for example, Deepdale Ltd receives a one-off special order from a customer who wishes by buy 500 units of product A at a price of £10 per unit. The cost-plus price of A is £18.40 per unit. Should the special order be accepted? If management applies the cost-plus criterion to this offer, it will reject the offer, as it will 'lose' £8.40 per unit on the order (i.e. £18.40 less £10). If however, management accepts the offer, what will happen? Five hundred units will be sold at a price of £10 per unit and the incremental costs of producing and selling each unit will be £8; a contribution of £2 per unit, or £1,000 in total, will be generated towards the fixed costs and profits of Deepdale Ltd. It seems that Deepdale Ltd should accept the special order. However, there are caveats which should be observed. Specifically management might ask the following questions:

1. Is this special order likely to use limited plant capacity which could be better employed manufacturing goods saleable at normal prices? If so, then the order is using the firm's scarce resources and, as we shall see in Chapters 9 and 10, further analysis of the problem is necessary.

2. Can the special sale be made without reducing sales at normal selling prices? For example, other customers for product A may also expect to buy it for £10 per unit if they become aware of sales to one customer at this price.

3. What will be the likely advantages and disadvantages of the sale on future relationships? The new customer may be so pleased with the purchase that other of the firm's products are purchased at prices well in excess of marginal cost. On the other hand, the new customer may expect future purchases of the firm's products to be at special 'reduced' prices.

If the answers to the above questions suggest that the overall effect is likely to be disadvantageous then perhaps Deepdale Ltd should not proceed with the order. It should still be stressed, however, that the contribution margin approach will always be based on the underlying notion of a minimum price. Whether or not that price

Table 8.7 Deepdale Ltd: product selling price data (2)

	Product A (£)	*Product B* (£)	*Product C* (£)
Variable costs:			
Direct material	3.00	4.00	5.00
Direct labour	2.50	2.00	3.50
Production overheads	1.50	2.00	1.50
Selling costs	1.00	0.50	0.75
P_1 total variable cost	8.00	8.50	10.75
Fixed costs:			
Production overheads	5.00	4.00	7.00
Selling costs	1.20	1.20	1.70
Administration	1.80	1.80	2.55
P_2 total cost	16.00	15.50	22.00
Profit margin (%)	2.40 (15)	1.55 (10)	4.40 (20)
P_3 cost-plus selling price	18.40	17.05	26.40

is ever charged will depend upon the other qualitative factors to be considered by management, which will vary from one pricing decision to another.

To conclude our discussion of cost-based pricing, let us return again to the data for Deepdale Ltd, presented in rearranged cost–volume–profit form in Table 8.7. Table 8.7 shows three possible price structures (denoted by P_1, P_2 and P_3 respectively) for the three products A, B and C. We might delineate these possible prices as follows:

P_1 is the *minimum short-run price*, represented by the variable (incremental) costs of production and sale. Fixed costs are not covered by price P_1, as they will be incurred anyway, and thus are not relevant to short-run decisions. P_2 is a *minimum long-run price*, based in this instance on a predetermined level of fixed costs and an (arbitrary) allocation method. It should be stressed that other allocation methods will yield other minimum long-run prices, all of which will be arbitrary to some extent. In the long run both variable and fixed costs must be recovered from selling prices if the firm is to generate sufficient cash flows to survive. We might say that in the long run all costs, however classified, are incremental costs. P_3 is the *normal desired long-run price* for each product. It includes an expected profit margin reflecting management's quantified perception of the various factors (e.g. possible total demand, elasticity of demand, quality of the product) unique to each product. The possible range of prices for each product is:

	Product A (£)	*Product B* (£)	*Product C* (£)
P_1 = minimum short-run price	8.00	8.50	10.75
P_2 = minimum long-run price	16.00	15.50	22.00
P_3 = normal long-run price	18.40	17.05	26.40

The range gives management some idea of its flexibility in setting prices. For instance, if Deepdale Ltd is selling B in a monopolistic market, then it may be able to obtain a price near to £17.05, the desired long-term price; if, for example, there is a great deal of competition for C, then Deepdale Ltd. may have to be satisfied with a price no greater than £22, and possibly less.

In short, we may say that pragmatic pricing should begin with a knowledge of these three price structures. As we discussed earlier in this chapter, the eventual pricing decision is likely to be the result also of a consideration of broader marketing strategies which involve the use of information outside the normal realm of the accountant. Nevertheless, the accountant's contribution in providing timely and relevant cost information and in analysing the implications of alternative selling price–output combinations is an essential ingredient of the whole process.

Discussion topics

1. 'Supply and demand models of pricing are too difficult to put into practice.' Discuss.
2. Discuss the relationship between optimal output levels and optimal selling prices.
3. 'Pricing should be related to competitive market situations, rather than to internal cost structures.' Discuss.
4. Discuss some of the possible dangers facing an organisation associated with contribution margin pricing.
5. 'Past costs are irrelevant to rational pricing policies.' Discuss.
6. Discuss any possible relationships between 'short-run' and 'long-run' pricing policies.

Exercises

8.1 Mr Sisley runs a small printing business. Each job is undertaken according to special instructions from the customer. Mr Sisley uses a system recommended by his trade association to fix the price he charges to his customers. He estimates what he paid for the paper used (he keeps large stocks of paper) and adds a standard percentage for 'consumables' (ink etc.). He estimates the number of labour hours required for the job and values them at the appropriate wage rate; he adds a standard percentage to cover fixed overhead costs. The sum of all these items gives a 'total cost' for the job and he adds 10% to total costs for his profit. The standard percentages are set equal to the actual percentage relationships between corresponding total costs during the previous financial year.

Actual results for last year ran as follows:

		£
Sales		26,000
Cost of paper used	2,400	
Consumables	300	
Wages	12,000	
Fixed costs	9,600	24,300
Net profit		2,300

Last year Mr Sisley's employees were fully occupied. During the current year just ending, however, business has fallen by 15% – measured in labour hours required. No one has been laid off. Mr Sisley has simply paid for idle time. Total wage costs for the current year and total fixed costs are the same as last year; cost of paper used is £2,200 and cost of consumables £225. No special prices have been charged on any jobs during the year. Mr Sisley is surprised to find, however, that he has made a loss on his business even though each job has shown a satisfactory profit.

(a) Prepare a calculation showing the amount of the loss for the current year.

(b) Explain how the loss has arisen and comment critically on Mr Sisley's pricing system.

8.2 Schmitt plc, which is a good customer of Schein Ltd, has asked Schein to produce 400 units of a special variation of one of the standard products that it buys from Schein. The estimated full cost of producing each unit of the standard product is £30, of which £20 is variable cost and £10 is allocated fixed cost. The selling price is £36 per unit. Although Schein is not geared to make the modifications required it decides for 'customer relationship' reasons to agree to go ahead and supply the order. It will be possible to modify up to 100 of the special units each 40 hour week, without disrupting regular production, but special machinery will be required for the purpose. There are three alternative ways of obtaining this machinery. Details are as follows:

1. *Adapting existing machinery*
   The existing machinery which could be adapted is not being used at present although it is envisaged that in approximately three months it will be required in its present form for a contract currently being negotiated. Costs of adapting this machinery would be £1,500, and after the order has been completed it would cost £1,800 to remove the adaptations and replace worn parts, etc., in order to return the machine to its current value. The machinery which could be adapted originally cost £10,000 five years ago and is being depreciated at £1,000 p.a. A special insurance policy would have to be held while it was operated in its adapted form, the fixed annual premium associated with this being 2% of the value of the machine when adapted. The current value of the machine is £3,000. Variable operating costs associated with using the adapted machinery would be: labour £3 per hour and maintenance £1.50 per hour.

2. *Hiring specialist machinery*
   The charge for hiring suitable machinery, which includes maintenance and insurance, but no labour costs, is £5 per production hour with a minimum hire charge of £300 per week.

3. *Purchasing specialist machinery*
   To buy a new machine would cost £5,000. Operating, maintenance and insurance costs would be on the same basis as for the adapted one. The manufacturers of the machinery estimate that it loses value at the rate of £2.00 for every unit produced and on this basis they are prepared to repurchase any machinery sold by them, after deducting a further 10% of the residual value to cover transaction expenses.

(a) Prepare a report to the managers of Schein Ltd, advising them which of the alternative courses of action would be most beneficial, based upon the given information. Indicate ways in which your recommendation might be further improved. In your report suggest a price to be charged to Schmitt plc for the modified product, mentioning the factors which should be considered before a final decision is taken.

(b) Suppose that Schmitt plc was willing to place a continuing order for the modified product. In this new situation broadly explain the alterations needed to produce a long-run cost analysis of the alternatives.

8.3 Ravel Ltd manufactures two products, the renoir and the whistler. Each product is produced in a separate department. The company's budget for next year runs as follows:

	Renoir		*Whistler*
Selling price per unit (£)	4.00		5.00
Variable cost per unit (£)	2.50		3.00
Contribution per unit (£)	1.50		2.00
Planned production (and sales) – (units)	38,000		7,000
Total contribution (unit contribution × planned sales) (£)	57,000		14,000
Less Fixed departmental overhead costs (£)	37,000		25,000
Departmental contribution to general fixed costs (£)	20,000		(11,000)
Total contribution (£): Renoir		20,000	
Whistler		(11,000)	
		9,000	
General fixed costs (£)		8,000	
Budgeted profit (£)		1,000	

Fixed departmental overhead costs for either product could be avoided if the particular product was not produced. At all positive production levels they are fixed in total for each product.

The company is concerned that the whistler is apparently being produced at a loss and asks your advice. You learn that the company has recently commissioned a market research survey for both its products. The following figures are included in the survey report:

	Renoir				*Whistler*			
Selling price (£)	2	3	4	5	2.5	5	7.5	10
Maximum quantity likely to be demanded at price shown (000s units)	80	60	40	20	10	8	6	4

(a) Calculate the production levels for the renoir and the whistler, likely to maximise the company's profit in the coming year.

(b) Prepare a statement showing the improvement in expected profit if your suggested production levels are implemented. Include a note of any reservations you have about your figures.

8.4 Stamitz Ltd, makes two products, A and B. Last year the firm made a loss and the directors ask you as budget officer to provide them with a plan for the next year. You are given the standard costs per unit for products A and B:

	Product A (£)	*Product B* (£)
Direct cost:		
Material	0.200	0.125
Labour	0.150	0.125
Variable overhead	0.250	0.146
Total variable cost	0.600	0.396
Fixed overhead per unit (47% of total variable cost)	0.280	0.185
Total cost per unit	0.880	0.581

In previous periods, the actual direct cost for both A and B has been close to the standard except that there has been a persistent 10% unfavourable variance on material due to price increases.

Market research studies of the demand for the two products gives the following results:

	Product A				*Product B*			
Price in pence	50	37.5	25	12.5	60	45	30	25
Sales volume (000)	10	20	30	40	24	34	44	50

Fixed overhead recovery rates are calculated on the assumption that the firm will annually produce 10,000 units of A and 24,000 units of B. Supervisory labour is included in fixed overheads. Past data for this cost category are given below. The remaining fixed overheads, which consist of such items as rent and rates, are constant for all levels of production.

Production volume total for both products (units)	20,000	30,000	40,000	50,000	60,000
Supervisory labour (£)	0	500	1,000	1,500	2,000

(a) Advise Stamitz Ltd on its best production plan for the year, stating your reasons clearly.

(b) Write a special note on your treatments of fixed overheads.

(c) What long-term policy would you advise the directors to follow?

8.5 Sickert Ltd prints booklets. The costs of a proposed new booklet are estimated at:

Preparation: Composition, preparing blocks and letterpress, etc.: £390 (for any likely quantity).

Machining: £22.50 for first 1,000. Due to less spoilage, succeeding 1,000s cost £21 each.

Binding materials: £93 for each 1,000

(a) Prepare a table showing:

(i) the total cost for 1,000, for 2,000 and for 3,000 booklets;
(ii) the marginal (incremental) cost of each successive 1,000 booklets;
(iii) the average cost per booklet if output is 1,000, 2,000 and 3,000.

(b) Suppose that Stravinsky will buy and retail the booklets at 25p each, if supplied with them at a buying price which allows $33\frac{1}{3}\%$ profit on cost. How many booklets must Sickert print to cover costs?

(c) Suppose that large numbers are in fact printed. Most are sold, but a batch of 1,000 remains on hand after demand seems satisfied. A dealer offers to take it for £60. Explain what sort of arguments would affect the firm in deciding whether to accept.

8.6 The Smith Company manufactures specialist batteries for use in special equipment which is manufactured by another division of the same company. The batteries and equipment are marketed as a package – package bright – for which the relevant selling price details are as follows:

Package bright

Selling price: Equipment	£50 per unit	
Selling price: Batteries	£ 4 per set	(a set of 8 batteries is required for each unit of equipment)
Total package price	£54	

Selling price of replacement batteries is 50p per battery
Estimated life of a set of batteries is 24 hours.

A competitor has just launched an extensive advertising campaign for a new package – package light – which it has developed. Although this package is more expensive to purchase and the basic equipment does not have a longer life – the normal life for equipment like this is between 500 and 750 hours – it requires cheaper longer-life batteries and it is this latter point, cheapness and longer life, which forms the basis of the advertising campaign.

The Smith Company has called a sales meeting to discuss this development in general, and in particular to isolate the cost differences to the customer between bright and light. The relevant information for package light is as follows:

Package light

Selling price: Equipment	£125.00 per unit	
Selling price: Batteries	£ 2.40 per set	(a set of 12 batteries is required for each unit of equipment)
Total package price	£127.40	

Selling price of replacement batteries is 20p per battery
Estimated life of a set of batteries is 60 hours.

As management accountant you are required to calculate and comment briefly on:

(a) The equipment life in hours at which a customer should be indifferent to either package.

(b) The price and/or performance changes required to make bright competitive with light:
  (i) the maximum price to be charged for the equipment in package bright if battery price and performance remain the same;
  (ii) the maximum price to be charged for the batteries used in package bright if the equipment cost and battery performance remain the same;
  (iii) the life of batteries which should be aimed for in package bright, assuming no price adjustments are made.

(c) The effect on your calculations of a suggestion by the sales director that a special offer of 'a free set of batteries with every set of package bright purchased' should be made.

N.B. Where required for calculation purposes an estimated life of 700 hours for both equipment packages should be used.

8.7 Schumann Ltd manufactures a single product. Plans are being considered for the financial year 19X1. Estimates of cost and demand relationships are as follows:

1. A small factory is rented for £2,000 p.a. There is room for three machines and 20 'direct' employees at most. No additional space can be obtained for 19X1.
2. At most, ten direct employees with the requisite skills can be employed during 19X1. The normal working year is 2,000 hours and the wage paid is £3 per hour. No overtime is worked and the firm does not employ part-time labour.
3. Machines can be hired at a cost of £5,000 p.a. each. Machines operate unattended whilst the factory is open but not at other times, i.e. machines have a maximum operating time of 2,000 hours p.a.
4. Sales are made by an agent who is paid on a commission basis. Rates are £3 per unit for the first 2,000 units sold. £2 per unit for the second 2,000 units and £1 per unit for all other units.
5. One product unit requires 1 machine hour and 4 direct labour hours. Other variable costs are: materials £8 per unit and administrative costs £1 per unit.
6. General administration and factory supervision costs £12,000 p.a.
7. Sales price–volume relationships are estimated as follows:

Price (£)	*Sales* (units)
41	3,000
36	4,000
30	5,000

(a) Estimate the optimal output level for 19X1, assuming that one of 3,000, 4,000 and 5,000 units will be chosen.

(b) Prepare a statement of estimated income and expenditure if this level is chosen.

8.8 Turner Ltd is considering whether to manufacture a new product – rameau – for one year. Components for the product will be manufactured in a new factory to be specially leased for the purpose at £10,000 a year. Rameaus will be assembled in the existing factory, utilising the same production lines as the firm's other products. The estimated costs per rameau are:

	Component manufacture (£)	*Assembly* (£)
Material	0.20	–
Labour	0.20	0.10
Factory supplies	–	0.10
Variable overheads	0.30	0.30
Total direct cost	0.70	0.50
Fixed overheads (250% of direct labour)	0.50	0.25
Administrative overheads (50% of total direct cost)	0.35	0.25
Total cost	1.55	1.00
Add Total assembly cost	1.00	
Total cost per rameau	2.55	

When operating at maximum capacity, the components factory can supply sufficient parts for 24,000 rameaus p.a. Surplus capacity after meeting the assembly division's requirements will be used to produce sets of rameau components for a supermarket which will market them under a different name. The cost of such components will be identical to those produced for the assembly division's use. The supermarket is willing to pay £1 per set of components.

A market research study has suggested that only two prices for the rameau should be considered, £3.60 and £3.10 per unit. Sales at these prices are estimated to be 15,000 and 22,000 units respectively. Of the fixed overheads charged to rameaus, 20% relate to the historical cost depreciation of machinery. The machines in the assembly plant do not depreciate in use. The estimated total overhead costs of the component factory are: rent £10,000, other fixed overheads £1,000, administrative costs £5,000.

The machines needed to manufacture the components are available within the firm. They have a value of £10,000 in the firm's books and could be sold for £4,000. If retained on their existing work, they will need to be replaced (at a cost of £15,000) in one year's time. If transferred to rameau production, they will have to be scrapped (proceeds nil) at the end of the year.

Advise management as to whether they should manufacture rameaus and, if so, at what volume and price. Add a brief note on your treatment of fixed overheads.

8.9 Pisarro Ltd, manufactures a single product. The data given below indicate the likely cost–volume relationships for the coming four week period.

1. Materials – use $\frac{1}{4}$ ton per product unit. One hundred tons are already in stock at a cost of £10 per ton. Current market price is £12 per ton.

2. Labour – workforce works 40 hours per week. Current labour force of ten persons would not be reduced. Up to five more skilled workers could be employed; each would work up to 10 hours per week overtime. Basic wage £1 per hour, overtime wage £1.5 per hour. One product unit manufactured in 2 person-hours.

3. Rent of premises – £100 per week (room for up to fifteen machines).

4. Machinery – six hand-operated machines are leased on a long-term contract at £200 per machine, per week. Extra machines could be leased at £240 per week. Each product unit requires one hour of machine time.

5. Fuel – fixed charge of £100 per four weeks plus £0.2 per kWh for 400 kWh; £0.15 per kWh for next 500 kWh, and £0.1 per kWh thereafter. Each machine uses 1 kW per hour.
6. Supervisors – one can control the activities of five workers at most – fixed salary of £60 per week, no overtime paid.
7. Administration – fixed cost £500 per four weeks.
8. Selling expenses – fixed cost, £100 per four weeks plus sales force's commission: nothing on first 100 units per week, £1 per unit for second hundred, £0.5 on third hundred and £0.2 thereafter.

The managing director has prepared the following estimate of weekly sales volume attainable at various different price levels:

Price (£)	*Volume*
30	100
25	160
22	230
20	300
19	340
18	370

(a) Sketch a graph showing the relationship of each type of cost with volume of output.

(b) Draw a graph showing total costs and revenues and estimate the output level which would maximise profits (for a typical four week period).

(c) Prepare a calculation showing what profit would be made over a four week period if output equalled:
(i) maximum capacity;
(ii) 80% of capacity;
(iii) 60% of capacity;
(iv) the amount given in your answer to (b).

8.10 Princess plc produces a single product, the connaught. The connaught is perishable and no stocks are kept. During the previous month Princess's results were as follows:

	£000	£000
Sales (100,000 units)		400
Less Cost of goods sold:		
Basic wages	10	
Bonus	45	
	55	
Materials	200	255
Gross profit		145
Less Sales commission	50	
General administration	15	65
Profit		80

The company pays its labour force a basic wage per month irrespective of production level and a bonus (currently at the rate of 45p per unit produced). The sales commission is paid to a marketing company which sells the connaught on behalf of Princess. General administration is the only fixed overhead incurred by the company. For some time past there have been serious problems associated with materials usage. Recently a machine has become available which allows a higher quality material to be used and this will reduce waste. The effect is expected to be a halving of materials costs. The machine cannot be bought but can only be leased from the manufacturer on a monthly basis. The monthly rental is £55,000.

Princess has just completed a market research survey to clarify the conditions of demand for the connaught. The survey found that if price per unit were set at £5.00 no sales would be made. Alternatively, if the connaught were distributed free to customers the maximum distribution would be 500,000 units. If price were increased by 1p, sales would fall by 1,000 units at all prices within the stated range.

If the machine were leased it is estimated that basic wages would remain the same, but the bonus rate would increase to 50p per unit. However, there would be no change in general adminstration costs or in the sales commission arrangements.

The objective of the company is to maximise monthly profits, but hitherto the company has not used a formal pricing policy designed to ensure the achievement of that objective but has relied upon the judgement of the sales manager.

(**a**) Prepare calculations to determine whether or not Princess should lease the machine.

(**b**) Determine the range of prices over which Princess might expect to make profits if it decides to lease the machine.

(**c**) Comment upon the significance of your calculations in (a) and (b).

8.11 During the financial year beginning 1 August 19X4, Commercial Printers Ltd has been operating to full capacity. All customers have been charged according to the company's standard pricing formula. The charge for a typical day's printing work can be calculated as follows:

	£
Paper, 18,000 sheets at 1p per sheet	180
Ink and other consumables, at 0.1111p per sheet	20
Wages	160
Overheads (all fixed) (150% of wages)	240
Total estimated cost	600
Add 20% for profit	120
Charge to customer	720

For the second half of the year, the company expects demand to slow down, and it is believed that if prices are maintained at present levels, the company may lose a substantial amount of business. The following estimates have been prepared of the number of days' work (out of a maximum 125 days available) that would be obtained at different price levels.

Price (£)	720	570	420
Days' work obtained	60	90	120

The company is uncertain as to whether the fall-off in demand will be permanent. If it is not permanent, the directors wish to continue to pay all employees full-time even though there may be insufficient work for them. Otherwise they will lay off employees as necessary to respond to the fall in demand.

(**a**) Calculate the price at which profits will be maximised or losses minimised, the number of days' work obtained at that price, and the profit or loss for the six months ending 31 July 19X5:

(i) on the assumption that the existing work force will remain employed throughout the period; and

(ii) on the assumption that the existing work force will be laid off as necessary, without cost, to reflect the amount of work undertaken.

(**b**) Write a memorandum for the directors, explaining why it might be desirable to charge a price below the 'total estimated cost' for a typical day's work.

(**c**) Comment briefly on the reasons why cost-plus pricing may be used despite its theoretical shortcomings.

Further reading

Arnold, J., 'An approach to pricing and output decisions when prices are changing', *Journal of Business Finance and Accounting*, Winter 1977.

Baxter, W. T. and Oxenfeldt, A. R., 'Costing and pricing: the cost accountant versus the economist', *Business Horizons*, Winter 1961, reprinted in Solomons, D. (ed.), *Studies in Cost Analysis*, 2nd edn, Sweet & Maxwell, 1968.

Dorward, N., 'Overhead allocations and "optimal" pricing rules of thumb in oligopolistic markets', *Accounting and Business Research*, Autumn 1986.

Edwards, R. S., 'The pricing of manufactured products', *Economica*, August 1952.

Flower, J. F., 'The case of the profitable Bloodhound', *Journal of Accounting Research*, Spring 1966.

Hilton, R. W., Swieringa, R. J. and Turner, M. J., 'Product pricing, accounting costs and use of product-costing systems', *The Accounting Review*, April 1988.

Lere, J. C., 'Product pricing based on accounting costs', *The Accounting Review*, April 1986.

Oxenfeldt, A. R., 'A decision making structure for pricing decisions', *Journal of Marketing*, January 1973.

Pearce, I. F., 'A study in price policy', *Economica*, May 1956.

Simmonds, K., 'Strategic management accounting for pricing: a case example', *Accounting and Business Research*, Summer 1982.

Sizer, J., 'Pricing policy in inflation: a management accountant's perspective', *Accounting and Business Research*, Spring 1976.

Sizer, J., 'The accountant's contribution to selling price decisions', in Arnold, J., Carsberg, B. and Scapens, R. (eds.), *Topics in Management Accounting*, Philip Allan, 1980.

Skinner, R. C., 'The determination of selling prices', *Journal of Industrial Economics*, July 1970.

Tishlias, D. P. and Chalos, P., 'Product pricing behaviour under different costing systems', *Accounting and Business Research*, Summer 1988.

Chapter 9

Short-term operating decisions and scarce resources: linear programming

In earlier chapters we have stressed the importance of the differential future cash flow concept in determining whether costs and/or benefits are relevant for management decisions. This is true whatever the time period of the decision, i.e. whether the decision is long-term involving the commitment of resources to extend productive capacity, or is an operating decision involving the best use of existing capacity.

In this and the three succeeding chapters we shall look in more detail at how the notion of relevant costs might be applied to some specific types of decisions facing the firm. This chapter and the next will examine operating decisions; Chapters 11 and 12 will examine long-term investment decisions.

9.1 The nature of operating decisions

We might classify operating decisions as having two distinguishing characteristics. They usually involve time periods of less than one year (hence the need to take account of the time value of money is reduced) and are concerned with the use of existing physical resources. Examples of operating decisions might be as follows:

1. Which products should be produced? How many units of each product should be produced?
2. Should existing products be abandoned?
3. Should component parts for final products be manufactured internally or bought from outside suppliers?
4. How should scarce capacity be best used?

The analysis of these sorts of decisions proceeds in two stages. First, the accounting information, in the form of relevant future cash flows, is prepared. This is the more straightforward aspect of the analysis. Second, qualitative factors are identified as being important and in some cases may overrule a decision based purely on monetary figures. Our concern here is with the development of the accounting information relevant to operating decisions but, where appropriate, we will try to identify qualitative factors which are of obvious significance.

We will examine operating decisions from two perspectives. First, we will look at some particular types of decisions which do not involve the use of scarce resources (i.e. in this situation management can produce all it wishes of any product); second, we will see how the existence of scarce resources alters the analysis.

9.2 Short-term decisions with no scarce resources

Dropping a product or segment

The usefulness of differential cash flows can be seen clearly in situations where management is faced with the choice of dropping (or adding to) its product range. This choice will be quite a common one for managers of multi-product firms.

Let us begin the analysis by presuming that Bloomfield Ltd makes three products, A, B and C, income statements for which are presented in Table 9.1. On the basis of the given figures for Bloomfield Ltd in Table 9.1, management might think that it would be in the interests of the company to drop product C. After all, the income statement for the company shows that C makes a loss, whereas both A and B make a profit. But would the dropping of C be a wise decision? Suppose that for whatever reason Bloomfield Ltd will not produce any additional units of A and B, or alternatively, that sales of A and B would be unaffected by dropping C. How will the analysis now look? A comparison of the costs and revenues for Bloomfield Ltd under both alternatives (i.e. keeping or dropping C) may reveal that a different conclusion is warranted. The figures are shown in Table 9.2. The most important column is the final one, which shows the differential cash flows to the firm. If C is

Table 9.1 Bloomfield Ltd: income statement for the year to 31st December 19X1

	Product A	*Product B*	*Product C*	*Total*
Sales (units)	2,000	4,000	6,000	12,000
	(£)	(£)	(£)	(£)
Sales	20,000	32,000	42,000	94,000
Less Variable costs	8,000	12,000	30,000	50,000
Contribution margin	12,000	20,000	12,000	44,000
Less Separable fixed costs*	2,000	3,000	5,000	10,000
Less Non-separable fixed costs allocated on the basis of sales units	2,500	5,000	7,500	15,000
Profit/(loss)	7,500	12,000	(500)	19,000

* The separable fixed costs of producing each product are avoidable if manufacture of the product is discontinued.

Table 9.2 Comparison of cash flows under alternative decisions

	Keep A, B and C (£)	*Keep A and B and drop C* (£)	*Differential cash flows* (£)
Sales revenue	94,000	52,000	42,000
Less Variable costs	50,000	20,000	30,000
Contribution margin	44,000	32,000	12,000
Less Separable fixed costs	10,000	5,000	5,000
Less Non-separable fixed costs	15,000	15,000	0
Net profit	19,000	12,000	7,000

dropped from the range, the total cash inflow, here presumed to be the same as total net profit, is *reduced* by £7,000. This is made up as follows:

	£
Cash outflows avoided by dropping product C:	
Variable costs avoided	30,000
Separable fixed costs avoided	5,000
	35,000
Less Cash inflows lost	42,000
Differential loss in revenue	(7,000)

The decision to drop C would, at this stage, be unwise. This could have been seen clearly had the income statement for Bloomfield Ltd been recast so as to deal differently with the non-separable fixed costs. The bottom line of the income statement showing the profit or loss for the individual products is arrived at after allocating fixed costs which, by their very nature, can be allocated only on an arbitrary basis. A different format for the income statement of Bloomfield Ltd which avoids the problems of allocation and shows separately the contribution to general fixed costs for each product, is presented in Table 9.3.

But is this the end of the story? Should management simply accept the revised conclusion that production of C is worthwhile because of its contribution of £7,000 to total fixed costs and profit? Presumably C utilises factory space. Perhaps this space could, even temporarily, be rented out. The question then is how much rent would Bloomfield Ltd need to receive in order to make it profitable to drop C? The answer is obviously at least £7,000 p.a., as this is the minimum amount which would compensate for the loss of C's contribution. The same argument in terms of rental forgone might be applied equally to A or B, where the minimum amounts acceptable would be £10,000 and £17,000 respectively. If in fact renting out the space used by C for £7,000 p.a. is the only alternative given up by production, we would term the amount of £7,000 the *opportunity cost* of keeping C for the next year. Further, if a rent in excess of £7,000 was offered to Bloomfield Ltd then, based purely on the quantifiable factors of the decision, the offer should be accepted. However,

Table 9.3 Bloomfield Ltd: income statement for the year to 31 December 19X1

	Product A (£)	*Product B* (£)	*Product C* (£)	*Total* (£)
Sales	20,000	32,000	42,000	94,000
Less Variable costs	8,000	12,000	30,000	50,000
Contribution margin	12,000	20,000	12,000	44,000
Separable fixed costs	2,000	3,000	5,000	10,000
Product contribution	10,000	17,000	7,000	34,000
Non-separable fixed costs				15,000
		Net profit		19,000

consideration must be given to other aspects involved in the decision (e.g. how is C's labour force to be deployed?; what will happen to the plant and equipment used to produce C?).

Joint product decisions

A single manufacturing process often entails the simultaneous production of two or more separate, identifiable outputs. These outputs are referred to as *joint products* if they have significant sales value and *by-products* if they have small sales value in relation to the main products. The process which generates the products is termed a *joint process*. The essential characteristic of a joint process is that none of the products resulting from the process can be produced without also producing all the other products in the joint group, although it may be possible to vary the proportions. For example, refining crude oil can produce many different grades of petrol and fuel oil; the processing of animals can produce many different cuts of meat, as well as fats and hides – a pork chop cannot be produced without producing the rest of the pig!

A critical decision which faces manufacturers of joint products, and which concerns us here, is whether to sell the products when they emerge from the joint process at what is termed the *split-off* point, or whether to process them further and incur additional, but separable, processing costs. The diagrammatic representation in Figure 9.1 may clarify the decision. Figure 9.1 shows a possible situation in which three separate joint products A, B and C and one by-product D can be produced from a single joint process. If we assume that there is a ready market for the products at the point of split-off, the question then arises as to whether additional processing should be incurred to produce A_2, B_2 and C_2 or whether the products should be sold in their existing state as A_1, B_1 and C_1. The analysis should be conducted in terms of differential cash flows. The decision to process further a joint product depends neither upon the amount of joint costs (fixed or variable) incurred in the initial joint process, as having already been incurred they are irrelevant to future actions, nor on the way these may be assigned to individual products for stock valuation purposes. The decision to process further depends simply upon whether the additional revenue from sale is justified by the additional costs involved.

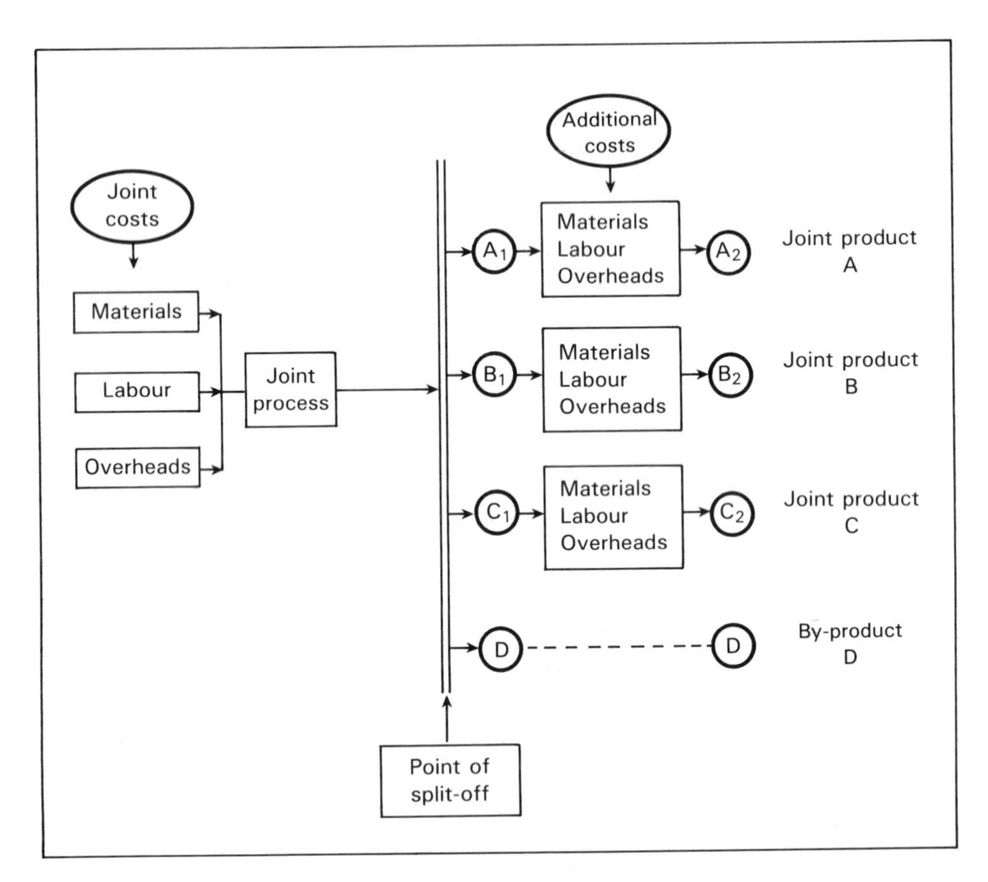

Figure 9.1 Joint products and by-products.

Consider the following example. Boundary Ltd produces two products, D and E, by means of a joint process. Both products have an intermediate market and thus can be sold at the split-off point. For every 100 lb of material used in the joint process, there is an output of 80 lb of D and 20 lb of E. The data relevant to selling prices and costs are:

	Product D	*Product E*
Selling price at the split-off point	£320 (£4 per lb)	£160 (£8 per lb)
Costs of additional processing	£200 (£2.5 per lb)	£60 (£3 per lb)
Selling price at final stage after processing	£560 (£7 per lb)	£200 (£10 per lb)

Should D and/or E be processed further? Analysing each in turn:

Product D: Further process or immediate sale?

	Immediate sale (£)	*Further process* (£)	*Difference* (£)
Sales revenue	320	560	240
Additional costs	0	200	200
Additional profit/(loss)	320	360	40

Product E: Further process or immediate sale?

	Immediate sale (£)	*Further process* (£)	*Difference* (£)
Sales revenue	160	200	40
Additional costs	0	60	60
Additional profit/(loss)	160	140	(20)

The differential analysis reveals that D should be processed further as the additional revenue per unit of £3 (£7 – £4) is greater than the additional cost per unit of £2.5, whereas E should be sold after split-off as the additional revenue of £2 per unit (£10 – £8) is less than the additional cost of £3 per unit.

We have not yet addressed ourselves to the question of whether the joint process should be operated in the first place. There is obviously no point in making decisions about the possible worthwhileness of incurring additional costs if it is unprofitable to make the products initially. Let us refer back to the example of Boundary Ltd and assume the following additional data. Each month the joint process incurs avoidable fixed costs of £1,000 and a variable cost per 100 lb batch for labour and raw materials used of £400. Further assume that ten batches are processed each month. We can now determine whether it is profitable to operate the joint process by analysing the data as follows:

	Product D (£)		*Product E* (£)	*Total* (£)
Sales (10 batches):				
Product D after additional processing (10 batches × £560)	5,600			5,600
Product E sold at split-off (10 batches × £160)			1,600	1,600
				7,200
Less Additional costs of processing Product D (10 batches × £200)	2,000			2,000
Surplus before costs of joint process	3,600		1,600	5,200
Less Additional costs of joint process:				
Avoidable fixed costs		1,000		
Variable costs (10 batches × £400)		4,000		5,000
Monthly surplus from whole process				200

The 'marginal' additional monthly surplus of £200 shows that the operation of the entire process appears to be worthwhile. If, of course, the monthly surplus for the process had been a negative amount (i.e. a loss had been incurred) then it would be unwise to proceed, even though both D and E show surpluses before deducting avoidable joint process costs.

9.3 Short-term decisions with one scarce resource

So far in our analysis we have assumed that there are no restrictions on the input factors needed for production. We have, for example, assumed that materials, machinery and labour are readily available and can be bought or hired in the desired quantities. In practice, however, it is quite likely that this assumption will not hold. A resource is scarce if the firm has insufficient supplies of it to accept all opportunities which are expected to generate positive contributions. Our analysis should therefore account for these constraints on production. We will examine the mode of analysis in two stages: first, by assuming that only one resource is scarce, and second, by extending the analysis to cope with the situation in which more than one resource is scarce.

Where only one resource is scarce, products competing for its use must be *ranked* so that the most efficient use is made of the scarce resource, i.e. so that the maximum total contribution is earned. This aim is achieved by ranking products according to the contribution they produce per unit of the scarce resource they require. The following example explains the procedure.

Prenton Ltd is considering its production plan for the next year. Four products, P, Q, R and S, are available for production and sale. The data relevant to the products are given in Table 9.4. Which products should Prenton Ltd produce? If no resources are in short supply, Prenton Ltd should produce all four products up to the level of their respective demands, as each one makes a positive contribution to fixed costs and profit.

Suppose now that Prenton Ltd is unable to obtain sufficient labour for next year to produce all four products to their demand limits (i.e. 120,600 labour hours). In

Table 9.4 Prenton Ltd: product data

		P		*Q*		*R*		*S*
Selling price (£)		230		150		160		130
Less Labour (£2 per hour)	140		52		48		28	
Materials (£1 per lb)	20	160	59	111	52	100	74	102
Contribution per unit (£)		70		39		60		28
Labour required per unit (hours)		70		26		24		14
Maximum expected demand at above selling price (units)		1,000		800		600		1,100

Table 9.5 Ranking of products on the basis of contribution per labour hour

Product	*Contribution per unit* (£)	*Labour hours per unit*	*Contribution per labour hour* (£)	*Ranking*
P	70	70	1.0	4
Q	39	26	1.5	3
R	60	24	2.5	1
S	28	14	2.0	2

fact only 41,500 labour hours are expected to be available. It is now necessary to see how efficiently the four products use available labour. The ranking according to their contributions per labour hour is shown in Table 9.5.

Table 9.5 shows that R, showing a contribution of £2.5 per labour hour, uses labour hours most efficiently and should be produced to its demand limit. Product S is the second most efficient and should also be produced to its demand limit. This process continues until all the 41,500 available labour hours have been used. Between them R and S require 29,800 labour hours (R requires 14,400 (600 × 24) and S 15,400 (1,100 × 14)). This leaves 11,700 available for Q, the third best on the ranking. But to produce Q to its demand limit would require 20,800 labour hours (800 × 26) which is more than the amount available. Production of Q is therefore restricted to 450 units (11,700 ÷ 26), and no labour hours remain to produce any units of P. The optimal plan for Prenton Ltd is set out in Table 9.6.

The optimality of the plan may be tested by considering the effect of transferring one of the scarce labour hours currently being used to help to produce one unit of Q (the least acceptable product included in the plan) to P (the only and therefore the best product excluded from the plan). We presume for illustrative purposes that all products are divisible and hence that we can measure contributions for fractions of products. Is the substitution worthwhile? The effect on total contribution will be as set out below:

	£
Increase in contribution from P through gain of one labour hour	1.0
Fall in contribution from Q through loss of one labour hour	1.5
Net decrease in contribution	0.5

The substitution is not worthwhile. Similarly it will not be worthwhile to substitute P for either of R and S, both of which use scarce labour hours more efficiently than Q.

The plan we have drawn up is the best available. We must stress here that we would *not* have obtained the same answer if we had ranked the four products according to their unit contributions. It is interesting to note that P, which has the

Table 9.6 Prenton Ltd: derivation of the optimal plan

Product	*Units produced*	*Labour hours required*	*Contribution (£)*
R	600	14,400	36,000
S	1,100	15,400	30,800
Q	450	11,700	17,550
P	0	0	0
		41,500	84,350

highest unit contribution (£70), also produces the lowest contribution per hour of labour, the scarce resource. Product S, on the other hand, has the lowest unit contribution (£28) but the second highest contribution per labour hour. In simple terms, the reason why contribution per unit of the scarce resource is a more appropriate means of evaluating products than is unit contribution is that ultimately a firm wishes to maximise its *total* contribution. So if Prenton Ltd had 140 labour hours available for production of either P or S it could make either 2 units of P, giving a total contribution of £140 (2 × £70) or 10 units of S, giving a contribution of £280 (10 × £28). Although P has the higher unit contribution, this is more than compensated for when labour is scarce by the fact that more units of S can be produced using a given number of labour hours. The same sort of reasoning would, of course, apply if the scarce resource in question was something other than labour time, for example raw materials, machine hours, factory space, or even cash.

9.4 Decision making with more than one scarce resource

Let us now extend the analysis by addressing the problem of decision making for a firm that is faced with constraints on the availability of at least two resources (e.g. labour and machinery). We have seen that it is possible to apply a ranking criterion based on contribution per unit of scarce resource to determine the best production plan if only one resource is in short supply. Can we apply the same criterion if two resources are scarce? The answer is that we can apply the ranking method, but it will give us the optimal answer only if it results in the same ranking for each constraining factor. If we do not get the same ranking for each constraining factor, then the plan will show that some resources are not being used to their best advantage. The best plan could be obtained by examining all possible combinations of product selection, but the sheer number of calculations involved will usually make this approach infeasible. What is needed is a method of analysis which limits the number of possible combinations of products to be examined and which ensures that the optimal plan is included in the set examined. In effect a method is needed to account for the relative use of scarce resources by different products. Such a method is provided by the technique of *linear programming*.

9.5 Linear programming: formulation

Linear programming is the most simple of the mathematical programming techniques available to the decision maker. It is widely used in fields other than production planning but it is this function, as an aid to the solution of business decision problems, that is of particular interest to us here. In order to illustrate the formulation, and subsequently the solution, of linear programming problems, we make use of an example.

Carrow Ltd manufactures two products, the widget and the didget. Each widget which is sold produces a contribution of £5 and each didget £4. All input factors required to manufacture the two products are readily available at their market prices with the exception of labour time, storage space and a special component, the justin. In the coming year Carrow Ltd expects to have available a maximum of 30,000 labour hours, 12,000 ft^2 storage space and 33,000 units of justin.

Each widget requires 15 labour hours, an average of two square feet of storage space per annum and 10 units of justin. Each didget requires 8 labour hours, an average of four square feet of storage space per annum and 12 units of justin. No restriction is expected on the demands for the two products. Carrow Ltd is seeking a production plan for the coming year that will maximise total contribution to fixed costs and profit from the two products. There is to be no production for stock.

Letting x_1 equal the number of widgets to be produced and sold in the coming year and x_2 the number of didgets, we may formulate the problem as a linear programme:

$$\text{Maximise } C = 5x_1 + 4x_2 \tag{9.1}$$

$$\text{Subject to} \quad \left.\begin{aligned} 15x_1 + 8x_2 &\leq 30{,}000 \\ 2x_1 + 4x_2 &\leq 12{,}000 \\ 10x_1 + 12x_2 &\leq 33{,}000 \end{aligned}\right\} \tag{9.2}$$

$$\left.\begin{aligned} x_1 &\geq 0 \\ x_2 &\geq 0 \end{aligned}\right\} \tag{9.3}$$

(9.1) is known as the *objective function* and is normally an equation (model) describing total profit or, more precisely, total contribution. We wish to maximise the value of this expression (C). In this case, total contribution is the sum of the contributions from widgets (£5 per unit multiplied by x_1 units) and didgets (£4 per unit multiplied by x_2 units). It is the object of the linear programming solution to find optimal values for x_1 and x_2, the quantities of each product to be produced and sold.

The other expressions are inequalities that define the *constraints* to be observed in maximising the value of the objective function. The constraints under (9.2) represent restrictions on the availability of input factors (resources). For example, 30,000 – the right-hand side of the first constraint – is the total amount of labour hours expected to be available in the coming year. The left-hand side of the constraint defines total labour hours required; 15 hours for each of the x_1 widgets to be produced and 8 hours for each of the x_2 didgets. Hence the constraint requires that total labour hours used ($15x_1 + 8x_2$) must be less than or equal to total labour hours available (30,000). Similarly the available amount of storage space and justin must not be exceeded.

In the case of Carrow Ltd, no constraints are expected on the demands for the two products. Demand constraints could easily be incorporated into the linear programming formulation. For example, suppose that Carrow Ltd expected to be able to sell no more than 1,500 widgets and 1,600 didgets during the coming year. As there is to be no production for stock, the company will not want to produce more of either product than it is able to sell and the demand constraints will be:

$$x_1 \leq 1{,}500$$
$$x_2 \leq 1{,}600$$

The constraints included under (9.3) are known as non-negativity constraints. They are technical requirements to ensure that negative production quantities for any of the products are not included in the optimal plan. Other refinements are possible within the general formulation and provided the expression may be stated in a linear form there is usually no reason why they should not be incorporated. The description 'linear programming' merely reflects that the equations and inequalities included are linear (i.e. they may be represented by straight lines – see Chapter 6 for examples of linear cost–volume–profit charts).

Linear programming, then, is suitable for solving problems where the objective is to maximise (or minimise) the value of some linear function subject to constraints (expressed as linear inequalities) which must not be violated.

9.6 Linear programming: solution

There are a number of techniques available for the solution of linear programming problems. All but the simplest problems are normally solved on a computer and it is not proposed to discuss the methods used in detail here.[21] Simple linear programming problems, e.g. where only two products are to be considered, may be solved with the aid of a graph. As this method of solution also serves to illustrate a number of the principles involved in more complicated methods of solution we shall apply it to the example of Carrow Ltd. Recall the linear programming formulation of the production problem facing the company:

$$\begin{array}{lrl}
\text{Max } C = & 5x_1 + 4x_2 & \text{(objective function)} \\
\text{subject to} & 15x_1 + 8x_2 \leq 30{,}000 & \text{(labour constraint)} \\
& 2x_1 + 4x_2 \leq 12{,}000 & \text{(storage space constraint)} \\
& 10x_1 + 12x_2 \leq 33{,}000 & \text{(justin constraint)} \\
& x_1, x_2 \geq 0 & \text{(non-negativity constraints)}
\end{array}$$

[21] Those interested in a further examination of the methods available for solving more complex problems might refer to W. J. Baumol, *Economic Theory and Operations Analysis*, 4th edn., Chapter 5, Prentice Hall, 1977, for the simplex method, or B. V. Carsberg, *Introduction to Mathematical Programming for Accountants*, chapters 4 and 5, Allen & Unwin, 1969, for an alternative description of the method, based on repeated substitution.

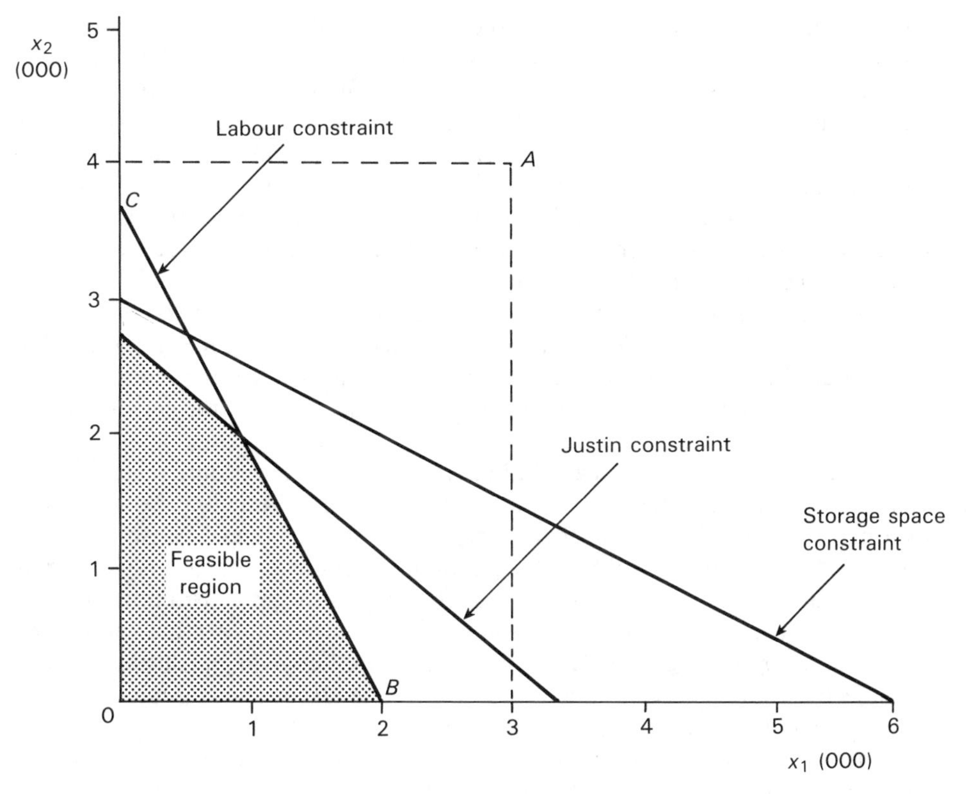

Figure 9.2 Definition of feasible region.

The first step in the graphical solution is to plot the various constraints. In Figure 9.2 we start by drawing axes representing possible production levels of widgets and didgets, x_1 and x_2. Any point on the graph represents a production plan. For example point A represents a production of 3,000 widgets (x_1) and 4,000 didgets (x_2). Our first task is to define a region, known as the *feasible region*, which covers all points, or solutions, that yield production plans not violating any of the constraints.

Consider first the two non-negativity constraints, $x_1 \geq 0$ implies that the solution must lie on or to the right of the x_2-axis. Similarly $x_2 \geq 0$ implies that the solution must lie on or above the x_1-axis. The boundary lines describing the other three constraints will all be linear as the constraints themselves are expressed as linear inequalities. If an input is utilised up to the limit imposed by the available amount of the resource then the inequality describing the constraint will become an equality. For example, if labour is fully utilised then the values of x_1 and x_2 will be such as to satisfy the equation

$$15x_1 + 8x_2 = 30{,}000$$

There is an infinite combination of values of x_1 and x_2 which satisfy this equation.

To construct the line which connects them all, we need only calculate two of the combinations as we know the line is straight. The two we shall calculate are shown as points *B* and *C* in Figure 9.2. Point *B* represents a value of zero for x_2 and consequently the expression above reduces to $15x_1 = 30{,}000$, i.e. $x_1 = 2{,}000$. Point *C* represents a value of zero for x_1 and hence a value of 3,750 (30,000/8) for x_2. By connecting these two points we construct a line representing the boundary imposed by the labour constraint; the solution must lie to the left of and below this line. By a similar process we may construct constraint lines for storage space and for the special component justin. The lines are shown in Figure 9.2.

To be acceptable a solution must not violate any of the five constraints. All such solutions lie within the shaded area, designated the feasible region, on the graph in Figure 9.2. They are known as *feasible solutions*. Any production plan represented by a point outside the feasible region will violate at least one of the constraints and will not be acceptable.

The next step is to find the solution, from within the feasible region, that is *optimal*, i.e. that gives the highest value to the objective function. To do this we shall make use of what are normally known as iso-profit lines. An iso-profit line connects all points on the graph that represent production combinations yielding the same profit. As our assumed objective is to maximise total contribution to fixed costs and profit our lines will connect all points representing production combinations producing the same total contribution, i.e. giving a constant value to the objective function. For example, the broken line *DE* on the graph in Figure 9.3 links all solutions that yield a total contribution of £20,000.

The construction of the line is similar to the method used to construct the constraint boundary lines; as the line is straight (because the contribution per unit for each product is constant at all production levels) we need only calculate two points lying on it to be able to draw the whole line. For simplicity we choose the two points representing a zero production of one product and a balancing figure for the production of the other. For the £20,000 constant contribution line, if $x_2 = 0$ then x_1 must equal 4,000 (£20,000/£5), and if $x_1 = 0$, x_2 must equal 5,000 (£20,000/£4). Similarly, we might construct an iso-profit line for a contribution of £10,000. This is the broken line *FK* in Figure 9.3.

There is an infinite number of (parallel) constant contribution lines, all having a negative slope equal to the ratio of the contribution from a widget to the contribution from a didget (5/4). The objective is to discover the product combination represented on the highest contribution line, i.e. the one which will yield the highest total contribution. From the graph it is apparent that line *HJ* is the highest profit line attainable that includes a product mix not outside the feasible region (0*GIF*, as drawn in Figure 9.3). The line *HJ* is tangential to the feasible region at point *I*. It is a general rule of linear programming solutions that the optimum will lie somewhere on the boundary of the feasible region: for any point within, but not on the boundary of, the feasible region, there exists another on the boundary having a greater contribution. Unless the iso-profit lines have the same slope as one of the constraint boundary lines there will always be a unique solution at the intersection of two constraint lines, as at the intersection of the labour and justin constraint lines in our example.

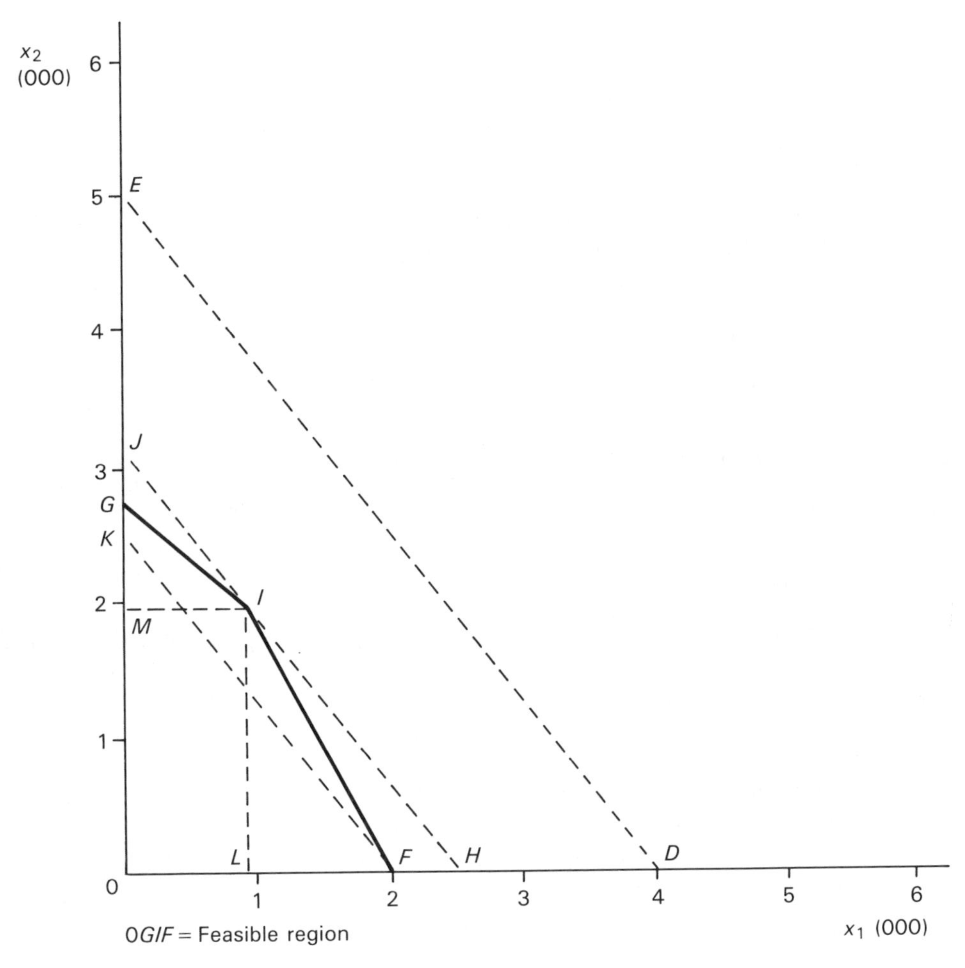

Figure 9.3 Identification of optimal solution.

The solution represented by point I is optimal. It is within the feasible region and yields a higher contribution than any other point in the feasible region. We might ascertain the production plan it represents by reading from the graph the value of x_1 and x_2 ($0L$ and $0M$ respectively). However, this method may lack precision and as an alternative we might utilise our new-found knowledge that the optimal plan involves using labour and the special component justin to their available limits. In other words, the inequalities describing these two constraints in the initial linear programming formulation become equalities at the optimal point, i.e.

$$15x_1 + 8x_2 = 30{,}000$$

$$10x_1 + 12x_2 = 33{,}000$$

Table 9.7 Usage of scarce resources

Labour	15(960) + 8(1,950) = 30,000
Storage space	2(960) + 4(1,950) = 9,720
Justin	10(960) + 12(1,950) = 33,000

Solving these as simultaneous equations we obtain values of $x_1 = 960$ and $x_2 = 1{,}950$. The optimal plan, then, is to produce 960 widgets and 1,950 didgets.[22]

Let us check that this plan will not lead to the violation of any constraints. The usage of the scarce resources implied by the plan is shown in Table 9.7. None of the constraints is violated. This confirms the feasibility of the plan. The total contribution expected from the plan may be determined by substituting the optimal values of x_1 and x_2 into the objective function:

$$\text{Total contribution} = £5(960) + £4(1{,}950) = £12{,}600$$

The optimality of this contribution could be confirmed by checking that there is no feasible substitution that would lead to a higher total contribution. Subject to the limitations of the method (discussed in the next section) the solution obtained by linear programming should be optimal.

Using the graphical framework, we might have calculated the optimal solution differently. As we know that the optimum solution(s) will lie at one of the corner points of the feasible region we might simply have calculated the contribution at each of these points and chosen the one with the highest contribution, thus avoiding the need for iso-profit lines. Alternatively, we could have dispensed with the graph altogether and calculated the values of x_1 and x_2 at the corner points by solving simultaneously all possible pairs of constraint equations, including the non-negativity constraints. After discarding solutions that violated other constraints, the solutions remaining would have represented the production plans at all corner points of the feasible region. From amongst them, we would have chosen the combination of x_1 and x_2 that yielded the highest contribution.

9.7 Limitations and assumptions of linear programming

There are a number of limitations to the linear programming approach, some of which stem from the assumptions implicit in the technique. The usefulness of linear programming models for decision making depends upon how well they simulate the conditions under which the firm operates.

[22] The simultaneous equations may be solved by multiplying through the first equation by 1.5 and subtracting from the answer the second equation. So:

$$\begin{aligned} 22.5x_1 + 12x_2 &= 45{,}000 \\ 10x_1 + 12x_2 &= 33{,}000 \\ \hline 12.5x_1 + 0 &= 12{,}000 \qquad \text{so } x_1 = 960 \end{aligned}$$

Substituting this value for x_1 into the original first equation gives:

$$15(960) + 8x_2 = 30{,}000 \qquad \text{so } x_2 = 1{,}950$$

As we have seen, linear programming models assume linear relationships between the variables. As such, they suffer similar limitations to the linear break-even charts discussed in Chapter 6. This has a number of practical implications. For example, one implicit assumption is that whatever the quantity of a particular product offered for sale, up to the level of any demand constraint which is included in the model, the selling price remains constant. The usual economic assumption is that the greater the number offered for sale, the lower will be the average price obtainable in the market (except in rarely found perfect markets). If a firm feels that it will be able to sell up to X units at a price of £Y it may include a constraint to this effect in its linear programming model. However, the optimal solution may suggest an output less than X units and it may be that the firm could sell this lower output at a price in excess of £Y. If the price is increased accordingly, the original plan may no longer be optimal. In this situation, the first formulation may be revised in the light of the first solution and the procedure repeated until a satisfactory position is reached.

A further implication of the linearity assumption is that each unit of output of a particular product requires a constant amount of each input factor, i.e. each successive unit of an input factor used on a particular product produces the same output quantity of that product. In the case of labour it is assumed that the workforce is equally efficient in all situations, ignoring the possibility that labour needs time to 'warm up' at the start of a production run or that people become more weary and less efficient towards the end of the run, and so on.

Furthermore, the model depends upon our being able to divide the total cost function of the firm into fixed and variable elements. Where step cost functions exist (see Chapter 6) they must be treated with care. Some may be reasonably approximated by a linear function while others may, within defined ranges, be regarded as fixed. Where neither of these treatments seem appropriate some improvisation may be necessary. For example, the programme may be run at different maximum output levels, corresponding to the points at which steps in total costs occur; step costs would be ignored in the formulation but adjusted manually in comparing contributions at each output level.

It is implied also that however many units of an input factor are bought, up to any constraint that may be assumed, the same price will be paid for each unit. This may fail to take account of discounts for bulk buying, increased prices as the available supply diminishes, and so on. Where these implied assumptions are not representative, or reasonably representative, of the actual conditions facing the firm, the use of a linear programming model may be inappropriate.

The linear programming solution may not be optimal if the input cost and price data used do not represent the relevant costs of the particular factors. For example, to maximise product contributions calculated on an historical cost basis may lead to a solution that is inconsistent with the maximisation of current cash resources.

We have not dealt explicitly with the problem of uncertainty. In practice, linear programming is a most useful aid to analysing the uncertainty problem. Once the initial programme is formulated, say on the basis of 'best estimates', the values of individual elements may be altered and the programme re-run rapidly on a computer to determine the effect of the change on total contribution. This sensitivity analysis enables the firm to form an opinion as to the sensitivity of total contribution to environmental changes or estimating errors in the value of individual input factors. Because much of the decision making cost is in the initial formulation of the problem, rather than in its solution, the incremental cost of undertaking the sensitivity analysis may be relatively low.

There are a number of other factors that may need to be considered. It is frequently the case that the solution to a linear programming problem involves fractional units of products (for example, with slightly different constraints the solution to Carrow Ltd's problem could have involved production of 960.5 widgets). It may be that the assumption that fractional units of products can be produced and sold is invalid. If so, the optimal solution will have to be in terms of integer output levels. Where fairly large output levels are involved, this may be achieved by rounding down any fractional output levels to the nearest whole number. Where small output levels are envisaged and each output unit is large relative to the total, such a process of rounding may not lead to a solution that is a good approximation to the optimum and a more refined form of programming may be required. This is known as integer programming and involves the inclusion of extra constraints to prohibit solutions involving fractional output levels.[23]

A further factor that was ignored in handling the problem of Carrow Ltd was the possibility of interdependence between the demands for widgets and didgets. Demand for the products, on the one hand, may be complementary. An example would be a firm manufacturing propelling pencils and the leads that are used in them. A fall in the number of pencils sold may lead to a fall in the number of leads demanded. Alternatively, the products may be substitutes for each other when a fall in the number of one product sold will be associated with a rise in the demand for others. An example would be an organisation manufacturing more than one sort of breakfast cereal. The implicit assumption of linear programming is that the demand functions for the various products under consideration are independent of each other. Where this is not a valid assumption a more refined mathematical programming approach is required.

An analogous problem may arise where there are interdependences between the input factors required to manufacture two or more of the products. For example, a farmer cannot produce milk, meat and hides independently of each other. They all come from the same input factor, the cow, and the final amounts produced are interrelated. In situations like this, the basic programming model may require development by the addition of extra constraints. Often, however, if the implied assumptions discussed in this section do not hold, we must resort to one of the non-linear programming techniques that are available.[24]

Finally, we mention three further points that are not strictly limitations of linear (and other) programming techniques but rather warnings to exercise care in their use. Similar caveats apply to many other mathematical business problem solving

[23] A detailed study of mathematical approaches is outside the scope of this text. For a good introduction to integer programming see Baumol, W. J., *Economic Theory and Operations Analysis*, 4th edn., Chapter 8, Prentice Hall, 1977.

[24] A good introduction to non-linear programming can be found in Baumol, W. J., *Economic Theory and Operations Analysis*, 4th edn., Chapter 7, Prentice Hall, 1977.

techniques as we have seen in previous chapters. The first concerns the existence of costs and benefits that are not readily quantifiable and hence cannot be easily incorporated into the linear programming formulation. For example, the firm may lose customer goodwill if it fails to produce a full line of products. It may be possible to treat this as a demand interdependence problem if the necessary quantification can be achieved. On the cost side, there is the possibility of industrial action if the optimal plan involves laying off part of the labour force. The uncertainties involved make it difficult to predict the likelihood and potential cost of a strike, for example. It may be that the firm wishes to ensure that the plan selected does not involve reducing the number of men employed on production below a specified minimum. In the case of Carrow Ltd, for example, a constraint is already included limiting the maximum number of labour hours. Suppose the firm also requires that a minimum of 18,000 hours be worked to reduce the probability of industrial action. This could be achieved by inserting a further constraint

$$15x_1 + 8x_2 \geq 18{,}000$$

which would ensure that at least 18,000 labour hours were required in the production plan.[25]

The second point is that linear programming will only yield a solution that is optimal for the available input data. Any opportunities that are not included in the formulation cannot be considered. It is important for the decision maker to ensure that a satisfactory range of feasible opportunities is taken into account unless there is some obvious reason for excluding any of them.

The final point concerns the implied rigidity of the constraints. As we are using a precise mathematical technique to solve our problem the input data must also be precise. A limit of 30,000 labour hours is interpreted in the solving of the problem at its face value, and not, for example, as 30,000 ± 10%. In practice, it is likely that the constraints will have some degree of flexibility, particularly if the possibility of paying increasing prices for further supplies is not rejected.

At first sight, the limitations of linear programming seem imposing. Yet many of them stem from the implied assumption of linear cost functions, and a number of statistical studies have presented evidence suggesting that within fairly wide relevant ranges firms are confronted with cost functions that may be reasonably approximated by linear expressions.[26] In addition many firms are already using linear

[25] If the requirement is merely that the labour should be employed for a minimum of 18,000 hours (not necessarily on productive work), the original constraint limiting the maximum number of labour hours becomes

$$15x_1 + 8x_2 \leq L$$

and the following additional constraints are included:

$$L \leq 30{,}000$$

$$L \geq 18{,}000 \text{ (or } -L \leq -18{,}000)$$

In addition, it will be necessary to amend the objective function to recognise the fact that the first 18,000 hours of labour employed is now a fixed cost.

[26] See, e.g. Johnston, J., *Statistical Cost Analysis*, McGraw-Hill, 1960, particularly Chapters 4 and 5.

programming techniques on a wide variety of business problems, with apparently satisfactory results.[27] The evidence suggests that linear programming is one of the more useful tools available to managers.

Discussion topics

1. 'Whatever the nature of the business decision, only differential future cash flows are relevant to the decision.' Discuss.
2. Give some specific examples of business decisions in which *qualitative* factors would likely determine the future outcome, and explain how such factors might affect the decisions.
3. Discuss some of the *social* implications of dropping a segment or division of a business. How should these implications be included in the decision process?
4. Discuss some possible disadvantages that might arise from the allocation of joint costs to individual products.
5. 'The results of linear programming are only as good as the assumptions of the model used.' Discuss.
6. 'The results of short-term decisions determine the organisation's future.' Discuss.

Exercises

9.1 Last year Prokoviev plc accepted an order for the supply of 100 ships (mini-destroyers) to the Martian Canal Company. The ships were part completed when a government order was issued banning all trading with Mars. Manufacture of the ships was abandoned and the ships remain in a partly completed condition. The Venusian Steamship Company has recently shown interest in the purchase of 100 passenger ships. Prokoviev plc is anxious to obtain the order because it wishes to get a foothold in the Venusian market. It is considering the possibility of adapting the partly completed destroyers. You are given the following additional information:

1. Expenditure to date on the destroyers has been: materials £2.4 million and labour £3.7 million.
2. Prokoviev plc does not expect to be able to use the ships on any other order. They could be dismantled and sold for scrap to realise £0.6 million. Dismantling would require 20,000 hours of highly skilled labour at a wage of £4.50 per hour; the workers would have to be taken off other work yielding a contribution of £2 per hour (over and above wage costs).
3. The following additional direct costs would arise in the course of converting and completing the ships:

   (i) Material A 5,000 tons required; 10,000 tons already in stock, carried in accounts at cost price £100 per ton. No other use is foreseen for the material. It could be resold for £80 per ton – net of transport costs; current market price is £110 per ton.

[27] For examples of some applications see Moore, P. G. and Hodges, S. D. (eds.), *Programming for Optimal Decisions*, Part 2, Penguin, 1970.

(ii) Material B 10,000 tons required; 8,000 tons already in stock, carried in accounts at cost price £120 per ton. This material is in common use by the company. Market prices of the material have fallen. Stocks could be resold for £75 per ton net of selling costs and current market buying price is £90 per ton.
(iii) Other materials would have to be purchased at a cost of £3.6 million.
(iv) Four million labour hours would be required. Enough workers are available to complete the work in normal working time at the average wage rate of £3 per hour. However, it is expected that another very profitable order will be received shortly, for speedy completion, and this will make it necessary for one million out of the 4 million hours on the Venusian job to be worked as overtime at £3.50 per hour.
(v) Other variable costs would be £2.3 million.

4. In setting prices, the company charges 25% of direct labour costs to cover fixed overheads – this effectively allocates all fixed costs to individual jobs at times of normal activity.

5. In setting prices, the company normally adds a profit margin of 10% to total cost.

Prepare calculations showing the minimum price which Prokoviev may quote to the Venusian Steamship Company without expecting to reduce the wealth of its shareholders.

9.2 The directors of Nicholson Department Store Ltd are concerned at the poor results achieved in its toy department. They have noted that it has earned an income of only £0.04 per £1 of sales, considerably less than the target set by the company. They are considering the closing of the department.

The income account of the department for the year just ended runs as follows:

	£	£
Sales		74,300
Less Cost of sales		47,800
Gross profit		26,500
Less		
Wages of sales assistants (2 @ £4,000)	8,000	
Salary of supervisor	7,000	
Establishment costs of the department (heating, repairs, insurance, etc.)	3,000	
Rent of store – allocated to department on basis of floor area occupied	2,500	
General overhead costs of store – allocation in proportion to sales in each department	3,000	23,500
Net income for the year		3,000

If the department were closed, the space it occupied could be used either for an extension of the clothing department, or for storage of inventory (in which case rent of £4,000 per annum for warehouse facilities could be saved). You are also given the following information:

1. The gross profit earned in the toy department would be expected to remain at the same level in future years. If the clothing department were extended, it would be expected to increase its sales by £45,000 and earn a gross profit of 50% on sales.

2. If the department were converted to storage, the sales assistants would be transferred to other departments at their present wages. This would avoid the need to employ new assistants at a wage of £3,500 per annum each to make good normal losses of staff. If the department were turned over to clothing, the assistants would be employed in the extended department at their present wages and no additional assistants would be required.
3. In either event, the supervisor of the department would be redundant; the new department would come under other supervisors, already employed. In accordance with company policy, however, the supervisor would not be dismissed but found employment in general administrative duties, at the present salary.
4. Establishment costs of the department would be:

if converted to storage	£1,500 p.a.
if converted to clothing	£2,000 p.a.

5. If the department were converted to storage, general administrative costs for the store would fall by £500. Otherwise, they would continue at the present level.
6. It is to be assumed that there would be no material capital expenditure associated with any of the possibilities.

(a) Prepare calculations to indicate to the board of directors the best course of action. You may make and specify any reasonable assumptions that you consider necessary for your answer and you may add a *short* note on any considerations not reflected in your calculations.

(b) Prepare a short note on the suitability of judging departments by their net income per £1 of sales.

9.3 Salazar Separators plc produce four products: maz, mez, miz and moz, by subjecting input chemical material (known as krudex) to an analytical process. The output proportions are maz 40%, mez 30%, miz 20% and moz 10%. The company has capacity to process 30,000 gallons of chemicals per four week period.

An output of 20,000 gallons per four week period represents the sales demand at prevailing prices which are:

Maz	£3.00 per gallon
Mez	£3.50 per gallon
Miz	£4.00 per gallon
Moz	£6.00 per gallon

and requires an input of 20,000 gallons of krudex which costs £1.50 per gallon. The labour cost of processing 20,000 gallons is £10,000. The company's fixed overhead at 50% to 100% of capacity working is £10,000 per four week period. Variable overhead has been found to be closely related to direct wages and an absorption rate of 50% thereof is applied.

The company is considering whether to subject any or all of the four products to further processing in order to produce more refined products which would be known as supermaz, supermez, supermiz and supermoz, and which would command higher prices, *viz*:

Supermaz	£3.50 per gallon
Supermez	£3.80 per gallon
Supermiz	£6.00 per gallon
Supermoz	£8.00 per gallon

Sales demands for the super products are not expected to exceed those for the products they would replace. For technical reasons, it is not possible to produce both the original and the refined versions of any of the four products during a four week period, though one or more of the products can be produced in the refined version and the others in the original version.

Additional material and labour costs for the more refined process have been estimated as follows:

	Supermaz (£)	*Supermez* (£)	*Supermiz* (£)	*Supermoz* (£)
Activating ingredients (of no significant weight or volume)	2,000	3,000	2,000	1,500
Direct wages	1,000	3,000	1,000	1,000

Present a report, submitting information on the basis of which a decision could be made as to whether to undertake the additional processing under consideration, and state your recommendations.

9.4 Spohr's accountant has drawn up the following statement to help the managing director in his decision on what to produce during the coming year:

	Product					
	A	*B*	*C*	*D*	*E*	*F*
Selling price (£)	135	177	123	129	153	135
Cost (£): Materials	30	45	36	54	81	72
Labour	36	45	30	24	18	15
Variable overheads	9	9	9	9	9	9
Fixed overheads	36	45	30	24	18	15
	111	144	105	111	126	111
Profit per unit (£)	24	33	18	18	27	24
Ranking	3=	1	5=	5=	2	3=
Estimated maximum demand p.a. (units)	500	700	600	1,000	400	600

Labour is all of one grade and earns £3 per hour; Spohr can hire only 22,000 labour hours during the coming year. All other resources can be obtained in the desired quantities. Materials are valued at expected cost; none is held in stock at present. Fixed overheads are charged at 100% of labour cost under the company's costing system.

(a) Criticise the accountant's statement as a basis for product selection and suggest an output plan for the coming year. Indicate how confident you are that your suggestion is optimal.

(b) Suppose that the price of materials has increased dramatically during the past year and that Spohr holds very large stocks purchased before the increase. Explain briefly how such materials should be valued for output decisions.

9.5 Mussorgsky Ltd manufactures two products, the hi and the fi. It sells the hi at £130 and the fi at £160. At these prices, the company is able to sell as many units of each product as it can produce. The variable cost of each hi is £90 and of each fi, £100. The company also incurs annual fixed costs of £95,000, the amount of which is unaffected by the production levels of hi and fi.

In the coming year Mussorgsky Ltd expects to have available only 28,000 hours of skilled labour time and 66,000 hours of machine time. The company does not expect to be able to exceed these amounts during the coming year. All other input factors are expected to be available in any likely quantities. Each hi produced requires 7 hours of skilled labour time and 33 machine hours. The requirements for each fi are 14 hours of skilled labour time and 22 machine hours.

The company wishes to determine a production plan which will maximise its expected profit for the coming year. No stocks of hi or fi are held at present and there is to be no production for stock during the coming year.

(a) Formulate the above problem as a linear programme.

(b) Calculate the optimal production levels for hi and fi during the coming year, and the company's expected profit if the optimal plan is implemented.

(c) Outline the limitations of linear programming in solving problems such as this in practice.

9.6 Paganini Ltd is drawing up production plans for the coming year. Four products are available:

		Product			
		A	*B*	*C*	*D*
Selling price per unit (£)		220	212	388	344
Cost of materials per unit (£)		68	100	152	88
Labour hours per unit –	Grade A	10	6	—	—
	Grade B	—	—	10	20
	Grade C	—	—	12	6
Variable overheads (£)		24	28	20	24

Fixed overheads of the firm amount to £142,000 per annum. Each grade of labour is paid £6 per hour, but skills are specific to a grade so that an employee in one grade cannot be used to undertake the work of another grade. The annual supply of each grade is limited to the following maxima:

Grade A – 9,000 hours
Grade B – 14,500 hours
Grade C – 12,000 hours

There is no effective limitation on the volume of sales of any product.

(a) Calculate the product mix which will maximise profit for the year, and state the amount of the profit.

(b) Calculate the minimum price at which the sale of product A would be worthwhile.

(c) Calculate the amount by which profit could be increased if the supply of Grade A labour were increased by one hour.

(d) Describe briefly the limitations of the technique you have used in answering (a).

9.7 Pamina owns a small highly skilled business which manufactures flutes and sets of pan-pipes. The following data are relevant to the two products:

	Flute (F)	*Set of Pan-pipes (P)*
Selling price per unit (£)	120	100
Variable cost per unit (£)	80	70
Contribution per unit (£)	40	30
Raw materials required:		
Special wood	1 'length'	2 'lengths'
High quality metal	0.2 kg	0.1 kg
Direct labour required (hours)	20	20

Estimates of the resource quantities available in a year are:

Special wood	1,000 'lengths'
High quality metal	100 kg
Direct labour	12,000 hours

(a) Advise Pamina how many flutes and sets of pan-pipes she should produce each year in order to maximise her profit.
(If a graphical solution is used, plot the number of flutes on the vertical axis.)

(b) Pamina has been discussing her selling prices with a musical friend who remarked that she should be able to sell a set of pan-pipes for the same price as a flute, i.e. £120 per set. Show how this new selling price would affect the optimal production quantities calculated in (a) and calculate the improvement in profit that would result.

(c) Discuss the limitations of the method of solution that you have used in parts (a) and (b).

9.8 Cumberland Manufacturing Ltd produces four products. Details of the sales price, material costs and labour requirements for each of the four products are provided below:

	Product			
	1	*2*	*3*	*4*
Sales price per unit (£)	65	27	60	46
Material cost per unit (£)	14	10	10	18
Labour hours per unit:				
Grade A	3	–	2	–
Grade B	–	2	–	4
Grade C	6	–	9	–

Each labour hour costs £4. The supply of all three categories of labour is restricted, and they are not interchangeable. The total number of hours available per month is as follows:

Grade A	6,000 hours
Grade B	10,000 hours
Grade C	18,000 hours

The company expects to be able to sell all units produced.

(a) Calculate the production plan which will maximise contribution for the month, and calculate the amount of contribution under this plan.

(b) Calculate the effect upon your answer to part (a) of the availability of an additional 900 hours of each grade of labour (consider the effect of additional hours of each grade separately).

(c) Discuss briefly any factors which you think might restrict the confidence of managers in the optimal plan calculated in answer to part (a).

Further reading

Carsberg, B. V., *An Introduction to Mathematical Programming for Accountants*, Allen & Unwin, 1969.

Dev, S., 'Linear programming and production planning', in Arnold, J., Carsberg, B. and Scapens, R. (eds.), *Topics in Management Accounting*, Philip Allan, 1980.

Dillon, R. D. and Nash, J. T., 'The true relevance of relevant costs', *The Accounting Review*, January 1978.

Gould, J. R., 'Opportunity cost: the London tradition', in Edey, H. C. and Yamey, B. S. (eds.), *Debits, Credits, Finance and Profits*, Sweet & Maxwell, 1974.

Gould, J. R., 'The economist's cost concept and business problems', in Baxter, W. T. and Davidson, S. (eds.), *Studies in Accounting*, 3rd edn., The Institute of Chartered Accountants in England and Wales, 1977.

Leininger, W., 'Opportunity costs: some definitions and examples', *The Accounting Review*, January 1977.

Salkin, G. and Kornbluth, J., *Linear Programming in Financial Planning*, Accountancy Age, 1973.

Chapter 10

Dual prices and opportunity costs

In the previous chapter we considered means of determining an optimal production plan where one or more of a firm's resources is scarce. In this chapter we consider ways of measuring the opportunity costs of scarce resources and the limitations and applications of such measures. To enable the reader to relate the arguments back to the analysis in the previous chapter, we continue to use the examples from that chapter, i.e. Prenton Ltd, to demonstrate the single scarce resource problem, and Carrow Ltd, to demonstrate the multiple scarce resource problem.

The most important message of this chapter is that the opportunity cost (the relevant cost for decisions) of using a scarce resource may be greater than the incremental cash flow directly associated with its purchase. Use of a scarce resource involves not only the cost of buying it but also the possibility that, because supply of the resource is limited, its use on one project may mean that another project cannot be undertaken even though it might have produced a contribution towards fixed costs and profit. It is this contribution forgone which provides the basis for measuring the *internal opportunity cost* of using a scarce resource.

10.1 Internal opportunity cost with one scarce resource

In order to illustrate the concept of internal opportunity cost with one scarce resource we return to the example of Prenton Ltd, introduced on p. 182. The relevant information relating to the company's production problem is reproduced in Table 10.1.

The figures in Table 10.1 show that the last product accepted into the optimal plan was Q, which has a contribution per labour hour of £1.5. It will not pay Prenton Ltd to substitute any other new product (say T, U or V) for Q unless it yields a contribution per labour hour of at least £1.5 (over and above the cash cost of one labour hour). This amount is the marginal return per labour hour within the framework of the optimal plan, and may be described as the *internal opportunity cost* of one labour hour.

Internal opportunity cost requires some clarification. Consider the value to

Table 10.1 Prenton Ltd: details of products

		P		*Q*		*R*		*S*
Selling price per unit (£)		230		150		160		130
Less Labour per unit (£) (2 per hour)	140		52		48		28	
Materials per unit (£) (£1 per lb)	20	160	59	111	52	100	74	102
Contribution per unit (£)		70		39		60		28
Labour (scarce resource) required per unit (hours)		70		26		24		14
Maximum expected demand (units)		1,000		800		600		1,100
Contribution per labour hour (£)		1		1.5		2.5		2
Ranking		4		3		1		2
Units produced		0		450		600		1,100
Labour hours required (total available is 41,500)		0		11,700		14,400		15,400

Prenton Ltd of one labour hour. If Prenton Ltd was deprived of one labour hour, production of Q (the marginal product) would have to be reduced by $\frac{1}{26}$ of a unit, as it takes 26 labour hours to produce one unit of Q. We assume that it is possible to produce fractions of a product. The effect on total contribution of this loss of one labour hour would be:

		£
Fall in total sales revenue [$\frac{1}{26} \times$ £150]		5.77
Less Saving on materials not used in producing one unit of Q [$\frac{1}{26} \times$ £59]	2.27	
Saving of one labour hour	2.00	4.27
Internal opportunity cost or fall in total contribution		1.50

An identical answer (of £1.50) would be obtained if we considered the *additional* contribution that would result from an extra labour hour.

Thus we can say that the *total opportunity cost* of one (scarce) labour hour, which determines its contribution to the optimal plan, is made up of two elements:

	£
Cash cost per labour hour (given)	2.0
Imputed internal opportunity cost (derived)	1.5
Total opportunity cost	3.5

This leads to an important decision rule in situations of scarce resources: a firm should accept new products into its production plan only if they yield positive contributions when the scarce resources they use are included at their total opportunity costs. The inclusion of scarce resources at these costs should ensure that they are always used efficiently.

The use of internal opportunity costs is often required in decisions involving the choice between buying in a component from an outside supplier or producing it within the firm, i.e. *make or buy decisions*. If there is spare productive capacity, the choice is simple; it is worth buying a component only if the additional cash flows incurred in production are greater in total than the buying-in price. If, however, the firm has no spare productive capacity, then other work must be displaced if the components are to be manufactured internally. In this case the comparison should be between the buying-in price and the additional cash flows from production plus the contribution lost because of the work displaced (the internal opportunity cost). The following example deals with a typical make or buy decision.

Bootham Ltd's accountant has estimated the cost per unit of making a component as:

	£
Direct material	10
Direct labour (4 hours)	5
Variable overhead	2
Fixed overhead	6
Total cost	23

The same component can be bought for £18. Should Bootham Ltd make or buy the component assuming:

(i) there is spare capacity?
(ii) there is no spare capacity?

The additional cash flows entailed in making the product are material + labour + variable overhead = £17, which is less than the buying-in price of £18. If there is spare capacity, the decision should be to make the component. Note that fixed overhead is omitted from the calculation of the price of manufacture, as it is not an additional cost.

If there is no spare capacity, then it will be necessary to determine the contribution which could otherwise be earned per hour of production, as this will be forgone in order to make the component and is thus a relevant cost of the decision. For example, assume Bootham Ltd's normal production is taken up with a product for which the following unit details are relevant:

		£
Selling price		10
Less Direct materials	2.50	
Labour (2 hours)	2.50	
Variable overhead	1.00	6
Contribution		4

Of the resources required for production, labour is in short supply. As it requires two labour hours to produce the normal product, then for every scarce labour hour used in making the component Bootham Ltd forgoes a contribution of £$\frac{4}{2}$ = £2 from normal production. In other words, labour is at present earning for the firm a contribution of £2 for every hour worked. The company must ensure that labour earns at least this amount if it is taken off normal production to work on the new component. Thus the full opportunity cost of labour is not represented by its cash cost. Because labour is in short supply the real cost is the cash cost *plus* the internal opportunity cost, and any new production should be charged this total opportunity cost to ensure that labour is allocated efficiently. The total opportunity cost of manufacturing one component for Bootham Ltd now becomes:

		£
Direct material		10
Variable overhead		2
Labour:		
Cash cost (4 hours × £1.25)	5	
Internal opportunity cost (4 hours × £2)	8	13
Total opportunity cost		25

When the internal opportunity cost for labour, represented by the contribution lost from displaced production (assumed to be its best alternative use within the firm) is brought into account, the decision is to buy the component, as the buying-in cost of £18 is lower than the total opportunity cost of manufacture of £25.

We should not leave the make or buy problem without mentioning some of the more obvious qualitative factors which may influence the decision. Suppose Bootham Ltd has no spare capacity and hence decides to buy rather than to make. One factor the company should consider is whether the future supply of the component is likely to be reliable. Unforeseen delivery problems could lead to production difficulties if the bought-in component is to be used within the firm or to loss of custom if it is to be sold. In either case, the company is likely to suffer a loss of contribution. Another factor is whether the quality of the bought-in component will always be satisfactory and, if it is not, whether Bootham Ltd will be able to exert pressure on the supplier to improve the quality. Inferior quality may lead to high wastage rates if the component is used on internal production or to customer dissatisfaction and consequent loss of future business if it is sold externally.

A third factor relates to the stability of the bought-in component's price. At current prices, buying seems a better alternative than making. But if the buying-in price increases more rapidly in the future than internal manufacturing costs, then the position may change. A similar argument may be made in respect of labour capacity. Although there is no current spare capacity, this situation may not persist. If spare labour capacity is expected in the near future it may be better for the company to make the component and suffer a short-term cost in terms of lost contribution in return for the gains which would be expected in the longer term from making rather than buying when there is spare labour capacity.

10.2 Internal opportunity cost with two or more scarce resources[28]

In the previous chapter we considered means of determining an optimal production plan where two or more of a firm's resources are scarce. In section 10.1 it was demonstrated that in the case of a single scarce resource the internal opportunity cost of one unit of that resource is given either by the extra return which could be secured if one extra unit were available or by the decline in contribution that the firm would suffer if it were deprived of one unit of the resource. We now turn to the problem of determining internal opportunity costs of resources where more than one is scarce.

Within the linear programming framework (see Chapter 9) there is a way of determining the marginal contribution of each scarce resource towards fixed costs and profit. This marginal return is known normally as the *dual price* or *shadow price* of the particular resource. Given the type of formulation used in the previous chapter, the dual price of a resource measures by how much total contribution will fall if the available amount of that resource falls by one (small) unit. If the linear programme is solved on a computer the dual price is normally readily available. Its calculation is part of the method usually used on computers for solving linear programming problems. However, we shall continue with the graphical method of solution to illustrate the principles involved in calculating dual prices, and the economic meaning which may be ascribed to them.

Let us continue with the case of Carrow Ltd, whose linear programming was formulated as follows:

$$
\begin{array}{llll}
\text{Max } C = & 5x_1 + 4x_2 & & \text{(objective function)} \\
\text{s.t.} & 15x_1 + 8x_2 & \leq 30{,}000 & \text{(labour constraint)} \\
& 2x_1 + 4x_2 & \leq 12{,}000 & \text{(storage space constraint)} \\
& 10x_1 + 12x_2 & \leq 33{,}000 & \text{(justin constraint)} \\
& x_1, x_2 & \geq 0 & \text{(non-negativity constraints)}
\end{array}
$$

We shall consider the effect on total contribution of reducing the availability of each of the three scarce input resources in turn. The total contribution from the original optimal plan was £12,600 (p. 190). In the first instance we shall consider the effect of reducing the availability of each resource by 1,000 units to avoid the infinitesimal figures that would result from a reduction of only one unit. To find the reduction that would be caused by a reduction of a single unit we may, in this case, divide the calculated loss in total contribution by one thousand. This method would not be valid if such a substantial reduction in resource availability were to lead to a change in the marginal product combination or in those resources representing an effective constraint on production (in the case of Carrow Ltd labour hours and units of special component justin) but the principles illustrated may be applied to smaller changes. The original constraint lines are shown on the graph in Figure 10.1. The

[28] The remainder of this chapter is based on Chapter 8 of John Arnold's *Pricing and Output Decisions*, Haymarket Press/Prentice Hall, 1973.

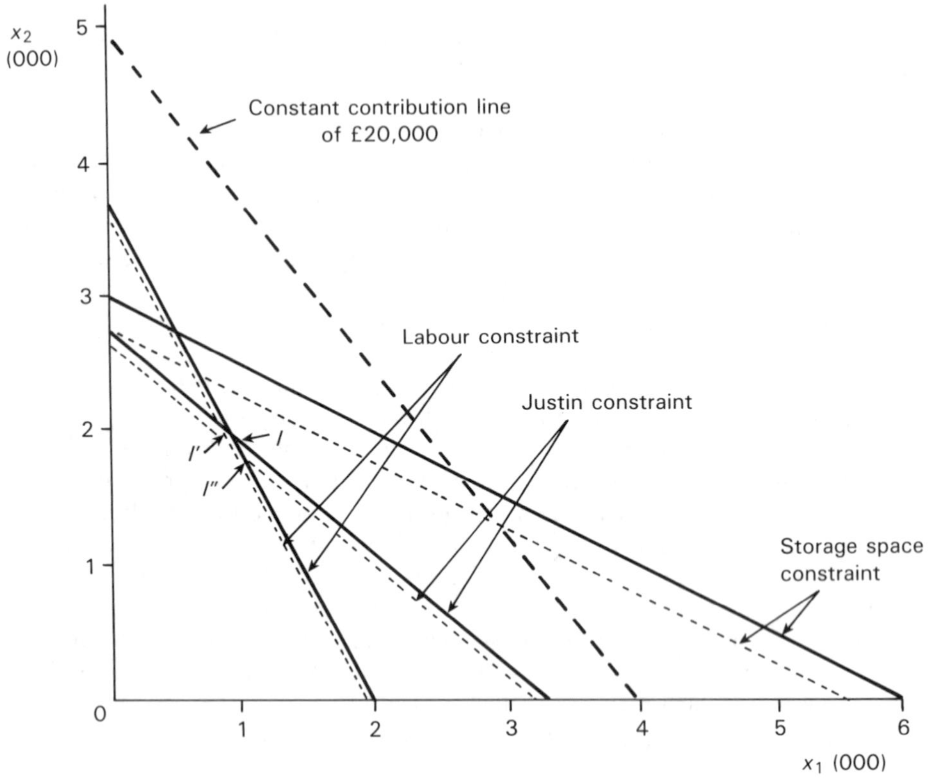

Figure 10.1 Carrow Ltd: original and revised constraint lines.

dotted lines represent the boundaries that would be operative if the available amount of each resource were to be reduced by 1,000 units.

Labour hours

Suppose that Carrow Ltd expects to have available only 29,000 labour hours in the coming year. The expected availability of the other two scarce resources is unchanged. The boundary line of the feasible region represented by the labour constraint will move downwards and to the left. It is apparent from the graph in Figure 10.1 that the new optimal production plan is represented by point I', where the revised labour constraint line and the original justin constraint intersect. To determine the production plan represented by this point we solve the following simultaneous equations:

$$15x_1 + 8x_2 = 29,000$$

$$10x_1 + 12x_2 = 33,000$$

This gives values of 840 for x_1 and 2,050 for x_2. The production plan is summarised in Table 10.2 which also shows that the new plan produces a total contribution of £200 less than the original. Correspondingly, a reduction of one hour in the amount of labour time available would lead to a fall in the value of the optimal plan of £0.2.

Table 10.2 Carrow Ltd: production plan revised for reduction in available labour

	Quantity	*Contribution per unit* (£)	*Total contribution* (£)
Widgets	840	5	4,200
Didgets	2,050	4	8,200
Revised total contribution			12,400
Original total contribution			12,600
Decrease due to a reduction of 1,000 in available labour hours			200
Decrease caused by a reduction of one in available labour hours	$£\frac{200}{1,000}=$	£0.2	

Storage space

It can be seen from Figure 10.1 that a reduction in the available storage space of 1,000 ft^2, the other two constraints remaining at their original levels, would not affect the optimality of the original plan. The optimal point would be I on the graph in Figure 10.1 and the total contribution £12,600. It follows that a reduction of one square foot in the available storage space would also lead to no fall in the value of the optimal plan.

Special component justin

A reduction of 1,000 units in the number of justin components available, amounts of labour time and storage space originally available remaining unchanged, would lead to an optimal plan represented by point I'', as may be seen from Figure 10.1. The boundary line of the feasible region described by the justin constraint moves downwards and to the left. The new optimum lies where the revised justin constraint intersects the original labour hours constraint. The relevant values of x_1 and x_2 are determined by solving the following simultaneous equations:

$$15x_1 + 8x_2 = 30,000$$
$$10x_1 + 12x_2 = 32,000$$

This gives values of 1,040 for x_1 and 1,800 for x_2, implying the production plan shown in Table 10.3. This plan yields a contribution £200 less than the original one. Correspondingly, a fall of one unit in the availability of justin would lead to a decrease of £0.2 in total contribution.

The reductions in total contribution caused by falls of one unit in the available supplies of the three scarce resources are summarised in Table 10.4. The figures measure the marginal return yielded by a single unit of each resource within the

Table 10.3 Carrow Ltd: production plan revised for reduction in available justin

	Quantity	*Contribution per unit* (£)	*Total contribution* (£)
Widgets	1,040	5	5,200
Didgets	1,800	4	7,200
Revised total contribution			12,400
Original total contribution			12,600
Decrease due to a reduction of 1,000 in available units of justin			200
Decrease caused by a reduction of one in available units of Justin		$£\frac{200}{1,000} = £0.2$	

Table 10.4 Carrow Ltd: dual prices of resources

Resource	*Fall in total contribution if amount available decreases by one unit (dual price)* (£)
Labour time	0.2
Storage space	0.0
Special component justin	0.2

framework of the optimal plan. Their use as measures of the internal opportunity cost of the resources is discussed in the next section.

10.3 Interpretation of dual prices

It is worthwhile to note first the equivalence of the dual price of a scarce resource and its marginal return (when it is the only scarce resource), as discussed in section 10.1. The latter is no more than a special case of a dual price and could equally well have been determined by solving the single scarce resource problem as a linear programme. Both measure the amount by which total contribution would fall if the firm were deprived of one unit of the scarce resource. Provided the scarce resource remains an effective constraint on production, both also measure the amount by which total contribution would rise if an additional unit of the resource were available. As we noted earlier when we discussed the opportunity cost of using a single scarce resource, the total opportunity cost of using a marginal unit of a resource is the sum of its external price and its internal opportunity cost. The latter is given by its dual price.

Two further observations on dual prices may be of interest. We have seen that costs that are fixed regardless of the decision to be taken have no relevant external cost. However, if these costs represent a scarce resource there may be a relevant cost attached to that resource: the total opportunity cost of using one unit will equal its dual price.

In the problem of Carrow Ltd, the dual price of storage space was zero (Table 10.4). The same is true of any resource that does not represent an effective constraint on production, even if the available supply of the resource is expected to be limited.[29] Neither a marginal increase nor a marginal decrease in the available amount of the resource will lead to any change in the optimal plan. The cost of using such a resource is its relevant external cost which reflects the only sacrifice involved in utilising it.

10.4 Limitations of dual prices

As dual prices are the products of a linear programming framework they suffer the same limitations and are based on the same assumptions as are relevant to linear programming (see pp. 190–4). Within these limits, they are useful indicators of the internal opportunity cost of using scarce resources.

However, there is a further reason for caution when dual prices are being used. They measure contribution changes resulting from marginal increases or decreases in resource availability. A large increase in the availability of a particular resource may mean that it is no longer an effective constraint on production and its dual price becomes zero. Consider the case of Carrow Ltd finding a supplier who is willing to provide up to an extra 11,000 units of the special component justin. The company has to decide how much over and above the market price previously charged it would be willing to pay for extra units. It might be argued that as the dual price of a resource measures the maximum amount a firm would be willing to pay, over and above the external opportunity cost, to obtain one further unit of that resource, then Carrow Ltd should be willing to pay a premium of up to 20p (the dual price) for each of the extra 11,000 units of justin.

If we re-calculate the optimal plan, reflecting the increased availability of justin but ignoring, at present, the surcharge that will be paid on all units used over 33,000, then the increase in total contribution will measure the maximum amount, over and above the present market price, that Carrow Ltd should be willing to pay for however many extra units of the special component are required. The revised justin constraint boundary is shown as a dotted line in Figure 10.2, and it is clear from the graph that justin is no longer an effective constraint. The optimal point is now I', where the labour time and storage space constraints intersect. The relevant values of

[29] Strictly, the supply of all of a firm's resources will be limited in an absolute sense by the amount of the resource available in the world. For practical purposes, however, a resource need only be regarded as scarce if its supply is limited within the range of any production plan a firm is likely to adopt.

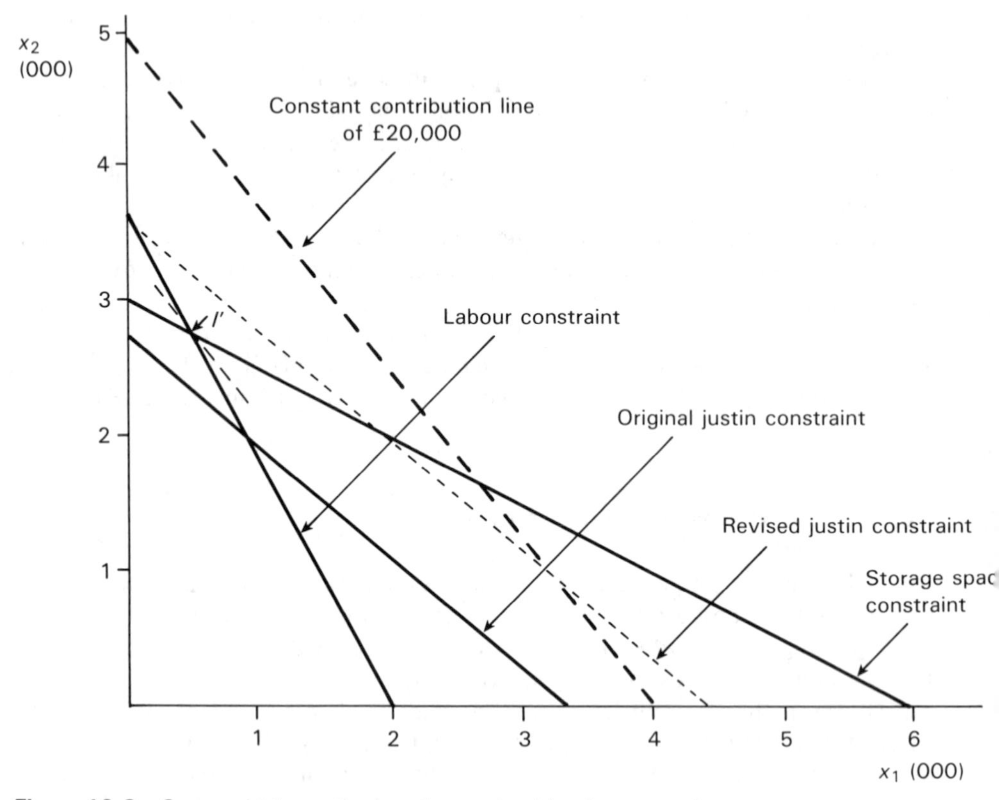

Figure 10.2 Carrow Ltd: graph showing revised justin constraint.

x_1 and x_2 are found by solving the following simultaneous equations:

$$15x_1 + 8x_2 = 30{,}000$$
$$2x_1 + 4x_2 = 12{,}000$$

This gives values correct to one decimal place of 545.5 for x_1 and 2,727.3 for x_2, implying the revised production plan shown in Table 10.5.

The extra contribution under the new plan is £1,037, and the plan requires an extra 5,183 units of justin.[30] The extra 5,183 units required increase total contribution by £1,037, an average of £0.2 per unit. The extra contribution obtainable from each unit of justin up to the amount required under the new plan remains equal to the dual price of 20p. But any units obtainable above this level do not increase total contribution at all as justin is no longer an effective constraint. Consequently it assumes a dual price of zero.

[30] Each widget requires 10 units of justin and each didget 12 units. Under the new production plan shown in Table 10.5 a total of 38,183 units of justin are required (10[545.5] + 12[2,727.3]). The previous plan required the maximum then available of 33,000 units and hence an additional 5,183 units are needed.

Table 10.5 Carrow Ltd: production plan revised for increase in available justin

Product	*Quantity*	*Contribution per unit* (£)	*Total contribution* (£)
Widgets	545.5	5	2,728
Didgets	2,727.3	4	10,909
Revised total contribution			13,637
Original total contribution			12,600
Increase in total contribution			1,037

Dual prices alone are of little help in tackling problems like this where the change in resource availability is not marginal. The example suggests that we need to re-solve the problem incorporating the revised constraint(s) and compare the new optimal solution with the original plan.

10.5 Applications of dual prices

Provided the limitations mentioned in the previous section are borne in mind dual prices, discriminately applied, have a number of uses. First they provide an indication of which constraints are the most severe. In the original example of Carrow Ltd, whose dual prices are given in Table 10.4, it does not seem worthwhile endeavouring to find new storage space. The zero dual price attached to this resource indicates that it is not an effective constraint on production. The company might usefully seek ways of relieving each of the other constraints, for a relaxation of either of them will lead to an increase in total contribution. It may be misleading to argue that as the special component justin and labour time both have the same dual price then it is, in some sense, equally worthwhile to relieve either of them. The units chosen for measuring the constraint will affect the size of the dual price. For example, had we chosen labour weeks of 35 hours each instead of labour hours as the measure of labour time, the dual price would have been 35 times higher, i.e. £7, considerably greater than the justin dual price. The dual price per unit of the resource will be a good indicator of where effort should be directed to relieve constraints only if the expected cost per unit of relaxation is the same for each resource constraint.

A second application of dual prices may arise when new opportunities, not in the original plan, are presented for consideration. Dual prices reflect the best marginal use of resources within the framework of the optimal plan and, to be acceptable, a new opportunity should use the resources at least as profitably as this marginal use; in a situation of scarce resources the new opportunity, if accepted, will displace one or more of the opportunities included in the optimal plan. The new opportunity is a worthwhile substitute if it yields a surplus when the resources it requires are valued at total opportunity cost, including the dual price values of any scarce resources needed. However, dual prices alone will not reveal precisely how the production levels of opportunities within the optimal plan should be adjusted: to determine this the firm must adopt some approximate method or re-formulate and re-solve the linear programme. The dual prices act merely as a screening device for new opportunities, a useful function as it avoids the firm having to re-run the linear programme for every new opportunity that emerges.

A third use arises when all decisions are not taken by a central decision making body with access to the linear programme. Decentralised decision making may be in evidence particularly in divisionalised firms where each division enjoys a certain amount of decision taking autonomy. To reduce the chance that resources are used suboptimally, they should be charged to those responsible for decisions at their total opportunity cost. As this includes the dual price value of scarce resources, only projects at least as efficient as those included in the optimal plan should be accepted. Problems facing divisionalised firms are discussed in Chapter 16.

Discussion topics

1. Discuss the importance of internal opportunity cost in the context of managerial decision making.
2. Suppose that management has decided to make a product internally rather than buy it on the open market, which appears to be the cheaper option. Discuss some possible reasons for this apparently irrational choice.
3. Explain what you understand by the dual (or shadow) price of a resource. What role does it play in determining the opportunity cost of using the resource?
4. Discuss the usefulness of dual prices in managerial decision making and explain their limitations. Illustrate your answer by reference to particular decisions.
5. List the major places so far in this book where the linearity assumption has been discussed. What conclusions do you draw about the importance of the linearity assumption?

Exercises

10.1 Zemlinsky plc, a manufacturer of scientific instruments, has been working on the manufacture of blue noise detectors under a contract with the government of Utopia. The government has just cancelled the contract and paid compensation of £50,000. The company has now 1,000 partly completed detectors on hand. It sees two alternative courses of action: (a) completion of the detectors and their sale to the Ruritanian government for £200 each, or (b) sale of the detectors for scrap in their present state for £20 each. You are given the following additional information:

1. Zemlinsky has spent £60,000 on the scientific development of the detectors; the resulting plans and specifications could be sold for £35,000 if and only if the detectors were sold for scrap.
2. 1,000 lb of material X has been purchased for production of the detectors at a cost of £30 per lb: 300 lb has already been used in production. The remaining 700 lb is in stock and could not be used in its existing state on other work in the company. It could be sold for £25 per lb; alternatively it could be put

through a special process at a cost of £5 per lb and used as a substitute for material A which has a current price of £32 per lb. Material A is in common use by Zemlinsky.

3. 5,000 lb of material Y has been purchased for production of the detectors at a cost of £10 per lb. 3,000 lb has already been used and 2,000 lb is in stock. Each finished detector requires 10 lb of Y. If the detectors are scrapped the material in stock would have to be sold as there is no alternative use for it in the company. The current buying price of Y is £12 per lb, but it could be sold for only £6 per lb and Zemlinsky would have to pay removal costs of £8 per lb in the event of sale.
4. Each detector requires 15 hours of Grade A labour. Zemlinsky has increased its labour force to provide the required time. Five thousand hours (out of the required total of 15,000 hours) have already been used. Grade A labour is paid £3 per hour. If the manufacture of detectors is discontinued, the labour would be used on less skilled work and save the employment of additional persons at a wage of £2.50 per hour (for dismissal of the employees would be contrary to company policy).
5. Each detector requires 20 hours of Grade B labour, which has a current wage rate of £3.50 per hour and which is in short supply. Each hour spent on the detectors would make it necessary to give up other work earning a surplus of £0.50 after charging all costs including wages. No Grade B labour has yet been used.
6. Under the company's costing system, all jobs are assigned an additional cost, equal to 75% of direct labour cost, to cover overheads. The manufacture of the detectors has not and will not cause any actual increase in overhead costs.

Prepare calculations showing which course of action is preferable. Describe the ingredients of your calculations clearly. Mention *two* factors which might influence the decision but are not reflected in your calculations.

10.2 Munter Ltd produces and sells cassette tape recorders to store groups Q, R, S and T. The recorders are manufactured in four buildings on the firm's single factory site. A different recorder is produced in each building, all of which have the capacity to produce 100 recorders per month. Each store group has contracted to take 100 recorders per month and the firm faces stiff penalties for non-delivery. The store groups have differing quality requirements for the recorders they buy from Munter and they sell these under their own house brands Q, R, S and T respectively.

The plant in any of the four buildings can readily be adapted to produce any model of recorder. The comparative profit schedule for the recorders when the factory is operating at full capacity is:

	Q (£)	*R* (£)	*S* (£)	*T* (£)
Revenue (i.e. contract prices)	20	17	22	30
Direct materials	7	6	5	8
Direct labour (note 1)	3	1	2	6
Variable overhead	1	3	4	5
Fixed overhead (note 2)	6	2	4	12
Total costs	17	12	15	31
Profit (loss)	3	5	7	(1)

Notes: Labour is paid £1 per hour; fixed overheads are based on the month's fixed costs and absorbed using direct labour hours; and during May the factory was operating at full capacity.

The prices at which Munter can buy in recorders suitable to enable them to fulfil their contracts are

Q–£17, R–£14, S–£19, T–£27

On the night of 31 May 19X0, one of the Munter Ltd factory buildings was burnt down. The following morning the directors of the company are trying to decide which tape recorder they will have to buy in to enable them to fulfil their contracts. The production director has been arguing for some time that the firm has been making a loss of £1 on every unit of model T it produces and sells; it is argued that this model could have been bought in for £27 instead of the £31 that it costs to make, which would have provided a £3 profit per unit on resale. The production director insists that model T is the one that they should buy in.

(a) State whether you agree with the production director. Support your answer with calculations.

(b) Discuss the factors which the directors of Munter Ltd should consider in deciding whether to rebuild the burned down building.

10.3 Macke Ltd manufactures a high fidelity amplifier, one of the components of which is loudspeaker B717. A specialist loudspeaker manufacturer has quoted £30 each for the supply of the 5,000 B717s which will be required during the forthcoming year. You have been asked to advise the board whether to accept the quotation or continue to manufacture and have ascertained the following facts:

1. The costs of producing the 4,000 B717s used last year were:

	£
Direct material	104,000
Direct wages	28,000
Plant depreciation	4,800
Plant insurance	4,400
Plant maintenance contract	5,200
General fixed overhead apportioned to this production	20,000

2. The following unit cost increases are anticipated for the forthcoming year if the company continues to manufacture B717s:

   Direct material £1.20
   Direct wages 40p

3. If it is decided to discontinue the production of B717s, then the plant currently used would be sold.

4. If the B717s are purchased, the following costs will be incurred in addition to the basic price charged by the supplier:

   Inspection and storage £8,000 p.a.
   Carriage and insurance £2 each

(a) Prepare a statement to enable you to advise the board whether to continue manufacturing B717s or to buy them.

(b) Prepare a summary of any other matters that the board should consider in arriving at its decision.

10.4 Vivaldi plc is considering its production plan for 19X8. At present it manufactures and sells four products, A, B, C and D. Some of the company's resources are expected to be in short supply during 19X8 and the directors are considering ceasing production of one or more of the existing products in order to make the most efficient use of available resources. The company accountant has produced the following statement to help the directors make a decision:

	A (£)	*B* (£)	*C* (£)	*D* (£)
Variable costs per unit:				
Materials: XK7 (units)	(3)6.00	(4)8.00	(1)2.00	(5)10.00
Others	41.00	65.00	38.00	21.00
Labour: Skilled (hours)	(2)30.00	(1)15.00	(3)45.00	(2)30.00
Unskilled (hours)	(2)20.00	(6)60.00	(1)10.00	(3)30.00
Variable overheads	42.00	54.00	26.00	63.00
	139.00	202.00	121.00	154.00
Selling price per unit	200.00	250.00	160.00	220.00
Contribution per unit	61.00	48.00	39.00	66.00
Fixed costs (40% of variable costs)	55.60	80.80	48.40	61.60
Profit/(loss) per unit	5.40	(32.80)	(9.40)	4.40

Total fixed costs are not expected to be affected in 19X8 by any decision regarding particular products. However, the company accountant argues that as all products are expected to yield positive contributions some other method must be used to eliminate one or more of them. The accountant suggests that the most profitable products are those that recover a fair share of fixed costs. Consequently, fixed costs have been allocated to each product at a rate of 40% on total variable costs. This percentage is based on the company's accounts for 19X6, which showed total variable costs of £2,000,000 and total fixed costs of £800,000. The accountant recommends that products B and C should not be produced in 19X8 as they do not recover a fair share of fixed costs; only products A and D should be manufactured.

The directors are uneasy about discontinuing both B and C in 19X8 and seek advice from a firm of consultants. The consultants recommend the use of linear programming to solve the problem, and duly formulate the programme taking account of scarce resources expected and including as the objective function the maximisation of total contribution, using the unit contribution figures from the accountant's statement.

The solution to the linear programme reveals the following dual prices for 19X8:

Material XK7	£5 per unit
Skilled labour	£8 per hour
Factory space	£10 per yd^2 per annum

Usage of factory space during 19X8 is expected to be:

Product A	3 yd^2 per annum per unit
Product B	2 yd^2 per annum per unit
Product C	1 yd^2 per annum per unit
Product D	4 yd^2 per annum per unit

The dual prices of all resources other than the three mentioned above are zero.

(a) On the basis of the information given, which products should Vivaldi plc plan to produce in 19X8? (Note: You are *not* required to calculate production quantities.) Give your reasons.

(b) Explain the economic significance of dual prices and discuss the limitations to their usefulness.

10.5 Liza Beck runs a small but successful pottery business. She has only two products, an ornate bowl and a classically proportioned jug. At the present moment she is producing 10 bowls and 15 jugs each week. One of the reasons that her production is limited is that she does not want to spend more than 7.5 hours per day making pottery in a five day working week; each bowl and each jug requires 1.5 hours of her time. There is also a limited amount of kiln space available to fire the pottery. A bowl takes up 1.5 times as much space as a jug and the total capacity of the oven is equal to 30 jugs or 20 bowls. Liza uses a special clay in order to give her pottery its distinctive feel. This clay is in much demand and Liza is only able to obtain a maximum of 84 lb per week. A jug requires 3.5 lb of the clay whereas a bowl requires 2.4 lb. At the present, Liza sells her bowls for £11.80 each and her jugs at £16 each. The clay costs equal £2 for each bowl and £3 for each jug. Her weekly fixed costs total £25.

(a) Calculate the number of bowls and jugs that Liza should manufacture and calculate the improvement in her profit. (If you use a graph as part of your solution, plot the number of *jugs* on the *vertical* axis.)

(b) Explain what is meant by the term 'dual price' (or shadow price) and indicate which of the three constraints in your solution has a zero dual price.

10.6 Susanna is in charge of a small chemical plant which uses two surplus by-products (code named A10 and B11) transported by pipeline from a large refinery. The daily supply of the two by-products is limited to 25 tonnes of A10 and 37.5 tonnes of B11, any surplus being collected by a local dealer. The dealer pays Susanna £90 per tonne for A10 and £70 per tonne for B11. The plant managed by Susanna converts the by-products into two new chemicals sold under the names of siroe and ezio. Both chemicals are in great demand and Susanna can sell as much as she produces. Given below are details of the two chemicals:

	Siroe	*Ezio*
Tonnes of A10 required for 1 tonne	1	3
Tonnes of B11 required for 1 tonne	3	1.5
Plant hours required for 1 tonne	1	1
Selling price of 1 tonne (£)	540	660

The plant is currently operated for 13 hours per day and the production costs for siroe and ezio are both £80 per hour. The plant has to be kept operational for the remaining 11 hours of each day at a cost of £20 per hour. The net costs of disposing of the waste products from the production process are included in the £80 per hour production cost figures.

(a) Calculate how many tonnes of siroe and ezio Susanna should produce in order to maximise the profits of the plant. Calculate the contribution that will result if your suggestion is followed.

(b) Calculate the dual prices of the resources used.

(c) Discuss the likely practical usefulness of the calculations undertaken in parts (a) and (b).

Further reading

Arnold, J., 'On the problem of interim pricing decisions', *Accounting and Business Research*, Spring 1973.

Dev, S., 'Linear programming dual prices in management accounting and their interpretation', *Accounting and Business Research*, Winter 1978.

Samuels, J. H., 'Opportunity costing: an application of mathematical programming', *Journal of Accounting Research*, Autumn 1965.

Chapter 11

Long-term decisions: the net present value rule

In previous chapters we have discussed the appropriateness of costs and benefits for particular short-term decisions. These decisions will, of necessity, entail the use of such assets as factories and plant and equipment, the purchase of which, at some earlier date, constituted a decision by the firm to commit resources for a long time period. Thus the ability of the firm to operate at different levels of activity is determined largely by the nature of the long-term (or fixed) assets at its disposal. For example, a firm cannot produce beyond a certain level unless it invests further funds in productive equipment; it may not be able to exploit new market opportunities if it fails to invest in new technology; it may fail to take advantage of prospective customers in the USA unless it contemplates the purchase of an American company. These types of long-term investments constitute the basis for the firm's future success, and must be evaluated in a way consistent with the firm's objectives. In this chapter and the next we look at different methods available to evaluate long-term investments in such a way.

Throughout this book we have assumed that the firm's strategy is to maximise the (present value of) cash flows from its operations. In practice firms seek to do this in a variety of different ways, by employing more specific and more operational strategic aims. For example, United Biscuits plc devotes two pages of its 1987 annual report to listing its corporate objectives and showing whether they have been met. The company's primary stated objective is 'providing shareholders with a good return on their money', and this is to be achieved by a variety of quantitative measures such as 'maintaining the quality of fixed assets by investing not less than 4p per £ sales annually' and 'achieving a minimum return of 20% and a target return of 25% on average capital employed'.

Other companies express their aims in less precise ways. Thus, for example, the chairman of ICI plc, Denys Henderson, notes in his statement supporting the 1987 annual report that part of ICI's strategy is represented by 'a shift towards higher added-value, science intensive, world competitive products'. This may seem a far cry from the production of basic commodity chemicals, with which ICI is more traditionally associated. The modern, competitive firm is continually on the lookout for opportunities which are consistent with its strategy, and the stage of evaluating the financial costs and benefits of opportunities which meet strategic objectives may in fact be of a relatively low level of importance in the investment decision process. Consider Figure 11.1, which offers a possible sequence of five stages in that process.

The process seeks to show that capital investment decision making is not an instantaneous process. Investments do not appear out of thin air. Thus at Stage 1, ICI's search for opportunities consistent with its high value-added strategy has led to major US purchases in both paints and agrochemicals. The chairman states that 'we are now the world's largest supplier of paints and specialised coatings ... and our agrochemicals ... now rate as number three in the world league'. We might note also that, in the same report, the chairman explains that 'as part of our re-shaping strategy we divested our commodity chemicals business in the USA'. But how do we know if the investment opportunities in Stage 1 should undergo rigorous evaluation techniques to determine their acceptability? Two intermediate steps are necessary. Before a major evaluation is undertaken, preliminary screening should try to iron out potential problems relating, *inter alia*, to the feasibility of the project, the level of risk involved and the availability of resources to carry out the project.

After the project has been filtered and deemed worthy of further investigation (i.e. it has passed Stage 2), it is likely that a more detailed specification will be made. This will entail an analysis of the project's technical and financial characteristics, and will probably necessitate engineering expertise. The nature and sophistication of this analysis will, to a large extent, depend on the type of project. Thus, for example,

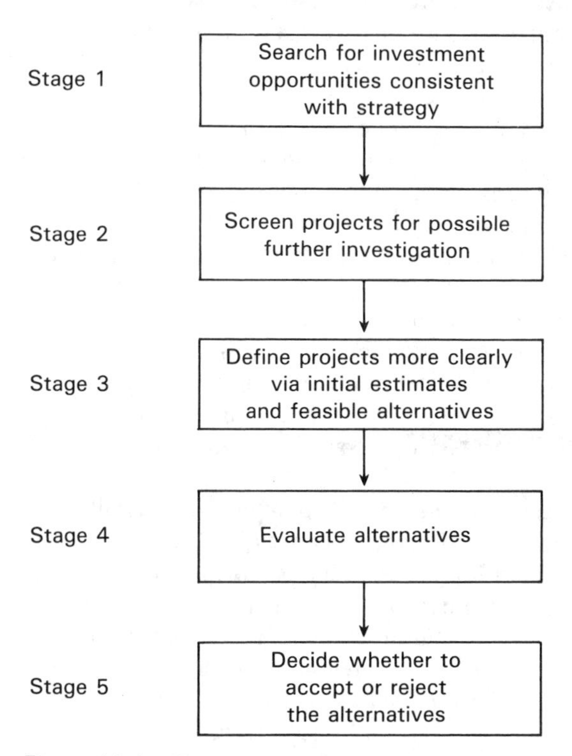

Figure 11.1 The investment decision process.

new strategic proposals may have ill-defined technical characteristics but may be thought necessary to keep the firm at the cutting edge of business (e.g. investments in advanced manufacturing systems); projects which simply replace labour with capital (e.g. the installation of robotic equipment) may be capable of well-defined specifications; replacement projects, which seek to replace existing assets with similar ones may also be easy to specify; welfare projects, such as the installation of air-conditioning to improve the immediate working environment, may be justified if they meet certain minimum cost requirements.

It is only after the investment has been found, screened and defined that the accountant's functional role becomes significant. It is at the evaluation stage that the accountant draws together the cash flow analysis relating to the costs and benefits of the project and seeks to determine its financial acceptability. Information relating to production, sales, purchasing and organisational costs and the effects of external factors on these, will probably be compiled by the accountant in discussion with those in charge of the functional areas to which the project relates. Thus quantification of the additional sales revenue generated by the project will reflect the judgements of both the sales director and the management accountant; production costs and capacity use will be determined by the production director and the accountant, and so on. If the financial analysis suggests the project is worthwhile, the decision at Stage 5 may well be acceptance of the investment.

Having set out the five stage process, we should stress here that the evaluation criteria for long-term investment decisions differ from those applicable to short-term decisions in only one important respect. When cash flows arise in different periods, it is necessary to incorporate into the analysis a means of taking account of the differences in their timing. The importance of the time value of money was explained in Chapter 3. The method of analysis to be used in this chapter is the net present value (NPV) method, the underlying rationale of which was also explained in Chapter 3. In essence, the difference between short- and long-term decisions is one of time; and the biggest technical problem in long-term decision making is how to deal with the time factor (including the impact of risk and uncertainty) in the analysis.

In other respects, the principles appropriate for both short- and long-term decisions are identical. Both are directed to the same overall goal (to maximise the present value of cash resources) and both use the differential future analysis principle for determining relevant cash flows (i.e. whatever the time period covered by the decision, only cash flows that change as a result of a decision are relevant to that decision).

Let us suppose that a firm is considering the possible purchase for £2 million of a new machine which is likely to enhance its operating capacity considerably. How should the firm decide whether purchase of the machine is worthwhile? The first thing to note is that although the uncertain benefits from the machine will arise in the future, the decision must be made now. Future benefits are always uncertain, because the future is always uncertain. (See Chapter 4 for a discussion of the problems of risk and uncertainty in decision making.) The decision involves a trade-off between the uncertain future returns and the certain present cost of £2 million. Management should use a method of analysis which deals with all costs and benefits of the decision in terms of the present, when the decision has to be taken. This complicates the analysis. Suppose management's best estimates of the quantifiable benefits (inflows less outflows) from the investment are £400,000 p.a. for ten years. Is purchase worthwhile? If we simply add up the ten annual money cash inflows, we can see readily that the total of £4 million is greater than the £2 million cost of the machine.

But such a simplistic approach completely ignores the point that future cash benefits are less attractive than present ones, because cash has a value dependent upon the time at which it arises. This time value arises from the existence of opportunities to lend and borrow at positive rates of interest. To incorporate the time value of money, we use a *discount factor*, based on the firm's relevant interest rate or *cost of capital*, to bring all future cash flows to the present decision date. How we might derive a cost of capital for the firm on which to base such a discount factor will be examined later in this chapter; for now we assume that the cost of capital is 10% p.a. How does this change the analysis? Will the purchase of the machine still be worthwhile? The annuity discount factor for ten years at 10% p.a. is 6.145;[31] thus the discounted present value of the yearly future cash flows is £400,000 × 6.145 = £2.458 million, which is greater than the investment cost of £2 million. Purchase of the machine is worthwhile. The machine has a positive NPV (the difference between the discounted future net cash inflows and the investment cost) of £458,000. Although purchase is worthwhile, the net benefit of £458,000 is considerably smaller than the gain of £2 million calculated from undiscounted cash flows.

Note that the application of the NPV method yields a *cash* figure, the maximisation of which is consistent with the organisation's assumed overall objective. In the absence of scarce resources, an organisation should accept all opportunities with positive net present values and reject those with negative net present values. We can summarise the NPV decision criterion as involving the following three basic steps:

1. Estimate the date and amount of the relevant future cash inflows and outflows (including the investment cost) arising from each decision alternative.
2. Discount these cash flows at an appropriate discount rate.
3. Decide whether the alternative(s) is acceptable, by use of the NPV rule.

We now turn to a consideration of each of these three basic steps.

11.1 Estimation of cash flows

Cash flows and accounting profits

All cash inflows and outflows which change because of the undertaking of a project are relevant to the project, and should be discounted to determine its present value.

[31] See the appendix to Chapter 3 for an explanation of compounding and discounting factors.

Table 11.1 Income statements using straight line depreciation

	Year 1 (£)	Year 2 (£)	Year 3 (£)
Net cash inflows	8,000	8,000	8,000
Less Depreciation $\frac{£15{,}000}{3}$	5,000	5,000	5,000
Net income	3,000	3,000	3,000

Strictly this means that not only should all relevant operating cash revenues and costs be included, but also any changes in taxation payments and investment grants which arise through undertaking the project.

It is very important to remember that all relevant cash flows should be included in a project assessment, on the date at which they *arise*, irrespective of the period to which they *relate*. For example, suppose that a firm buys an asset for £15,000 which will produce additional net cash inflows of £8,000 p.a. for three years. After three years the asset will be worthless. For purposes of external reporting the firm uses straight line depreciation for all its assets.[32] We might draw up yearly income statements for the asset as in Table 11.1, based on conventional accounting procedures for measuring income (we assume that all net cash inflows will be included in income in the year in which they are received).

The purpose of the depreciation charge in conventional accounting is to spread the cost of the asset, £15,000, over its estimated three year life. It allocates the cost against the revenue to which it relates, in order to produce a yearly income figure. Other possible depreciation methods could involve different patterns of charges to the income statement and hence different yearly income figures. If for example, the firm uses the sum-of-the-years'-digits method,[33] the yearly income statement shown in Table 11.2 would result for the same asset.

Table 11.2 Income statements using sum-of-the-years'-digits depreciation

	Year 1 (£)	Year 2 (£)	Year 3 (£)
Net cash inflows	8,000	8,000	8,000
Less Depreciation	7,500	5,000	2,500
Net income	500	3,000	5,500

[32] That is, the cost of an asset is written off against income in equal parts for each year of its life.

[33] Using the sum-of-the-year'-digits method of depreciation, the cost of the asset is spread between accounting periods in the ratio $n:n-1:n-2\ldots\ldots:1$, where n is the original life expectancy of the asset. So for an asset with an expected life of three years, the ratio is 3:2:1, i.e. 1/2 in the first year, 1/3 in the second year and 1/6 in the third year.

The point of these two examples is very simple. Irrespective of the accounting depreciation method used, and the accounting income reported, the estimated cash inflow arising from the asset will be £8,000 p.a., and the estimated cash outflow will be £15,000, the purchase price of the asset. These are the only cash flows associated with the machine, and the only amounts to be included in the NPV calculation for managerial decision purposes. The allocation of the investment cost of £15,000 may be necessary to measure accounting income for external reporting purposes: as we explained in Chapter 5, it is not necessary, and indeed it may be misleading, to include a non-cash allocation such as depreciation in internal decision making calculations. Managerial decision analysis makes no distinction between capital and income items. The purpose of managerial decision making is to maximise the present value of future cash flows, not allocated accounting profits.

The range of possible cash flows

Because many of the cash flows associated with long-term investment decisions arise far into the future, the prediction of their exact amount is often very difficult. The use of single-point estimates of future cash flows is unlikely to be an adequate means of describing their uncertainty. We might more usefully attempt to incorporate elementary probability theory into our analysis, so as to produce expected cash flows. The following example explains how we might do this. (Chapter 4 deals in some detail with expected values.)

Griffin plc is contemplating an investment project, the cash flows from which are uncertain. On the basis of management's expectations, a range of probable cash flows has been drawn up. This suggests that there is a 20% probability of a yearly net cash inflow of £7,000, a 50% probability of £8,000 p.a., and a 30% probability of £10,000 p.a. What is the expected yearly future cash flow for Griffin plc?

Possible cash flows p.a. (£)	*Probability of occurrence*
7,000	0.20
8,000	0.50
10,000	0.30
	1.00

The expected yearly cash inflow is the sum of each possible cash flow, multiplied by the probability of its occurrence. Thus, the expected cash flow is 7,000 (0.20) + 8,000 (0.50) + 10,000 (0.30) = £8,400.

The percentage figures used to assess the probability of the cash flows may be based on past experience of similar projects. Alternatively, if no similar investment has been undertaken previously, as will inevitably be the case with investments at the leading edge of technology, the estimates will be 'best guesses' which incorporate all the available evidence on factors which determine cash flows, e.g. the anticipated level of demand for the product being sold and the likely changes in the firm's levels of costs associated with the investment.

The impact of working capital

The decision to undertake a long-term investment will frequently involve necessary outlays on current assets (e.g. stocks and amounts owing by customers) and current liabilities (e.g. amounts owing to suppliers) in order to support the higher level of activity brought about by the new investment. For example, additional cash may be needed to fund the higher levels of raw materials, finished goods and amounts owing by customers resulting from new activity levels: in turn, some of the finance may be provided by suppliers. If these items of current assets and liabilities (which make up the additional *working capital* required) are needed for the entire life of the investment, then the working capital will not be released until the project is finished, and calculations of the acceptability of the investment must incorporate the cash flows associated with changes in working capital.

11.2 The cost of capital

Use of the NPV method entails the determination of an appropriate interest rate of discount rate to discount future cash flows to their equivalent present value. This discount rate is usually referred to as a *cost of capital*; this is a simple concept to understand, but notoriously hard to measure. Indeed there are many conflicting views on just how the cost of capital should be computed.

Our view is that the cost of capital should measure the minimum return required by providers of long-term funds. Most firms raise their long-term funds from two main sources, *equity capital* and *debt capital*. Equity capital represents the funds provided by the owners of the firm. Payments made to the owners of equity capital (called *dividends*) vary, amongst other things, according to how well the firm is doing. No dividends can be paid to equity holders until the firm has met its obligations to the providers of debt capital, although there is then no limit on the amounts which can be paid, subject to the firm having sufficient income and cash resources from which to make the payment. The equity capital itself is rarely repaid until the firm is liquidated.

The returns paid to debt holders (called *interest*), on the other hand, are usually fixed by contract, and must be paid regardless of the size of the firm's income or cash resources. Furthermore, much debt capital is *redeemable*, i.e. a date (or dates) is specified by which the capital must be repaid. If no provision is made for repayment, the debt is termed *irredeemable*. Failure to pay interest or repay capital on the due dates often results in control of the firm being passed to the debt holders.

As debt capital and equity capital carry different levels of risk relating both to interest and dividend payments and to capital repayment, they often have different costs. In other words, the holders of debt capital generally require a lower return than do the holders of equity capital, because the interest paid to them and the repayment of their capital both take preference over payments to the owners of equity capital. Thus to calculate a cost of capital which incorporates both the cost of equity capital and the cost of debt capital, it is necessary first to calculate the individual costs of the different sources, and second to combine them into a weighted average cost of capital. We deal with each stage in turn.

Cost of equity capital

There is a variety of models available for calculating the cost of equity capital – the minimum return required by shareholders. We will discuss the two most widely advocated models, the dividend growth model and the capital asset pricing model (CAPM).

The dividend growth model

Under this model the cost of equity capital is derived from the basic valuation model which we first introduced in Chapter 3. This model defines the value of equity capital as the present value of the future dividend stream. It can be expressed as:

$$V_E = \frac{d_1}{(1 + K_E)} + \frac{d_2}{(1 + K_E)^2} + \frac{d_3}{(1 + K_E)^3} + \cdots + \frac{d_n}{(1 + K_E)^n}$$

where V_E is the present value of equity capital, *ex div* (i.e. just after a dividend has been paid); d_1 is the dividend to be paid after one year, d_2 is the dividend to be paid after two years, and so on; K_E is the cost of equity capital or the minimum annual return required by the providers of equity capital and n is the last time at which a dividend will be paid. If the dividend stream is expected to be constant throughout all future periods, then, as n (the time period) approaches infinity, the valuation model may be simplified to a perpetuity, i.e.:

$$V_E = \frac{d}{K_E}$$

Rearranging to derive the cost of equity gives:

$$K_E = \frac{d}{V_E}$$

Suppose the market value of equity is £200,000, and the firm intends to pay dividends of £20,000 p.a. indefinitely. What is the cost of equity capital?

$$K_E = \frac{d}{V_E} = \frac{£20{,}000}{£200{,}000} = 0.1 \text{ or } 10\%$$

If dividends are expected to grow at a constant per annum rate (g) over future periods, the basic valuation model becomes:

$$V_E = \frac{d_0(1 + g)}{(1 + K_E)} + \frac{d_0(1 + g)^2}{(1 + K_E)^2} + \cdots + \frac{d_0(1 + g)^n}{(1 + K_E)^n}$$

As n approaches infinity the valuation model can be simplified to:

$$V_E = \frac{d_0(1 + g)}{K_E - g} = \frac{d_1}{K_E - g}$$

Rearranging to derive the cost of equity gives:

$$K_E = \frac{d_1}{V_E} + g$$

Suppose the market value of equity is £420,000, the dividend just paid is £20,000 and the expected future growth rate is 5% p.a. What is the cost of equity capital?

$$K_E = \frac{d_1}{V_E} + g = \frac{£20{,}000(1.05)}{£420{,}000} + 0.05$$

$$= 0.1 \text{ or } 10\%$$

Capital Asset Pricing Model

Under the CAPM the approach to the cost of equity capital is very different. Here the cost of equity capital is calculated by reference to the return required in a single period by the company's investors. This return comprises two elements – an element which is risk free and thus represents a fixed minimum level of return, and an element (or premium) which depends on the relative risk associated with the performance of the company's shares. This split of return into a riskless and risky element is a very useful way of understanding why different investments offer different returns. The greater the level of risk, the higher the promised return. In principle it is not difficult to calculate these two parts of the shareholder's return. The risk-free rate can be defined as the current return from long-term government securities (e.g. the return on Treasury Bills). This return is risk free in the sense that it is most unlikely that the government will default on its borrowing commitments. The relative risk of the company's shares is determined by relating two factors:

(i) the average return available from all listed shares (i.e. from the market portfolio); and
(ii) the relative risk of the company's shares compared to the average for all listed shares.

The CAPM formula which is used to derive the cost of equity by incorporating the above data is as follows:

$$K_E = r_f + (r_m - r_f)\beta$$

where K_E is the cost of equity capital, r_f is the return on a risk-free security (e.g. on Treasury Bills), r_m is the return on the market portfolio (e.g. the return on the *Financial Times* All Share Index); and β is the variability of the company's return in relation to that of the market portfolio.

Let us see how it works. Suppose the current return on Treasury Bills is 10%, the return on the *FT* All Share Index is 19% and the variability of the company's return, as determined by a series of past observations, is 80% or 0.8 that of the market (i.e. if the *FT* All Share Index were to increase by 10%, this particular company's return would increase by 8%). We can calculate the cost of equity capital for the company – the minimum return required by shareholders – as follows:

$$K_E = r_f + (r_m - r_f)\beta$$
$$= 0.10 + (0.19 - 0.10)\ 0.8$$
$$= 0.10 + (0.9)\ 0.8 = 0.172 \text{ or } 17.2\%$$

It can be shown that, if the capital market is in equilibrium, these two models should give similar results, though some slight differences may occur because of their respective time horizons – i.e., the CAPM is a single-period model, whereas the dividend valuation model covers periods longer than one year.

The following example shows in more detail how different costs of equity capital can be calculated for the same company.

Ayrsome plc is an all-equity financed company whose shares are listed on the London Stock Exchange. It has paid dividends per share over the past five years of 7.5p, 8.3p, 8.7p, 10.4p and 12p. Its current market price per share is £2.40. The company's financial analyst has collected data on the returns on Ayrsome plc's shares and those on the *FT* All Share Index over the past five years and has estimated the company's beta factor as 0.7. The analyst has also estimated the average return on the All Share index to be 15% and the return on Treasury Bills to be 8%.

With the above information we can calculate Ayrsome plc's cost of equity capital under each of the two methods as follows:

1. *Dividend growth model*

$$K_E = \frac{d_1}{V_E} + g$$

$$d_1 = 12\text{p}(1 + g), \text{ where } g \text{ (see below) is } 12.5\%$$
$$= 12\text{p}(1.125)$$

$$V_E = £2.40$$

$$g = \sqrt[4]{12/7.5} = 12.5\%$$

$$K_E = \frac{12(1.125)}{240} + 0.125 = 0.181 \text{ or } 18.1\%$$

2. *CAPM*

$$K_E = r_f + (r_m - r_f)\beta$$
$$= 8 + (15 - 8)\ 0.7 = 12.9\%$$

What meaning can we derive from these very different estimates? We might begin by stressing the inherent differences between the two models.

The CAPM is a single-period model and therefore the rate obtained is the return expected over the next time period. The K_E estimated using the dividend growth model is the average return in perpetuity. It should also be remembered that strictly both models depend on the existence of a perfect capital market. Where market imperfections exist it cannot be assumed that they will affect both models equally or in the same way. It is possible that some of the difference observed is due to the effect of such imperfections.

In addition, the difference in the observed results may be caused by defects in one or both of the models and/or errors in their application. A major reservation with respect to the growth model is its very assumption of constant dividend growth. While there is some evidence to show that firms attempt to pursue stable dividend policies, such an assumption inevitably represents a weakness in the model. There are further problems in estimating the values of the variables included in the calculation of K_E. The greatest difficulties are associated with determining the dividend growth rate. Past growth patterns may be an indicator of future growth but they must be interpreted with care. The data given in the question are typical. Although average growth over the period has been 12.5%, this has not occurred in any year. Actual growth rates over the four year period have been 10%, 5%, 20% and 15%.

The major reservation in principle with the CAPM is the assumption that required returns are entirely determined by the company's beta factor. One way of regarding the beta factor is as a reward for the risk which is determined by the movement of the company's share price with the movement of the market index – i.e. as a reward for the risk which cannot be diversified away. This is consistent with the assumption of a perfect capital market in which rational and risk-averse investors will not hold risk that can be diversified away. However, if the capital market is imperfect it is possible that share prices may be influenced by more than undiversifiable risk. Other assumptions underlying the CAPM may give rise to further reservations about the results. In particular the CAPM assumes that shares are completely characterised by information about their expected single-period return and the standard deviation of possible returns about the expected return. In other words, information about return and standard deviations is all that is required by the market in arriving at a share price. If, in practice, other factors influence share prices then the results from the CAPM may be suspect.

Further, the estimate of beta is based on historic data. For decision making purposes beta values should be based on *what is going to happen*, not what has happened.

One further consideration must be borne in mind in comparing the results. The CAPM return of 12.9% is calculated without direct reference to the current market value of the ordinary shares in Ayrsome plc. In the dividend growth model the share price, V_E, should be the equilibrium value. If the current value is not in equilibrium this could explain the difference between the two results. If the CAPM result is 'correct', Ayrsome is currently undervalued and would be a good investment.

Cost of debt capital

The cost of debt capital is easier to determine than the cost of equity because the annual interest payments and the final capital repayment (if any) are fixed by the terms of the contract. The cost of debt, K_D, can be determined from the following valuation expression:

$$V_D = \frac{C}{(1 + K_D)} + \frac{C}{(1 + K_D)^2} + \cdots + \frac{C + R}{(1 + K_D)^n}$$

where V_D is the current market value of debt, *ex interest* (i.e. just after an annual interest payment has been made); C is the annual interest payment; R is the capital amount payable on redemption at time n; and n is the number of years to redemption.

If the debt capital is irredeemable, the redemption payment is zero and n approaches infinity. The valuation expression simplifies to:

$$V_D = \frac{C}{K_D}$$

Rearranging gives the formula for the cost of irredeemable debt capital:

$$K_D = \frac{C}{V_D}$$

Suppose that a firm has issued £500,000 of 8% irredeemable debt capital, which now has a market value of £440,000. The next annual interest payment of £40,000 (8% of £500,000) is due shortly. In order to estimate the cost of the debt capital it is first necessary to calculate its *ex interest* value by subtracting the current interest payment due from the current market value. This gives an estimate of what the value will be just after the interest has been paid and complies with the *ex interest* assumption in the valuation expression. The revised value may then be included in the cost of capital formula:

$$K_D = \frac{£40,000}{£(440,000 - 40,000)} = 0.1 \text{ or } 10\%$$

If debt capital is redeemable, no simple rearrangement of the valuation expression is possible and the cost of debt must be found by trial and error. A simple computer program will usually complete the calculation very quickly. The valuation expression may be rewritten using the symbols $A_{\overline{n}|}$ and $V_{\overline{n}|}$, introduced and explained in the appendix to Chapter 3:

$$V_D = C \times A_{\overline{n}|} K_D + R \times V_{\overline{n}|} K_D$$

In words, the *ex interest* value of redeemable debt is equal to the present value of the annual interest payments (the present value of an annuity of £C per annum for n years) plus the present value of the redemption payment, £R.

Suppose that a firm has issued £1 million of 7% debt, redeemable in 20 years at £102%, i.e. each £100 of debt will be redeemed for £102. The current market value of the debt, *ex interest*, is £50%. What is the cost of the debt capital? The current total market value of the debt is £500,000 (£50 multiplied by 10,000 units of £100 each). Annual interest payments are £70,000 (7% of £1 million) and the redemption payment is £1.02 million (£102 multiplied by 10,000 units of £100 each). Substituting these numbers in the simplified valuation expression gives:

$$£500,000 = £70,000 \times A_{\overline{20}|} K_D + £1,020,000 \times V_{\overline{20}|} K_D$$

We must find the value for K_D which sets the right-hand side of this equation equal to £500,000 (the current value of the debt).

At 15%: $(£70,000 \times 6.2593) + (£1,020,000 \times 0.0611) = £500,473$

At 16%: $(£70,000 \times 5.9288) + (£1,020,000 \times 0.0514) = £467,444$

The cost of redeemable debt capital is just over 15%. If a more accurate indication than this is required we may use a procedure known as *linear interpolation* to estimate where the cost lies between 15% and 16%. This procedure is explained in the next chapter (p. 255).

The weighted average cost of capital

Having computed the costs of the specific sources of capital, it is then necessary to weight the costs according to the market values of the sources of capital. Market values and not book values should be used because they are both current and observable. Furthermore they measure the amount sacrificed by investors in a company as a result of their continuing to own equity or debt which could otherwise be sold at its market value. In other words, they indicate the opportunity cost to investors of being investors in that particular company. The need to use a weighting arises because the aim of the cost of capital calculation is to offer a minimum acceptable return for *all* projects undertaken by the firm. If projects were expected to earn returns which corresponded to the cost of *individual* sources of capital, for example if each project was financed by a specific loan taken out for that purpose, a firm might increase its cheapest source of capital, debt capital, to unreasonable levels. This would ultimately imperil the position of equity shareholders (as interest payments would bite more deeply into the profits available for dividends) who would increase the return they required from their investment to compensate for their additional risk. This could mean that a firm's overall cost of capital would increase, or at least would not decrease, if it issued substantial amounts of apparently cheap debt. Also, any attempt to match the uses and sources of long-term funds would result in different discount rates for projects which may otherwise be identical.

The weighted average cost of capital (WACC) can be derived by substituting the values for K_E (cost of equity) and K_D (cost of debt) into the following formula:

$$\text{WACC} = \left[K_E \times \frac{V_E}{V_T}\right] + \left[K_D \times \frac{V_D}{V_T}\right]$$

where V_E is the total market value of equity; V_D is the total market value of debt, and V_T is the total market value of debt and equity.

We are now in a position to show how we might compute the weighted average cost of capital for a firm. We will use the following data for Portman plc for the purpose.

Portman plc has a capital structure as follows:

3 million ordinary (equity) shares of £1 each (£)	3,000,000
7% debt (redeemable at par in seven years' time) (£)	1,300,000

The ordinary shares have a current market value of £3 each *ex div*; an annual dividend of £900,000 has just been paid. Dividends have grown steadily at 6% p.a. over past years, and are expected to grow at the same rate in future years. The debt has a current market value of £77.177% *ex interest*.

Using the formulae for each specific source of capital, Portman plc's weighted average cost of capital is as follows:

1. *Cost of equity* (using the dividend growth model):

$$K_E = \frac{d_1}{V_E} + g = \frac{£900{,}000(1.06)}{3{,}000{,}000 \times £3} + 0.06$$

$$K_E = 0.106 + 0.06 = 0.166 \text{ or } 16.6\%$$

2. *Cost of debt*

$$V_D = \frac{C}{(1+K_D)} + \frac{C}{(1+K_D)^2} + \cdots + \frac{C+R}{(1+K_D)^n}$$

$$1{,}300{,}000\ (0.77177) = 91{,}000 \times A_{\overline{7}|}K_D + 1{,}300{,}000 \times V_{\overline{7}|}K_D$$

$$\text{at } 12\%\ V_D = 91{,}000\ (4.5638) + 1{,}300{,}000\ (0.4523) = £1{,}003{,}300$$

$$= £1{,}300{,}000\ (0.77177)$$

$$\therefore K_D = 12\%$$

3. *Weighted average cost of capital*

Total market value of equity (£)	9,000,000
Total market value of debt (£)	1,003,300
Total market value of Portman plc (£)	10,003,300

$$\therefore \text{WACC} = 16.6\% \times \frac{9{,}000{,}000}{10{,}003{,}000} + 12\% \times \frac{1{,}003{,}300}{10{,}003{,}300} = 16.14\%$$

The illustration shows that the minimum rate to be used by Portman plc in project appraisal is 16.14%. A word of caution: note that such a rate will be applicable to all projects only if all projects are subject to the same degree of risk. If different projects attract different levels of risk, more sophisticated treatment may be necessary. One possibility is to use portfolio analysis, which was introduced and explained in Chapter 4.

11.3 The net present value decision rule

Having determined the relevant future cash flows, and derived a weighted average cost of capital, the firm is now in a position to decide whether the project should be undertaken, based on a calculation of its net present value. The following example shows how such a decision might be reached.

Layer Ltd is considering the introduction of a new product to add to its present range. A feasibility study costing £7,000 has been carried out. This suggests that a selling price of £5 per unit should be set, at which price demand is expected to be 50,000 units p.a. Manufacture requires a new machine costing £200,000, which will be worthless when demand for the product ceases in four years' time. Variable costs of producing the new product are estimated at £3 per unit; additional overheads will be £25,000 p.a. if manufacture takes place. The directors estimate that Layer Ltd's cost of capital is 10% p.a.

If we assume that all cash inflows and outflows will arise on the final day of each year, with the exception of the cost of the machine which will be payable at the start of the first year, we can prepare a schedule to determine the worthwhileness of the proposed investment, as in Table 11.3. The investment shows a discounted NPV of + £37,750 and thus is acceptable. Note that the cost of the feasibility study of £7,000 is ignored in the calculations as it has already been incurred.

However, because the estimated cash flows arise over a future period of four

Table 11.3 Schedule of future cash flows

	£
Net cash inflows:	
Annual contribution £(5 – 3) × 50,000	= 100,000
Less Annual fixed costs	25,000
	75,000
Present value of annual cash inflows:	
£75,000 × $A_{\overline{4}|}$ 10%	
= £75,000 × 3.17	237,750
Net present value of investment:	
Present value of cash flows	237,750
Less Cost of machine	200,000
Net present value	37,750

years, the directors may wish to know how 'wrong' they can be in their estimates of each of the variables before NPV becomes negative and the project unacceptable. This is obviously important as it may reveal which variables are most critical to the success of the project.

11.4 Sensitivity analysis

A useful technique for determining how sensitive the NPV is to errors in estimation is known as *sensitivity analysis*. This involves calculating the expected NPV (or contribution or other measure of worthwhileness) from a project on the basis of most likely outcomes and subsequently investigating the implications of various deviations of actual outcomes from forecast. For example, the value that a particular variable will take if the NPV expected from the project is to be reduced to zero may be ascertained and the difference in value expressed as a percentage of its most likely value. This provides an indication of the sensitivity of the project's expected NPV to changes in the value of individual variables and points to those estimates in which a small deviation may be critical for the success or failure of the project. These estimates should be examined most carefully before a decision is made on the project. The increased availability of sophisticated inexpensive computers has made this method generally practicable.

We shall illustrate the usefulness of sensitivity analysis by examining in turn the sensitivity of Layer Ltd's new project's NPV of £37,750 to errors in estimating some of the variables which contribute to the NPV – selling price, annual volume of sales, variable cost per unit, annual fixed costs and the life of the product.

For each of these components of the NPV figure we shall calculate the percentage change in its value which can occur before the NPV becomes zero. This is known as the *sensitivity margin* (SM). First, in order to provide a basis for assessing the various sensitivity margins, it is helpful to calculate the break-even annual net cash flow and the break-even annual contribution:

$$\text{Break-even annual net cash flow} = \frac{\text{investment cost}}{\text{discount factor}} = \frac{\pounds 200{,}000}{3.17} = \pounds 63{,}091$$

$$\begin{aligned}\text{Break-even annual contribution} &= \text{break-even annual net cash flows} \\ &\quad + \text{annual fixed costs} \\ &= \pounds 63{,}091 + \pounds 25{,}000 \\ &= \pounds 88{,}091\end{aligned}$$

We can now calculate the various sensitivity margins:

1. *Selling price*

   Break-even selling price = x, where

   $$\pounds(x - 3) \times 50{,}000 = \pounds 88{,}091$$
   $$\therefore\ x = 4.76$$

   The selling price can fall from £5 to £4.76 and the product will still break even. This reveals a sensitivity margin (SM) of

   $$\frac{\pounds(5 - 4.76)}{\pounds 5} = 0.048 \text{ or } 4.8\%$$

2. *Annual volume of sales*

   Break-even annual volume = x, where

   $$\pounds(5 - 3) \times x = \pounds 88{,}091$$
   $$\therefore\ x = 44{,}045$$

   The annual sales volume can drop by 5,955 units (i.e. from 50,000 to 44,045), and the product will still break even. Thus the SM is

   $$\frac{50{,}000 - 44{,}045}{50{,}000} = 0.119 \text{ or } 11.9\%$$

3. *Variable cost per unit*

   Break-even variable cost = x, where

   $$\pounds(5 - x) \times 50{,}000 = \pounds 88{,}091$$
   $$\therefore\ x = \pounds 3.24$$

   Variable cost per unit can increase from £3 to £3.24. The SM for variable cost per unit is

   $$\frac{\pounds(3.24 - 3)}{\pounds 3} = 0.08 \text{ or } 8\%$$

4. *Annual fixed costs*
   Fixed costs can rise by £(75,000 − 63,091) = £11,909 before NPV = 0. The SM

for annual fixed costs is therefore

$$\frac{£11,909}{£25,000} = 0.476 \text{ or } 47.6\%$$

5. *Product life*
The NPV for the current four year life is £37,750. Suppose only a three year life was anticipated. In that case NPV would be $-200,000 + 75,000A_{\overline{3}|}$ $10\% = -£13,250$ (where $A_{\overline{3}|}$ $10\% = 2.49$). The break-even product life is somewhere between three and four years. If NPV changes linearly with product life we may estimate the break-even life as follows. The increase in NPV as product life increases one year, from three to four years, is £51,000 (from $-£13,250$ to $+£37,750$). Thus the increase in product life above three years necessary to give an NPV of zero is 13,250/51,000 of one year. The break-even life is $3 + (13,250/51,000) = 3.26$ years. The SM is $(4 - 3.26)/4 = 0.185 = 18.5\%$.

What conclusions can we draw from the sensitivity analysis applied to the new product? We can say initially that the NPV is most sensitive (the lowest percentage SM) to errors in the estimation of selling price, where only a 4.8% error is needed to eliminate the positive NPV. The margins of error on variable cost per unit (8%) and annual sales volume (11.9%) are also critical and particular attention should be directed to these estimates. Note that the estimate of annual fixed costs is not particularly critical – in fact it may be increased by as much as 47% before the project becomes unacceptable.

There are, however, certain factors which should be considered when interpreting the results of sensitivity analysis, and indeed of net present value calculations in general. First, the final investment decision must depend ultimately upon the particular risk of the project and the firm's attitude to it. Second, sensitivity analysis ignores the possibility of combination errors which could arise because two or more components of the overall calculation are interdependent. For example, the sensitivity margins on sales volume and selling price should not be viewed in isolation from each other, as it is likely that they are connected closely (see Chapter 8). Third, different acceptable safety margins may be applicable to each component, depending upon the decision maker's confidence in the various estimates. For example of 2% safety margin on a rent payment which is fixed by contract may be more acceptable to a firm than a 20% margin on the costs of raw materials which are purchased in extremely volatile markets. In summary, we might say that sensitivity analysis is intended as an aid in investment decisions, not as a definitive answer to the problem of risk and uncertainty.

11.5 The problem of scarce capital

One problem that frequently arises in practice is concerned with the acceptance of long-term investments when the amount of available capital is rationed. Capital rationing can be said to occur when a company has more projects showing a positive net present value when discounted at the prevailing cost of capital than can be financed from available funds.

It is, however, important to distinguish between two different types of capital rationing, sometimes termed 'hard' and 'soft' rationing. The distinction between the two is determined by the cause of the rationing (i.e. by what is meant by 'availability of funds'). Thus if the company wishes to impose its own constraints on the level of capital expenditure, the situation is one of soft rationing. However when the constraint is imposed externally by the capital markets, hard rationing is taking place. In this situation the company cannot raise the necessary additional finance for acceptable projects at any price.

Why might a company choose to impose internal rationing? It may seem irrational not to accept projects with positive net present values when discounted at the cost of capital. But such seeming irrationality may be necessary to comply with the company's objectives. Perhaps the owners are quite happy with their existing returns and have little desire to expand via new capital investments; perhaps funds are available but managerial ability to manage the new investments is not; perhaps also the reluctance to raise external funds for 'good' projects may be due to the fear of loss of control over the running of the company. There is much evidence that companies do impose internal restrictions on their capital budgets, and thus there is a necessity to understand how the choice of investments might be made in such circumstances.

Whether hard rationing really exists is a more debatable issue. It has been argued that hard rationing is no more than a temporary imperfection in the market for funds, and is due to lack of information on the part of those seeking finance – in other words, any company which puts enough effort into looking for finance, and is prepared to pay the prevailing rates, will find a supplier. The contrary view is that, for small expanding companies at least, access to finance for investment is difficult because of gaps in the institutional framework of the provision of funds. This very issue was addressed in some detail by the Wilson Committee in its 1980 *Report to Review the Functioning of Financial Institutions*. The Committee found that although an 'equity gap' could be identified for smaller growing firms, there was in general little evidence of a shortage of finance for industry at prevailing rates of interest and levels of demand. A recent study by Pike (1982) bears out these findings. In examining constraints on 126 companies' investment programmes, Pike observed the following as being the most significant:

	%
Lack of profitable investment opportunities	19.8
General economic uncertainty	18.7
Unwillingness to increase level of borrowings	19.0
Lack of capital available	8.7
Lack of trained managers to implement investment opportunities	7.4

Source: R. H. Pike, *Capital Budgeting in the 1980s*, CIMA, 1982.

Table 11.4 Expected cash flows from projects

Project	*Cash flows*			
	19X0 (£)	*19X1* (£)	*19X2* (£)	*19X3* (£)
A	– 60,000	+ 30,000	+ 25,000	+ 25,000
B	– 30,000	– 20,000	+ 25,000	+ 45,000
C	– 40,000	– 50,000	+ 60,000	+ 70,000
D	0	– 80,000	+ 45,000	+ 55,000
E	– 50,000	+ 10,000	+ 30,000	+ 40,000

For our purposes the question is how the NPV criterion should be modified to incorporate this scarcity of capital, be it hard or soft. The following illustration considers the problem.

Sincil Ltd is considering its capital expenditure programme for 19X0 and 19X1. The company's directors have reduced their initial list of projects to five, the expected cash flows of which are set out in Table 11.4.

None of the five projects can be delayed. All are divisible (i.e. cash outlays may be reduced by any proportion and inflows will then be reduced in the same proportion). All cash flows arise on the first day of the year. The minimum return required by shareholders of Sincil Ltd is 15% p.a. Which projects should Sincil Ltd accept if the capital available for investment is limited to £100,000 on 1 January 19X0 but readily available at 15% p.a. on 1st January 19X1 and subsequently?

The problem may be solved in two steps: first, we calculate the NPV of each project, and secondly, we use these NPVs to determine the allocation of the £100,000 investment capital.

Step 1 – calculation of NPV

$$\text{A} \quad -60{,}000 + 30{,}000\,(0.87) + 25{,}000\,(0.76) + 25{,}000\,(0.66) = +1{,}600$$

$$\text{B} \quad -30{,}000 - 20{,}000\,(0.87) + 25{,}000\,(0.76) + 45{,}000\,(0.66) = +1{,}300$$

$$\text{C} \quad -40{,}000 - 50{,}000\,(0.87) + 60{,}000\,(0.76) + 70{,}000\,(0.66) = +8{,}300$$

$$\text{D} \quad 0 - 80{,}000\,(0.87) + 45{,}000\,(0.76) + 55{,}000\,(0.66) = +\ 900$$

$$\text{E} \quad -50{,}000 + 10{,}000\,(0.87) + 30{,}000\,(0.76) + 40{,}000\,(0.66) = +7{,}900$$

All five projects show positive NPVs and, under conditions of no capital rationing, all would be accepted. However, by totalling the cash required at 19X0, we can see that Sincil Ltd needs £180,000 capital at 1st January 19X0 to undertake all five projects. Only £100,000 is available and no project can be delayed. How should Sincil Ltd allocate the £100,000 capital? Project D may be accepted as it has a positive NPV and requires none of the scarce capital. The remaining four projects should be ranked on the basis of the NPV they produce per £ of investment required at the date on which capital is rationed, i.e. on 1 January 19X0. The procedure is analogous to that described in Chapter 9 for allocating a single scarce resource. The aim is to apply available capital to those projects which use it most efficiently, i.e. that produce the highest NPV for each £ of scarce capital they require.

Step 2 – ranking on the basis of NPV per £ of investment cost

Project	*NPV per £ of outlay on 1 January 19X0*	*Ranking*	*Fraction accepted*	*Capital needed on 1 January 19X0* (£)
A	$\frac{1,600}{60,000} = 0.027$	4	0	0
B	$\frac{1,300}{30,000} = 0.043$	3	$\frac{1}{3}$	10,000
C	$\frac{8,300}{40,000} = 0.207$	1	1	40,000
E	$\frac{7,900}{50,000} = 0.158$	2	1	50,000
		Total available capital		100,000

The application of the ranking per £1 of investment outlay thus gives us a criterion for choice in situations of scarcity. Sincil Ltd should accept projects D, C and E completely, and one third (presuming projects are divisible) of project B. Project A should be rejected, even though it shows a positive NPV; more efficient uses are available for the capital which would be required to undertake it.

This method of allocating scarce capital is valid only if no other resources needed by the firm, including capital at any time other than 1st January 19X0, are scarce. Otherwise it is necessary to use mathematical programming methods to deal with problems of scarcity, similar to the linear programming method discussed in Chapter 9. The following example of Valley Ltd shows how this might be done.

Valley Ltd is a private limited company which is financed entirely by ordinary shares. Its effective cost of capital, net of tax, is 10% per annum. The directors of Valley Ltd are considering the company's capital investment programme for the next two years, and have reduced their initial list of projects to four. Details of the projects are set out in Table 11.5.

None of the projects can be delayed and all projects are divisible. No project can be undertaken more than once. Valley Ltd is able to invest surplus funds in a bank deposit account yielding a return of 7% per annum, net of tax.

Which projects should Valley Ltd accept if capital available immediately is limited to £500,000, capital available after one year is limited to £300,000 and capital is available thereafter without limit at a cost of 10% per annum?

We can now draw up a mathematical programming formulation to help the directors choose projects on the basis of capital scarcity at different points in time.

Table 11.5 Cash flows (net of tax) and NPVs

£000	*Immediately*	*After 1 year*	*After 2 years*	*After 3 years*	*NPV*
Project					
A	−400	+50	+300	+350	+156.3
B	−300	−200	+400	+400	+149.3
C	−300	+150	+150	+150	+73.0
D	0	−300	+250	+300	+159.3

Let a, b, c, d be the proportions of projects A, B, C and D accepted and x be the amount in £000 placed on deposit immediately.

The resultant formulation would be as follows:

Maximise $156.3a + 149.3b + 73.0c + 159.3d - 0.027x$

Subject to $400a + 300b + 300c + x \leq 500$

$200b + 300d \leq 300 + 50a + 150c + 1.07x$

$a, b, c, d, x \geq 0$

$a, b, c, d \quad \leq 1$

We can interpret the formulation as follows. The objective function is to maximise the positive net present values of the four projects (a, b, c and d). To complete the information in the objective function it is necessary to calculate the NPV (at 10%) per £1 of external investment for one year:

Amount received after one year from £1 invested at 7% (£)		1.07
Discounted at 10%: 1.07 × 0.909	=	0.973
Less Original investment	=	1.000
NPV per £1 =		−0.027

We now have to consider the two cash availability constraints. The cash available immediately is £500,000. All projects except D require immediate cash outflows. The first constraint is thus:

$$400a + 300b + 300c + x \leq 500$$

The cash limit after one year is £300,000, by which date the investment of surplus funds will include one year's interest at 7% to augment the cash available. Projects A and C also generate inflows on that date. Projects B and D both require further outflows. The constraint thus becomes:

$$200b + 300d \leq 300 + 50a + 150c + 1.07x$$

The final two sets of constraints, $a, b, c, d, x \geq 0$, and $a, b, c, d \leq 1$, reflect the situation that projects are divisible but cannot be undertaken more than once. Solution of the linear programme would give the optimal plan for Valley Ltd.

11.6 The impact of inflation on long-term decisions

Throughout our analysis of long-term decision making we have made no explicit reference to the possible impact of inflation on the estimates of future cash flows and on the cost of capital. This has been a deliberate omission. It is necessary to understand the basic method of long-term decision making before adding any refinements. But of course in any real world situation, the existence of inflation is likely and presents a problem to decision makers. Quite apart from the difficulty of predicting future levels of inflation and, more particularly, their effect on the prices of resources used by the firm, decision makers face the problem of how to incorporate inflation into project appraisal. For instance should inflation be incorporated into estimates of future cash flows? Or into the cost of capital rate? Or both? This section briefly tackles these particular issues.

Brisbane Ltd is considering a project which will cost £10,000, have a life of three years, and reduce labour costs by £4,000 p.a. for each of the three years. The company's cost of capital is 10% p.a. For simplicity, assume that labour costs are paid annually in arrears. No increases in any prices are expected in the future.

In this case the project is marginally unacceptable, as follows:

$$\begin{aligned} \text{NPV} &= -£10{,}000 + £4{,}000\ A_{\overline{3}|}\ 10\% \\ &= -£10{,}000 + £9{,}948 = -£52 \end{aligned}$$

Now suppose that general inflation is anticipated at 15% p.a. compound and that all specific prices (i.e. all the costs of Brisbane Ltd) are expected to change in line with general inflation. In other words, no real relationships change. The existence of expected inflation will affect both the cash flows and the cost of capital.

The initial investment outlay of £10,000 remains unchanged as it occurs at the decision date, but the three yearly cost savings of £4,000 must be increased in money terms to reflect the expected increase in labour costs of 15% p.a. Thus the cost savings become:

$$\begin{aligned} &\text{Year 1 } £4{,}000 \times (1.15) = £4{,}600 \\ &\text{Year 2 } £4{,}000 \times (1.15)^2 = £5{,}290 \\ &\text{Year 3 } £4{,}000 \times (1.15)^3 = £6{,}084 \end{aligned}$$

With the existence of inflation, a larger return than previously will be required by suppliers of funds, to compensate them for the loss of purchasing power of their funds. Thus if the return required after one year on each pound supplied is £1.10 without inflation, it will be necessary to pay £1.10 (1.15) = £1.265, if inflation is expected at 15% p.a. compound, implying a discount rate of 26.5% p.a.

The appraisal of the project may now proceed as previously using cash flow estimates and a discount rate which incorporates inflation. The NPV is computed as follows:

Year	*Cash flows* (£)	*Discount factor at 26.5%*	*Present value* (£)
0	– 10,000	1.0000	– 10,000
1	+ 4,600	$\frac{1}{(1.265)} = 0.7905$	+ 3,636
2	+ 5,290	$\frac{1}{(1.265)^2} = 0.6249$	+ 3,306
3	+ 6,084	$\frac{1}{(1.265)^3} = 0.4940$	+ 3,006
		Net present value	– 52

The calculation of the NPV shows that in this case nothing has changed relative to the original situation, because all prices are affected equally by the existence of inflation. The measuring scale is different, but the NPV is still the same. The project is still marginally unacceptable. The illustration gives us a basis for clarifying some basic ideas of long-term decision making under inflation. Cash flows which are estimated as actual cash sums to be paid or received in future periods are referred to as *money cash flows*: a discount rate which converts money cash flows into present values and which allows for both the time value of consumption potential (i.e. the time value of money if no inflation is expected, in our example 10% p.a.) and the effect of inflation (in our example 15% p.a.) is referred to as a *money discount rate* (in our example 26.5%). In most countries, virtually all interest rates are expressed in money terms with no distinction being made between that part of the rate which represents the time value of consumption potential and that part which represents compensation for expected inflation. Because no split is readily available between the two components of the money discount rate it is usually more convenient to undertake NPV calculations in money terms – discounting money cash flows at a money discount rate – than to attempt to disaggregate the observed money interest rate into its two component parts and adopt an alternative NPV calculation.

Nevertheless, it is possible, even if not preferable, to express cash flows in *real* terms (i.e. in units having a constant purchasing power), and discount these at a *real discount rate*. We might define a real cash flow as the cash amount we would have to pay now, in today's pounds, to buy the same amount of goods as we will be able to buy with any given future cash amount when we receive it. The real discount rate is computed by:

$$K = \frac{i - h}{1 + h}$$

where K is the real discount rate, i is the money discount rate, and h is the expected rate of inflation.

We can use our basic example to illustrate the computation in real terms of the NPV. The figures are as follows:

Year	Money cash flows (£)	×	Deflation factor at 15%	=	Real cash flows (£)	×	Real discount factor at 10%*	=	Present value (£)
0	− 10,000		1.0000		− 10,000		1.0000		− 10,000
1	+ 4,600		$\frac{1}{(1.15)} = 0.8696$		+ 4,000		0.9091		+ 3,636
2	+ 5,290		$\frac{1}{(1.15)^2} = 0.7561$		+ 4,000		0.8264		+ 3,306
3	+ 6,084		$\frac{1}{(1.15)^3} = 0.6575$		+ 4,000		0.7513		+ 3,006
							Net present value		− 52

$$^*K = \frac{0.265 - 0.15}{1 + 0.15} = 0.1 \text{ or } 10\%$$

The NPV is still − £52, as in the previous computation when money cash flows and a money discount rate were used. This demonstrates that NPV calculations may be carried out either in money terms or in real terms. Provided that inflation is dealt with correctly in computing cash flows and discount rates, both methods will yield the same answer. The essence of the argument is consistency; money cash flows to be discounted at a money rate, real cash flows at a real rate. However, as we have noted, it is usually preferable to undertake calculations involving inflation by using money cash flows and money discount rates for two main reasons. First, the use of money discount rates avoids the necessity of splitting the discount rate into an inflationary element and an element for the real rate, and thus necessitates fewer calculations. Second, and more importantly, money interest rates are the ones used in almost all financial dealings and can thus be observed, whereas real rates cannot, as they are determined by (possibly variable) predictions of inflation.

One final point of great importance warrants mention. In our simple example we have assumed that all prices change in line with general inflation and consequently that cash flows in real terms are identical to cash flows at current prices. In practice, it is quite likely that inflation will affect different resources in different ways, and thus that real relationships between resources will change. Let us alter our example to make it somewhat more realistic. Suppose now that specific wage rates are expected to increase at 20% p.a., although the general rate of inflation is still expected to increase at 15% p.a. Money and real costs of capital are as previously (26.5% and 10% respectively). Our analysis in *money* terms for Brisbane Ltd will now be as follows:

Year	*Cash flows at current prices* (£)	×	*Specific inflation at 20%*	=	*Money cash flows* (£)	×	*Money discount factor at 26.5%*	=	*Present value* (£)
0	−10,000		1.00		−10,000		1.0000		−10,000
1	+4,000		1.20		+4,800		0.7905		+3,794
2	+4,000		$(1.20)^2$		+5,760		0.6249		+3,599
3	+4,000		$(1.20)^3$		+6,912		0.4940		+3,415
							Net present value		+808

The new calculation incorporating the differential impact of inflation on the labour costs saved, and the cost of capital, results in a positive NPV of £808 and a sign for acceptability. The sign has changed from negative to positive because the cost of labour is increasing over time *relative* to other prices, and hence cash savings are increasing in real terms. The same conclusion would of course hold if the appraisal had been undertaken using real cash flows – as opposed to savings at current prices – and a real discount rate. The point of the more realistic example using differential price change rates is this: if we had simply estimated cash savings at current prices (i.e. £4,000 p.a.) and applied a real discount rate (i.e. 10%), the answer would have shown a negative NPV of £52, and the project would probably have been rejected. This would be a wrong decision because the benefits of the labour cost savings would be under-estimated. For purposes of investment appraisal under inflation it is essential that net benefits (the cash flows) are expressed in terms comparable with the discount rate. Calculating net benefits on one basis and the discount rate on a different basis may well lead to incorrect investment recommendations.

Finally let us suppose that Brisbane Ltd is tackling a trickier problem. The company is deciding whether to introduce a new product with a three year life. The investment cost will be £30,000 at 1.1.19X0 and 10,000 units of the product are expected to be sold each year for £5 in current prices. Because of severe competition in the market, Brisbane Ltd expects price increases to be limited to 5% per annum. Brisbane Ltd's money cost of capital is 15% per annum. The following variable costs per unit, expressed in current prices, will be incurred:

	£
Labour	1.00, increasing at 8% per annum
Raw material	1.50, increasing at 12% per annum
Overhead	0.75, increasing at 8% per annum

The example poses a variety of costs, prices and inflation rates. To determine whether the project should be accepted we should compute the relevant money cash flows over its life and discount them at the money discount rate. Of vital importance is tabulating and ordering the data in an easily understandable way, to ensure we compare like with like. We might proceed as follows:

Brisbane Ltd
Money Cash Flows (£)

	1 January 19X0	*31 December 19X0*	*31 December 19X1*	*21 December 19X2*
Investment cost	(30,000)			
Revenue:				
50,000 × (1.05)		52,500		
50,000 × $(1.05)^2$			55,125	
50,000 × $(1.05)^3$				57,881
Labour:				
10,000 × (1.08)		(10,800)		
10,000 × $(1.08)^2$			(11,664)	
10,000 × $(1.08)^3$				(12,597)
Raw material:				
15,000 × (1.12)		(16,800)		
15,000 × $(1.12)^2$			(18,816)	
15,000 × $(1.12)^3$				(21,074)
Overheads:				
7,500 (1.08)		(8,100)		
7,500 $(1.08)^2$			(8,748)	
7,500 $(1.08)^3$				(9,448)
Net cash flow	(30,000)	16,800	15,897	14,762
Discount factor at 15% per annum	1	0.8696	0.7561	0.6575
Present values	(30,000)	14,609	12,020	9,706

Net present value is +£6,335 and the project is worthwhile.

Discussion topics

1. Contrast the type of information required for long-term decisions with that required for short-term decisions. Are there any essential differences?
2. Why is it necessary to build a discount factor into long-term decision making?
3. Evaluate the role of depreciation in long-term decision making.
4. Discuss some of the difficulties of measuring the firm's weighted average cost of capital.
5. 'Sensitivity analysis is a most powerful technique in project appraisal.' Discuss.
6. Compare and contrast the different methods available for dealing with inflation in investment decisions.

Exercises

11.1 Rousseau Ltd uses electricity as a source of power for its machines and for lighting and heating its factory. The local electricity board has offered Rousseau a choice of two tariffs on the basis of which the charges for the electricity used may be calculated. Details of these tariffs are as follows:

	Fixed annual charge (£)	*Variable charge per unit used* (£)
Tariff A	500	2.0
Tariff B	3,000	0.5

Whichever tariff Rousseau chooses will be put into effect as from the 1 January 19X1. Accounts will be rendered annually by the electricity board and will be payable on the 31 December in the year to which they relate. Under the terms of the contract offered by the electricity board, Rousseau Ltd must choose one of the tariffs for a minimum period of four years.

Rousseau Ltd estimates that it will require 700 units of electricity during 19X1, 1,200 units during 19X2, 2,000 units during 19X3 and 3,000 units during 19X4. The company's cost of capital is 15% p.a.

(a) Prepare a calculation showing which of the two tariffs the company should choose.

(b) Note any other factors not included in your calculation which may influence the decision.

11.2 Mr Suppe is proposing to install central heating in his house. He intends to sell the house in about five years time and he feels that whichever system is installed will add some £1,500 to the resale value. Mr Suppe estimates that the costs of installing and running the various possible systems will be:

1. Installation costs (payable immediately)

	£
Gas	1,500
Oil	2,100
Solid fuel	1,200

2. Annual fuel costs (payable at the end of each year)

	£
Gas	450
Oil	300
Solid fuel	510

3. Maintenance costs (payable at the end of the year in which they are incurred)

	£
Gas	60 p.a.
Oil	75 p.a.
Solid fuel	300 during the fourth year

Mr Suppe feels that each of the systems is equally efficient for heating purposes. He can both borrow and lend money readily at 10% p.a.

(a) Prepare a calculation showing which central heating system should be installed.

(b) Note any other factors not included in your calculation which may affect the decision.

11.3 Tartini Ltd is considering a proposal that it should commence the manufacture of lunets. It has already spent £4,800 on a study of the feasibility of the activity and is satisfied that the necessary skills are available. The manufacture of lunets would require the use of a machine already owned by Tartini. It was purchased two years ago for £11,500 and currently stands in the firm's balance sheet at £7,500 (after deducting depreciation). Tartini has no other use for the machine, but it could be sold for £5,200 if lunets were not manufactured.

Demand for lunets is expected to last for six years. Maintenance costs of the machine would be £200 p.a. for the first three years, and £300 p.a. for the second three years; the machine would be sold for £700 at the end of year 6. A special advertising campaign would be mounted during the first year of the sale of the product at a cost of £7,000.

Tartini's accountant has produced the following estimate of selling price and costs (excluding machinery) per unit of lunets:

	£	£
Selling price		25
Less Materials – 6 lb @ £1.50	9	
Labour – 1 hour @ £4	4	
Variable overheads	2	
Fixed overheads – 1 hour @ £3 per labour hour	3	
		18
Surplus		7

It is expected that 500 lunets would be sold each year.

Tartini requires a rate of return on investment of 10% p.a. (at which rate it can borrow or lend large sums). Assume that annual receipts and payments arise at the end of each year.

(a) Prepare a calculation showing whether the manufacture of lunets is worthwhile and by how much.

(b) Explain briefly the rationale of your method of allowing for the fact that cash flows arise at different times.

11.4 Poulenc and Nielsen each own 50% of the issued ordinary share capital of Mozart Ltd, but neither plays any part in its management. The company presently has £3,000 available on bank current account which it is proposing to invest in a project expected to produce cash inflows of £800 after one year, £1,000 after two, and £1,700 after three. No other cash flows are expected to be associated with the project. If the £3,000 is not used on this project it will be paid out as a dividend to Poulenc and Nielsen. If the project is accepted the cash inflows it produces will be paid out in full as dividends as they arise.

Nielsen is in agreement with the company investing in the proposed project, but Poulenc wishes to take his wife on a world cruise and claims that the company is not acting in his best interests if it fails to pay the money as dividend to enable him to do so. Mozart Ltd is able to both lend and borrow funds freely at 5% p.a.

(a) Calculate the net present value of the proposed project to Mozart Ltd.

(b) Explain whether the company is acting in the best interests of *both* its shareholders by accepting the project if
(i) Poulenc and Nielsen may both borrow freely at 5%;
(ii) Poulenc and Nielsen may both borrow freely at 10%.

(c) Comment briefly on the implications of your answers to (a) and (b) above for capital investment theory.

11.5 Reger plc is considering the introduction of a new product, the trump, to its range. A feasibility study, recently undertaken at a cost of £10,000, suggests that a selling price of £50 per unit should be set for the trump.

Manufacture of the trump would require a specialised machine costing £150,000. The machine is expected to be capable of producing trumps for an indefinite period, although due to its specialised nature it is not expected to have any resale or scrap value when production of trumps ceases. Variable costs of manufacturing trumps are estimated at £30 per unit, and overhead costs are estimated at a fixed level of £40,000 p.a., avoidable only if no trumps are manufactured or sold. At a selling price of £50, it is estimated that 5,000 trumps will be demanded and sold each year. Demand for trumps is expected to cease after four years.

All expenses and revenues will be paid or received in cash at the end of the year in which they arise, with the exception of the cost of the machine which will be payable at the beginning of the first year in which trumps are manufactured. The directors of Reger plc estimate the company's cost of capital at 10% p.a.

(a) Calculate the net present value expected from the introduction of the proposed new product, based on the estimates given.

(b) Prepare a statement showing in percentages how sensitive the net present value is to errors of estimation in each component of your calculation in (a).

(c) Comment briefly on the results of your calculations in (a) and (b).

11.6 Manet Ltd has been offered a contract which, if accepted, will begin on 1 January 19X7. It will last for three years. The price offered is £45,600, of which £12,000 is payable on 31 December 19X7, £12,000 on 31 December 19X8 and £21,600 on 31 December 19X9.

Four items of cost are relevant to the contract:

1. Materials: only one type of material, material X, will be used on the contract. 1,000 units will be required in all, 500 as soon as the contract is commenced and 500 at the end of 19X7. At present, 500 units of material X, which cost £18 per unit in 19X6, are in stock. The material is in regular use and stocks are replaced as they are used. Payment for replacement stock is made when the order is placed. The current buying price (at 1 January 19X7) is £18.60 per unit, and this is expected to increase by 5% by 31 December 19X7.

2. Labour: three unskilled workers will each spend three years on the contract. Their current wage rate is £90 per week each. In additional, a supervisor will be required to spend 13 weeks on the contract in 19X7 and 13 weeks in 19X9. At present, he is paid £140 per week. The firm intends to give a 10% wage increase to all employees on 1 January 19X8 and a further 10% increase on 1 January 19X9.

3. Machinery: the machinery required for the contract will be leased by the firm at an annual rental of £2,400 payable in arrears and fixed for three years. The machinery will be required for the full three years of the contract.
4. Overhead expenses: overhead expenses are normally recovered at a rate of 50% on labour cost. The level of total overhead expenses will be unaffected by undertaking the contract.

Assume that none of the firm's resources is in short supply and that all cash flows (excluding the purchase of the first 500 units of material X) arise on the last day of the year in which they fall due. The general price level index presently stands at 100, and is expected to increase at the rate of 7% p.a. compound for the indefinite future. Manet Ltd has a cost of capital, in 'money' terms, of 11% p.a.

(a) Prepare calculations showing whether acceptance of the contract is worthwhile.

(b) Justify the method you use for appraising the contract; deal particularly with your treatment of inflation.

11.7 Nono plc is financed by three types of capital:

1. 1 million 50p ordinary shares each having a current market value of £5.20 *cum div*. The current annual dividend, which is due to be paid shortly, is 20p per share. The dividend has grown steadily in the past at a compound annual rate of 15% and is generally expected to continue doing so indefinitely.
2. £200,000 redeemable 8% debt, having a current value of £50% *ex interest*,
3. £2 million 10% debt, redeemable in twenty years at a price of £110%. The current market value is £80% *ex interest*.

Nono is considering a new project having the same risk characteristics as existing projects, which would require an immediate outlay of £150,000 and would produce annual net cash inflows of £30,000 indefinitely.

Prepare calculations showing whether acceptance of the new project is worthwhile.

11.8 Vitali Ltd is considering the replacement of a group of machines used exclusively for the manufacture of one of its products, the yeti. The existing machines have a book value of £65,000 after deducting straight line depreciation from historical cost; however, they could be sold for £45,000 only. The new machines would cost £100,000. Vitali expects to sell yetis for four more years. The existing machines could be kept in operation for that period of time if it were economically desirable to do so. After four years, the scrap value of both the existing machines and the new machines would be zero.

The current costs per unit of manufacturing yetis on the existing machines and the new machines are as follows:

	Existing machines (£)		*New machines* (£)
Materials	22.00		20.00
Labour (8 hours @ £5)	40.00	(4 h @ £5)	20.00
Overheads (8 hours @ £2.40)	19.20	(4 h @ £7.20)	28.80
Total cost	81.20		68.80

Overheads are allocated to products on the labour hour rate method. The hourly rates of £2.40 and £7.20 comprise £1 and £2.50 for variable overheads and £1.40 and £4.70 for fixed overheads, including depreciation.

Current sales of yetis are 1,000 units p.a. at £90 each; if the new machines were purchased, output would be increased to 1,200 units and selling price would be reduced to £80. Vitali requires a minimum rate of return on investment of 20% p.a. in money terms. Materials costs, overheads and selling prices are expected to increase at the rate of 15% p.a. in step with the index of retail prices. Labour costs are expected to increase at the rate of 20% p.a. Assume that annual receipts and payments would arise annually on the anniversary of the installation of the new machinery.

(a) Give calculations to show whether purchase of the new machines would be worthwhile.

(b) Explain shortly your treatment of inflation.

11.9 Sati Ltd is considering which, if any, of four projects to accept. The cash flows, which are all paid out or received at the end of the year in question, are shown below. All the projects are regarded as equally risky. The company's capital budget for year 0 is restricted to £6,000; at later times funds will be readily available at the firm's cost of capital rate of 10% p.a. All the projects must be commenced at time 0 or abandoned; they cannot be postponed. Parts of a project may be accepted, but no project can be accepted more than once.

Projects	*Initial investment (£)*		*Receipts (£)*			
Years	*0*	*1*	*1*	*2*	*3*	*4*
A	1,000	2,000	–	1,500	1,500	1,500
B	5,000	–	2,000	2,000	2,000	2,000
C	4,500	–	1,750	1,750	1,750	1,750
D	1,750	1,400	–	1,500	1,500	1,500

(a) Provide reasons and calculations showing which, if any, of the projects should be adopted by Sati Ltd.

(b) If it was anticipated that the amount of funds available for capital investment in future years would be limited, would your answer differ? Explain *briefly* the techniques available to solve the multi-period rationing case.

11.10 Franzl is a contract engineer working for a division of a large construction company. He is responsible for the negotiation of contract prices and the subsequent collection of instalment monies from customers. It is company policy to achieve a mark-up of at least 10% on the direct production costs of a contract, but there is no company policy on the speed of customer payment. Franzl is presently engaged in deciding upon the minimum acceptable price for contract K491, which will last for 24 months. He has estimated that the following direct production costs will be incurred:

	£
Raw material	168,000
Labour	120,000
Plant depreciation	18,400
Equipment rental	30,000
	336,400

On the basis of these costs Franzl estimates that the minimum contract price should be £370,000. Payment would be received in four equal instalments, six-monthly in arrears. The raw material and labour costs are expected to rise evenly over the period of the contract and to be paid monthly in arrears. Plant depreciation has been calculated as the difference between the cost of the new plant (£32,400) which will be purchased for the contract and its realisable value (£14,000) at the end of the contract. Special equipment will be rented for the first year of the contract, the rent being paid in two six monthly instalments in advance. The contract will be financed from head office funds, on which interest of 1% per month is charged or credited according to whether the construction division is a net borrower or net lender.

(a) Calculate the net present value of contract K491 assuming that Franzl's minimum price and normal payment terms are accepted.

(b) Assuming that the customer agrees to pay the instalments in advance rather than arrears, calculate the new contract price and mark-up that Franzl could accept so as to leave the net present value of the contract unchanged.

(c) Prepare two statements to show that the eventual cash surpluses generated in (a) and (b) are identical. The statements need show *only* the total cash received and paid for each category of revenue and expense.

(d) Discuss the factors that should influence the tender price for a long-term contract.

11.11 The directors of Anhang plc are considering how best to invest in four projects, details of which are given below

	Project			
	I	*II*	*III*	*IV*
Net present value (£000)	+80	+40	+120	+110
Beta factor of project	1.0	1.0	0.8	1.2
Initial payment (£000)	50	40	90	55

The net present values of the projects have been calculated using specific, risk-adjusted discount rates. The directors' choice is complicated because Anhang plc has only £90,000 currently available for investment in new projects. Each project must start on the same date and cannot be deferred. Acceptance of any one project would not affect acceptance of any other and all projects are divisible. The directors at a recent board meeting were unable to agree upon how best to invest the £90,000. A summary of the views expressed at the meeting follows:

1. Wendling argued that as the presumed objective of the company was to maximise shareholder wealth, project III should be undertaken as this project produced the highest net present value.

2. Ramm argued that as funds were in short supply investment should be concentrated in those projects with the lowest initial outlay, that is in projects I and II.

3. Ritter suggested that project III should be accepted on the grounds of risk reduction. Project III has the lowest beta, and by its acceptance the risk of the company (the company's present beta is 1.0) would be reduced. Ritter also cautioned against acceptance of project IV as it was the most risky project; he pointed out that its high net present value was, in part, a reward for its higher level of associated risk.

4. Punto argued against accepting project III, stating that if the project were discounted at the company's weighted average cost of capital, its net present value would be greatly reduced.

   (a) Write a report to the directors of Anhang plc advising them how best to invest the £90,000, assuming the restriction on capital to apply for one year only. Your report should address the issues raised by each of the four directors.

   (b) Explain why the criteria you have used in (a) above to determine the best allocation of capital may be inappropriate if funds are rationed for a period longer than one year.

   (c) Describe the procedures available to a company for the selection of projects when capital is rationed in more than one period.

11.12 Thamos plc is a successful food retailing company. Over the last five years it has increased its share of the UK food retail market by 30%. Thamos plc makes no use of debt and has financed its operations entirely from retained earnings. Thamos plc has a current price/earnings ratio of 28 compared with the food retailing sector average of 19. Other financial data relating to Thamos plc are shown below:

	1982	*1983*	*1984*	*1985*	*1986*
Earnings per share (p)	16.1	19.2	24.7	30.5	35.8
Net dividend per share (p)	4.86	5.86	7.5	9.0	11.0
Book value of equity per share (p)	103	124	142	165	190

(a) Estimate the cost of equity capital for Thamos plc using the following:
(i) dividend growth model;
(ii) capital asset pricing model. (You should assume a risk-free rate of interest of 10%, a beta of 0.8 and a market premium for risk of 9%.)

(b) Discuss whether the assumptions underlying the models used in part (a) are realistic and explain how the effects of using these assumptions are reflected in the results obtained.

(c) Explain why managers need to know the cost of the equity capital of their companies.

Further reading

Adelson, R. M., 'Discounted cash flow, can we discount it?', *Journal of Business Finance*, Summer 1970.

Arditti, F. D. 'The weighted average cost of capital: some questions on its definition, interpretation and use', *Journal of Finance*, September 1973.

Bromwich, M. 'Capital budgeting – a review', *Journal of Business Finance*, Autumn 1970.

Duvall, R. M. and Bulloch, J., 'Adjusting rate of return and present value for price level changes', *The Accounting Review*, July 1965.

Fairchild, K. W. and Bline, D., 'Capital investment analysis: the index method', *Issues in Accounting Education*, Spring 1988.

Grinyer, J. R., 'An alternative to maximisation of shareholders' wealth', *Accounting and Business Research*, Autumn 1986.

Hall, W. K., 'Changing perspectives on the capital investment process', *Long-Range Planning*, February 1979.

King, P., 'Is the emphasis of capital budgeting theory misplaced' *Journal of Business Finance and Accounting*, Spring 1975.

Modigliani, F. and Miller, M. H., 'The cost of capital, corporate finance and the theory of investment', *American Economic Review*, June 1958.

Pike, R. H., 'A review of recent trends in formal capital budgeting processes', *Accounting and Business Research*, Summer 1983.

Piper, J. 'Classifying capital projects for top management decision-making', *Long-Range Planning*, June 1980.

Porterfield, J. T. S., *Investment Decisions and Capital Costs*, Prentice Hall, 1965.

Rappaport, A. and Taggart, R. A., Jr, 'Evaluation of capital expenditure proposals under inflation', *Financial Management*, Spring 1982.

Chapter 12

Long-term decisions: internal rate of return and other methods

In the previous chapter we discussed the net present value (NPV) approach to long-term capital investment decisions. We believe that technically it is the best approach currently available. As we explained in Chapter 3, NPV is linked directly to the measurement of present wealth or value. Under certain circumstances, a firm which accepts a project with a positive NPV should enjoy an immediate increase in its value, equal to the amount of the project's NPV. It is this direct link with our assumed objective of managerial decision making – the maximisation of the present value of the firm's net cash inflows – which makes the NPV decision rule so attractive as a criterion for the evaluation of capital investment opportunities. NPV is, however, only one of many possible approaches to long-term decision making. In this chapter we consider other methods and contrast them with the NPV method. First, we consider one appraisal method (the internal rate of return) which incorporates the time value of money and then we consider two methods (the payback method and the accounting rate of return) which do not. Finally we discuss how managers actually evaluate investments and compare practice with theory.

12.1 The internal rate of return

The internal rate of return, or yield, method, entails the discounting of future cash flows to the present date, and as such bears some similarity to the NPV method. The internal rate of return (IRR) of a project may be defined as the discount rate at which the present value of all future cash flows, positive and negative, is equal to the investment cost of the project. Phrased differently, we may say that the IRR method, unlike the NPV method, does not seek to generate a cash figure to determine whether an investment should be undertaken, but rather it seeks to find the discount rate at which the NPV of a project is zero. It signals acceptance or rejection of an investment in percentage terms, not in cash terms. Because it is a relative measure, expressing net returns as a percentage of investment cost, it takes no account of the absolute size of a project's required investment cost or of its cash returns. This is an important difference between the NPV and IRR methods, and we shall return to examine its implications later in this chapter.

To be acceptable under the IRR criterion, a project must have an internal rate of return greater than some other rate, which we might term a 'hurdle' or 'cut-off' rate. This rate should be the same as the discount rate suggested for use in NPV calculations, i.e. the weighted average cost of capital (WACC), which reflects all long-term sources of funds used by a firm.

Internal rates of return are usually determined by a process of trial and error. (Computers perform the necessary calculations very speedily.) Consider the following cash flow profile for a particular project, + and − denoting positive and negative flows respectively:

Year 0	*Year 1*	*Year 2*	*Year 3*
− £9,514	+ £1,000	+ £5,000	+ £9,000

What is the internal rate of return of the project? The answer is not obvious, so we might begin by choosing any discount rate as the potential IRR. (Remember: we are trying to find a rate which equates cash inflows of £1,000 in year 1, £5,000 in year 2 and £9,000 in year 3 with one cash outflow, the project cost of £9,514 at the start of year 1.) Let us begin by choosing a rate of 10% p.a. The NPV of the project at this rate is:

$$-9{,}514 + 1{,}000(0.909) + 5{,}000(0.826) + 9{,}000(0.751) = +£2{,}284$$

However, we are trying to find a discount rate which shows neither a positive nor a negative net present value. Thus 10% is too low. Let us try a rate of 15%. The NPV for the project now becomes:

$$-9{,}514 + 1{,}000(0.870) + 5{,}000(0.756) + 9{,}000(0.657) = +£1{,}049$$

15% is still too low. Let us try 20%:

$$-9{,}514 + 1{,}000(0.833) + 5{,}000(0.694) + 9{,}000(0.579) = 0$$

By trial and error we have found that the IRR of the project is exactly 20%. To determine whether this is an acceptable project we of course need the additional information on the hurdle rate. If the hurdle rate is less than 20% the project should be undertaken; if it is greater than 20%, the project should be rejected.

In general, the IRR for any project is represented by r in the following equation:

$$\frac{a_1}{(1+r)} + \frac{a_2}{(1+r)^2} + \cdots + \frac{a_n}{(1+r)^n} - I_0 = 0$$

where $a_1, a_2, \ldots, a_n$ are the cash flows at the end of years 1, 2, ..., n respectively and I_0 is the project cost payable immediately. Using the actual cash data from our example, we can rewrite the equation as

$$\frac{1{,}000}{(1.2)} + \frac{5{,}000}{(1.2)^2} + \frac{9{,}000}{(1.2)^3} - 9{,}514 = 0$$

This can be interpreted roughly to mean that if cash flows of £1,000, £5,000 and £9,000 are received at the end of years 1, 2 and 3 of a project's life, then, if the initial cost is £9,514, the project is 'yielding' a percentage return of 20% p.a. Hence the common use of the term 'yield' to mean the same as internal rate of return.

In situations where management must decide whether to accept or reject a single project, the IRR criterion always gives the same advice as NPV, provided that the cash flow pattern is *orthodox* (i.e. that one or more cash outflows is followed by a series of cash inflows).

Figure 12.1 depicts the NPV of a project with an orthodox cash flow pattern, expressed as a function of the discount rate. The intercept of the NPV line with the horizontal axis is denoted by point r. This point is the project's IRR (i.e. the rate at which the project shows a zero net present value). For any point on the graph where the NPV is positive (to the left of point r and above the horizontal axis), the cost of capital must be less than the IRR (point r). For example, if the cost of capital is i_A, the project's NPV is positive and equal to £A. Similarly for any point on the graph where the NPV is negative (to the right of point r and below the horizontal axis), the cost of capital must be greater than the IRR (point r). For example, if the cost of capital is i_B the NPV is negative and equal to $-$£B.

Thus both methods, NPV and IRR, give the same solutions to most normal accept/reject decisions. However, there are situations in which the application of the two methods is not so straightforward, and which may lead to conflicting advice.

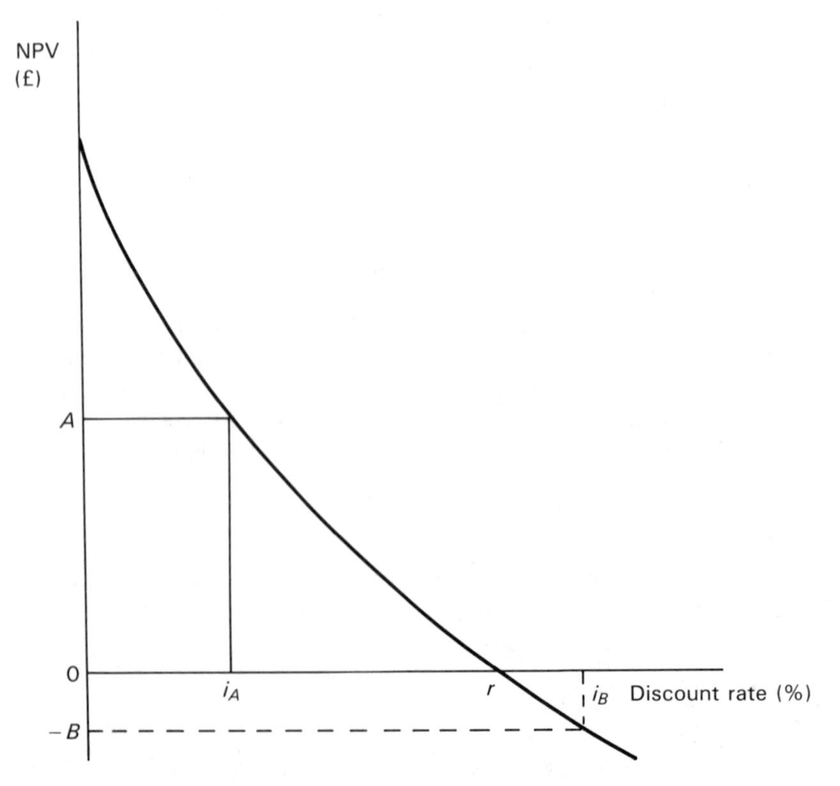

Figure 12.1 The relationship between IRR and NPV.

We now examine some of these situations and explain why the NPV method is, in each case, to be preferred.

12.2 Mutually exclusive projects

Suppose that Loftus Ltd is in a situation where it has three possible investment projects, but it may accept only one of these three. The firm's cost of capital is 10% p.a. The cash flow profiles of the three projects are as follows:

	Cash flows (£)			
	Year 0	*Year 1*	*Year 2*	*Year 3*
Project A	−9,514	+1,000	+5,000	+9,000
B	−9,514	+7,000	+5,000	+1,000
C	−9,514	+4,500	+4,500	+4,500

Let us begin by computing the NPVs of the three projects, as follows:

$$\text{Project A} \quad -9{,}514 + 1{,}000(0.909) + 5{,}000(0.826) + 9{,}000(0.751) = +£2{,}284$$

$$\text{B} \quad -9{,}514 + 7{,}000(0.909) + 5{,}000(0.826) + 1{,}000(0.751) = +£1{,}730$$

$$\text{C} \quad -9{,}514 + 4{,}500(2.487) = +£1{,}677$$

The answer is clear and unambiguous. As the projects are mutually exclusive, Loftus Ltd should accept A, as it has the highest net present value of the three available projects, when discounted at the cost of capital of 10% p.a.

Now let us see how the IRR rule would rank the three projects: project A gives an IRR of exactly 20%, as we have seen from our previous illustration of the computation of the IRR.

The IRR for project B is more difficult. Trying a rate of 20% we have:

$$-9{,}514 + 7{,}000(0.833) + 5{,}000(0.694) + 1{,}000(0.579) = +£366$$

This shows that 20% is too low. (Figure 12.1 shows that NPV usually decreases as the discount rate increases.) Trying a rate of 25% we have:

$$-9{,}514 + 7{,}000(0.800) + 5{,}000(0.640) + 1{,}000(0.512) = -£202$$

The negative NPV found when applying a rate of 25% shows that the IRR must lie somewhere between 20% and 25%. Where it lies may be approximated by using the technique of *linear interpolation*, which we mentioned in the previous chapter.

The solution is only approximate as it is based on the assumption that NPV changes linearly as the discount rate changes, an assumption which is not strictly correct as can be seen from the graph in Figure 12.1. [34] IRR is estimated as follows.

[34] Our interpolation is based on NPVs at 20% and 25%. Greater precision would be achieved by undertaking further calculations prior to interpolation to find the two integer discount rates that give NPVs closest to zero: the lower discount rate will give a positive NPV and the higher one a negative NPV.

For a 5% increase in the discount rate (from 20% to 25%), NPV falls by £568 (from +£366 to −£202). We have to calculate what increase in the discount rate is needed to reduce NPV by £366, i.e. to zero. This increase is added to 20% to find the IRR. If a 5% increase leads to a fall of £568 in NPV, the increase necessary for a fall of £366 is (5 × 366/568). The IRR for project B is approximately:

$$20 + \left(5 \times \frac{366}{568}\right) = 23.22\%$$

The IRR for Project C is easier to determine, as the yearly cash flows are constant. It is solved as follows:

$$9514 = 4500\ A_{\overline{3}|}r$$

$$\therefore A_{\overline{3}|}r = 2.114$$

Using interpolation, we have:

$$A_{\overline{3}|}\ 19\% = 2.140$$

$$A_{\overline{3}|}\ 20\% = 2.106$$

$$\text{IRR} = 19 + \frac{2.140 - 2.114}{2.140 - 2.106} = 19.76\%$$

The IRRs and NPVs of the three projects are:

	IRR (%)	*NPV* (£)
Project A	20.00	+2,284
Project B	23.22	+1,730
Project C	19.76	+1,677

The rankings of A and B are clearly quite substantially different. If Loftus Ltd uses the NPV rule, it will choose A; if the IRR rule is used, it will choose B. In this situation the choice of NPV or IRR is critical. But why has this situation arisen at all? The answer is because the two methods do not always rank projects in the same way, and in any situation in which the choice of one project precludes the acceptance of others, the ranking of projects is vital.

Figure 12.2 illustrates the nature of the problem. The graph shows the NPVs of A and B as functions of the discount rate. The two functions intersect at point *Y* where the discount rate is 15.47% p.a. For discount rates below 15.47% the NPV rule favours A; for rates greater than 15.47%, B is better. What meaning can we ascribe to these figures?

Let us begin by looking at the differences between the cash flows of A and B. These are as follows:

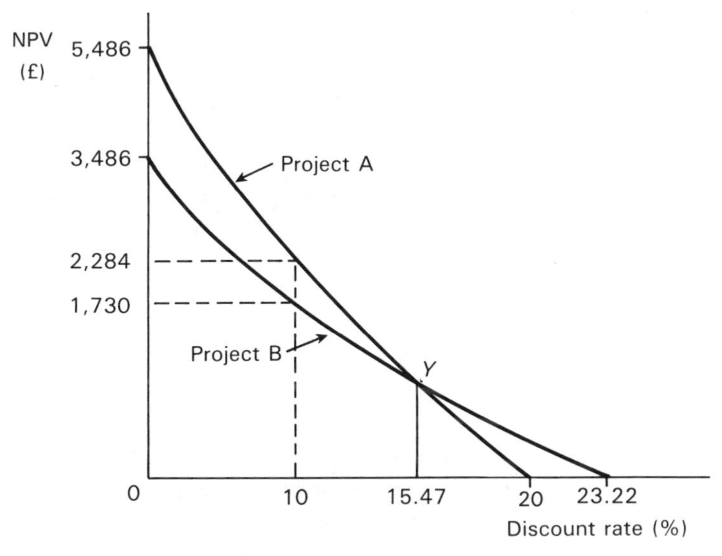

Figure 12.2 NPV and IRR of projects A and B.

	Year 0 (£)	*Year 1* (£)	*Year 2* (£)	*Year 3* (£)
Project A	−9,514	+1,000	+5,000	+9,000
Project B	−9,514	+7,000	+5,000	+1,000
Difference	0	−6,000	0	+8,000

The cash flow from B is greater by £6,000 in year 1, and the cash flow from A is greater by £8,000 in year 3. Suppose Loftus Ltd provisionally accepts A. What would happen if it did this? In cash flow terms, it would *give up* the incremental return of £6,000 from B in year 1 to receive an extra £8,000 in year 3. Would this be worthwhile? The answer is that it would if the extra return were greater than the firm's cost of capital (here 10%). To answer this, we need to compute the return on the additional cash outflow of £6,000 which will generate a cash inflow of £8,000 in two years' time. Thus the return (r) is derived from the formula:

$$6{,}000 = \frac{8{,}000}{(1+r)^2} \qquad \text{where } r = 15.47\%$$

The return of 15.47% represents the point at which the two NPV curves intersect, as shown by Figure 12.2 (i.e. the discount rate at which both projects have the same NPV and at which Loftus Ltd would be indifferent between them). As 15.47% is greater than the firm's cost of capital of 10%, the firm should invest in project A rather than B.

Because the very nature of the NPV method ensures that the additional cash flows are compared with the cost of capital, it accounts for the size of the investment in its recommendations. The IRR method does not account for size in its recommendations. IRR measures the average annual return earned on the amount remaining invested in the project at the start of each year. Hence, in our example, although project A earns a lower average return (20.00%) over its life than does B (23.22%) it does so on a *higher* average sum invested – much more of the capital invested in B is repaid after only one year (£7,000) than is the case with A (£1,000); hence A is preferable. This preference is quite rational – most people would rather have a return of 50% p.a. on an average annual investment of £1,000, than a 100% return on an average annual investment of £100.

12.3 The problem of unorthodox cash flows

Up to now we have discussed the IRR criterion in the context of orthodox cash flow patterns, in which negative investment outflows are followed by positive cash inflows. In these cases a unique IRR can always be calculated. There are, however, investment projects in which the cash flow signs change from positive to negative and vice versa during the life of the project. For example, consider the case where replacement of equipment is concentrated into only a few years of a project's life; or where a mine has to be made safe (involving cash costs) after excavations have been completed. In these cases technical problems may arise with the use of the IRR; for example, there may be more than one IRR for a project or, alternatively, there may be no meaningful IRR at all. Consider the following two projects with attendant cash flows:

		Cash flows (£)	
End of	*Year 0*	*Year 1*	*Year 2*
Project D	−2,000	+5,100	−3,150
Project E	+1,000	−2,000	+2,000

The internal rates of return (r) are as follows:

$$\text{Project D} \quad -2{,}000 + \frac{5{,}100}{(1+r)} - \frac{3{,}150}{(1+r)^2} = 0$$

where $r = 5\%$ or 50%

$$\text{Project E} \quad +1{,}000 - \frac{2{,}000}{(1+r)} + \frac{2{,}000}{(1+r)^2} = 0$$

$$1{,}000(1+r)^2 - 2{,}000(1+r) + 2{,}000 = 0$$

$$1{,}000 + 2{,}000r + 1{,}000r^2 - 2{,}000 - 2{,}000r + 2{,}000 = 0$$

$$1{,}000r^2 = -1{,}000$$

$$r^2 = -1$$

$$r = \sqrt{-1}$$

It is difficult to imagine how a decision maker could *not* be confused by these solutions. A hurdle rate for D of anywhere between 5% and 50% may indicate acceptance or rejection. Whatever the hurdle rate for E, it is hard to see how an internal rate of return of $\sqrt{-1}$ could lead to any conclusion as to acceptability! We might note here that both D and E still generate unambiguous net present values. Project D has a positive net present value at all costs of capital between 5% and 50%, and E has a positive net present value at any discount rate. In view of the technical difficulties associated with IRR, it is always preferable to use NPV to evaluate projects with unorthodox cash flows.

12.4 The payback method

It would be wrong to assume that all managers use the relatively sophisticated discounted cash flow techniques embodied in both the NPV and the IRR methods. In practice, other less sophisticated and, as we shall see, less 'correct' methods are used to evaluate long-term investments. It is important to bear in mind that non-discounting methods have been employed in practice for many years. The use of discounting techniques in managerial decision making is substantially an innovation of the 1960s and 1970s. The simplest of the non-discounting methods is known as the payback method.

The payback criterion involves estimating the time period, usually the number of years, over which the cost of any particular investment is 'paid back'. This time period – the *payback period* – is then compared to some standard period to decide whether the project is to be accepted. If a number of projects are being ranked, the most acceptable will be the one which has the shortest payback period. The method thus looks at the return *of* investment, rather than the return *on* investment, and the criterion for choice is expressed as a period of time rather than as either a cash figure or a percentage. Consider three projects K, L and M, with the following cash flows:

	Project K	*Project L*	*Project M*
Initial cost (£)	– 15,000	– 15,000	– 15,000
Cash flows by year (£):			
Year 1	+ 1,000	+ 1,000	+ 11,000
Year 2	+ 3,000	+ 3,000	+ 3,000
Year 3	+ 11,000	+ 11,000	+ 1,000
Year 4	0	+ 10,000	+ 10,000

All have payback periods of three years. Are they equally worthwhile?

We might make the following observations about the three projects. First, under a strict interpretation of the payback rule, management would be indifferent as between the three projects as each pays back its initial investment cost of £15,000 in three years. Yet it should be immediately obvious that differences exist between the projects for two reasons:

1. The cash flows from K cease at the end of the payback period (at the end of year 3), whereas the cash flows from L and M continue for one year after the end of the payback period.
2. The cash flows from M are much larger in the earlier years, and therefore are more attractive than the cash flows of L or K, in view of the time value of money.

This example illustrates the two main problems with the use of the payback method. It ignores both the existence of cash flows arising after the payback period, and the timing of the cash flows within the payback period. Why then is this method used in practice when it has such major faults? The answer may well be that because payback does not entail the use of the sophisticated methodology of discounting methods, it may be easy, and not too misleading, to apply it to small investment projects where the prediction of longer-term cash flows is not critical to the acceptance decision; or even if discounting methods are to be used, payback may be a rough screening device which gives some clue at an early stage whether the project is likely to be acceptable. If it becomes evident after using the payback rule that there is very little chance of acceptance of the project, then the more detailed and time consuming calculations are avoided. This is particularly true for projects whose cash flows are subject to great uncertainty in the longer term. A short payback period may provide some assurance that acceptance of the project is unlikely to have serious consequences for the firm. However, use of the payback method is no substitute for the application of more refined methods of handling risk, such as those discussed in Chapters 4 and 11.

12.5 The accounting rate of return

The accounting rate of return is another non-discounting method of project appraisal which enjoys quite wide acceptance. It has several synonyms; for example, 'unadjusted' rate of return, 'book' rate of return or, most simply, return on investment (ROI). The accounting rate of return (ARR) can also be computed in many different ways, all of which rely on traditional accounting profit numbers, rather than on cash flow numbers. The ARR may for instance be computed by dividing a prospective investment's annual net profit by either the *total* investment cost, or the *average* book value of the investment. Because the ARR method necessitates the use of accounting profits, accrued revenues and costs, rather than yearly cash flows, enter the calculations. Accounting profits also involve depreciation charges, which are non-cash items.

Assume a project (fixed asset) with an initial cost of £100,000, an estimated life of five years and nil scrap value, which is to be depreciated using the straight line method (i.e. at the rate of £20,000 p.a.). The asset is expected to generate operating cash flows of £30,000 p.a. The accounting rate(s) of return can be computed as follows:

$$\text{ARR on total investment } \frac{30{,}000 - \text{depreciation } 20{,}000}{100{,}000} = 10\%$$

$$\text{ARR on average investment } \frac{30{,}000 - \text{depreciation } 20{,}000}{100{,}000 \div 2} = 20\%$$

The faults of the method are obvious. It uses accounting profits rather than cash flows, and it does not consider the time value of money (i.e. profits arising in the final year of the asset's life are weighted equally with profits arising in the first year). Further, like the IRR method, the ARR method deals in ratios, and thus says nothing about the size of the projects. As we have seen in the IRR section, this can present problems if projects are mutually exclusive.

Consider the following data on two alternative projects, P and Q, both of which have an initial investment cost of £100,000 and are expected to last for three years, at the end of which each investment will be worthless. The cost of capital is 10%.

1. *Net yearly cash flows*

	P (£)	*Q* (£)
Year 1	70,000	20,000
Year 2	50,000	30,000
Year 3	10,000	80,000

We will examine their potential acceptability under the NPV and the ARR methods.

2. *Net present value method*

Project P $\quad -100{,}000 + 70{,}000(0.909) + 50{,}000(0.826) + 10{,}000(0.751)$

$= +£12{,}440$

Project Q $\quad -100{,}000 + 20{,}000(0.909) + 30{,}000(0.826) + 80{,}000(0.751)$

$= +£3{,}040$

Clearly P is the more acceptable project.

3. *Accounting rate of return method (based on total investment cost)*

$$\text{ARR} = \frac{\text{annual cash flow} - \text{annual depreciation}}{\text{total investment cost}}$$

$$\text{Project P: ARR} = \frac{\dfrac{70{,}000 + 50{,}000 + 10{,}000}{3} - \dfrac{100{,}000}{3}}{100{,}000}$$

$$\text{ARR} = \frac{43{,}333 - 33{,}333}{100{,}000} = 10\%$$

$$\text{Project Q: ARR} = \frac{\dfrac{20{,}000 + 30{,}000 + 80{,}000}{3} - \dfrac{100{,}000}{3}}{100{,}000}$$

$$\text{ARR} = \frac{43{,}333 - 33{,}333}{100{,}000} = 10\%$$

Using ARR, the two projects are indistinguishable, as each shows a return of 10%. Furthermore both apparently produce a return no higher than the cost of capital. This shows that incorrect decisions can be taken by using the ARR method, based on arbitrary accounting profits, caused by arbitrary depreciation figures, and other accounting allocations.

12.6 Long-term decisions in practice

We have looked in some detail at various methods which might be used to decide on the worthwhileness of long-term projects. Some are technically sophisticated, some costly to implement and some, which are neither sophisticated nor costly, are intuitively appealing. Whatever their apparent merits and demerits, it would be wrong to conclude this chapter by failing to mention which methods are used by corporate decision makers. Is there wide acceptance by decision makers of apparently superior methods? Several recent studies of the practice of long-term decision making have been undertaken in both the UK and the USA. Two UK studies are of particular interest. The first, conducted by Carsberg and Hope in 1975, looked at the evaluation methods used by 325 of the top 1,000 UK firms. [35] The results of the survey showed the most widely used methods to be:

(i) qualitative judgement;
(ii) IRR;
(iii) payback;
(iv) NPV;
(v) accounting rate of return.

Given the preceding discussion, the pre-eminence accorded to qualitative judgement might seem somewhat surprising. But should we really be surprised to find that managers use their judgement extensively in making decisions which shape the firm's future? Throughout this book we have frequently stressed that the qualitative aspects of business decisions are very important, even if difficult to quantify. So why might 'qualitative judgement' be of primary importance in long-term decision making? Perhaps because of the uncertainty attached to the outcomes of long-term decisions. It is likely that the results of such decisions will be affected by some unexpected features – and thus exclusive reliance on numerical forecasts might expose managers to criticism if those forecasts are not met. In other words, judgemental decision making may be in the managers' own interests.

[35] See Carsberg, B. V. and Hope, A., *Business Investment Decisions Under Inflation*, Institute of Chartered Accountants in England and Wales, 1976.

The second survey, conducted in 1982 by Pike[36], looked at the practices of 150 of the larger UK firms and found a substantial measure of agreement with the findings of Carsberg and Hope. Thus Pike confirmed the weight attached to judgemental issues, noting that 63% of his respondents considered qualitative judgement to be 'important' or 'very important' in decision making. However, Pike's ranking of the more formal methods of appraisal used by his respondents gives a changed ordering from that of Carsberg and Hope, as follows:

(i) payback;
(ii) IRR;
(iii) ARR;
(iv) NPV.

Pike also found that where firms used more than one method of appraisal, IRR was the most popular. Only 17% of respondents considered NPV to be the most important evaluation method.

Both surveys show that the decision makers clearly prefer IRR to NPV. Nor is this situation peculiar to the UK. A series of American studies have also confirmed the practical preferences for IRR. How are we to explain this apparent conflict between the prescriptions of theory and the choices of decision makers? We probably cannot argue that decision makers are unfamiliar with the arguments concerning the merits of the methods. Academic writers have been presenting the case of NPV in more or less sophisticated fashion for the last thirty years, and it is not likely that all of these presentations have remained unheard and unread. Perhaps the explanations lie not at a technical level, but rather at a more practical level, one which reflects the comparative ease of understanding the data. Here we offer, in no particular order, three possible explanations for the practical superiority of IRR over NPV.

First, in contrast to the NPV rule, the IRR method does not require an explicit cost of capital calculation *at the start of the analysis*, although the *final* decision on acceptability should be based on a comparison of the IRR and the cost of capital. What may happen in practice is that the IRR may be measured finally against a series of possible hurdle rates (whether costs of capital or otherwise) chosen on a subjective basis. Thus use of the IRR allows the manager to incorporate qualitative judgement into the analytical framework. A series of possible hurdle rates could also be tested using NPV, by calculating a range of NPVs at different discount rates. However this procedure may well appear more cumbersome and less readily understandable to a manager.

Second, there is evidence to suggest that managers may be more 'at home' in dealing with percentage measures than with absolute cash flows when comparing investments and investment returns. The use of IRR allows them to make use of this familiarity.

Finally, and somewhat more tentatively, we suggest that many managers may prefer IRR because it enables them to allow for the different risk levels associated

[36] See Pike, R. H., 'A review of recent trends in capital budgeting processes', *Accounting and Business Research*, Summer 1983.

with particular investments, by examining the differences in the margins of safety as measured by the difference between the IRR and the required return. Although this appears a rather more unsophisticated treatment of risk than others we described in Chapter 4, it is easier to implement and allows a more obvious use of qualitative managerial judgement, an attribute which we have seen to be attractive to many managers.

How also are we to explain the continued popularity of the non-discounting methods? For example, Pike's survey showed that 70% of large UK firms use the payback method and of those firms which use multiple evaluation criteria, over 90% use payback as one of the methods. These are significant percentages. A number of factors may be suggested for such popularity. For example, many managers may feel that the uncertainty inherent in the cash flow estimates renders complex evaluation methods superfluous. Why make an elaborate analysis when the underlying data themselves are unreliable? At least payback has the advantages of simplicity and understandability. It may also be the case that the popularity of payback is in part due to management's concern with short-term liquidity rather than longer-term profitability. Finally, we might stress that one theoretical justification for the use of discounting depends both on the existence of a perfect capital market and on the belief that share prices represent the present value of the anticipated dividend stream. It is possible that the capital market is imperfect (or at least that managers believe it to be so) and that the value of shares is affected by (short-term) variables other than anticipated dividends. This point is worth exploring further as it may do much to explain the continued importance in investment appraisal not only of payback, but of other profit-based measures such as ARR.

Insofar as managers believe that variables such as reported profits, asset cover and current ratios influence share prices, they ignore at their peril the effects of long-term decisions on these variables. Nor should we forget that many managers have their own compensation and bonuses tied to the firm's (or the division's) performance, as measured typically by a variant of the accounting rate of return, the return on investment (ROI). ROI is by far the most popular method used to evaluate performance within the organisation. There is an obvious incentive for managers to accept projects which are successful when evaluated by the same criteria (ARR or ROI) against which they themselves are assessed. This may be the case even if these criteria give different signals (and therefore entail the choice of different projects) from those given by the NPV method. At the root of the conflict may well lie the managers' belief that they are constrained in their long-term decision making by the short-term view adopted by the capital markets. They are less willing to accept long-term projects which do little to enhance short-term profits. Long-term projects with long gestation periods which depress accounting profits in the early years, may make the firm vulnerable to bids from third parties or may otherwise threaten the positions of managers, if these lower accounting profits have adverse effects on the share price. The moral may be that if investors worry about the quality and quantity of short-term profits then, to maintain the company's share price (and their own positions), so should the managers. The following example relating to project choice poses the sort of dilemma faced by managers.

Mr Race, the chief executive of Course plc, is concerned about the share price of his company, fearing that unless it improves over the next two years, the company may be subject to an unwelcome takeover bid. Mr Race is currently choosing between two alternative ways (A and B) of marketing a new product. The sales of each product will last for four years. A market research survey has suggested that the annual net cash receipts (R) for the new product, before advertising and special packaging costs, will be the same whichever marketing alternative is chosen, and will be determined by the equation:

$$R = 600{,}000y - 100{,}000y^2$$

where y represents the relevant year, e.g. in the second year ($y = 2$), R = £800,000.

The equipment required by each marketing alternative has a four year life and zero scrap value and costs £1,000,000 for alternative A and £800,000 for alternative B. The initial two years' advertising costs will be the same for both alternatives, namely £400,000 in the first year and £200,000 in the second year. For alternative A, the advertising costs compared to the second year will increase at 20% p.a. compound for the third and fourth year. No further advertising costs will be incurred in alternative B after the second year. Alternative B necessitates the use of special display packaging, the cost of which is equal to 20% of the annual net cash receipts (R).

The purchase of the equipment will take place on the first day of the first financial year and all other cash flows can be assumed to take place on the last day of each financial year. The effective after-tax cost of capital of Course plc is 10%.

On the basis of the above data, which alternative should Mr Race choose? Alternative A or alternative B? Let us begin our analysis by determining the effect of each alternative on the reported profitability of Course plc. Tables 12.1 and 12.2 show the profits generated by alternatives A and B over the four year period of the investment.

Though both alternatives show an accounting loss in the first year, the net improvement in profitability over the first two years, the period of Mr Race's expressed concern, is much greater for alternative A. Alternative A increases reported profit by £200,000 in the first two years; alternative B by only £40,000. The signal given to Mr Race might be to choose alternative A, as this is likely to have a more favourable short-term impact on the company's share price. But how would the alternatives be ranked under our preferred NPV criterion? Would the same

Table 12.1 Alternative A – effect on profits in £000

	Years							
		1		*2*		*3*		*4*
Net revenues (£)		500		800		900		800
Less Advertising (£)	400		200		240		288	
Depreciation (£)	250	650	250	450	250	490	250	538
Net profit (£)		(150)		350		410		262

Table 12.2 Alternative B – effect on profits in £000

				Years				
		1		*2*		*3*		*4*
Net revenues (£)		500		800		900		800
Less Advertising (£)	400		200		—		—	
Packaging (£)	100		160		180		160	
Depreciation (£)	200	700	200	560	200	380	200	360
Net profit (£)		(200)		240		520		440

preference be expressed? Tables 12.3 and 12.4 show the NPV calculations over the full life of the projects.

Examination of the results shown in Tables 12.3 and 12.4 reveals clearly Mr Race's dilemma. The NPV model, which discounts the cash flows arising over the project's entire life, signals alternative B as the appropriate choice. If Mr Race wishes to maximise the wealth of Course plc's shareholders he should choose alternative B. The relative benefits of alternative B are the superior cash flows in the later years related to the lower investment cost. Reconciliation of conflicts such as these are major problems for corporate managers, and we should not ignore such problems. Perhaps shareholders in Course plc might prefer alternative A if they also believed the future independence of their company to be more secure via the short-term benefits produced by this investment. Perhaps also Course plc has shareholders who have invested for short-term capital gains rather than for a longer-term dividend stream – in which case they might also prefer alternative A. But for the purpose of developing a theory of long-term decision making, we must presume that shareholders are primarily interested in the long-term future of the

Table 12.3 Alternative A – net present value calculation in £000

			Periods		
	0	*1*	*2*	*3*	*4*
Machine cost (£)	(1,000)				
Operating cash flows (£) (Net revenues *less* advertising)	—	100	600	660	512
Net cash flow (£)	(1000)	100	600	660	512
Discount factor at 10%	1.000	0.9091	0.8264	0.7513	0.6830
Present values of cash flows (£)	(1,000)	91	496	496	350
	Net present value + £433,000				

Table 12.4 Alternative B – net present value calculation in £000

	Periods				
	0	*1*	*2*	*3*	*4*
Machine cost (£)	(800)				
Operating cash flows (£) (Net revenues *less* advertising and packaging)	—	—	440	720	640
Net cash flow (£)	(800)	—	440	720	640
Discount factor at 10%	1.000	0.0901	0.8264	0.7513	0.6830
Present values of cash flows (£)	(800)	—	364	541	437
	Net present value + £542,000				

organisation, and that they expect to receive a stream of dividends as reward for their investment. On this basis it is difficult to argue against the NPV method. We conclude this chapter by reiterating why we believe the NPV method is the best available and why it should be used in all cases which demand relatively complex and sophisticated treatments. Its virtues can be expressed as follows:

1. It is clear, simple to understand and unambiguous.
2. It focuses on the maximisation of the present value of future cash flows, which is the objective assumed for business decision making.
3. It uses a discount rate (the cost of capital) which reflects the returns required by the suppliers of funds.
4. It avoids the many technical problems of the IRR method, and because it accounts for the time value of money, it is superior to any non-discounting method.

Even though the NPV method has not yet gained the wide acceptance by business which it deserves, this situation may change as managers come to realise that the use of the method leads to optimal decision making, at least in the sense that the present value of the firm's cash resources will be equal to or larger than the present value of cash resources resulting from the use of any other method.

Discussion topics

1 'The net present value technique offers more practical advice for managers than the internal rate of return method.' Discuss.

2 Explain the situations in which the IRR technique may lead to different conclusions from the NPV method. Are these situations likely to arise often?

3 Many studies have shown that, in practice, IRR is preferred to NPV. Why is this? Do you believe that accounting writers should rethink their theories in the light of such practices?

4 'Any appraisal technique which uses discounting is likely to be more effective than any technique which does not.' Discuss.

5 'The accounting rate of return is riddled with inconsistencies such as to make its usefulness very doubtful.' If you accept this proposition, why do you think that the accounting rate of return is still used in practice?

6 'The future is so uncertain that the use of any technique which requires the precise identification of future yearly cash flows is an unwarranted luxury. In inflationary times, such techniques are simply academic.' Discuss.

Exercises

12.1 Marc plc is considering the selection of one of a pair of mutually exclusive investment projects. Both would involve purchase of machinery with a life of five years. Project 1 would generate annual cash flows (receipts less payments) of £200,000; the machinery would cost £556,000, and have a scrap value of £56,000. Project 2 would generate annual cash flows of £500,000; the machinery would cost £1,616,000 and have a scrap value of £301,000.

Marc uses the straight line method for providing depreciation. Its cost of capital is 15% p.a. Assume that annual cash flows arise on the anniversaries of the initial outlay, that there will be no price changes over the project lives and that acceptance of one of the projects will not alter the required amount of working capital.

(a) Calculate for each project:
- (i) the accounting rate of return (ratio, over project life, of average accounting profit to *average book value of investment*) to nearest 1%;
- (ii) the net present value;
- (iii) the internal rate of return (DCF yield) to nearest 1%;
- (iv) the payback period to one decimal place.

(b) State which, if any, project you would select for acceptance, giving reasons for your choice of criterion to guide the decision.

12.2 Sullivan Investments Ltd is considering which, if any, of four projects to undertake. The forecast cash flows for each project are listed below; receipts arise at the end of the year.

Projects	*Immediate outlay* (£)	*Net inflows* (£) *Year 1*	*Year 2*	*Year 3*
1	−2,500	+1,000	+1,000	+1,000
2	−1,000	+ 100	+1,400	—
3	−1,000	+ 800	+ 600	—
4	−4,000	—	—	+5,000

Cash is readily available at the company's cost of capital of 10% p.a.

(a) Indicate which projects the company should accept. State clearly the reason for your decisions.

(b) How would your conclusions in (a) above differ if 2 and 3 were mutually exclusive? The internal rate of return of 2 is 23%, and that of 3 is 27%. Would it be valid to choose between projects 2 and 3 on the basis of their expected internal rates of return? If not, present revised calculations so that the internal rate of return method and the method you have used in (a) above lead to the same, unambiguous conclusions.

12.3 Strauss Ltd is considering three projects each of which, if accepted, would commence on 1 January 19X7. Cash flows expected from the projects are as follows:

		Project	
	A (£)	*B* (£)	C (£)
1 January 19X7	−5,000	−10,000	−6,000
31 December 19X7	+4,000	+ 1,000	+2,200
31 December 19X8	+1,500	+ 1,000	+2,200
31 December 19X9	+1,100	+13,900	+2,200

Projects A and B are mutually exclusive (i.e. only one of them may be accepted). The company's accountant has calculated the approximate internal rate of return of each project as follows:

Project A	20%
Project B	18%
Project C	5%

The accountant advises that project A should be accepted rather than B as it has a higher internal rate of return, and that C should be accepted as it shows a positive rate of return. Strauss Ltd is able both to lend and borrow funds freely at 10% p.a.

(a) Prepare calculations showing which projects Strauss Ltd should accept. If your recommendations differ from those of the accountant, explain and justify the differences.

(b) Prepare revised calculations so that the internal rate of return method of appraisal and the method you have used in (a) above, lead to the same conclusions.

12.4 Moore plc manufactures and sells a wide range of consumer durable goods. The sales of one of its products, alpha, have been increasing in recent years. The current selling price of each alpha is £40 and the variable costs are £35 per unit. Fixed costs directly attributable to alpha are currently £140,000.

Over the next four years it is anticipated that the sales will be as follows:

	Unit sales
Year ended 31 December 19X7	73,000
19X8	81,000
19X9	89,000
19Y0	97,000

Selling prices will increase by 5% each year over this period, whereas variable costs will increase by 7% p.a. and fixed costs by 5% p.a.

In anticipation of the management accountant presenting figures which may show a decline in profits for alpha, the sales manager has proposed an extensive advertising campaign to boost sales of this product. Such a campaign would cost an additional £150,000 at the beginning of the first year and a further £50,000 at the beginning of the second year. The expected benefits are reflected in the revised sales forecast as follows:

	Unit sales
Year ended 31 December 19X7	93,000
19X8	107,000
19X9	112,000
19Y0	118,000

After 19Y0 alpha is expected to be superseded. The sales increase would require an additional investment in working capital of £80,000 during the first year and a further £20,000 during the second year. This working capital would all be disinvested during the final year in which alpha is made and sold.

The general manager is willing to consider such a campaign, although there is some concern as to how this will be reflected in the annual profitability statements, particularly in the years when additional advertising expenditure will be incurred. It is company practice to charge all advertising and sales promotion expenditure to the current income statement and not to defer the expense.

(a) Prepare a statement showing the estimated profitability of alpha over the next four years, assuming the additional advertising expenditure is not incurred.

(b) Prepare a statement showing whether or not the increased advertising expenditure can be justified in the light of the company's target return on investment of 15% p.a.

(c) Prepare a statement showing the profitability of alpha over the next four years, assuming the advertising campaign is undertaken.

12.5 Pyne Ltd has been offered a contract to manufacture and supply 500 cridgets per annum for two years. The price would be £150 per unit for the first year; it would be increased in line with the retail price index for the second year. The customer would pay £25,000 now, £75,000 a year later and the balance on completion. Pyne would normally expect a higher price, but it is interested in the contract as a means of using spare capacity following cancellation of another contract.

The following information is available about resources required to manufacture cridgets.

1. *Materials*

Type of material	*Quantity per cridget* (kg)	*Amount in stock now* (kg)	*Original purchase price of stock per kg* (£)	*Current purchase price per kg* (£)	*Purchase price per kg after one year* (£)	*Net realisable value per kg now* (£)
PS	5	–	–	6.0	7.5	5.5
EQ	2	1,000	5.0	6.0	6.6	4.0
DZ	3	2,000	8.0	10.0	11.0	7.0

PS would be purchased immediately. The stock of EQ could not be used by Pyne for any purpose other than the manufacture of cridgets. DZ is used frequently by Pyne. Additional supplies of EQ and DZ, if required for the contract, would be purchased after one year.

2. *Labour*

Grade of labour	*Hours per cridget*	*Normal wage rate* First year (£)	*Second year* (£)
Skilled	5	4.00	4.80
Semi-skilled	3	3.00	3.60
Unskilled	4	2.50	3.00

There will be a shortage of skilled labour only during the first year of the contract so that acceptance of the contract would then make it necessary to give up other work on which a contribution of £5 per hour would be earned, net of wage costs. Pyne currently has a surplus of semi-skilled labour paid at the normal rate but doing unskilled work. The employees concerned could be transferred to provide sufficient labour for the manufacture of cridgets and would be replaced by unskilled labour. Additional labour would be employed to provide unskilled labour and skilled labour in year 2.

3. *Overheads*
Overhead costs are normally charged to contracts at £14 per machine hour used (£4 for variable costs and £10 for fixed costs). Depreciation is included as a fixed cost and amounts to £3 per hour. Two machines are available to meet the requirements for manufacture of cridgets. If they were not used on the contract they would be sold immediately for £2,500 each. However, their current book values are £6,500 each. At the end of two years they would have to be scrapped for £500 each. Output of each cridget requires four hours of machine time.

The retail price index is expected to be 15% higher on average in the second year of the contract than in the first. The cost of capital of Pyne is 15% p.a. Assume that payments for labour and overheads would be made at the end of the year to which they relate.

(a) Prepare calculations to show whether the proposed contract is worthwhile and by how much.

(b) Add a short note on other factors, not reflected in your calculations, which might influence the decision.

12.6 Verdi Ltd is considering its investment programme for 19X8 and 19X9. The following projects are available:

	Project A (£)	B (£)	C (£)	D (£)
Cash flow at:				
1 January 19X8	−30,000	−60,000	−24,000	−15,000
1 January 19X9	−90,000	−15,000	−24,000	−30,000
1 January 19Y0	+120,000	+90,000	+40,000	+90,000
1 January 19Y1	+70,000	+40,000	+40,000	+10,000

No other projects are expected to be available for commencement on 1 January 19X8 or 1 January 19X9. None of the above projects can be delayed.

Verdi Ltd is financed entirely by ordinary shares, and has a cost of capital of 14%. The company is able to invest surplus funds in a bank deposit account at an annual rate of 8%. Assume that fractions of projects may be undertaken, although no project can be undertaken more than once.

(a) Provide calculations showing which projects Verdi should undertake if capital is expected to be freely available at 14% during all future periods.

(b) Show how your answer to (a) above would change if capital at 1 January 19X8 was limited to £60,000, and expected to be freely available at 14% from 1 January 19X9.

(c) Provide a mathematical programming formulation to assist the directors of Verdi Ltd in choosing investment projects for 19X8 and 19X9, if capital available at 1 January 19X8 is limited to £60,000, capital at 1 January 19X9 is limited to £45,000, and capital is freely available at 14% from 1 January 19Y0.

12.7 Mrs Capricorn is proposing to purchase a machine to manufacture widgets. She plans to manufacture 1,000 widgets per annum and sell them at £2 per unit; materials and other variable costs would amount to 50p per unit and there would be no fixed costs. The machine would cost £4,000 and have a life of five years after which it would be sold for scrap for £100. The machine would require an overhaul at the end of year 3 at a cost of £1,000. Assume that sale proceeds and variable costs arise at the end of each year. Mrs Capricorn requires a return of 7% p.a. on investment; she does not expect there to be any change in relevant prices over the foreseeable future.

(a) Prepare a calculation showing whether the purchase of the machine is worthwhile.

(b) Assume that Mrs Capricorn can borrow and lend as much as she wants at 7% p.a. She decides that she will arrange her affairs so that she spends the same amount on living expenses each year and has £4,000 in hand for the purchase of a new machine in five years' time. Calculate how much she can use for living expenses each year.

(c) Prepare a calculation of accounting profits (according to usual conventions), balance sheets and rates of return on capital employed over the life of the asset, assuming that Mrs Capricorn implements the plan found in your answer to (b).

(d) Comment on the usefulness of conventional accounting calculations for purposes of investment decision making.

12.8 Stadler is an ambitious young executive who has recently been appointed to the position of financial director of Paradis plc, a small listed company. Stadler regards this appointment as a temporary one, enabling him to gain experience before moving to a larger organisation. His intention is to leave Paradis plc in three years' time, with its share price standing high. As a consequence, he is particularly concerned that the reported profits of Paradis plc should be as high as possible in his third and final year with the company.

Paradis plc has recently raised £350,000 from a rights issue, and the directors are considering three ways of using these funds. Three projects (A, B and C) are being considered, each involving the immediate purchase of equipment costing £350,000. One project only can be undertaken and the equipment for each project will have a useful life equal to that of the project, with no scrap value. Stadler favours project C because it is expected to show the highest accounting profit in the third year. However he does not wish to reveal his real reasons for favouring project C and so, in his report to the chairman he recommends project C because it shows the highest internal rate of return. The following summary is taken from his report:

	Net cash flows (£000) Years									Internal rate of return
Project	*0*	*1*	*2*	*3*	*4*	*5*	*6*	*7*	*8*	%
A	−350	100	110	104	112	138	160	180	—	27.5
B	−350	40	100	210	260	160	—	—	—	26.4
C	−350	200	150	240	40	—	—	—	—	33.0

The chairman of the company is accustomed to projects being appraised in terms of payback and accounting rate of return, and is consequently suspicious of the use of internal rate of return as a method of project selection. Accordingly, the chairman has asked for an independent report on the choice of project. The company's cost of capital is 20% and a policy of straight line depreciation is used to write off the cost of equipment in the financial statements.

(a) Calculate the payback period for each project.

(b) Calculate the accounting rate of return for each project.

(c) Prepare a report for the chairman with supporting calculations indicating which project should be preferred by the ordinary shareholders of Paradis plc.

(d) Discuss the assumptions about the reactions of the stock market that are implicit in Stadler's choice of project C.

Further reading

Bromwich, M., *The Economics of Capital Budgeting*, Penguin, 1976.

Carsberg, B. V. and Hope, A., *Business Investment Decisions under Inflation*, Institute of Chartered Accountants in England and Wales, 1976.

Coulthurst, N. J., 'The application of the incremental principle in capital investment project evaluation', *Accounting and Business Research*, Autumn 1986.

Coulthurst, N. J., 'Accounting for inflation in capital investment: the state of the art and science', *Accounting and Business Research*, Winter 1986.

Hirshleifer, J., 'On the theory of optimal investment decision', *Journal of Political Economy*, October 1958.

Jones, C. J., 'Financial planning and control practices in UK companies: a longitudinal study', *Journal of Business Finance and Accounting*, Summer 1986.

Kee, R. and Bublitz, B., 'The role of payback in the investment process', *Accounting and Business Research*, Spring 1988.

Klammer, T., 'Empirical evidence on the adoption of sophisticated capital budgeting techniques', *Journal of Business*, July 1972.

Lerner, E. and Rappaport, A., 'Limit DCF in capital budgeting', *Harvard Business Review*, September/October 1968.

Luckett, P. F., 'ARR vs IRR: a review and an analysis', *Journal of Business Finance and Accounting*, Summer 1984.

Mao, J. C. T., 'Survey of capital budgeting: theory and practice', *Journal of Finance*, May 1970.

Pike, R. H., 'A review of recent trends in capital budgeting processes', *Accounting and Business Research*, Summer 1983.

Pike, R. H., 'Owner–manager conflict and the role of the payback method', *Accounting and Business Research*, Winter 1985.

Pike, R. H., 'An empirical study of the adoption of sophisticated capital budgeting practices and decision-making effectiveness', *Accounting and Business Research*, Autumn 1988.

Primrose, P. L., Bailey, F. A. and Leonard, R., 'The practical application of discounted cash flow to plant purchase using an integrated suite of computer programs', *Accounting and Business Research*, Winter 1984.

Sarnat, M. and Levy, H., 'The relationship of rules of thumb to the internal rate of return: a restatement and generalisation', *Journal of Finance*, June 1969.

Scapens, R. W. and Sale, J. T., 'Performance measurement and formal capital expenditure controls in divisionalised companies', *Journal of Business Finance and Accounting*, Autumn 1981.

Chapter 13

The budgeting process

In previous chapters we have examined in some detail the types of decisions, both short- and long-term, typically undertaken by management, and we have set out the criteria to be used to ensure that such decisions are consistent with the assumed goals of the organisation. Throughout these chapters we have stressed the importance of the concept of *differential analysis* as the basis of managerial decision making. Our primary aim has been to look at individual decisions in isolation so as to highlight the main principles of decision analysis. We have not considered explicitly the interdependences which exist between the different functions within an organisation.

In practice, managerial decisions frequently involve the simultaneous use of factors which draw on a number of functions of a business, for example the marketing, production, purchasing and financing functions. Such functions do not operate independently of each other. Decisions which utilise these functions are interdependent decisions. For example, suppose that the management of a manufacturing firm decides to sell x units of product Y. Unless the firm holds large stocks of Y and does not wish to replace these stocks when they are used, the decision to sell will involve a decision to produce more units of Y, which in turn may entail a further, simultaneous decision to purchase raw materials, hire labour and incur overhead costs, each of which will affect the firm's financial resources.

A vitally important task for management is to coordinate these various interrelated aspects of decision making. This helps first to ensure that the final results are consistent with the organisation's goals and, secondly, to prevent suboptimisation within the organisation by ensuring, as far as is possible, that individual managers are working towards the same end. This is a difficult and time consuming task. Individual managers may pursue targets which appear good for themselves but which, from the firm's viewpoint, are not optimal. For example, the manager of the assembly department may wish to buy components externally rather than rely on internal manufacture, perhaps because external components are currently cheaper than the price charged to the assembly department by the manufacturing department. However, for the firm as a whole this choice may be suboptimal when other social and economic factors are considered. We consider this particular issue in Chapter 16.

One way for management to coordinate these activities is to prepare detailed and explicit financial plans of action for specific future periods, both for individual units within the firm, such as manufacturing and assembly divisions, and for the firm as a single entity. These detailed plans are usually referred to as *budgets*, and the coordinating activity is usually termed the *budgetary process*. The overall plan for the firm is termed the *master budget* or *comprehensive budget*. The general objective of budgeting is thus to provide a formal, quantitative and authoritative statement of the firm's plans, expressed in money terms. (We will discuss the validity of purely financial budgets in the concluding section of this chapter). This rather wide-ranging definition covers a multitude of different possible sub-objectives. At least six, some of which are overlapping, are worthy of further analysis.

1. Budgeting forces managers to plan. The existence of formal budgets compels busy managers to think coherently about their position in the firm and their contribution to its future. Thus budgeting forces managers to stand back from their regular activities and to consider the goals of the firm, as well as the more detailed ways of achieving them.

2. Budgeting reveals new data about the firm's future and thus reduces the risks inherent in its operations. For example, the extent of the different, and joint, claims on resources from managers of decentralised activities may not be obvious until they are brought together in the budget. This may then show the existence of scarce or surplus resources, which, in turn, may lead to improved measures (e.g. opportunity costs) of the costs of using such resources.

3. Budgeting encourages communication and the coordination of activities. Budget procedures allow information about the proposed activities of the firm to be communicated to different managers in different locations, and may thus help in the reconciliation of claims to, and availability of, significant resources. In addition, where responsibilities are geographically and functionally separate, it may be difficult to communicate the performance targets expected of individuals – formal budgeting seeks to mitigate this problem. Whether or not all employees should participate in the setting of such targets is an important issue which we discuss later in this chapter.

4. Budgeting provides a guide to action. The physical process of budgeting of itself gives information to management about the feasibility and appropriateness of particular activities. If activities are seen to be infeasible or inappropriate, the signal is given for corrective action, and once the budget has been approved, managers are given a clearer indication of the tasks and targets expected of them.

5. Budgeting acts as a basis for measuring and evaluating performance. This aspect of budgeting is regarded by many writers as being its most important feature. The preparation and subsequent agreement of the budget offers a benchmark against which the performance of all entities within the firm, as

well as the firm itself, can be measured. Managers can be held responsible for their own particular portion of the overall budget. Budgets thus facilitate management by exception, as it is only necessary for managers to investigate those aspects of performance which are significantly different from expectations.

6. Budgeting aids goal congruence. The process of planning and controlling is a constantly reiterative process which helps greatly to marry the firm's goals with those of its individual parts, i.e. it helps the achievement of goal congruence between each part of the firm (the managers and the divisions) and the firm itself.

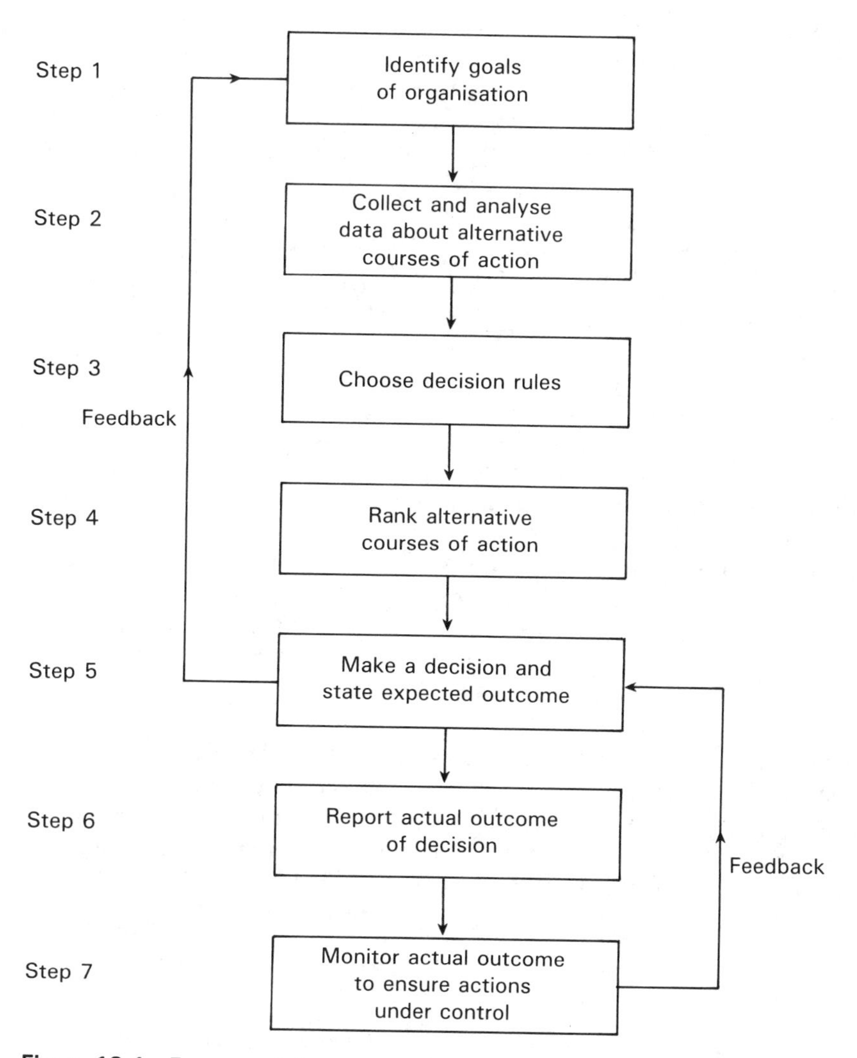

Figure 13.1 Framework for managerial planning, decision making and control.

In order to understand the budgetary process more clearly, we should explain how it fits into the overall framework for managerial planning, decision making and control, which we first set out in Chapter 1. The framework is produced again here (see Figure 13.1). The budgetary process begins with Step 5 of the managerial framework, i.e. once decisions have been taken to commit resources to specific plans of action, forecasts are made of the expected outcomes of these plans, in the form of budgets. Budgets thus embody the expected outcomes of particular decisions; and because decisions take account of the interdependences within the organisation, budgets include the impact of these interdependences.

As we have just seen, the use of budgets is integral to the *planning process*. But the importance of budgeting does not stop with planning. In order to ensure that plans are correctly implemented, that stated targets are reached and that information is available to aid future planning, actual performance must be regularly reported and monitored, by comparison with expected performance (Steps 6 and 7 of the framework). These two steps are commonly known as the *control process*. Thus the use of budgets is important also as an aid to performance evaluation and control. We might add a third main use of budgets as a device for *motivation*. In Chapter 14 we show how we might prepare a master or comprehensive budget for the firm. Chapter 15 looks in detail at the control system provided by standard costing (the most commonly used accounting system for budgetary control which we introduced in Chapter 5), and Chapter 16 looks at budgeting and planning in decentralised organisations.

13.1 Budgeting and planning

In order to better aid the pursuit of organisational goals, explicit, formal plans should be drawn up. If this is not done, then managers can use only crude, intuitive measures to judge whether their operations are successful, and their targets achieved. Budgets represent the financial expression of formal plans, and, as with successful planning, successful budgeting should also be formalised. But what is planning? It is a difficult question to answer easily, as firms engage in different forms of planning. We might classify business plans as falling under one of the following headings.

1. Operating plans: these are short-term plans which relate directly to the achievement of the firm's objectives. Thus the annual production and sales plans, as well as the plans to finance them would be examples of operating plans. As we will see, most of the firm's budgeting activities are taken up with short-term operating plans.
2. Administrative plans: these are 'tactical' plans concerned with the creation of the organisational structure, under which budgets and performance levels can be determined for appropriate functions.
3. Long-term strategic plans: these plans are concerned with the long-term development of the firm's strategy, and are likely to be expressed in quite general terms.

The objectives of the budget, and the means of attaining them, should be stated explicitly. The level of sophistication and detail of any budget should be a function of the size of the organisation and also the position of the particular budget within the organisation. For example, the top management of a large organisation is not likely to wish to consider detailed budgetary data concerning proposed expenditure on spare parts in one of many factories within the organisation: rather it might wish to concern itself with the proposed total expenditure for the forthcoming period for the whole factory. This implies a structure of responsibility centres within the organisation, each accountable for a specific level of detail within the total budgetary process. We look at this notion of responsibility accounting and its corollary activity, management by exception, in the next section dealing with budgeting and control. It is very important to point out here that, as with other aspects of the planning and control process, the benefits of any system of budgeting should be judged in relation to the costs of setting up and operating the system. No managerial activity should be viewed in isolation from its attendant costs and benefits. There are, however, two interdependent aspects of the relationship between budgeting and planning which we should consider in more detail: the method by which budgets are prepared, and the time periods covered by budgets.

The preparation of budgets

Budgets do not appear out of thin air; they represent the product of much organisational thinking and, often, internal dissension. Most large organisations commit considerable human resources to the preparation of budgets. A budget director or controller, who usually takes no part in the detailed preparation of individual budgets, is responsible for overall budget preparation and coordination, often being assisted by a budgeting committee consisting of members of top management from each of the organisation's functional divisions. The task of the committee is to set general guidelines to be followed by individual managers in building up their own budgets, to resolve differences among them and to submit a final comprehensive budget for approval by the board of directors.

In effect, budgeting constitutes a system of authority within the organisation. The structure of budget organisation and responsibility is important. Budgeting is a complicated process and in practice seldom starts with a 'clean sheet'. Such general factors as last year's budget and actual level of performance, the profit or return on investment objectives of the firm, and the relative bargaining strengths of interested groups will influence the process. Ideally these influencing factors will result in a budgeting procedure which sets targets that are neither over- nor under-demanding, so that challenges are offered but fears of unfavourable variances are calmed. We will discuss these issues further in the final section of this chapter.

As can be imagined, only infrequently will figures be immediately accepted without controversy. Rather, an iterative process is involved by which the plans, intentions, ambitions and constraints of individual managers throughout the organisation are submitted, reviewed, changed and ultimately, by reason of the authority of the budget controller and the budget committee, agreed. Budgeting, in short, is a bargaining process in which individual goals are traded off for (it is hoped) the overall benefit of the organisation and, as in most bargaining situations, the end product is often radically different from the original submission. The end product of the whole budgeting process takes the form of the organisation's expected position at some future point in time (a *budgeted balance sheet*) and the means of reaching that position (a *budgeted income statement*). A statement of the sources and applications of the organisation's funds may accompany the two main statements. The budgeting process will typically begin well in advance of the period covered by the budget. For example, the preparation of detailed budgets for a firm with a year end of 31 December may well begin in the summer of the previous year, and be completed by October of that year. The budget statements are usually vague single-valued estimates of the future, derived from individual budgets for sales, purchases, cash flow, etc., and as such are static. We query the usefulness for control purposes of such static budgets in the following section.

In preparing detailed budgets it must be recognised that the activities of the organisation are likely to be limited by certain constraints. In consequence, the recognition of both the level of constraints, and the time at which they are likely to arise, is of critical importance. For example, if 4,000 units of a particular product can be produced with the available equipment and workforce, but only 3,000 units can be sold, then obviously the principal limiting factor for the firm is the level of consumer demand. In this case, it will be necessary to prepare first the sales budget and then to prepare the other budgets in the light of estimated sales. Similarly, situations may arise in which productive capacity, short- or even long-term cash may prove to be the constraining factor. If one constraint cannot be relaxed, then all budgets must be geared to the one representing the constraining factor. If it is anticipated that two or more constraining factors are likely to be in force simultaneously then the procedure is more complicated, although the underlying principles are similar, and the organisation should use an optimising technique such as linear programming (see Chapter 9) to derive its best budgetary plan.

The time periods covered by budgets

Budgets are financial plans for future periods. But which future periods? In general, planning horizons will depend largely on the uncertainty of the business environment and management's need for control information. It is normal however to distinguish between two types of budgets, short-term and long-term, because they may seek to serve different purposes and because the level of detail they incorporate may differ widely.

Short-term budgets

These are related to current conditions and usually cover a period of one year. Such annual budgets are, in turn, broken down into quarterly, monthly, four weekly or even weekly periods. The actual level of disaggregation of the annual budget is a function of the particular business, but at least some disaggregation is usually necessary. For instance, management will wish to monitor progress throughout the year, and to take any corrective action as soon as possible rather than wait until the end of the year when the final results are known. Equally, management will need information during the year to adjust current budgets for the remainder of the period if the situation warrants such changes.

Although the time period chosen for a short-term budget is often one year, this may vary from firm to firm. For example, the appropriate period for a short-term budget of a firm engaged in the fashion trade may be considerably less than one year, whereas a similar budget for a construction company may be prepared for a longer period.

In general the period selected will depend upon such factors as the following:

1. The life cycle of the firm's products: the shorter the life cycle the more frequent will be the need for operating decisions.
2. The type of customer: in industries where buying and selling relationships are very close (e.g. between food manufacturing and food retailing), both parties may prefer to enter into longer-term contracts to encourage stability.
3. The stability of demand for the firm's product: most firms have some degree of seasonality of sales and thus the season (e.g. the Christmas season for retailing) may influence the budget period as much as the financial year.
4. The existence of any constraints on operations: as we have discussed, certain constraints (e.g. shortage of labour, materials or funds) may necessitate more regular control reports and, if of sufficient severity, a rescheduling of operations.
5. The characteristics of the industry: some production processes involve such a level of technological sophistication that short-term alterations to budget will be impossible.

The above discussion suggests that, at the very least, the importance of the multi-purpose budget demands that revisions should be frequent enough to accommodate situations in which the original assumptions in the budget, both in relation to the current and to future periods, have proved to be invalid. The necessity and direction of such revisions will be determined in large part by the stability of the firm's environment, but failure to revise budgets properly may diminish quickly their relevance to managerial decision making. One means of incorporating such revisions is by way of a *rolling* or *continuous* budget. A continuous budget is formulated initially for a period of, say, one year. As each monthly, four weekly, or quarterly period passes, two actions take place within the budgetary process. First a budget for the corresponding period of the following year is prepared, thus ensuring that a short-term budget is always in existence for the immediate future twelve months; second, the budget for the following eleven months (or 48 weeks or three quarters if appropriate) is revised in the light of the results of the period which has just elapsed (in particular, of any changes in expectations regarding costs etc.) so ensuring that the current budget is revised constantly and kept up to date.

Long-term budgets

These are budgets which relate to the development of the business over many years, and, as such, are unlikely to be changed very often. They reflect a long-run appreciation of the firm's objectives and are usually drawn up in very general terms covering, *inter alia*, the nature of the business, its position in the industry, the expected level of inflation and its impact on the business. The targets covered by long-term budgets are often expressed as overall company goals – for example to produce a return on shareholders' funds of 20%. Achievement of this target will in turn entail the setting of more detailed sub-goals for individual divisions and managers. Thus, to achieve the 20% return on shareholders' funds, the production department's goal might involve a target quota of 10,000 components per week.

Long-term budgets are typically drawn up for a period of between three and ten years, and will deal particularly with the firm's likely requirements for long-term assets, and the appropriate mix of debt and equity finance.

13.2 Budgeting and control

A second major purpose of budgeting is its usefulness for control purposes. The control process follows the planning process, i.e. once plans have been agreed,

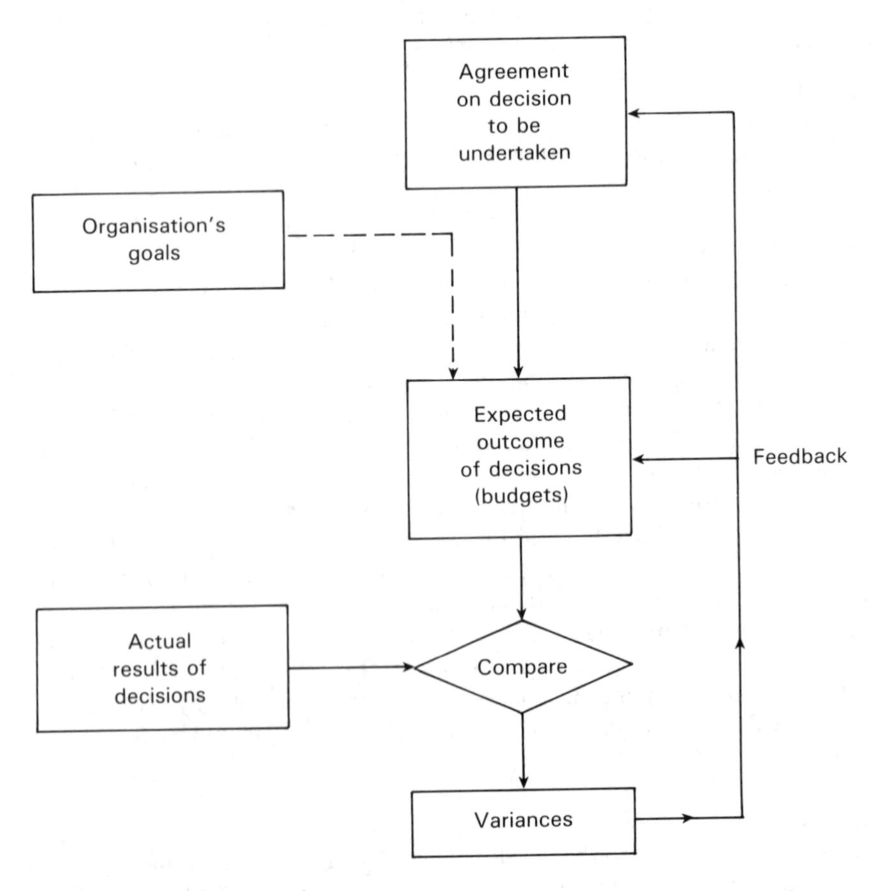

Figure 13.2 The control process.

decisions are implemented and reports are prepared to determine whether events are going according to plan. We might say that the control process involves three sequential, but interrelated stages: the recording of actual performance, the comparison of actual performance with expected performance and, as a linking stage, the provision of regular feedback to allow continual monitoring of events. These three steps are brought together in Figure 13.2, which shows an abbreviated view of the control process.

Differences between budgeted and actual performance are termed *variances*. The generation of variances provides the feedback which entitles us to term the whole process a *control system*. Notice that the diagram of the control process takes the appearance, via the feedback mechanism, of a loop, or continuous process. This is because any time scale has been omitted from the diagram. The budget for the current period is compared with the actual performance of the current period and the variances are calculated accordingly. These variances will be useful both as a spur to immediate, remedial action if actual performance is less good than expected and also as input into the budgetary process for future periods. We now examine each of the three aspects of the control process in more detail.

Recording actual performance

We have seen that the decisions giving rise to the formulation of plans and budgets are carried out for different areas of activity within the organisation. If such budgets are to be used to assess and evaluate individual performance, managers need some criteria to determine exactly what constitutes a particular area of activity. To achieve this end, budgets should reflect *areas of responsibility* within the firm, so that individuals are charged *only* with those costs and revenues for which they can be held responsible, i.e. for those costs and revenues which they control. Thus we might define a responsibility area, or centre, as an area of activity within an organisation which has control over particular resources for a specified period.

It is vital that such areas are explicitly defined, so that managers and employees know precisely what is expected of them. Conceptually, this is easy to acknowledge; in practice it is very difficult to apply. The difficulty lies in determining which costs should be assigned to specific responsibility centres. We can do no better than to cite guidelines for deciding which costs should be assigned to responsibility centres (first drawn up in the USA in 1956).[37]

1. If the person has authority over both the acquisition and the use of the services, he should be charged with the cost of such services.
2. If the person can significantly influence the amount of cost through his own action, he may be charged with such costs.
3. Even if the person cannot significantly influence the amount of cost through his own action, he may be charged with those elements with which the management desires him to be concerned, so that he will help to influence those who are responsible.

[37] Report of the Committee on Cost Concepts and Standards, *The Accounting Review*, April 1956, p. 190.

Table 13.1 Responsibility accounting reporting system

Overall responsibility		Budget This month (£)	Budget Year to date (£)	Variance* F(U) This month (£)	Variance* F(U) Year to date (£)
	Level 1 Managing director's monthly performance report				
Managing director	General administration costs	X	X	X	X
	Financial director	X	X	X	X
	Production director	125,000	470,000	(7,630)	(40,150)
	Sales director	X	X	X	X
	Total controllable costs	174,000	666,000	(7,480)	(39,750)
	Level 2 Production director's monthly performance report				
Production director	Manufacturing administration costs	X	X	X	X
	Factory A	51,000	193,000	(4,000)	(19,000)
	Factory B	X	X	X	X
	Factory C	X	X	X	X
	Supervision: personnel and scheduling	X	X	X	X
	Total controllable costs	125,000	470,000	(7,630)	(40,150)
	Level 3 Factory A's monthly performance report				
Factory supervisor	Manufacturing dept	18,000	78,000	(3,600)	(9,800)
	Assembly dept	X	X	X	X
	Packing dept	X	X	X	X
	Total controllable costs	51,000	193,000	(4,000)	(19,000)
	Level 4 Manufacturing dept's monthly performance report				
Department supervisor	Machine operators	X	X	X	X
	Direct materials	X	X	X	X
	Material handlers	X	X	X	X
	Other variable overheads	X	X	X	X
		18,000	78,000	(3,600)	(9,800)

* F signifies a favourable cost variance, i.e. actual is less than budget; U signifies an unfavourable variance, i.e. actual is greater then budget.

Responsibility centres are usually cost centres, profit centres or investment centres. The nature of the organisational structure will determine the type(s) of responsibility centre. A cost centre is the smallest area of responsibility for which costs are accumulated, for example, a single department of a firm employing few people. A manager in charge of a cost centre is held accountable only for the controllable costs of his centre. He has no control over, and is therefore not accountable for, revenues earned. A profit centre, such as an autonomous division within a firm, is a section of business for which both costs and revenues are accumulated. Thus, a manager in charge of a profit centre is responsible for the profit, or contribution margin, earned by his section of the business. The manager of an investment centre is responsible for the return on the assets under his control. We will deal more fully with some of the problems caused by accounting for divisional responsibility centres in Chapter 16.

Table 13.1 provides an example of a reporting system based on the notion of responsibility accounting. For purposes of simplicity it deals only with the costs for which each centre is responsible. In this example, there are four levels of responsibility within the organisation. As the managing director is responsible for the running of the whole organisation (Level 1), he receives reports concerning the four functional areas of the firm – general administration, finance, production and sales. The reports show both the monthly and accumulated figures for the organisation's budget, and the variances which have arisen to date. Obviously, the managing director will wish to look only at those variances representing significant departures from plan and so demanding his attention. Other variances can, if necessary, be examined by his subordinates. This is known as *management by exception*.

We shall demonstrate the notion of responsibility accounting by tracing responsibility for the costs of one of the functional areas, production, from Level 2 to Level 4. The production director's cost budget is made up by reference to the five areas directly under his control. Table 13.1 shows that factory A contributes costs of £51,000 to an overall monthly cost budget of £125,000. The total budget of factory A (Level 3) is then broken down further into the budgets for the three departments within the factory which are under the control of the factory supervisor. We can see that the manufacturing department of factory A contributes costs of £18,000 to the total budget of £51,000. Finally, the total budget of the manufacturing department of factory A is broken down (Level 4) into the elements of production within the department, for which the departmental supervisor is responsible. The system of responsibility accounting is intended to generate control reports which reflect the decentralisation of authority within the firm. In our example we have delineated four levels of managerial responsibiity, from board level to department foreman. The system has the advantage of allowing responsible officials to react speedily to any changes in their own area of responsibility, with the result that the flow of reports through the firm will allow corrective action to be taken at the appropriate level.

Comparison of actual and expected performance

When a single, fixed budget (e.g. the organisation's master budget) is prepared for planning purposes, the level of activity used to determine the costs and revenues relevant to the budget will reflect the level which is most likely to be attained. But fixed budgets may not serve equally well for control purposes. For control purposes it is necessary to compare like with like, i.e. to compare actual and budgeted costs at the level of activity achieved during the period. This ensures that valid comparisons and inferences can be made when the budgeted activity level is not attained. If the organisation's output tends to vary across a range of levels, then a number of different, flexible budgets should be prepared (see Chapter 6). They show the effects on costs (and contributions) of producing at various activity levels, and thus put the management in a better position to evaluate performance and take appropriate action. The key to flexible budgeting is, as we have seen, the separation of fixed and variable costs. If costs are split in this way it becomes much easier to gauge the impact of changes in the activity level on the period's results.

In practice this split may not be easy to achieve. Very few of the firm's costs are 'fixed' over the long term, and very few costs are 'variable' in the short term. Thus the time period chosen in preparing the flexible budget is very influential in determining the usefulness of the control system's output and thus its ultimate success. The problems of cost classification alluded to here are likely to be accentuated in the future as many organisations replace labour with capital, and invest more heavily in high technology equipment. We can envisage situations in which the *only* short-term variable costs under the manager's control will be represented by raw material and energy costs. It is certainly difficult to describe the minimal labour force employed to supervise the workings of robots and flexible manufacturing systems as being variable in relation to the level of production. And as firms plan their production around computer-integrated manufacturing systems, the classification of labour as 'direct' may cease to have any relevance at all. The following example explores the issue of budgeting for control.

Bramall Ltd produces one product, and activity levels vary widely from month to month. The following statement shows Bramall Ltd's production budget based on an average level of output of 20,000 units per four week period, and the actual results for a four week period during October.

	Budgeted production for 4 week period	*Actual production for 4 week period*
Number of units produced	20,000	17,600
Costs	(£)	(£)
Variable labour costs (£1 per unit)	20,000	19,540
Variable cost of small parts (4p per unit)	800	1,000
Other variable costs (21p per unit)	4,200	3,660
Fixed costs	18,000	16,000
Total costs	43,000	40,200

The arithmetic difference, or total variance, between the total costs expected (£43,000) and the costs actually incurred for the same period (£40,200) is £2,800. As costs incurred are less than those expected, we might say initially that this difference of £2,800 represents a favourable (F) variance. But before we make that statement, we must ask ourselves why we have prepared these figures, and how we should use the differences which they reveal. If we are trying to assess the effectiveness of the production manager in controlling his costs *once the planning decision to produce 17,600 units has been made*, then the favourable variance of £2,800 is meaningless. Why is this? Simply because we are failing to compare similar aspects of the same decision. For control purposes we should compare the actual costs of producing 17,600 units with the budgeted costs of producing the same number of units. If we do this, as in Table 13.2, a very different pattern is revealed.

Table 13.2 shows the breakdown of the total variance of £2,800 into two separate variances for which different managers may be responsible. These separate variances arise because the budget has been 'flexed' to the actual level of activity. The difference between the original budget of 20,000 units and the flexed budget of 17,600 units gives rise to a *budget revision variance* or *volume variance*. This variance reflects the expected change in costs due to the change in activity level. As the revised budget entails a fall in production of 2,400 units, Bramall Ltd expects a reduction in costs of £3,000 (i.e. 2,400 units at £1.25 per unit). The cost per unit

Table 13.2 Bramall Ltd: budgeting for control*

	Original (fixed) budget 20,000 units	*Revised (flexible) budget 17,600 units*	*Actual results 17,600 units*
Costs:			
Labour costs (£1 per unit)	20,000	17,600	19,540
Small parts (4p per unit)	800	704	1,000
Other variable costs (21p per unit)	4,200	3,696	3,660
Fixed costs (£)	18,000	18,000	16,000
Total costs (£)	43,000	40,000	40,200
	3,000 (F)		200 (U)

Budget revision variance
2,400 units at £1.25
= £3,000 (F)

Control variance

Cost of labour	1,940 (U)
Cost of small parts	296 (U)
Cost of other variable overheads	36 (F)
Expenditure on fixed costs	2,000 (F)
	200 (U)

* See Table 13.1 for definition of F and U.

avoided represents the variable cost of production, £1 plus 4p plus 21p. Fixed costs are not expected to change with the level of activity and so remain at £18,000 in the revised budget. The second variance, representing the difference in costs at the actual level of activity, is the *control variance*. This tells top management whether the production manager has been able to meet the revised budget (i.e. control the revised level of costs) for the actual level of activity. We shall discuss how we might determine the causes of, and thus the responsibility for, these different kinds of variance in Chapter 15.

We can now see that the production manager exceeded his budget for the production of 17,600 units by £200, i.e. the control variance is unfavourable (U). A breakdown of the control variance reveals that the variable costs of both labour and small parts were greater than expected, whereas the cost of other variable overheads were lower than budgeted. Expenditure on fixed costs was considerably less than expected. It is apparent that attention should be directed to the labour variance; not only is it large within the context of the labour budget, but it also seems worthy of investigation within the context of the total budget. Attention should also be paid to the fixed cost variance. It is possible that the original budget for fixed costs was set at too high a level and that a more realistic figure might improve the quality of future plans.

Because it will seldom be possible to determine the precise activity level in advance, flexible budgeting is an important tool in cost control. It sets out a series of alternative budgets for various possible levels of activity. It is similar to the technique underlying the construction of break-even charts and profit–volume graphs, explained in Chapter 6, although in practice flexible budgeting is less likely to assume linear cost and revenue behaviour.

Provision of feedback information

Timely and regular feedback is vital to a successful control system, as an aid to both managers and employees. For example, managers need speedy information on significant deviations from budget in order to take effective action to correct such deviations and to amend future plans, in so far as deviations signify a change in longer-term circumstances; employees need equally speedy information to know whether or not they have achieved their targets, and whether their performance is satisfactory. Delay in giving information on employee performance may lead to a loss of motivation, to the detriment of future performance.

The regularity with which control information is generated determines in large measure the success of the entire control process. Regularity will be largely dependent upon the activity under consideration and on the position of the activity within the entire organisation. For example, departmental supervisors will require feedback immediately if machinery breaks down, or materials are faulty; plant supervisors will require daily information on the levels of output reached; whereas for the performance of divisions within the organisation, and the performance of the organisation as a whole, the provision of formalised monthly reports will usually be adequate. But we must stress again that reports of variances do not necessarily tell the management why deviations have occurred, nor do they offer advice as to how deviations are to be acted on. For example, suppose that the production department of a large manufacturing organisation reports a favourable variance on labour cost. Is this necessarily an indication to top management that labour efficiency has increased and that the supervisor responsible should be encouraged to sustain the situation? The answer depends upon the cause of the variance and on its consequence elsewhere. It may be that the favourable variance has been achieved by labour working more quickly but less carefully than budgeted, with the result that material wastage is substantially greater than was expected. The unfavourable variance in respect of material usage should be compared to the favourable variance on labour cost before it is decided to continue with the new increased speed of working. It is one of management's most important tasks to interpret and evaluate variance information.

13.3 Budgeting and motivation

All budgeting processes involve relationships between people, for example manager–employee, director–manager and manager–manager relationships, and all interpersonal relationships generate, to some extent, behavioural problems. Thus budgeting entails behavioural problems. We must state quite categorically that the present state of knowledge concerning the behavioural implications of accounting is such that even very broad generalisations can be dangerous. Individuals, whatever their formal position within the organisation, differ in their behaviour in any given situation, and organisational settings vary widely from firm to firm.

The earlier sections of this chapter may have given the impression that budgeting is a somewhat mechanistic exercise. We described it there as a means of stating individual and collective expectations, and of ensuring operational and administrative control. We suggested its purpose might include planning, evaluating performance, reducing uncertainty, achieving goal congruence, providing a guide to action and communicating and coordinating activities. In practice many of these courses are likely to be in direct conflict. Requests for additional funds from individual managers may be mutually incompatible, especially when resources are limited. This problem is accentuated when managers, in the expectation that their requests will be cut back, propose overly optimistic budgets. The final agreed budgets may be determined as much by the managers' political skills as by the merits of their cases. This involvement in the process is likely (and perhaps intended) to influence the individual behaviour and action of the participants. As we earlier intimated this conflict of aims is likely to be at its most acute when budgets are used both for planning and for motivation. We now consider this issue further.

In determining the basis to be used in evaluating performance for any budget period, two related behavioural questions have given rise to considerable debate and elicited much research output.[38] First, how tightly should budgets be set in order to

[38] See e.g. Hofstede, G. H., *The Game of Budget Control*, Tavistock, 1968; Argyris, C., 'Human problems with budgets', *Harvard Business Review*, January/February 1953; Hopwood, A. G., *Accounting and Human Behaviour*, Prentice Hall, 1976.

induce maximum performance from employees, and second, what degree of employee participation in the budgeting process should be encouraged?

To clarify some of the issues under these two headings we shall say something about the forms of organisational structure which can exist within individual firms. In order to illustrate the main points, it is useful to identify two forms of organisational structure which lie towards opposite ends of the spectrum of possible structures: the *classical* and the *modern* structure.[39] The classical structure supposes the existence of formal relationships within a hierarchical organisation, which exists simply to maximise profits. Employees, who are characterised as being basically inefficient and antagonistic to management, are presumed to be motivated purely by monetary rewards. The classical idea views the imposition of pressure upon an alien workforce as being the best way to achieve the desired results.

The modern view of organisational structure views matters from a different perspective. The firm is seen as being a partnership or coalition of managers and employees who are not motivated solely by notions of profit and cash, but also by psychological and social needs. This view recognises that individuals within an organisation have different goals and levels of aspiration, and it is only by harnessing these to the particular situations facing the organisation that an increased sense of commitment to the goals of the organisation is achieved. (See Chapter 1 for an extended discussion of this view.) The modern view incorporates the idea of budgetary slack representing a degree of padding introduced into budgets so as to guard against possible failure to attain targets. It is deemed necessary to do this because failure to attain budget levels is seen as a social stigma which affects the individual in such a way that it reduces aspiration levels, goals and, eventually, performance.

Slack exists within even the most efficient and well-run organisations. It exists because human nature requires it to exist. It is argued that if individuals are given no room to manoeuvre within a budgetary constraint, then conflict will quickly arise between the individual's personal goals and those of the firm. The type of organisational structure possessed by the firm, whether classical, modern or some intermediate structure will have a direct bearing on the behavioural questions we have raised.

Consider now the first of the two questions posed above: how tightly should budgets be set so as to encourage maximum performance? For example, if budgets are set at too high a level, individuals may become discouraged in their tasks and not attempt to meet targets; alternatively, if budgets are pitched at too low a level, individuals may become self-satisfied and inefficient, and thus perform below their real potential.

The setting of budgets should therefore seek to reflect individuals' need for achievement and their perception of the probability of succeeding, together with the level of reward appropriate for the level of success, whilst, at the same time, recognising individuals' need to avoid failure, and the cost to the firm of such failure. It is a delicate balance. The above analysis suggests that the relationship between budgets and performance should recognise the aspiration levels of

[39] See Caplan, E. H., *Management Accounting and Behavioural Science*, Addison Wesley, 1971.

individuals. To be good motivators, budgets must be closely linked to such aspiration levels and incorporate personal perceptions of success and failure. Two types of budgets are frequently referred to in this context: ideal budgets and currently attainable budgets.

Ideal budgets are intended to act as a powerful incentive to performance by making no allowance for such mitigating factors as machine breakdowns, material shortages or labour strikes. In effect, they assume that the firm can operate at maximum capacity with maximum efficiency. Under normal operating conditions they are not likely to be achieved. Research has shown that ideal budgets are unlikely to represent the best form of motivation if the employees view them as being unreasonable and unachievable.[40]

Currently attainable budgets represent those which can reasonably be achieved under normal working conditions. They allow for normal breaks and suppose less than perfect efficiency. The problem for managers is to define 'reasonable achievement' and 'normal working conditions' in such a way that the standards set are tight enough to prevent inefficiency while at the same time generating a feeling of satisfaction on achievement. It is a difficult feat to accomplish. Evidence suggests that defined, quantitative targets are more likely to induce higher levels of performance. Aside from the technical problems involved, it requires from the management a thorough knowledge of the workforce, much previous experience in the area and, most of all, a great deal of common sense.

The research studies on budgeting and behaviour raise a potentially serious problem, to which we briefly referred earlier. It may be desirable to set the budget at a particular level in order to motivate the individual to achieve some other level, e.g. to set the budget slightly above reasonable expectations; such a budget may elicit maximum performance from the employee, but it will not be a suitable basis for planning what is likely to be achieved. Thus it may be inconsistent to use the same budget for both planning and motivational purposes.

The second question we posed earlier was: what degree of employee participation in the budgeting process should be encouraged? We should perhaps begin by defining our terms. Participation is a process of joint decision making in which the interests of all participants are fairly reflected, and where the outcome is a decision to which all parties are committed. Participation in the setting of budgets should improve performance where group decision making results in the reconciliation of goals and commitment to budgets. There is now a considerable body of research showing that in general better performance can be expected from employees if they have some say in the construction of the budgets to be used to evaluate their performance (i.e. that participative budgets are more likely to succeed than are authoritative, imposed budgets)[41] Indeed, common sense suggests that participation by individuals who have detailed knowledge of the particular problems associated with any given task is likely to increase the realism of budgets. But as with most topics which involve the interaction of human relationships, the relationship

[40] See Hofstede, G. H., *The Game of Budget Control*, Tavistock, 1968; Hopwood, A. G., *An Accounting System and Managerial Behaviour*, Saxon House, 1973.

[41] See the references quoted in Footnote 38.

between the optimum level of participation and the optimum level of performance is not without complexities. A word of caution is warranted, prompted by recent research in this area. Researchers have found that, *inter alia*:

1. Participation may not be 'real', in the sense that the purpose of joint discussions may simply be a ratification of previous management decisions.
2. The results of participation in the budgeting process may be of less benefit to non-numerate managers. The important point underlying this caveat is that the communication and understanding of financial information may be of equal benefit to all parties only when all have equal competence in its analysis.
3. Participation will be more effective in situations where changes in the working environment are possible. In machine controlled settings, where most decisions are programmed, the effect of participation is minimal.

One other issue should be addressed before we leave our initial discussion of budgeting. Throughout this chapter we have assumed budgets to be expressed purely in financial terms. But need we necessarily rely only on monetary measures? Certainly there are compelling arguments for monetary measures – after all budgets are a part of the firm's management control system, and control information is inevitably expressed quantitatively. It is also reasonable to demand consistency of measurement between internal targets and budgets and objectives expressed in financial terms (e.g. maximisation of the firm's cash flows). Further arguments for the use of monetary measurements might include the following:

1. Much of the quantitative information used in budgeting is already produced by the management accounting system for other purposes, for example for reporting to shareholders.
2. Such measurements are easily understood by managers and relate directly to the firm's reward structure.
3. Such measures represent the only common basis on which the comparative performance of managers, and divisions, can be analysed.
4. Production of non-monetary statements may prove to be a very costly exercise.

But should we simply accept these views without challenging their underlying assumptions? At their heart is the implicit assertion that monetary measures are the most relevant available. We might argue however, that certain important concepts of the firm's, and the manager's, performance cannot easily be measured in money terms, and that we should therefore try to develop different or additional measures. Indeed the nature of the existing budget system may well demand this, if, in seeking to meet budget targets, costs are incurred, which by their nature are not easily measurable and which therefore do not appear directly in the budget statements.

The possible range of non-monetary or qualitative measures which could be introduced into the budget system varies considerably in ease of measurement. For example, such items as the amount of time devoted to training, labour turnover rates, and levels of absenteeism can be relatively easily measured; whereas the measurement and interpretation of individual attitudes and interpersonal judgements is complicated by the lack of appropriate evaluation methods. Perhaps the best situation is to argue for a compromise – the inclusion of relevant non-monetary measures (e.g. those relating to quality, reliability, service, satisfaction of employees) as supplementary information to conventional budget statements – after all budgets themselves are no more than output statements, and do not normally offer a detailed explanation of actual performance. The introduction of more qualitative measures more accurately reflects the complexity of the managerial environment and the notion that performance must encompass a variety of objectives rather than a single monetary target.

We conclude this chapter with some general comments on budgets and budgeting. As we have seen, budgets seek to serve many different and often conflicting aims and, as such, it is unlikely that all will be achieved with equal success. To prevent dissatisfaction with the system a priority ranking of the budget's aims may be useful. Such a ranking should involve a review of budgeting procedures and may result in better data for future budgeting decisions and an improvement in the attitudes of managers to the whole budgeting process.

We have also attempted to portray budgeting as a complex process which is not susceptible to simple economic models or simple accounting rules, but whose influence, as a system of authority, pervades organisational behaviour. Its role is well summarised by Cyert and March.

> Within rather large limits, the organisation substitutes the plan for the world – partly by making the world conform to the plan, partly by pretending that it does. So long as achievement levels continue to be satisfactory, budgeting decisions are exceptionally dependent on decisions of previous years, with shifts tending to reflect the expansions and inclinations of sub-units rather than systematic reviews by top management.

Discussion topics

1. Specify and comment on the objectives of budgeting.
2. Outline the differences and similarities between budgets for planning and budgets for control.
3. 'Cost information which is prepared for one purpose can be misleading when used in another context.' Discuss the extent of the validity of this comment, and give illustrations of two management reports which may contain the same basic cost data.
4. A major problem in applying a control system based on flexible budgeting lies in identifying and measuring an appropriate basis of activity with which to 'flex' the budget. Comment on the necessary attributes of such an activity measure.
5. 'Budgetary control can provide a bridge which links the resources of an organisation to the behaviour of the people within the organisation.' Discuss.

6 'Responsibility accounting is the essence of a successful managerial control system.' Discuss.

7 'Planning and control systems do not themselves exercise control. That is the prerogative of management.' Explain how management might use such systems for control purposes.

Exercises

13.1 An important concept in management accounting is that of responsibility accounting.

(a) Define the term 'responsibility accounting'.
(b) What are the conditions that must exist for there to be effective responsibility accounting?
(c) What benefits are said to result from responsibility accounting?
(d) Listed below are three charges found on the monthly report of a division manufacturing and selling products primarily to outside companies. Divisional performance is evaluated by the use of return on investment, i.e. the ratio of profit to total assets. You are to state which, if any, of the following charges are consistent with the responsibility accounting concept. Support each answer with a brief explanation.

(i) A charge for general corporation administration at 10% of division sales.
(ii) A charge for the use of the corporate computer facility. The charge is determined by taking actual annual computer department costs and allocating an amount to each user based on the ratio of departmental hours of use to total corporate hours of use.
(iii) A charge for goods purchased from another division. The charge is based upon the competitive market price for the goods.

13.2 As the management accountant in a company producing, selling and distributing a wide range of products, you are considering possible improvements in the current system of budgetary control. The existing system of annual budgets produces unrealistic variances because of the rapidly changing conditions in which the company operates. As an alternative you are proposing to adopt a system of continuous budgeting on a quarterly cycle.

Write a report to your financial director explaining the procedure required to operate the proposed continuous budgeting system and indicate the benefits likely to arise.

13.3 As the newly appointed controller of Telemann Foods, you have been asked to design a budgetary control system for the firm. Being of some experience, you have witnessed the introduction of budgetary control systems in several organisations and feel that a carefully considered framework is an essential first step if such systems are going to be successful. The technical detail of budgetary control (e.g. the methods of variance calculation) should, you have found, follow only after such a framework has been considered.

Telemann Foods are take-away restaurants whose profits have been growing by 40% annually for the last five years. There are now 29 restaurants located in England. Each is run by a manager who has considerable freedom in relation to the type of food sold, its selling price, the nature and extent of advertising and staffing policies. Because of the variety in types of location and the nature of local competition (which is generally intense) each restaurant is encouraged to have its own style and character. The central organisation of Telemann Foods provides the finance to set up and sustain each take-away restaurant. It also purchases the supplies and food for the restaurant and provides accounting, legal and administrative services for the restaurants.

All managers are paid a basic salary of £25,000 per year, and commission, computed quarterly, amounting to 20% of the excess of their stores' profits over the budget profit. (At present, the budgetary control system merely comprises a quarterly meeting of each store manager with the chief executive of Telemann Foods, when agreement is reached as to the next quarter's profit budget.)

Develop a framework for the design of a budgetary control system. Use the above information about Telemann Foods in your analysis, and indicate the nature of any further information which you might need to complete your design.

Further reading

Bromwich, M., 'Standard costing for planning and control' in Arnold, J., Carsberg, B. and Scapens, R. (eds), *Topics in Management Accounting*, Philip Allan, 1980.

Brownell, P. and McInnes, M., 'Budgetary participation, motivation, and managerial performance', *The Accounting Review*, October 1986.

Caplan, E. H., *Management Accounting and Behavioural Science*, Addison Wesley, 1971.

Chenhall, R. H., Harrison, G. L. and Watson, D. J. H. (eds), *The Organisational Context of Management Accounting*, Pitman, 1981.

Choudhury, N., 'Responsibility accounting and controllability', *Accounting and Business Research*, Summer 1986.

Cooper, D., 'Organizational aspects of budgetary control', in Lewis, J. E. and Dickinson, G. (eds), *Handbook of Financial Management*, Kluwer Harrap, 1977.

Cooper, D., 'A social and organizational view of management accounting' in Bromwich, M. and Hopwood, A. G. (eds), *Essays in British Accounting Research*, Pitman, 1981.

Hirst, M. K., 'The effects of setting budget goals and task uncertainty on performance: a theoretical analysis', *The Accounting Review*, October 1987.

Hofstede, G. H., *The Game of Budget Control*, Tavistock, 1968.

Hopwood, A. G., *Accounting and Human Behaviour*, Prentice Hall, 1976.

Hopwood, A. G., 'Accounting and organisational behaviour', in Carsberg, B. and Hope, A. (eds), *Current Issues in Accounting*, 2nd edn, Philip Allan, 1984.

Hopwood, A. G., 'Organisational and behavioural aspects of budgeting and control', in Arnold, J, Carsberg, B and Scapens, R. (eds), *Topics in Management Accounting*, Philip Allan, 1980.

Lyne, S. R., 'The role of the budget in medium and large UK companies and the relationship with budget pressure and participation', *Accounting and Business Research*, Summer 1988.

Merchant, K. A., 'The design of the corporate budgeting system: influences on managerial behavior and performance', *The Accounting Review*, October 1981.

Otley, D. T., 'Budgets and managerial motivation', *Journal of General Management*, Autumn 1982.

Otley, D. T., 'The contingency theory of management accounting', *Accounting, Organizations and Society*, 1980, pp. 413–428.

Otley, D. T. and Berry, A. J., 'Control, organisations and accounting', *Accounting, Organizations and Society*, 1980, pp. 231–246.

Otley, D., *Accounting Control and Organizational Behaviour*, Heinemann, 1987.

Pope, P. F., 'Information asymmetries in participative budgeting: a bargaining approach', *Journal of Business Finance and Accounting*, Spring 1984.

Ronen, J. and Livingstone, J. L., 'An expectancy theory approach to the motivational impacts of budgets', *The Accounting Review*, October 1975.

Schiff, M. and Lewin, A., 'The impact of people on budgets', *The Accounting Review*, April 1970.

Chapter 14

The master budget and the cash budget

In the previous chapter we discussed how managerial decisions can often involve the simultaneous use of factors with draw on the marketing, sales, production, purchasing and financial aspects of business; and we stressed the importance of management's task of coordinating all these various, interrelated aspects of decision making. This chapter considers how the ultimate production of this coordinating activity, the master plan or master budget for the firm, is pieced together. The master budget represents the firm's blueprint for the forthcoming period(s). It brings together, usually in the form of a budgeted income statement and a budgeted balance sheet, the various individual budgets prepared within the organisation.

No organisation of any size or complexity should proceed without an overall plan, and, in practice, most large organisations prepare some form of master budget. The format may vary from firm to firm (there is no standard mode of preparation), but the need to prepare a master plan is usually cited as a prerequisite for success. It is useful because, as we argued in the last chapter, it both sets out the organisation's targets for the coming period in a quantifiable, easily understood form, and provides a basis for coordinating the organisation's detailed operating budgets which are essential ingredients of the control process.

14.1 Preparation of the master budget

The preparation of a master budget is rarely an easy task. The speed with which agreement can be reached on the final budget figures depends upon the size of the organisation, the number of different responsibility centres, the degree of divisionalisation and so on. But even within a small organisation, detailed discussion, argument and persuasion may be necessary at all levels before the master budget can be drawn up. The art of preparing the master budget lies in the ability of the budget committee to piece together at minimum cost and maximum agreement the various parts of the corporate jigsaw. The analogy with a jigsaw is worth pursuing. The most time consuming part of putting together a jigsaw is knowing where to start. The more pieces in the jigsaw the harder is this task. Likewise in preparing the firm's master budget the most difficult tasks for the budget committee may lie in knowing which of the individual functional budgets (e.g. sales, purchasing, production) to use as the starting point for the total plan. Preparation of the budget may entail a number of different submissions before final agreement is reached. The procedure might thus involve an initial budget for an individual responsibility centre, which may be revised prior to submission to the budget committee. This committee may in turn require further amendments on seeing the budgets from other centres.

Management will usually be aided in its choice of the initial jigsaw pieces by recognising that the range of the firm's activities is likely to be inhibited by certain constraints; more specifically that there is likely to be at least one critical factor which determines the firm's appropriate output level. It is a primary function of management to determine the nature of this critical factor(s) and decide whether the costs of alleviating the constraint(s) are worth incurring. The critical factor could be one of many; for example, the firm may suffer restrictions on its productive capacity, its supply of labour, its availability of cash, or perhaps most likely in a competitive situation, the demand for its products at a particular price. For purposes of exposition this chapter will presume demand quantity to be the constraining factor, and thus the sales budget will determine, within reasonable bounds, the levels of the other functional, allied budgets. (If there is more than one constraining factor, a more refined technique such as mathematical programming will be necessary for piecing together the jigsaw.) In the remainder of this chapter we show how, in a much simplified situation, management may gradually build up a master budget for the firm. A separate section at the end of the chapter is devoted to the important topic of cash budgeting.

The example of Windsor Ltd is used for illustrative purposes throughout the chapter. Windsor Ltd produces and sells only two products, Y and Z. Its actual balance sheet as at 31 December 19X0, is shown in Table 14.1. The balance sheet is a statement of a firm's position at a particular point in time, usually at the end of an accounting period. It shows the firm's assets, conventionally at their original cost adjusted for depreciation where appropriate, less liabilities. The difference between assets and liabilities represents the interest in the firm of the providers of long-term funds (see pp. 224–31).

We have already noted that the master budget often takes the form of a budgeted income statement and a budgeted balance sheet. As such, it provides a forecast of what the firm's published income statement and balance sheet will look like for the period covered by the budget. This may be of interest to managers as the published income statement and balance sheet will be one means of communication between those responsible for running the firm (the managers) and others with an interest in its performance (e.g. shareholders and other providers of long-term funds). Insofar as the master budget is intended to forecast the contents of the firm's published accounting reports it should be prepared on the same basis as will be the published accounting statements. Hence the conventions used in preparing the budgeted income statement and balance sheet for inclusion in the master budget will often be identical to those used in preparing the firm's external accounts. We discussed some of these conventions briefly in Chapter 5 (pp. 86–9) and pointed

Table 14.1 Windsor Ltd: balance sheet as at 31 December 19X0

	(£)	(£)	(£)
Fixed assets (at cost less depreciation)			260,000
Current assets:			
Stocks of finished goods at 'full' cost:			
500 units of product Y at £7.50	3,750		
500 units of product Z at £7.50	3,750		
	7,500		
Work-in-progress	8,000		
Raw materials at cost:			
5,000 lb at £1.00	5,000	20,500	
Debtors (accounts receivable)		24,000	
Cash		22,500	
		67,000	
Less Current liabilities (creditors)		12,000	
Net current assets			55,000
Total net assets			315,000
Represented by:			
Issued share capital			240,000
Retained income			75,000
Total long-term funds			315,000

out that, whatever their merits in external reporting, they often result in figures that are only partly relevant to managerial decision making. In particular, the use of historical costs and the allocation of fixed costs between products may not provide measures of the relevant costs of using resources. Our main purpose in this chapter is to illustrate how a master budget might be built up from a series of subsidiary budgets. For convenience, we adopt accounting conventions that are often used in the preparation of external accounting reports. However, it is crucial to recognise that the resulting figures may not be the best available for internal decision making; the figures most relevant for that purpose have been discussed in previous chapters. In other words, our main purpose in this chapter is to forecast the impact on a firm's income statement and balance sheet of decisions taken on the bases we have recommended previously.

14.2 The sales budget

The sales budget for an organisation is derived from estimates of the demand for (and the ability to supply) its different products at particular prices. These estimates are, in turn, determined on the basis of sales forecasts. Thus sales forecasting precedes sales budgeting.

The purpose of sales forecasting is to estimate the organisation's sales revenue for the budget period. Two interdependent factors make up sales revenue: the volume of sales and the selling price(s) – we examined the relationships between the two in Chapter 8. Some of the variables which may affect the organisation's pricing policy are:

(i) extent of market competition;
(ii) general economic and industrial conditions;
(iii) organisational cost structure.

Sales volume will be determined both by the chosen pricing policy and by some or all of the following additional factors, some of which may be uncontrollable:

(i) level and effectiveness of advertising and other promotional policies;
(ii) quality of the sales force;
(iii) past sales volume, and the relationships with suppliers and customers;
(iv) any seasonal and cyclical influences;
(v) decisions of competitors.

The sales forecaster might use the above variables to predict first the level of regular business, comprising contracts already placed and the normal demand of regular customers; second, the level of non-regular business, comprising the likely demand from new customers and other non-repetitive sources (i.e. although certain individual transactions may not be repeated regularly, the total amount of such business may be stable from year to year) and finally the level of unstable business or unexpected demand which, by its very nature, is difficult to forecast.

Sales forecasting procedures can be very sophisticated and a detailed discussion of them lies outside the scope of the text.[42] However, we note below some approaches that a forecaster might use in deriving his expectations:

1. Assessments by sales department staff: estimates of sales demand might be made by the individual salespersons and subsequently be passed upwards for consideration by the sales managers. This approach has the advantage that individual salespersons can offer advice on the basis of detailed knowledge of the particular factors peculiar to their own areas.

2. Mathematical analysis of past sales figures: the purpose of such an analysis, of whatever degree of sophistication, is to indicate trends in the relationship between selling price and quantity demanded and, where possible, patterns of seasonal variation. This information can then be adjusted for known factors, such as the level of future advertising or changes in the degree of market competition, to produce future sales forecasts.

3. Senior management judgement: the meeting of the senior management team, which might include representatives of production management, purchasing and administration, as well as senior sales executives, may bring a wider variety of expertise to the forecasting exercise.

On the basis of sales forecasts we can draw up the sales budget for Windsor Ltd as per Table 14.2. Note that although the 'conventionally' calculated production

[42] But see Chapter 8 for a more comprehensive discussion of selling price–demand relationships.

Table 14.2 Windsor Ltd: sales budget for the year to 31 December 19X1

	Units to be sold	*Price* (£)	*Total sales revenue* (£)
Product Y	40,000	10.00	400,000
Product Z	16,000	12.50	200,000
			600,000

cost of the two products is the same (£7.50) their selling prices differ. This is a common occurrence in practice. It may result from certain products being advertised more heavily than others, from differences in the competitiveness of markets in which different products are sold, or from differences between the relevant incremental costs of products even though their costs calculated according to normal accounting conventions are the same.

When the sales budget has been prepared, it is a relatively straightforward task to estimate the appropriate selling and distribution costs, i.e. those costs which depend upon the level of sales. The make-up of the selling expenses budget is shown in Table 14.3. Of the items making up the selling expenses budget only sales commission (5% of £600,000) varies directly with sales revenue; the remainder of the costs are fixed for the following year, although their actual amounts are, to a large extent, determined by the expected volume of sales.

Table 14.3 Windsor Ltd: selling expenses budget for the year to 31 December 19X1

	(£)
Sales commission (5% × £600,000)	30,000
Salaries	27,000
Travelling expenses	15,000
Advertising and promotion	23,000
	95,000

14.3 The production budget

In order to meet its sales demand, the organisation requires a continually available stock of saleable finished goods. It must attempt to plan its manufacturing cycle so as to ensure the availability of stock. Production planning is of particular importance if the organisation has seasonal peaks in its sales levels. It is also likely that the management will wish to have a minimum stock of finished goods at any point in time, not only to meet future sales targets but also to meet unforeseen orders and to alleviate possible difficulties in meeting existing orders if any production breakdowns occur – although many companies are currently looking closely at their production and stock relationships to try to minimise the level of stock and work-in-progress held by the firm, thereby saving warehouse and interest costs. Attempts to make suppliers deliver raw materials only when the firm needs them (known as just in time delivery), cut down dramatically the need for excess buffer stocks. To accomplish this properly the firm must reorganise its production activities – usually via computer aided techniques. Hence we might say that the production budget for the period (the amount of finished goods to be produced during the period) is determined by the sales budget and by the stock of finished goods required by the organisation. If we further suppose, as in the case of Windsor Ltd, that the organisation possesses a stock of finished goods at the start of the period, we can generalise the number of units to be produced by solving the following simple equation:

$$\text{Units to be produced} = \text{Units to be sold} + \text{Units to be in closing stock} - \text{Units in opening stock}$$

Table 14.4 shows Windsor Ltd's production budget in units for the year to 31 December 19X1, on the assumption that 1,200 units of Y and 800 units of Z are required at the year end, and that there will be no change in the quantity or cost of work-in-progress (i.e. partially completed units) which will remain constant at £8,000.

Having determined the required levels of production for the year, the management can now proceed to determine the costs of producing the required units of finished product. In practice it is unlikely that levels and costs of production will be determined independently of each other. For ease of exposition we presume such independence. We will classify the costs of production under four separate headings, raw materials, direct labour, manufacturing overhead and capital expenditure, each of which gives rise to a separate budget.

Raw materials budget

In Windsor Ltd's case we assume that there is only one type of raw material which is used in the production of both Y and Z. It is a major task of the purchasing manager to ensure that raw materials are available whenever required. This may entail 'bulk buying' at particular times during the year, with the attendant possibility of holding

Table 14.4 Windsor Ltd: production budget (in units) for the year to 31st December 19X1

	Y (units)	*Z* (units)
Budgeted sales (as per Table 14.2)	40,000	16,000
Budgeted closing stock	1,200	800
Total requirements	41,200	16,800
Less Opening stock (as per Table 14.1)	500	500
Required production	40,700	16,300

Table 14.5 Windsor Ltd: raw materials budget for the year to 31 December 19X1

	Units of production	*Quantity required per unit* (lb)	*Total quantity required* (lb)	*Price per unit* (£)	*Total cost* (£)
Needed for production of:					
Y (as per Table 14.4)	40,700	2	81,400	1.00	81.400
Z (as per Table 14.4)	16,300	2	32,600	1.00	32,600
Total to be used in production			114,000		114,000
Add Budgeted closing stock			7,000	1.00	7,000
Total requirement			121,000		121,000
Less Opening stock (as per Table 14.1)			5,000	1.00	5,000
Total to be purchased			116,000		116,000

large raw materials stocks which take up extra warehouse space and have a cost to the firm in terms of the finance which is invested in them. However, one result of bulk buying may be the ability to negotiate a lower price for the materials purchased, which thus acts as a countervailing benefit to the extra storage and finance costs. The raw material budget might therefore be useful for estimating the warehouse space needed and for determining re-order levels, as well as agreeing any constraints on raw material expenditure.

We assume that both products use 2 lb of raw material to produce a single unit, and that the price to be paid for the raw material is £1 per lb. We also assume that management requires 7,000 lb of raw material to be in stock at the year end. We can now prepare the raw material budget for the year as per Table 14.5.

Direct labour budget

If the organisation does not make different specialised products, direct labour requirements (i.e. labour which is readily traceable to particular units of production) can be determined from previous experience or by using time and motion studies. These figures can then be applied to the production target to ascertain labour requirements. If the production mix is intricate, the determination of direct labour cost is trickier, as labour is then regarded as a 'pool' to support production generally. Direct labour budgets might be used for a variety of purposes, amongst the most important of which are:

(i) to help the development of recruitment policies;
(ii) to identify training and education needs;
(iii) to provide a framework for wage negotiations, for both skilled and unskilled labour.

We assume that production of each unit of Y and Z is expected to require half an hour of direct labour, and that the rate payable is £6 per hour. This yields a budget for direct labour as shown in Table 14.6.

Table 14.6 Windsor Ltd: direct labour budget for the year to 31 December 19X1

	Units of production	*Labour hours per unit*	*Total hours*	*Total budget at £6 per labour hour* (£)
Y (as per Table 14.4)	40,700	$\frac{1}{2}$	20,350	122,100
Z (as per Table 14.4)	16,300	$\frac{1}{2}$	8,150	48,900
			28,500	171,000

Manufacturing overhead budget

Manufacturing overhead represents those expenses which, unlike raw materials and direct labour, cannot easily be identified with separate units of production. However some manufacturing overhead, which in the case of Windsor Ltd is represented by indirect labour and a part of the total cost of power, varies with the level of production and must be assigned both a basis of allocation and a rate of allocation. We assume in our example that indirect labour and a part of the total cost of power are variable costs and are allocated to production on the basis of a budgeted level of activity of 57,000 units of production, as calculated in Table 14.4; and that indirect labour is charged at a rate of £1 per unit of production, and power of 20p per unit of production. The remaining manufacturing overhead is composed of fixed costs. Table 14.7 shows the make-up of the manufacturing overhead budget for the year. Depreciation is calculated using the straight line method and represents a writing off of part of the original cost of fixed assets.

The total production costs may now be summarised in a cost of goods sold budget, shown in Table 14.8. This is a step in the summarising process leading to the preparation of the master budget.

Table 14.7 Windsor Ltd: manufacturing overhead budget for the year to 31 December 19X1

	£	£
Fixed costs:		
Power	3,600	
Supervision	22,000	
Maintenance	13,500	
Rent, rates and insurance	25,000	
Depreciation	10,000	74,100
Variable costs:		
Indirect labour (57,000 units at £1 per unit)		57,000
Power (57,000 units at 20p per unit)		11,400
Total		142,500

Table 14.8 Windsor Ltd: cost of goods sold budget for the year to 31 December 19X1

	From Table	£	£
Materials (to be used in production)	14.5		114,000
Direct labour	14.6		171,000
Manufacturing overhead	14.7		142,500
			427,500
Add Stock of finished goods at 1 January 19X1 (as per Table 14.1)			7,500
			435,000
Less Stock of finished goods at 31 December 19X1			
Y, 1,200 units at £7.50* per unit		9,000	
Z, 800 units at £7.50* per unit		6,000	15,000
Cost of goods sold (56,000 units as per Table 14.2 at £7.50* per unit)			420,000

* The calculation of the 'full' unit cost of finished goods is as follows:

		(£)
Raw materials (2 lb at £1 per lb)		2.00
Direct labour ($\frac{1}{2}$ hour at £6 per hour)		3.00
Manufacturing overheads (as per Table 14.7)	$\frac{£142,500}{57,000 \text{ units}}$	2.50
		7.50

The method of stock valuation which allocates total manufacturing overhead to products is known as *full* or *absorption* costing. Under this method, which is widely used for external reporting, some fixed manufacturing overheads are carried forward to the next period as part of closing stock. The determination of the basis of allocation is an arbitrary choice and thus different bases can lead to different unit costs of finished goods. As we noted earlier, this method of stock valuation may not be the best available for managerial decision making.

Capital expenditure budget

The capital expenditure budget will usually be prepared for a longer period than other budgets, say from three to five years, and is used to indicate the expenditure required to cover both capital projects already in place and those to be undertaken. Thus the budget should be geared to the current production budget, future expected levels of output and the long-term development of the business, and the industry, as a whole. It may be convenient to classify projects in the capital expenditure budget under separate headings, for example:

(i) cost reduction and replacement expenditure;
(ii) expenditure on the expansion of existing product lines;
(iii) new product expenditure;
(iv) health, safety and welfare capital expenditure.

Table 14.9 Windsor Ltd: capital expenditure budget for the year to 31 December 19X1

Project number	*Estimated date of payment*		*Cost* (£)
153	30 January	Replace machine M 75	25,000
154	31 May	Purchase new machine N 23	10,000
		Total capital expenditure	35,000

The reason for making this differentiation lies in the method(s) of appraisal used for their justification. The first three categories are susceptible to the types of capital investment appraisal techniques discussed in Chapters 11 and 12, whereas projects in the last category arise generally from policy decisions of top management, or from sources such as mandatory government regulations.

The administration of the capital budget is usually separate from that of the other budgets. Indeed in most large companies there is a capital projects committee which has overall responsibility for the authorisation and monitoring of capital projects, and for the preparation of the capital budget. Thus for example, projects costing over £100,000 may require authorisation by the board of directors, those between £50,000 and £100,000 may need approval by divisional management, and those below £50,000 may be approved by individual divisional managers. The capital expenditure budget for Windsor Ltd is set out in Table 14.9.

14.4 The general and administrative budget

In most organisations there is a block of costs, usually fixed in amount, which relate to the non-production and non-sales aspect of business. Table 14.10 itemises these costs for Windsor Ltd.

Table 14.10 Windsor Ltd: general and administrative expenses budget for the year to 31 December 19X1

	£
Office wages	21,000
Executive salaries	35,000
Office supplies	4,000
Miscellaneous	5,000
Total	65,000

14.5 The cash budget

Having prepared detailed budgets for each of the functional aspects of the business, we now draw up one of the most important budgets of all – the cash budget. The ability of the firm to generate cash flow represents its ability to pay dividends, and to succeed and grow in the future. The preparation of the cash budget aids management in its planning and in its desire to minimise unwanted, and non-productive, cash balances, while at the same time ensuring that, wherever possible, expensive borrowing to overcome short-term deficiencies is not incurred. Most organisations draw up their cash budgets on, at least, a monthly basis, and we will show how this can be done in the concluding section of this chapter; for the purposes of determining the master budget of Windsor Ltd we show simply the total cash amounts for the full year. We assume in our analysis that debtors (amounts owed by customers) will increase over the year by £6,000, and that creditors (amounts owed to suppliers) for raw materials will increase by £5,000. Finally, we assume no other outstanding liabilities exist at 31 December 19X1. The cash budget for the year is shown in Table 14.11.

Table 14.11 Windsor Ltd: cash budget for the year to 31 December 19X1

	From Table	£
Opening cash balance (per opening balance sheet)	14.1	22,500
Add Receipts:		
Collections from customers		
(sales less £6,000 increase in debtors)	14.2	594,000
Total cash available		616,500
Less Payments:		
For materials		
(purchases less £5,000 increase in creditors)	14.5	111,000
For selling expenses	14.3	95,000
For direct labour	14.6	171,000
For manufacturing overhead*	14.7	132,500
For capital equipment	14.9	35,000
For general expenses	14.10	65,000
Total cash needed		609,500
Closing cash balance		7,000

* Note that the cash payment for manufacturing overheads excludes the depreciation expense of £10,000, as depreciation is a non-cash item.

14.6 Budgeted income statement and balance sheet

We explained at the start of this chapter that the master budget often takes the form of a budgeted income statement and balance sheet. We are now in a position to prepare these two documents for Windsor Ltd. Because we have reached the stage in the budgeting process where the attention of management will be directed towards the way in which the expected results of the forthcoming year will be shown in the company's external accounting reports, we shall present the income statement and balance sheet in a form suitable for publication. Details are given in Table 14.12.

Table 14.12 Windsor Ltd: budgeted income statement and balance sheet

	From Table	£	£
Budgeted Income Statement for the year to 31 December 19X1			
Sales	14.2		600,000
Less Cost of goods sold	14.8		420,000
Gross profit			180,000
Less Selling expenses	14.3	95,000	
General and administrative expenses	14.10	65,000	160,000
Budgeted net income			20,000
Budgeted Balance Sheet as at 31 December 19X1			
Fixed assets (net)*			285,000
Current assets:			
Stocks: Finished goods	14.8	15,000	
Work-in-progress		8,000	
Raw materials	14.5	7,000	
		30,000	
Debtors (£24,000 + £6,000)		30,000	
Cash	14.11	7,000	
		67,000	
Less Creditors (£12,000 + £5,000)		17,000	
Net current assets			50,000
Total net assets			335,000
Represented by:			
Issued share capital	14.1		240,000
Retained income at 1 January 19X1	14.1		75,000
Budgeted net income for the year			20,000
Total long-term funds			335,000

* The fixed asset balance is computed as follows:

	(£)
Balance as at 1 January (as per Table 14.1)	260,000
Capital additions (as per Table 14.10)	35,000
	295,000
Less Depreciation (as per Table 14.7)	10,000
Balance as per closing balance sheet	285,000

14.7 Summary of the master budget

The budgeted income statement and balance sheet represent the summarised plans for the whole organisation for the forthcoming period.

Certain decisions and inferences might be made by top mangement on the basis of the projected figures. For example, management might calculate certain key ratios to determine whether the position revealed by the budgeted statements is satisfactory. *Profitability* ratios would examine the relationships between net income and turnover, and net income and capital employed. Focus on Windsor Ltd's *liquidity* situation would question whether the projected cash balance is adequate, whether the debtors are likely to pay on time, whether the stocks of finished goods and work-in-progress are likely to prove saleable, whether the relationship between the totals of fixed assets and current assets is satisfactory, and whether the current assets/current liabilities ratio is optimal. Attention to the funds employed by the business might query the rationale of *financing* operations without any debt capital.

The two budgeted statements as we have presented them are static, deterministic budgets. They show the projected results of operating only at a single expected level of activity. They should be interpreted with caution as it is unlikely that the firm will operate at exactly the level of activity embodied in the budgets. For control purposes it is imperative, as explained in the previous chapter, that the management supports the fixed master budget with a series of flexible budgets showing the expected results of operating at different levels of activity, and perhaps also with budgets showing, for example, the effects of changes in input and output prices.

In addition the conventions used to prepare the budgeted accounts are those commonly applied to the preparation of accounts for publication. For example, cost of goods sold includes allocated fixed costs and a charge for using fixed assets (a depreciation charge) based on an allocation of the original cost of assets. Hence, as we explained in Chapter 5 and subsequently, the figure for cost of goods sold may be a poor approximation to the expected relevant, opportunity cost of the goods to be sold. As an indication of what Windsor Ltd's published accounts will look like if actual performance for the year accords with budgeted performance, the budgeted income statement and balance sheet are satisfactory. However, insofar as they are used as a basis for preparing more detailed operating budgets, care must be taken to ensure that proper attention is paid to the sort of decision rules we have discussed in previous chapters.

14.8 Formal planning models

By the very nature of the world they face, all businesses prepare their plans and budgets in an uncertain environment. How should they best incorporate the possible effects of such uncertainty into their formal planning? Many firms now construct alternative budgets which incorporate different assumptions about the variables critical to their success. The need to know quickly the results of different strategic and tactical decisions prepared under different assumptions makes alternative budgeting an indispensable component of successful planning. This recognition has led many managers to develop formal models to simplify and hasten planning procedures. In particular two broad-ranging types of model have been developed.

1. *Mathematical programming models*. These models are used to develop *optimal* measures (e.g. of production and sales quantities and prices, of financing sources and costs) for the firm. They are characterised, like the linear programming models we discussed in Chapters 9 and 10, by statements of objective functions, binding constraints and explicit relationships between variables. Their use generates a series of equations which, in turn, produce a series of optimal transactions. These optimal transactions are then used to construct the master budget. Important as these characteristics are, the real benefit of such models lies in their ability to produce 'shadow' or 'dual' prices, which give information on the results of slight changes in the model's constraints – information which can then be used to evaluate the usefulness of possible changes to the firm's plan, for example that of extending or contracting production capacity, with its concomitant effect on the firm's cost structure.
2. *Simulation models*. These relatively recently developed models rely on the data processing capacity of sophisticated computers to generate the results of a large number of alternative scenarios over different periods. Such models can combine other endogenous and exogenous variables (those within and those outside the control of the business) and thus relate directly assumptions about the business with those of the external world.

Choice of model will depend on a number of factors, among which we might cite two in particular. The first is the desire of the firm either to develop an integrated model of its entire activities or, as is more common, to break down its requirements into a series of functional modules such as those relating to production, sales and finance. The second is whether the firm wishes to develop a deterministic or a probabilistic model. There is little doubt that the latter is of more use but, because of its high cost, and the problem of determining appropriate probabilities of different operating aspects, deterministic models are more frequently used.

14.9 Cash budgeting

We should not leave the subject of budgeting without a further, more detailed look at cash budgeting. Short-term cash budgeting focuses attention directly on the most critical aspect of short-term financial management – the day to day handling of cash resources. It entails making detailed estimates of when cash will be received from cash and credit sales and when cash will be paid to the various suppliers of materials, capital, overheads and labour. Indeed the cash budget indicates the effect of the budgeted activities of all the functional areas of business on the flow of the firm's liquid resources, which represent the lifeblood of the organisation. Thus cash budgets are invariably prepared and revised at intervals not exceeding one month.

Why is cash budgeting so important? An organisation needs cash to facilitate its daily transactions, but it naturally wishes to avoid the accumulation of idle cash balances which represent a non-productive (wasteful) use of resources. For example, cash can be used to earn interest for the organisation by investment in short-term loans and bank deposits. The cash budget assists the financial manager in pointing out whether there is likely to be sufficient cash available for the (profitable) budgeted levels of activity. Equally the cash budget helps to indicate the periods, if any, in which cash resources are likely to be inadequate, thus allowing the manager to arrange additional finance as soon as possible to meet the cash bottleneck. The following example shows how a detailed cash budget might be prepared so as to reveal likely periodic surpluses and deficits.

The information below relates to Kenilworth Ltd for the six month period to 30 June 19X1.

1. On 1 January cash on hand and at the bank is expected to total £5,000.
2. Debtors normally pay one-half of the amount due at the end of the month following sale, and one-half at the end of the second month after sale, whereas Kenilworth Ltd pays its creditors at the end of the month after purchase of the goods.
3. Budgeted sales and purchases are as follows:

	Sales (£)	*Purchases* (£)
November 19X0	20,000	10,000
December	25,000	12,000
January 19X1	25,000	22,000
February	27,000	19,000
March	30,000	18,000
April	30,000	18,000
May	30,000	18,000
June	30,000	18,000

4. General expenses of £5,000 will be paid at the end of each month.
5. A machine costing £18,000 is to be acquired and paid for at the end of March.

We can now prepare the cash budget as detailed in Table 14.13. The layout of the cash budget is of great importance, and should highlight the expected cash position month by month. Total monthly receipts and total monthly payments are itemised separately and a balance representing either a cash surplus (as in January, April, May and June) or a cash deficit (as in February and March) is struck at the end of each month. This surplus (deficit) is added to (deducted from) the opening balance for the month, to form the month's closing balance. Cash receipts represent half the sales of the preceding month, and half the sales of the pre-preceding month (e.g. the receipt of £22,500 in January is made up of £10,000 from November sales

Table 14.13 Kenilworth Ltd: cash budget January–June 19X1

	January (£)	*February* (£)	*March* (£)	*April* (£)	*May* (£)	*June* (£)
Cash receipts						
(A) Sales (debtors)	22,500	25,000	26,000	28,500	30,000	30,000
Cash payments:						
Purchases (creditors)	12,000	22,000	19,000	18,000	18,000	18,000
Expenses	5,000	5,000	5,000	5,000	5,000	5,000
Cost of machine	—	—	18,000	—	—	—
(B)	17,000	27,000	42,000	23,000	23,000	23,000
Net cash receipts for the month (A–B)	5,500	(2,000)	(16,000)	5,500	7,000	7,000
Cash balance at start of month	5,000	10,500	8,500	(7,500)	(2,000)	5,000
Cash balance at end of month	10,500	8,500	(7,500)	(2,000)	5,000	12,000

and £12,500 from sales in December). Cash payments to creditors are lagged by one month (e.g. the payment of £12,000 in January relates to the purchases made in December).

The example clearly reveals that cash shortages will occur during the six month period, and that additional finance will be required during March and April to ensure the continuance of trading. As the shortage is apparently short-term, arising because the machinery payment is to be made during March, it may be possible to finance it by a variety of means. For instance, Kenilworth Ltd might negotiate with its bank for temporary overdraft facilities during the relevant period, it might attempt to negotiate stricter terms for debtor payments, or it might try to delay payments to creditors for an extra month. Alternatively it might, depending upon the level of stocks it holds, consider some short-term reduction in stock levels. It is one of the biggest advantages of a monthly cash budgeting system that it draws attention not only to cash surpluses and deficits, but also to the whole notion of optimal working capital management. It raises questions, as in the example of Kenilworth Ltd, concerning the period of credit allowed to debtors, the level of stocks held by the organisation, and the payment period allowed by creditors.

Discussion topics

1. Describe and analyse the main functions of the organisation's master budget.
2. Describe the relationship between the organisation's master budget and its cash budget.
3. Explain the differences and relationships between a sales forecast and a sales budget.
4. You are the production director of a large organisation. Discuss the various interrelationships between your yearly budgets and the budgets of other functions within the organisation.

5 You are the sales director of a large organisation. Discuss the various interrelationships between your yearly budgets and the budgets of other functions within the organisation.

6 'The success or failure of a business depends on its ability to manage cash. Thus the cash budget is of the utmost importance.' Discuss.

7 The firm's cash budget reveals a short-term funds requirement for two months in the coming year. Discuss some possible ways of raising short-term cash to finance the temporary deficit.

Exercises

14.1 The balance sheet of Mendelssohn Ltd at 1 January 19X0 is expected to be as follows:

Capital and liabilities	(£)	(£)	*Assets*	(£)	(£)
Ownership interest:			Fixed assets, at cost		870,000
Share capital		500,000	*Less* Accumulated		
Reserves		135,000	depreciation		210,000
		635,000			660,000
8% loan stock		200,000	Current assets:		
			Stock	150,000	
			Trade debtors	70,000	
			Cash	55,000	275,000
Current liabilities:					
Dividend due	40,000				
Trade creditors	60,000	100,000			
		935,000			935,000

The following is a summary of the transactions expected by the company during the year ending 31 December 19X0.

1. Sales are expected to amount to £800,000. All sales are on credit and Mendelssohn Ltd expects that 12% of the annual sales will not have been paid for at 31 December 19X0.
2. All purchases of stock are on credit and are expected to amount to £650,000. The company expects to owe its suppliers £65,000 at 31 December 19X0. It expects to have stocks on hand at that date of £250,000 at cost price.
3. New fixed assets are expected to be purchased for cash during the year, costing £150,000. No fixed assets will be sold. Depreciation is to be provided on all fixed assets (including those bought during the year) at the rate of 10% on cost.
4. Interest on the loan stock is payable annually in arrears on 31 December.
5. Operating expenses for the year (other than those mentioned above) are expected to amount to £65,000, payable as they are incurred.
6. The dividend due at 1 January 19X0 will be paid during the year, and the company intends to provide for a dividend of a similar amount at 31 December 19X0.

(a) Prepare a budgeted income statement for the year ending 31 December 19X0, and a budgeted balance sheet as at that date.

(b) Comment on the figures revealed by your budgets.

14.2 Mr Vermeer forms a company to start a new business on 1 January 19X4. He plans to provide the necessary capital in the form of £1 ordinary shares. The following estimates are made about the first six months' business:

	£
Equipment bought for cash, January	3,000
Stock of goods bought for credit, January	5,500
Sales per month, January–March	2,800
Sales per month, April–June	7,600
Rent p.a., payable quarterly in advance	800
General expenses, per month, cash outlay	350
The estimated gross profit percentage is 25% on sales value	
Stock is to be maintained always at £5,500	
Creditors will allow one month's credit. Customers are to be allowed two months' credit.	
An interim dividend of £1,000 is, if profit allows, to be paid at the end of June.	

Assume all payments will be made at the end of the month in which they fall due. Depreciation on equipment for the half-year is to be £150.

(a) Calculate the capital Vermeer should pay if the *maximum* financial need in the first six months is to be met, but no more.

(b) Draft the final accounts for the half-year (income statement and balance sheet), on the assumption that Vermeer pays in the necessary capital, as calculated in (a), on 1 January.

14.3 Paderewski plc has the following (summarised) balance sheet as at 30 April 19X2:

	£000	£000
Share capital		1,000
Revenue reserve (undistributed profit)		754
		1,754
4% debenture stock (long-term loan)		300
Current liabilities:		
Trade creditors	1,200	
Inland revenue (for tax)	30	
Bank overdraft	300	1,530
		3,584
Freehold land and buildings at cost		320
Manufacturing equipment, tools, dies, etc.		560
		880
Current assets:		
Stock of raw materials, work in progress and finished goods at cost or under		1,300
Trade debtors		1,404
		3,584

Estimates prepared in the accounting department for the following three months are as follows:

	£000
Sales on credit, spread equally over the three months (sales are on deferred terms: the debtors will pay in twelve equal instalments, the first falling in the month in which the debt is incurred)	576
Purchase of raw materials, spread equally over the three months (purchases will all be for cash, as suppliers will not give any more credit)	114
Manufacturing wages (payable in cash weekly): total for three months	228
Other expenses (non-manufacturing wages and salaries, insurance, heating and lighting, rates etc.) (These will be payable in cash and arise evenly over the three months)	237
It is estimated that it will be possible to collect in each month about $\frac{1}{6}$ of the debts due to the company at 30 April	
It is expected that $\frac{1}{3}$ of the trade creditors at 30 April will have to be paid in each of the three months	
The tax is payable immediately	
The expected sales will absorb finished goods at a book value (based on manufacturing labour and materials only) of	342
The bank overdraft limit (i.e. the maximum advance allowed) is	600
One quarter's interest on the debenture stock must be paid in July	

(a) Prepare a clear statement for the directors of the company showing month by month, the estimated cash receipts and payments of the company for the next three months.

(b) Prepare an estimated income statement for the period and an end-period balance sheet. (Write £14,000 off equipment for depreciation.)

(c) Comment on the situation revealed by these statements.

14.4 You have been appointed management accountant to a company which has been operating at a low profit level over the last few years. The company does not operate a budgetary planning system, but based on present performance plus allowances for price and other cost increases, a preliminary profit forecast for the next twelve months shows the following:

Estimated sales	£3,750,000
Estimated net income	£5,000

The managing director is most perturbed and comments as follows:

> It looks as if we are finished. At least £50,000 is needed to replace our old equipment. We have been putting this off for years and can now delay no longer. We are already overdrawn at the bank, and there is nothing to use as security. The directors, who between them own all of the shares in the company, are unable to provide the extra finance required and even if they could it wouldn't be worthwhile investing for the income we look like making.

(a) Comment on the managing director's statement.

(b) Suggest areas of investigation which might disclose possible sources of finance within the company and the matters which would have to be considered in respect of these.

14.5 The directors of Rossi Ltd have been concerned about the problems of cash shortages. The company sells on both cash and credit terms. Credit customers who pay their accounts within 15 days are given a cash discount of 5%, and likewise Rossi Ltd always pays cash on receipt of purchases in order to obtain a 4% discount.

Forecast sales for the next three months are:

	June (£)	*July* (£)	*August* (£)
Credit sales	80,000	80,000	90,000
Cash sales	20,000	25,000	27,000
Total sales	100,000	105,000	117,000

The profit mark-up on sales gives a gross profit margin of 50% on gross cost. It is estimated that the above sales will require a stock of goods of £90,000 in sales value to be maintained.

An analysis of customer accounts discloses that 80% of credit customers pay in time to take advantage of the cash discount, 10% pay at the end of 30 days and the remainder at the end of 60 days. There are virtually no bad debts in this business. On average 25% of the credit sales in any one month to customers who take the benefit of the cash discount will be in debtors at the end of the month.

The estimated other expenses payable monthly are:

Fixed	£14,000 per month
Variable	10% of gross sales

Included in the fixed expenses is a depreciation charge of £3,000. A capital payment of £20,000 is required to be made during July.

The balances at the beginning of June are:

Cash	£16,000
Stock	£50,000
Debtors	£18,000

Credit sales for May – a low sales month – were £35,000 of which £14,000 were still outstanding at the end of the month. The remainder of the debtors represent April sales.

Prepare a cash budget for June–August and comment on the results.

14.6 Respighi Plastics Ltd, a manufacturer of moulded plastic containers, determined in October 19X8 that it needed cash to continue operations. The company began negotiating for a one month bank loan of £100,000 on 1 November at 12% interest. In considering the loan, the bank requested a projected profit statement and a cash budget for the month of November.

The following information is available:

1. Sales were budgeted at 120,000 units per month in October 19X8, December 19X8 and January 19X9, and at 90,000 units in November 19X8.
2. The selling price is £2 per unit. Sales are invoiced on the 15th and the last day of each month. Terms are 2% discount if payment is made within 10 days, otherwise the full amount is to be paid within 30 days. Past experience

indicated sales are made evenly throughout the month. Fifty per cent of the customers pay the invoiced amount within the discount period. The remainder pay at the end of 30 days, except for bad debts, which average 0.5% of gross sales.

3. The stock of finished goods on 1 October was 24,000 units. The finished goods stock at the end of each month is to be maintained at 20% of sales anticipated for the following month. The production process is such that there is no work-in-progress.
4. The stock of raw materials on 1 October was 22,800 kg. At the end of each month the raw materials stocks are to be maintained at not less than 40% of production requirements for the following month. Materials are purchased locally. Minimum quantity is 25,000 kg per shipment. Raw material purchases of each month are paid in the next month. Terms are net 30 days.
5. All salaries and wages are paid on the 15th and last day of each month for the period ending on the date of payment.
6. All manufacturing overhead and selling and administrative expenses are paid on the 10th of the month following the month in which the expenses are incurred. Selling expenses are 10% of gross sales. Administrative expenses, which include depreciation of £500 per month on office furniture and fixtures, total £33,000 per month.
7. The standard cost of a moulded plastic container, based on normal production of 100,000 units per month, is:

	£	
Materials, $\frac{1}{2}$ kg	0.50	
Labour	0.40	
Variable overhead	0.20	
Fixed overheads	0.10	(total budgeted = £10,000)
Total	1.20	

8. Fixed overhead includes depreciation on factory equipment of £4,000 per month. Over- or under-absorbed overhead (i.e. difference between £10,000 and the amount applied to production) is included in cost of sales.
9. The cash balance on 1 November is expected to be £10,000.

Assuming the bank loan is granted:

(a) Prepare schedules calculating stock budgets by months for
(i) finished goods production in units for October, November and December;
(ii) raw materials purchases in kg for October and November.

(b) Prepare a projected income statement for the month of November.

(c) Prepare a cash forecast for November showing the opening balance, receipts (itemised by dates of collection), payments and the closing balance.

14.7 You are the cost accountant of a company making three different items of office furniture. The following information is given:

1. Estimated sales in units:

Products	X	*Products sold* Y	Z
January 19X6	5,000	4,000	7,000
February	6,000	3,000	7,000
March	7,000	4,000	6,000
April	6,000	6,000	6,000
May	4,000	6,000	8,000
June	3,000	5,000	12,000
Selling price per unit (£)	57	62	58

2. Direct material standards:

	Price per square yard (£)	*Square yards per unit* X	Y	Z
DM1	4.00	3	5	—
DM2	2.50	2	—	3
DM3	3.20	1	2	7

3. Direct labour standards:

	Rate per hour (£)	X	*Hours per unit* Y	Z
DL1	3.00	4	6	4
DL2	3.20	2	—	3
Direct expense per unit		£5.40	£7.60	£7.50
Overhead absorbed as % of direct cost		$12\frac{1}{2}$%	5%	20%

4. Products are made in the month prior to the month of sale. There are no stocks of part finished items.
5. Labour is paid in the month of manufacture.
6. Materials are purchased in the month prior to manufacture and 50% are paid for in the month of purchase and the balance in the following month.
7. Of the direct expense, £120,000 p.a. is an internal charge for depreciation; the remainder is for outside charges paid in the month after production.
8. Overhead costs are paid 20% in the month prior to sale; 40% in the month of sale and 20% in each of the two months following.
9. Customers' remittances in respect of sales are received as follows:

   60% in month of sale, less $2\frac{1}{2}$% cash discount;
   30% in month after sale;
   10% is second month after sale.

(a) Prepare an estimated profit statement for each item for the period of 3 months ending 31 March, 19X6.

(b) Provide a forecast of cash receipts and payments for the month of March 19X6.

(c) State briefly the most important point revealed by the results reported in (a) and (b).

14.8 It is April 19X6. The Trade Union Coordinating Committee has just walked out of the room. There is going to be a strike starting on the first day of May 19X6. It is thought that the strike may last two months.

The company's budget for 19X6 is as follows:

	£000												
	Total	*Jan.*	*Feb.*	*Mar.*	*Apr.*	*May*	*June*	*July*	*Aug.*	*Sep.*	*Oct.*	*Nov.*	*Dec.*
Material consumed	320	22	23	29	32	26	28	30	32	34	24	20	20
Direct wages	179	14	14	15	16	17	17	16	16	15	13	13	13
Other factory variable expenses	20	1	2	2	2	2	2	2	2	2	1	1	1
Factory fixed expenses:													
Depreciation	40	3	3	4	3	3	4	3	3	4	3	3	4
General	150	12	13	12	13	12	13	12	13	12	13	12	13
Head office fixed expenses	170	14	14	14	14	14	14	14	14	15	14	14	15
Selling expenses:													
Commission	55	2	2	3	4	5	6	7	8	9	4	3	2
Fixed	60	5	5	5	5	5	5	5	5	5	5	5	5
	994	73	76	84	89	84	89	89	93	96	77	71	73
Profit (loss)	71	(3)	(1)	(4)	(4)	6	11	21	32	44	3	(11)	(23)
Sales	1,065	70	75	80	85	90	100	110	125	140	80	60	50
Stock of materials (end of month)		20	25	20	30	30	35	35	40	25	20	20	20

Assumptions

1. Payment is made to suppliers of material one month after delivery. No materials will be bought during the strike.
2. The lag in payment of wages is $\frac{1}{8}$ of a month.
3. Factory variable and general expenses, head office expenses and fixed selling expenses are paid during the month incurred.
4. Sales commission is paid one month in arrear.
5. Debtors take two months' credit.
6. Cash balance at 30 April 19X6 is estimated at £14,000.
7. There will be no production during the strike. Sales lost in the strike will not be recovered subsequently. If the strike ends on 30 June it will not be possible in the succeeding months to produce more than originally budgeted and the costs and stock levels will be as budgeted.
8. There is no work-in-progress or finished stock as the product is delivered daily.

(a) Assuming the strike lasts two months, prepare a statement of cash flow (showing the opening and closing cash balances) for each of the four months May, June, July and August.

(b) Assuming the strike is not settled, prepare a statement of cash flow on a monthly basis showing in which month the bank account goes into overdraft.

(c) Assuming that the strike lasts two months, prepare a statement showing the effect on budgeted profit for the year to 31 December 19X6.

Further reading

Amey, L. R., 'Budget planning: a dynamic reformulation', *Accounting and Business Research*, Winter 1979.

Gershefski, G., 'Building a corporate financial model', *Harvard Business Review*, July/August 1969.

Ijiri, Y., Kinard, J. C. and Putney, F. B., 'An integrated system for budget forecasting and operating performance with a classified budgeting bibliography', *Journal of Accounting Research*, Spring 1968.

Steiner, G. A., *Top Management Planning*, Macmillan, 1969.

Welsch, G. A., *Budgeting: Profit-Planning and Control*, 3rd edn, Prentice Hall 1971.

Chapter 15

Variance analysis and standard costing

In the previous two chapters we have examined the initial stage of the budgetary control process – its budgeting aspect. We now turn our attention to the subsequent stages of the process, namely the measurement of actual performance and the comparison of this performance with budget expectations. Our approach will focus on one of the accountant's most frequently used systems of control, standard costing, to which we have referred in a number of previous chapters. In this chapter we consider the purposes of standard costing, explain how variances might be calculated and consider their interpretation and usefulness. We also discuss the particular problem of dealing with inflation in a standard costing system.

15.1 The purposes of standard costing

Standard costing is the term used to describe a management system which applies budgeting concepts for purposes of control. Typically, standard costing systems possess the following significant elements:

1. Procedures for setting up and updating standards.
2. A recording system, which may be separate from the firm's 'financial accounting' records, which gathers both standard and actual cost (and revenue) information, and computes differences, known as *variances*.
3. The determination of the unit costs of the firm's products, divided into their raw material, labour, variable and fixed overhead elements.
4. The use of a budgeting period, for example one year, subdivided into smaller (e.g. four weekly) time periods which are used as the vehicle for comparing standard and actual costs.
5. Procedures for investigating material variances, and apportioning such variances to responsibility centres.

The primary purposes of a standard costing system are threefold:

1. To provide the management with a yardstick for the evaluation of performance.
2. To give information on those aspects of business operations which are not proceeding according to plan. This purpose recognises the importance of controlling both actual results and planning procedures.
3. To generate information which may be useful for future planning, e.g. for the setting of future standards. This purpose is especially important in a changing environment, for example in times of rapid technological change or high inflation.

There are other less obvious purposes of a standard costing system. For example, because the proper setting and revision of standards requires a knowledge of all the functional areas of the business and their contribution to overall success, standard costing may encourage managers to understand more fully the nature of their business. By concentrating attention only on significant deviations from plan, as detailed by regular variance reports, managers do not waste valuable time on those areas of activity which are proceeding normally, or engage in random testing of different areas covered by the control system.

To best meet its purposes, a standard costing system should embody realistic standards. Hence most systems employ currently attainable standards rather than ideal standards as the yardstick for assessment and evaluation (see Chapter 13, pp. 289–93, for a discussion of currently attainable and ideal budgets). Currently attainable standards reflect the cost expected to be incurred under normally efficient working conditions.

We argue later in this chapter that if conditions change significantly during the period, then the attainable standards may no longer be current and should be changed, otherwise the system will fail to produce useful variances.

Figure 15.1 shows the breakdown of the profit variance (the difference between the expected and actual profit for the year) into its component cost and revenue variances. The main purpose of this chapter is to suggest how these variances might be calculated and what meaning might be ascribed to the resultant calculations. However, at this stage, a few preliminary views on the possible causes of variances are necessary, in order to give some background to the later analysis. It is important to try to identify the *causes* of particular variances, as different variances may call for different remedies. Bromwich has identified *five* major causes of variances, as follows:[43]

1. Inefficiency in operation e.g. failure to obtain a reasonable standard in the prevailing circumstances, through inability in one form or another, or through lack of motivation.

[43] See Bromwich, M., 'Standard costing for planning and control', in Arnold, J., Carsberg, B. and Scapens, R. (eds.), *Topics in Management Accounting*, Philip Allan, 1980.

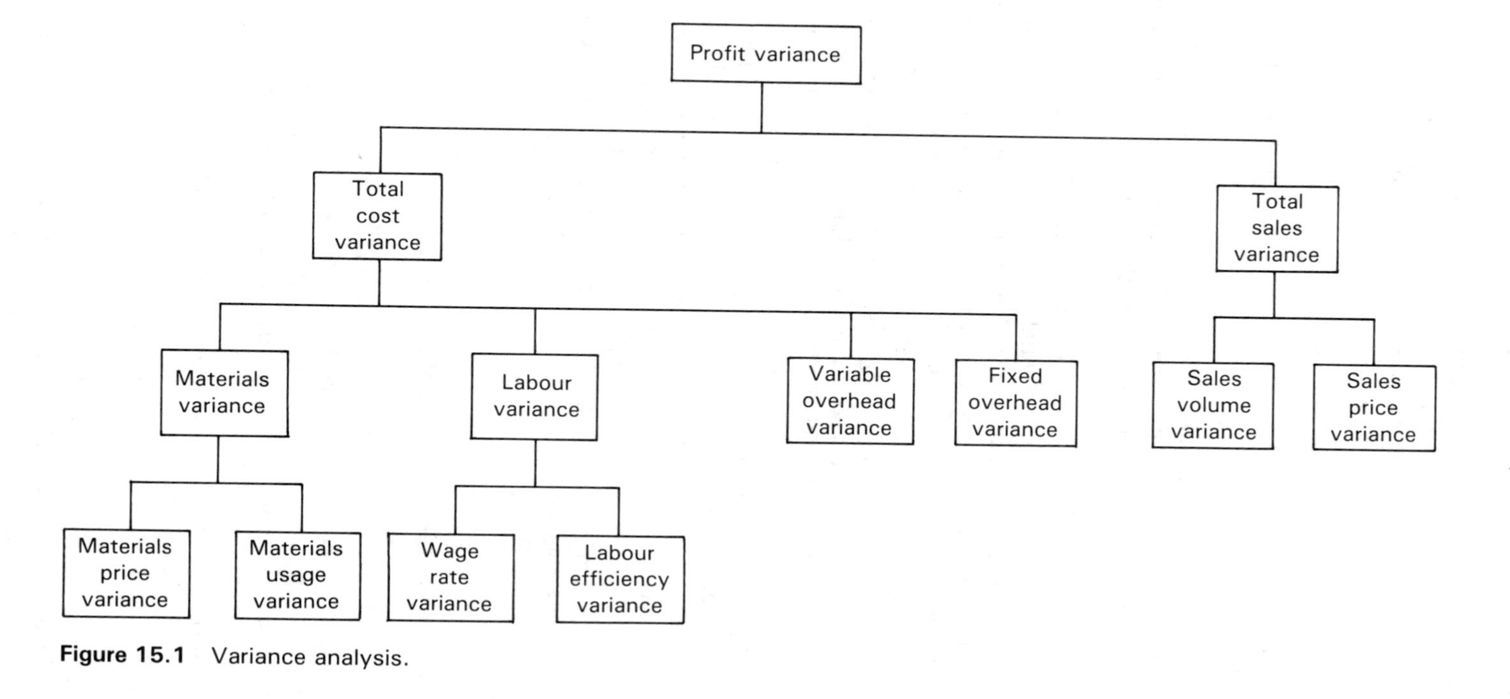

Figure 15.1 Variance analysis.

2. Incorrect original plans and standards, or originally correct plans and standards that have been invalidated by environmental changes (here, the reporting of variances may result in the revision of plans, and the process of variance analysis for planning can be described as being educational).

3. Poor communication of standards and budgetary goals.

4. Random fluctuations around standards and goals which are likely to be average targets.

5. If in budgeting (and in decision making) the interdependence of departments has not been taken into account, then action taken by one department may cause variances elsewhere within the firm (the suboptimisation problem).

Our primary concern in this chapter is with the identification of the first two causes, and the recognition of the potential importance of the fifth cause. To best achieve these purposes, we conduct our analysis in two stages; first, we identify any variances due to changes in *volume* during the period. Because this necessitates a revision or flexing of the budget to the actual volume attained, we term this volume difference a *budget revision* variance. Second, we analyse the differences between the revised budget and the actual figures. We term these differences *control* variances (this distinction between budget revision and control variances was introduced in Chapter 13, pp. 286–8). Control variances should indicate whether managers have achieved the best possible performance in the light of the (revised) budget, as only then will variances be based on a comparison of like with like. In addition, they should exclude as far as possible any factors not within the control of the person to be held responsible for the variance. A main reason for the split between budget revision and control variances is that their causes will probably be different, and will reflect the responsibility of different managers. For example, budget revision variances may reflect the forecasting and planning abilities of managers, whereas control variances are more likely to be caused by operating efficiencies and inefficiencies.

15.2 The mechanics of variance analysis

We shall use an example to illustrate our approach to the calculation and interpretation of variances. Victoria Ltd is a manufacturing company which produces and sells motor car components. It employs a standard costing system for planning and control. Table 15.1 shows the budgeted and actual results for the year to 31 December 19X0.

The following information is also relevant. Usage of both material P and material Q was expected to vary directly with each unit of output, as were the number of unskilled and skilled labour hours, and the element of variable overhead. Victoria Ltd followed its normal practice during the year to 31 December 19X0 of maintaining stocks at a constant level.

Our method of analysis of the difference between expected profit (£7,050) and actual profit (£6,281) rests on an understanding of the role of flexible budgeting.

Table 15.1 Victoria Ltd: budgeted and actual results for the year to 31 December 19X0

	Budget			*Actual*	
	(£)	(£)		(£)	(£)
Total revenues					
Sales (15,000 unis at £5 per unit)		75,000	(14,000 units at £5.25 per unit		73,500
Less Total costs:					
Raw materials:					
Material P (15,000 lb at 55p per lb)	8,250		(14,500 lb at 55p per lb)	7,975	
Material Q (30,000 lb at 80p per lb)	24,000		(28,000 lb at 85p per lb)	23,800	
Labour:					
Unskilled (7,500 hours at £2.50 per hour)	18,750		(6,875 hours at £2.75 per hour)	18,906	
Skilled (1,500 hours at £4 per hour)	6,000		(1,400 hours at £4 per hour)	5,600	
Variable overhead (15,000 units at 25p per unit)	3,750			3,438	
Fixed overhead	7,200	67,950		7,500	67,219
Net profit		7,050			6,281

Table 15.2 First estimation of variances

		(1) Budgeted volume Standard prices		(2) Actual volume Standard prices		(3) Actual volume Actual prices	(4) Remaining variances (2)–(3)
Volume (units)		15,000		14,000		14,000	
		(£)		(£)		(£)	(£)
Sales	(£5)	75,000	(£5)	70,000	(£5.25)	73,500	3,500 (F)
Materials:							
P	(55p)	8,250	(55p)	7,700		7,975	275 (U)
Q	(£1.60)	24,000	(£1.60)	22,400		23,800	1,400 (U)
Labour:							
Unskilled	(£1.25)	18,750	(£1.25)	17,500		18,906	1,406 (U)
Skilled	(40p)	6,000	(40p)	5,600		5,600	—
Variable overhead	(25p)	3,750	(25p)	3,500		3,438	62 (F)
		60,750		56,700		59,719	3,019 (U)
Contribution		14,250		13,300		13,781	481 (F)
Fixed overhead		7,200		7,200		7,500	300 (U)
Profit		7,050		6,100		6,281	181 (F)

Flexible budgeting plays a vital role in generating useful control variances, because for control purposes, it is essential that actual costs and revenues incurred are compared to budgeted costs *at the actual level of activity*. Control and responsibility should go hand in hand in the standard costing system. Individual managers should be held responsible only for variances under their control.

It is therefore necessary to first flex the original budget of 15,000 units to the revised budget of 14,000 units. This eliminates any differences due to changes in volume, and allows us to compare actual performance with expected performance at a level of 14,000 units. Table 15.2 shows how we might achieve this.

The difference between columns (1) and (2) of £950 is the difference in profit (and contribution) due to the shortfall in sales volume: it is the difference generated by flexing the budget to the revised volume of 14,000 units. It thus represents the decline in volume of 1,000 units multiplied by the standard contribution per unit of 95p. The standard contribution per unit is calculated as follows:

	£	£
Selling price		5.00
Less P (1 lb at 55p)	0.55	
Q (2 lb at 80p)	1.60	
Unskilled labour		
($\frac{1}{2}$ hour × £2.50)	1.25	
Skilled labour		
(1/10 hour × £4.00)	0.40	
Variable overhead		
(1 unit at 25p)	0.25	4.05
Standard contribution per unit		0.95

Note that the expected level of fixed overhead, which does not enter the standard contribution per unit calculation, is unchanged for both volume levels. We shall suggest some possible causes for the loss of contribution of £950 in Section 15.3.

We are now in a position to undertake the second stage of the analysis of variances – the comparison at the revised volume level of 14,000 units of the expected profit of £6,100 with the actual profit of £6,281. This favourable difference of £181 is broken down into its constituent parts in column 4 of Table 15.2. We now deal with each of the constituent parts in turn.

Sales variance – £3,500 (F)

Column 4 shows a favourable sales variance of £3,500, i.e. the actual revenue generated from the sale of 14,000 units was greater by £3,500 than the expected revenue at that volume. It can be readily seen that this variance is due to the increase in price of 25p multiplied by the 14,000 units sold. We can express this sales price variance (SPV) by means of the following formula:

$$\text{SPV} = \text{AQ} \times (\text{AP} - \text{SP})$$

where AQ = actual quantity sold, SP = standard price, AP = actual price.

Thus, in our example we have:

$$\begin{aligned} SPV &= 14{,}000 \times (5.25 - 5.00) \\ &= £3{,}500\ (F) \end{aligned}$$

Note that we do not need to calculate a separate variance due to the change in sales volume, as we have already implicitly calculated the sales volume variance in arriving at the revised profit figure in column 2. Whether the sales price variance and the volume variance are useful for planning and control and whether they should be viewed independently, we shall discuss in the following section.

Raw material and labour variances

Raw material and labour variances are often referred to as direct cost variances. They are based on both monetary and non-monetary measures. For example the use of raw materials will probably be measured first in terms of tons, kg or lb used. Similarly, the efficiency with which the labour force performs its task might be expressed initially in a time dimension in terms of hours or minutes.

Managers could exercise control by focusing solely on the quantity of materials used, or the time taken to perform the job, and comparing these non-monetary totals with the budget figures for material quantity and labour time. But how much information would this provide? Remember that one purpose of the control exercise is to monitor the effect of the firm's operations on the budgeted profit for the period. As profit is expressed in money terms, it is necessary to translate the non-additive hours, tons, litres etc. into money values. Thus at the very root of direct cost variance analysis is a recognition of the effects of changes due to price and changes due to quantity, both of which must be expressed in cash terms.

Price variances (or *rate variances*) measure the difference between the amount the firm expected to pay for the actual quantity bought and the amount it did pay. *Usage variances* (or *efficiency variances*) measure the difference between the quantity of a resource the firm expected to use for the actual activity level and the quantity it did use. This difference in quantity is usually expressed as a money amount by multiplying it by the standard price per unit. The total of the price and usage variances (or the rate and efficiency variances) is equal to the difference between the actual cost of a resource and the cost expected for the actual output level.

Price variances are not concerned with differences between the standard and actual purchase quantities of a resource, but rather with the differences between the standard and actual purchase price per unit of the quantity bought. They should be calculated at the time of purchase rather than at the time of use, in order to provide the quickest possible feedback for control purposes. The price variance (PV) is defined as the difference in price (standard price (SP) less actual price (AP)) multiplied by the actual quantity bought (AQ). It may be expressed by a formula similar to the one used to calculate the sales price variance:

$$PV = AQ \times (SP - AP)$$

The quantity variance (QV) is not concerned with price changes. It represents the difference between the standard quantity for the actual output (SQ) and the actual quantity used (AQ), multiplied by the standard cost price (SP). It may be expressed as:

$$QV = SP \times (SQ - AQ)$$

We can now use these definitions of price and quantity variance to analyse the differences arising in respect of raw materials and labour for Victoria Ltd.

1. *Material P – £275 (U)*: the price paid for P was 55p per unit. As this was the expected price, no price variance arises. However, as Table 15.1 shows 14,500 lb of P were used to produce 14,000 units – 500 lb more than expected. Thus a material quantity or usage variance arises. We can calculate the effect of this by using the formula for quantity variances given above. This gives:

$$\begin{aligned} \text{QV (Material usage variance)} &= SP \times (SQ - AQ) \\ &= 55p \times (14{,}000 - 14{,}500) \\ &= £275\ (U) \end{aligned}$$

2. *Material Q – £1,400 (U)*: The price paid for Q was 85p per unit. This is greater than the standard price of 80p per unit. Thus a price variance arises, calculated according to the price variance formula:

$$\begin{aligned} \text{PV (Material price variance)} &= AQ \times (SP - AP) \\ &= 28{,}000 \times (80p - 85p) \\ &= £1{,}400\ (U) \end{aligned}$$

   Note that no usage variance arises for Q. At an output level of 14,000 units, Victoria Ltd expected to use 28,000 lb of Q, which in fact represented the actual usage. The usefulness of these price and usage variances will be considered in the next section.

3. *Unskilled labour – £1,406 (U)*: Victoria Ltd expected to pay unskilled labour a standard rate per hour of £2.50. The actual rate paid was £2.75 per hour, and thus an unfavourable price (or rate) variance arises. Using the price variance formula, and substituting actual hours worked (AHW = 6,875 from Table 15.1) for actual quantities, we can calculate the cash effect of this variance as follows:

$$\begin{aligned} \text{PV (labour rate variance)} &= AHW \times (SP - AP) \\ &= 6{,}875 \times (£2.50 - £2.75) \\ &= £1{,}718\ (U) \end{aligned}$$

   Elimination of the price variance leaves a further favourable difference of (£1,718 – £1,406) = £312. This further difference is explicable in terms of the usage (or efficiency) of labour. On the basis of an output of 14,000 units, unskilled labour was expected to work for 14,000/2 = 7,000 hours. However, only 6,875 hours were needed to produce the 14,000 units, and thus labour 'saved' 125 hours. We can calculate the effect of this extra efficiency by using the quantity variance formula, and by substituting the standard hours (SH) and the actual hours worked (AHW) for the standard and actual quantities. Thus we have:

$$\begin{aligned} \text{QV (Labour efficiency variance)} &= \text{SP} \times (\text{SH} - \text{AHW}) \\ &= £2.50 \times (7{,}000 - 6{,}875) \\ &= £312 \text{ (F)} \end{aligned}$$

Note that no price or quantity variances arise in respect of skilled labour. The rate paid of £4 per hour is the standard rate for skilled labour, and the production of 14,000 units in 1,400 hours, the actual time taken, represents the expected level of efficiency.

Variable overhead – £62 (F)

Variable overhead for Victoria Ltd is expected to be incurred at a rate of 25p for each unit produced. Thus any variances between the variable overhead expected to be incurred at the actual level of output and the actual overhead incurred are due to favourable or unfavourable expenditure differences. The formula for calculating variable overhead expenditure variances is as follows:

$$\begin{aligned} \text{VO (expenditure variance)} &= \text{budgeted variable overhead at actual} \\ &\quad\ \text{output level} - \text{actual variable overhead} \\ &= (14{,}000 \text{ units} \times 25\text{p}) - £3{,}438 \\ &= £3{,}500 - £3{,}438 \\ &= £62 \text{ (F)} \end{aligned}$$

Fixed overhead – £300 (U)

As fixed overheads do not change with the level of output, it is not helpful (and indeed it may be misleading) to allocate them to individual units of production. The only meaningful variance for control purposes is the difference between the total amount expected to be spent on fixed overheads during the period and the actual amount spent. In the case of Victoria Ltd, this variance of £300 is the difference between £7,200 (budgeted fixed overheads) and £7,500 (actual fixed overheads).

We can now prepare a final control statement for Victoria Ltd, reconciling budgeted and actual contribution, and showing the actual profit figure as in Table 15.3.

15.3 The interpretation and usefulness of variances

Having explained the two-stage calculation of variances in the previous section we are now in a position to interpret their meaning and discuss their usefulness. Each variance shown in Table 15.3 will be discussed in turn *in the context of the purposes of the standard costing system* as outlined at the start of this chapter.

Table 15.3 Victoria Ltd: standard costing statement for the year to 31 December 19X0

	F (£)	*U* (£)	(£)
Budgeted contribution at budgeted volume (15,000 components at 0.95p)			14,250
Less Contribution lost due to reduction in volume (1,000 units at 95p)			950
Budgeted contribution at actual volume			13,300
Less Remaining variances:			
Sales price	3,500		
Unskilled labour efficiency	312		
Variable overhead expenditure	62		
P-usage		275	
Q-price		1,400	
Unskilled labour rate		1,718	
	3,874	3,393	481 (F)
Actual contribution (14,000 components)			13,781
Less Budgeted fixed costs		7,200	
Fixed costs expenditure variance (U)		300	7,500
Actual profit (as per Table 15.1)			6,281

Sales variances

Table 15.3 shows a favourable sales price variance of £3,500. Is the sales manager to be congratulated on this achievement? To begin to answer this question we should look at the other side of the sales coin – the number of units sold. Victoria Ltd expected to sell 15,000 units, but in fact sold only 14,000 units, i.e. the price increase was accompanied by a fall in volume, as the workings of a competitive market would suggest.[44] Should we then equally blame the sales manager for failure to achieve the budgeted volume? If the shortfall of 1,000 units on sales was due entirely to the price increase, the benefit from the additional selling price per unit should be abated to some extent by the contribution lost on the shortfall, i.e. by £950. In other words, the net benefit from increasing selling price would be £2,550 (£3,500 minus £950).

Further consideration should convince us that we need more information about the state of the market place before we can say how well the sales force performed in the circumstances. For example, if demand in the market place has declined rapidly since standards were set, then the sales department may have done very well to sell 14,000 units at the increased price of £5.25. Thus the favourable net sales variance of £2,550 may be an inadequate reflection of managerial performance. The sales managers of Victoria Ltd may have taken advantage of their opportunities as well as possible, and indeed, have performed better than sales managers elsewhere. In this

[44] See Chapter 8 for a more detailed discussion of sales demand–price relationships.

situation the loss of volume of 1,000 units may have been totally uncontrollable, in which case it may be inappropriate to reduce the favourable sales price variance of £3,500 by the lost contribution of £950. Indeed, as we explain later in this section the loss of volume (and hence contribution) may be attributable to other factors for which *non-sales* managers *within the firm* are responsible.

If, however, demand for Victoria Ltd's goods has been particularly buoyant, then the loss of sales of 1,000 units may represent a controllable loss due to the inefficiency of the sales force. Or the price charged of £5.25 may have been too *low* at a volume level of 14,000 units. In this case sales managers may have failed to take advantage of the market situation. The real loss due to the fall in sales volume depends upon whether Victoria Ltd can recoup the sales in future periods. If sales are lost forever the real cost to the firm is the lost contribution from these sales; if sales are likely to be recouped in the future the only cost is one of *time*. Persistently favourable or unfavourable volume variances might offer indications to top management as to the direction it should take; for example, a regularly favourable volume variance might indicate that the firm should increase its production capacity to take advantage of profitable market opportunities.

How should the sales price variance be evaluated? This depends largely upon whether the firm can influence the prevailing market price. If the firm has no control over the price, and hence the sales price variance is largely uncontrollable, there is little advantage to be gained in holding the sales force responsible for the difference, favourable or otherwise. In this case the only useful information to be derived from the sales price variance is as an aid to future planning. If the sales price variance is controllable it should be used *in conjunction with* the volume variance (based on contribution lost or gained) in evaluating management. This underlines the important point that individual variances should not be viewed independently of their effects elsewhere in the organisation.

Raw materials variances

Table 15.3 shows two variances for raw materials – an unfavourable usage variance of £275 for P, and an unfavourable price variance of £1,400 for Q. Does this mean that the *buying* manager should be criticised for failure to secure the standard price for Q, and that the *production* manager should be penalised for inefficient use of P? Before we can answer these questions we need to explore a little further the possible interpretations of these two variances.

Material price variance

A primary aim of top management is to evaluate the success of the materials buying manager in obtaining a favourable price. Comparison of the actual price paid with the budgeted price may reflect an insufficient amount of time spent on evaluating the 'quality' of suppliers, slowness in taking advantage of discount, and changes in material quality. But such comparisons may not be the best way of evaluating success if there have been substantial changes in the price of raw materials between the date at which the budget is set and the date of purchase. If the price change is due to market factors, as is most likely, then such a change will be outside the control of the buying manager, and so to say that he had done well or badly in generating a price variance may convey little useful information as to his buying skills. Thus to show how well the buying manager has competed in the market, the appropriate comparison should rest between the price paid for raw materials and *the best estimate of the market price at the date of purchase*. This comparison attempts to remove any uncontrollable factors from the evaluation. The unfavourable price variance for Victoria Ltd may therefore be outside the control of the buying manager, and may reflect poor budgeting. If this proves to be the case, it should be charged to the planners rather than the buying manager. In Chapter 13, we discussed the issue of participation in budget setting. It may be that, in practice, the dichotomy between budget setters and budget achievers is not clear cut. If the person responsible for implementing a budget has also played a substantial role in setting it, then variances should be interpreted with particular care. It may, for example, be unwise in these circumstances to reward the achievement of a favourable price variance without, at the same time, investigating carefully whether the budget price was reasonable in the circumstances which existed at the time the budget was set.

The trend in material price variances may give useful information for future planning. For example a regularly favourable variance might suggest that the firm's planners are consistently pessimistic about future material prices, which may result in incorrect output level and selling price decisions (see e.g. Chapters 8 and 9). The price variance should not, however, be viewed in isolation from costs elsewhere in the firm. Consider the possible effects of (bulk) buying a large quantity of raw materials. A larger quantity demanded will often lead to a discount being offered by the supplier, i.e. a favourable price variance. This decision in turn may lead directly to the incurrence of interest costs in relation to the additional finance required for the purchase and warehouse (and supervision) costs for the material's storage. These extra costs are due to the particular action of the buying manager and all variances, wherever located in the organisation, due to this action should be attributable to the buying manager and not to other managers. Nor should material price variances be viewed in isolation from usage variances. For example, purchases of non-standard material at cheaper (or more expensive) prices may result in unfavourable (or favourable) usage variances. These interdependent variances, as far as they can be identified, should be attributable to the material buyer. In practice, the determination of such interdependences may be very difficult.

Material usage variance

The usage variance of £275 for P seems at first glance to be more controllable than the price variance for Q. After all, users of raw material are not as directly at the mercy of the market as are buyers. Thus inefficient use may be attributable to the production manager and may be due to such factors as changes in material quality, the efficiency of machine operators, changes in the material mix and non-standard production scheduling. But the usage variance may also hide some interdependences. We discussed in the previous paragraph how off-standard material, bought at off-standard prices, can make for usage problems. We must look also at *who* is using the material. For example, if the firm is employing unskilled instead of skilled labour, one consequence of this decision may be greater waste, resulting in an unfavourable material usage variance, which may not be the fault of the production manager but rather of the personnel department.

The joint variance

One area of difficulty in the evaluation of raw material variances concerns the combined or joint variance. Figure 15.2 gives a diagrammatic example of this variance. (This diagram is unrelated to the example of Victoria Ltd.) The solid rectangle represents the standard cost of raw materials (9,000 lb at £5 per lb), and the larger dashed rectangle represents the actual cost (9,500 lb at £5.50 per lb). The shaded area between the two rectangles reflects the total variances. Clearly there is an unfavourable usage variance of 500 lb at £5 per lb = £2,500; and clearly there is an unfavourable price variance of 9,000 lb at 50p per lb = £4,500. But how do we evaluate the joint variance of £250 (the extra use of 500 lb at the additional price of 50p per lb), denoted by the top right-hand corner of Figure 15.2. Who is responsible for this joint variance? In our analysis in the previous section we followed conventional practice and included the joint variance in the price variance, i.e. we based the price variance on the actual quantity used. In this example, that practice would give an unfavourable price variance of 9,500 × (£5.50 – £5.00) which equals £4,750. But should the buying manager be blamed for the increase in prices or should the production manager be blamed instead for excessive use of materials? Each manager might argue that the variance is due to the action of the other. Thus fair apportionment of responsibility for the joint variance may be impossible, and it may be more meaningful to divide the total price variance of £4,750 into a 'pure'

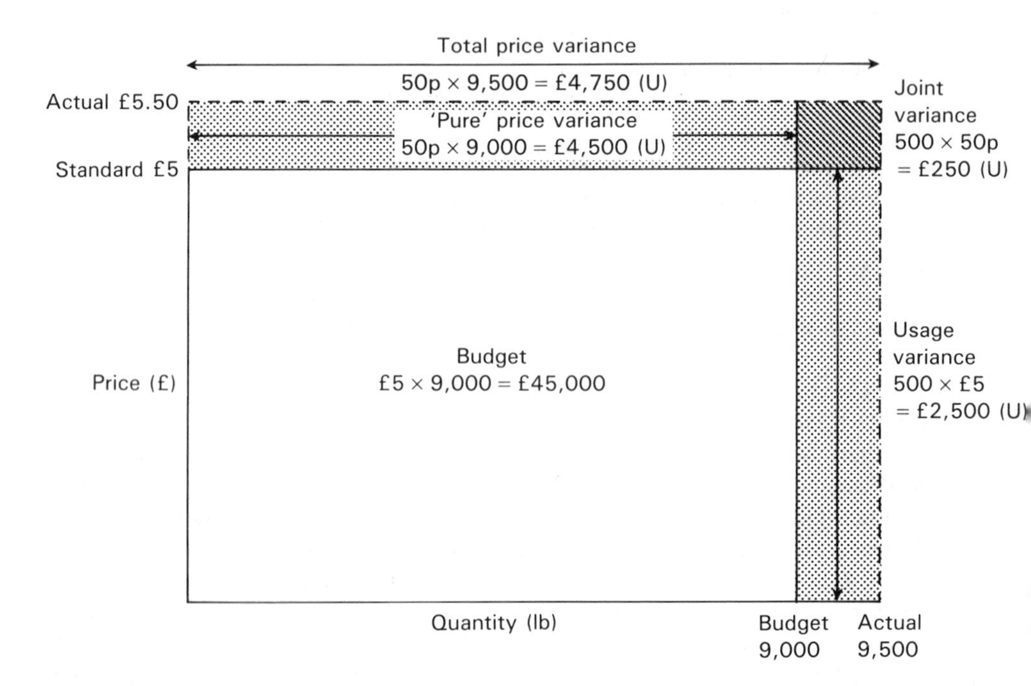

Figure 15.2 The joint variance.

variance of £4,500 and a joint variance of £250. Whether this refinement is necessary in practice depends upon how the variances are to be used by management and how significant are these joint variances in the context of total variances.

Labour variances

Table 15.3 reveals two types of variance for unskilled labour – an unfavourable rate variance of £1,718 and a favourable efficiency variance of £312. What interpretation can be placed on these figures?

Labour rate variance

As in the case of raw materials price variances, labour rate variances may be due entirely to external, uncontrollable factors, e.g. national and local wage awards for individual grades and skills. In these cases the personnel department cannot be held responsible for rate changes. Certain rate changes however may be within the firm's responsibility, e.g. changes in incentive schemes and changes in the class of labour used may be controllable, and, if so, should be charged to the responsible production manager. Regular variances in labour rate might give useful information for planning, and in particular might suggest some possible changes in the production process via the substitution of capital for labour or vice versa.

Labour efficiency variance

This arises because the labour force completed its task in more or less than the allotted time and may be due, *inter alia*, to lack of supevision, poor training, changes in material quality and changes in working methods. The setting of standards for labour efficiency or productivity can be a complex and time consuming task in itself – the notion of the correct 'time for the job' is one on which managers and workers may have very different views. Responsibility for these variances depends partly upon conditions prevailing in the labour market. If, for example, less skilled labour has to be used because skilled labour cannot be obtained, then the standard time for the job may have to be lengthened to permit meaningful evaluations. If the standard time for the job is representative of the actual conditions pertaining during the period, then the labour efficiency variance may be fairly attributed to the production manager.

Our calculation in Table 15.3 showed the labour efficiency variance to be the product of the difference in hours expected and achieved for actual output and the standard rate per hour. But will this calculation always measure adequately the cost of labour inefficiency (or the benefit from labour efficiency)? The real cost of labour inefficiency may in fact be greater than the conventional computation allows. If, for example, the result of labour inefficiency is a loss of production which, because the firm is working at full capacity, will never be recovered, then the real cost of inefficiency is the wage rate *plus* the lost contribution on the (unsold) production. Only if the firm has spare capacity will the conventional variance appropriately measure the cost of inefficiency, as only then may production be recovered in future periods. (Note that if the supply of materials or any other resource is limited, similar arguments to these apply in measuring the cost of inefficient usage or the benefit of efficient usage.)

Overhead variances

Table 15.3 shows two *expenditure* variances – a favourable variable overhead variance of £62, and an unfavourable fixed overhead variance of £300. These represent the only meaningful overhead variances for planning and control. They indicate whether the appropriate managers have kept their spending within the revised budget. It is inappropriate to compute any other overhead variances, of whatever form, for managerial decision making purposes.[45]

Budget revision (sales volume) variances

Table 15.3 shows a lost contribution of £950 arising from the failure to attain the budgeted level of sales of 15,000 units. We have not yet attempted to explore directly the cause of this fall in volume which we have termed a budget revision or volume variance. No information is given as to why it occurred. Several possible explanations might be offered, each of which might point to a different cause, and thus attract a different responsibility. Perhaps the sales manager had specified incorrectly the firm's demand–price relationship, and thus the original target figure of 15,000 units was unrealistic, even at the budget selling price of £5.00 per unit. Or perhaps the increase in selling price from £5.00 to £5.25 resulted in a decrease in the quantity demanded. The variance may thus be a planning error, to be charged to the sales planning manager, or a consequence of increasing selling price, to be set against the favourable sales price variance. Alternatively the volume change may be due to the failure of the sales force to meet a realistic target. In this case the variance arises from operating inefficiency and should be charged to the sales force. Other explanations might suggest that the loss of contribution was not caused by incorrect sales predictions or by the performance of the sales department but rather by a restriction on the quantity available for sale resulting, for example, from labour inefficiency, production breakdowns, strikes, or indeed a variety of less significant factors combining together to the detriment of the firm, each of which should be investigated to determine appropriate responsibility.

15.4 The investigation of variances

It is an art of good management to know when to investigate a variance. The need to investigate is not always self-evident. The important point to bear in mind when considering the investigation of variances is the cost involved relative to any benefits likely to be achieved. But this cost–benefit criterion for investigation poses a major

[45] Many managerial accounting texts devote considerable space to the calculation of overhead 'efficiency', 'capacity' and 'idle time' variances. As we believe that the cost of such factors is (for purposes of planning and control) more appropriately measured by lost contribution, we do not include a discussion of such overhead variances here.

practical problem. Although it may be possible to quantify with reasonable accuracy the costs of investigation, it is far less easy to put a value on the benefits. Thus it frequently happens that investigation is conducted on a subjective basis, in which educated guesswork is substituted for a more scientific or formal analysis.

The importance of investigating only material or significant variances is frequently stressed and we may agree intuitively that the expenditure of time and money on the examination of immaterial or insignificant variances is a pointless task. But the terms 'materiality' and 'significance' present large measurement problems. What is a significant variance? Some variances will be small in amount, others will be large. As we have seen, some variances arise because actual costs are different from planned costs at the predicted level of activity; some arise because errors are made in the identification and measurement of actual costs; some arise because the level of activity actually attained is different from the plan; and others occur because the plan has proved to be unrealistic in the light of changed circumstances. Given all these varying circumstances and varying amounts how is management to determine which variances are significant and thus worthy of investigation? We might offer at least two pieces of advice in deciding whether or not to investigate. First, managers should not necessarily be concerned with the absolute amount of any variance, but rather with the relationship of the variance to the costs of production if the particular variance is a cost variance, and the relationship of the variance to total sales revenue if the particular variance is a sales variance. Viewed in this light a labour rate variance of £1,000 might be considered insignificant and not worthy of investigation if the total labour costs are £200,000, whereas a labour rate variance of £1,000 in relation to total labour costs of £20,000 (a variance of 5%) would normally be considered significant.

Second, managers should be aware of the potential usefulness of certain statistical techniques in measuring materiality or significance. For example, techniques of statistical quality control are often used to lay down, on the basis of the mean and standard deviation of particular variables, certain limits for randomness. This helps management to know whether individual variances are likely to be uncontrollable chance factors, or whether variances fall outside the limits for random deviation and therefore require a more detailed scrutiny.

15.5 Inflation and standard costing

Throughout our exposition of standard costing and variance analysis we have referred only in passing to situations in which managers might need to review and update standards *during* the budget period. This exposition may be valid if no significant changes in the expected costs of input factors occur, and if expected sales prices do not change during the budget period, i.e. if managers have properly anticipated price changes in setting standards. If however, costs or sales prices do change, through the existence of such factors as *unanticipated* inflation, the pursuit of a new pricing policy, or other environmental changes, it becomes a matter of great importance for management to ensure that budgets and standards remain at a realistic level. Thus it becomes a major management decision to determine the frequency with which standards should be revised to reflect the impact of changes in prices and other factors. In this section we concentrate particularly on the impact of inflation on standard costing.

At this stage we should reiterate one of the basic purposes of the control exercise – the assessment of managerial effectiveness. To measure effectiveness in a meaningful way we must compare like with like; thus to measure managerial effectiveness we must compare actual costs and revenues with realistic standards existing at the time of incurring the costs and revenues. If this is not done individual managers may be unfairly advantaged or disadvantaged by being assessed on the basis of obsolete standards. In revising standards management should aim to strike a balance between the use of realistic standards for the performance evaluation and a desire not to confuse the implementation of the control system by excessively frequent changes. With this balance in mind some firms review and, if necessary, change standards half-yearly or quarterly or maybe monthly.

But how should the effects of inflation be incorporated? At least two possibilities present themselves. Managers can use either specific or general price indices to incorporate inflation. The use of specific indices for labour, material and overheads is preferable and this information can often be obtained if there exist nationally agreed wage rates, and if long-term contracts for materials and services have been secured. If managers feel the inflated wage rate is to some extent negotiable, they must then decide whether to use an expected rate or a maximum rate in the budget. The chosen rate may well depend upon their own negotiating ability. There is a variety of published indices which offer indicators of specific inflation rates, but their usefulness for control purposes depends upon their applicability to future (changing) circumstances, and even where such indices exist, they may be applicable only to very loosely defined categories of expense. It may well be the case that managers will need more detailed forecasts of specific prices, which may be obtainable from discussions with suppliers.

Where information on specific indices is either unobtainable or too expensive, managers may be driven to use such general indices as the Retail Price Index. If such an index is used, managers will need to be aware of those situations in which the prices of the firm's particular inputs have changed at a rate different from the chosen index. If both specific and general indices are available, managers may be provided with indicators of the efficiency of input mixes, and the ability of those responsible to 'beat' inflation.

Thus, in conditions of changing prices additional problems are presented to the management accountant. For example, at the *planning* stage of the standard costing exercise it may be that, as the budget passes through its various stages of preparation, individual managers add onto the budget a certain percentage to allow, in a rough and ready way, for the impact of inflation. In consequence, there is a danger of double-counting the effect of inflation. To avoid this it is necessary to spell out clearly the price change assumptions built into the budget. At the *control* stage it is important to analyse separately anticipated and unanticipated price changes and to distinguish those that are controllable from those that are not. This type of analysis may provide information on price changes of the firm's own input and output factors which can be used to improve future planning procedures.

The following example of Millmoor Ltd is designed to show how some of these difficulties might be avoided, and to present briefly one possible method of budgeting under inflation. We assume a budget period of one year although, as we have noted, a shorter period will probably be appropriate in practice if prices are changing. The principles involved are the same whatever the length of the budget period. Table 15.4 shows the 19X1 budgeted profit for Millmoor Ltd expressed in present prices (i.e. prices prevailing at the date the budget is set) and predicted prices (i.e. prices embodying management's best guess of future price changes).

Four adjustments are made to the original budget. These represent management's predictions of the impact of anticipated inflation on costs (numbers refer to superscripts in Table 15.4). They are as follows:

1. The price per lb of material is expected to rise during the year from 50p (the price included in the original budget) to 53p, and finally to 55p. 25,000 lb will be bought at 50p per lb, 50,000 lb at 53p per lb, and 25,000 lb at 55p per lb (i.e. Millmoor Ltd. needs 100,000 lb of material to produce 20,000 units).
2. The cost of labour is expected to rise from £2.55 per hour (the price included in the original budget) to £2.85 per hour. Each completed unit requires one hour of labour. Ten thousand units will require labour at the old rate of £2.55 per hour, and 10,000 units will require labour at the new rate of £2.85 per hour.
3. Variable overheads are expected to rise in line with the general level of inflation, which is expected to increase at 20% during 19X1. Hence the impact on Millmoor's variable overheads will be to increase them on average by 10% throughout the year.
4. Fixed overheads are also expected to increase in line with the general level of inflation during 19X1.

Table 15.4 Millmoor Ltd: budget for 19X1 in present and predicted prices

		Present prices (£)		*Predicted prices* (£)
Sales revenue (20,000 units at £9 per unit)		180,000		180,000
Less Variable costs:				
Material	50,000		52,750 (1)	
Labour	51,000		54,000 (2)	
Variable overhead	30,000		33,000 (3)	
Selling expenses	6,000	137,000	6,000	145,750
Budgeted contribution		43,000		34,250
Less Fixed costs		24,000		26,400 (4)
Budgeted profit		19,000		7,850

Table 15.5 Millmoor Ltd: comparison of revised budget and actual figures for 19X1

		Budget (at predicted prices) (£)		Actual (£)
Sales revenue (20,000 units)		180,000		185,000[1]
Less Variable costs:				
Material	52,750		58,300[2]	
Labour	54,000		51,750[3]	
Variable overhead	33,000		33,600[4]	
Selling expenses	6,000	145,750	6,000	149,650
Contribution		34,250		35,350
Less Fixed costs		26,400		28,000
Profit		7,850		7,350

Table 15.5 shows a comparison between the budgeted profit for the year, based on the predicted prices, and the actual profit for the year. The following information is relevant in explaining the actual figures for 19X1 (numbers refer to superscripts in Table 15.5):

1. The sales revenue of £185,000 arises from the sale of 10,000 units at £9 per unit, and 10,000 units at £9.50 per unit.
2. The cost of material is made up of 27,500 lb at 50p per lb, 55,000 lb at 53p per lb and 27,500 lb at 56p per lb.
3. The cost of labour is made up of 10,000 hours at £2.55 per hour and 8,333 hours at £3.15 per hour.
4. The general level of inflation increased by 24% during the year. Variable overheads increased in line with this rate, i.e. they amounted to £30,000 $\times \frac{112}{100}$ = £33,600.

We are in a position to analyse the difference between the profit figure based on predicted prices (column 1 of Table 15.5) and the actual profit for the year. Table 15.6 shows how we might do this by analysing the individual variances into two categories; those attributable to *unanticipated* price changes, over which managers have little control, and those attributable to other factors, which may be more directly controllable (numbers refer to superscripts in Table 15.6):

1. 10,000 units × £(9.50 – 9.00) = £5,000 (F).
2. 27,500 lb × (55 – 56)p = £275 (U).
3. (2,500 lb × 50p) + (5,000 lb × 53p) + (2,500 lb × 55p) = £5,275 (U).
4. 8,333 hr × (£2.85 – £3.15) per hr = £2,500 (U).
5. (10,000 – 8,333) hr × £2.85 = £4,750 (F).

Table 15.6 Millmoor Ltd: breakdown of total variances

	Total variance	*Attributed to:*	
		Unanticipated price changes	*Other factors*
	(£)	(£)	(£)
Sales price[1]	5,000 (F)	5,000 (F)	—
Material:			
Price[2]	275 (U)	275 (U)	—
Usage[3]	5,275 (U)	—	5,275 (U)
Labour:			
Rate[4]	2,500 (U)	2,500 (U)	—
Efficiency[5]	4,750 (F)	—	4,750 (F)
Variable overhead expenditure[6]	600 (U)	600 (U)	—
Fixed overhead expenditure[7]	1,600 (U)	480 (U)	1,120 (U)
Tòtal variance to explain (£7,350 – £7,850)	500 (U)	1,145 (F)	1,645 (U)

6. £33,000 – £33,600 = £600 (U).
7. Unanticipated price change = (26,400 – 24,000 × $\frac{112}{100}$) = £480 (U).
   Balance of variance (£480 – £1,600) = £1,120 (U).

This form of presentation is intended to offer some further insights into variance analysis which may be particularly useful for future planning, i.e. it should be viewed together with the interpretations suggested previously. For example, the column representing variances due to unanticipated price changes may give clues to the firm's future pricing policy (the sales price variance); and may, when used in conjuction with published indices and predictions, give information relevant to the estimation of future costs (the direct cost variances). The column representing variances due to other factors should be analysed and interpreted in the manner suggested in previous sections (e.g. recognition should be given to the possible effect of interdependences between price and usage variances).

Discussion topics

1. Why is it necessary to set standards for control purposes? What benefits accrue from having a workable standard costing system?
2. 'The technique of variance analysis is only useful if all variances associated with a particular decision can be identified.' Discuss.
3. 'Control and responsibility go hand in hand. No standard costing system should divorce the two.' Discuss.

4 'Price and quantity variances are at the heart of any managerial control system.' Do you agree with this? Can you cite any other types of variances which may generate useful information?

5 Explain any potential difficulties which might arise in apportioning responsibility for raw materials variances.

6 Can you suggest any forms of business in which standard costing systems may be of little use? What characteristics would these businesses possess?

7 'Planning variances and control variances seek to explain different aspects of the standard costing system, and should not be confused.' Discuss the above statement in the context of flexible budgeting.

8 Discuss the difficulties in identifying material (i.e. significant) variances which should be subject to investigation.

9 'Any standard costing system can become obsolete due to the impact of inflation.' Explain some of the problems which inflation presents for management control systems.

Exercises

15.1 Van Eyck Ltd manufactures and sells a single product. Its budgeted and actual results for the four week period ended 23 May 19X5 are summarised as follows:

	Budget (£)	(£)		*Actual* (£)	(£)
Sales 1,000 units @ £30		30,000	1,100 units @ £30		33,000
Less Materials 1,000 lb @ £5	5,000		1,150 lb. @ £5.20	5,980	
Labour 5,000 hours @ £2.30	11,500		5,000 hr. @ £2.40	12,000	
Fixed overheads	10,000	26,500		10,700	28,680
Net profit		3,500			4,320

At the time the budget was prepared (late 19X4), it was assumed that basic wage rates would have to be increased by 15% on 1 April 19X5. The actual increase was 20%; the average rate of wage increase in the industry was 18% over the same period. The supply of labour is limited to 1,250 hours per week.

Prepare a statement reconciling actual and budgeted results in whatever form you think will be most helpful to managers. Add a short note explaining what additional information you would seek to assess the performance of the sales manager who is responsible for pricing.

15.2 Moreno Ltd recently had a strike in its Leeds factory. By comparing budget and actual quantities for the period of the strike, the firm's accountant had prepared the following estimate of the cost of the strike:

Sales: Number of units below budget		70,000
Budget unit selling price (£)		2.50
Total revenue lost because of strike (£)		175,000
Less Cost savings (£):		
Material not used (70,000 units × budget unit material cost)	17,500	
Wages (70,000 units × budget unit labour cost)	35,000	52,500
		122,500
Add Wages paid during strike (not included in budget labour cost) (£):		
Supervisor	1,000	
Workers in trade unions unaffected by strike	2,000	3,000
Fixed overhead not recovered (£) (70,000 units × budget overhead recovery rate)		17,500
Total cost of strike (£)		143,000

The Leeds factory produces only one product, and keeps no stocks. At the time of the strike there was a temporary decline in demand for the product, and it is estimated that actual sales would in any case have been 20,000 units below budget. The sales manager has said that even to reach this volume of sales the price of the last 50,000 units sold would have had to be reduced to £2 per unit. The workers who came in during the strike were used in maintenance work usually undertaken by an outside contractor. Materials costing £2,000 had to be specially bought for the maintenance work. The normal charge by the contractor is £6,000. The budgeted fixed overhead rate is based solely on fixed costs that are unaffected by the activity of any one factory. It was agreed as part of the strike settlement to make up 20,000 of the units lost because of the strike by working exceptional overtime. For this work, there will be a special wage rate that will add 25% to budgeted unit labour cost.

(a) Prepare a report for Moreno's board of directors showing the opportunity cost of the strike explaining any assumption that you make.

(b) Add a brief note explaining your treatment of fixed overheads.

15.3 Scriabin Ltd, a company with two divisions, has recently installed a budgetary control system which is intended to help appraise managerial efficiency. The budget performance report for last month is:

	Division A	*Division B*
Sales in units: Actual	7,500	5,000
Budget	6,000	7,000
Price per unit (£): Actual	1.5	3.0
Budget	2.0	3.5
Total variable costs £:*		
Material (£): Actual	4,000	2,500
Budget	2,400	2,800
Labour (£): Actual	2,250	3,000
Budget	1,600	2,800
Total contribution to fixed overheads and profits (£):		
Actual	5,000	9,500
Budget	8,000	18,900

* Budget figures are based on budgeted sales

Additional information, covering all the factors which affected performance during the month, is given:

1. The firm produces to order and keeps no stocks. The demand conditions assumed in the budget for division A did in fact apply during the month. It was, however, expected that the sales of division B would be 2,500 units under the original budget at the budget price because of a temporary decline in the market. This shortfall in volume is expected to be recouped at the budgeted price in the next month by working exceptional overtime at a cost of £1,000. The sales manager of division B was able partially to offset the temporary decline in sales by cutting the price to below the budget figure.
2. Both divisions use the same raw material but each employs its own purchasing officer. Because of conditions in the world market, the price of the material rose at the beginning of the month by 50% over the budgeted price. The buyer in division B persuaded suppliers to pass on only half of this increase.
3. The production manager of division A has been able to cut material wastage by employing more skilled labour, costing £250 more than expected. A new factory has recently been built near division B, and by offering higher wage rates has attracted most of B's best workers. Scriabin Ltd has, as yet, not increased its wage rate and the personnel manager of B has been forced to employ workers who can only achieve 50% of the budgeted output per hour.

Prepare a statement explaining the difference between budgeted and actual performance during the month, in the way you think will best enable management to trace and eliminate inefficiency. As far as possible, try to include information which will enable management to appraise the performance of each of the executives mentioned. Such information may alternatively be given as a brief commentary to your statement.

15.4 Potter Co. operates a standard cost system. The variances for each department are calculated and reported to the department manager. It is expected that managers will use the information to improve their operations and recognise that it is used in turn by their superiors when they are evaluating performances.

Wally Williams was recently appointed manager of the assembly department of the company. He has complained that the system as designed is disadvantageous to his department. Included among the variances charged to the department is one for rejected units. The inspection occurs after the unit has been assembled. The inspectors attempt to identify the cause of the rejection so that the department where the error occurred can be charged with it, but some errors cannot be easily identified with a department. These are totalled and apportioned to the departments according to the number of identified errors. The variance for rejected units in each department is a combination of the errors caused by the department, plus a portion of the unidentified causes of rejects.

(a) Explain with reasons whether Wally Williams's claim is valid.

(b) Recommend what the company should do to solve its problem with Wally Williams and to deal with his complaint.

15.5 Morales Ltd manufactures rugby balls. As each ball is completed it is booked out to a subsidiary company Suk Ltd. Morales's budget for the seventh fourweekly control period of its financial year was as follows:

	£	£
Sales (6,000 units @ £24 each)		144,000
Variable costs:		
Bladders (6,000 @ £1.50 each)	9,000	
Leather (200 ten hide bales @ £228.00 each)	45,600	
Sundry and packaging materials	3,900	
Direct labour (5,000 hours @ £2.70 per hour)	13,500	
	72,000	
Fixed costs:		
Administrative and establishment expenses	12,717	
Staff and directors' salaries	24,783	109,500
Budgeted net profit		34,500

Due to water shortages during the summer drought, Morales was only able to manufacture during 60% of the budgeted production hours and was unable to sanction any overtime. Despite this the direct labour force was paid in full for the budgeted hours. Various other differences from budget occurred and the following are the actual figures for the period:

	£	£
Sales (4,000 units @ £27 each)		108,000
Variable costs:		
Bladders (4,000 @ £2.10 each)	8,400	
Leather (100 ten hide bales @ £400 each)	40,000	
Sundry and packaging materials	2,600	
Direct labour (5,000 hours @ £3 per hour)	15,000	
	66,000	
Fixed costs:		
Administrative and establishment expenses	13,155	
Staff and directors' salaries	24,945	104,100
Actual net profit		3,900

(a) Prepare a statement reconciling the budgeted contribution with the actual contribution, stating the variances in the way which you think will be most helpful to management. Present your calculations as schedules with references to the main statement.

(b) Comment briefly on any apparent interrelationships between the variances.

15.6 A small manufacturing company in Yorkshire is organised in three main functions, under a managing director, as follows:

Accounting and administration	–an accountant in charge with six staff
Marketing and sales	–a sales manager in charge with one representative and two clerical staff.
Production	–a works manager in charge of three productive cost centres, a drawing office and a stores. The direct labour force numbers 40.

The company has recently introduced a system of budgetary control and standard costing and, using this system, the board of directors has agreed a profit plan for the year to 30 June 19X7. The board considers that the most important factors influencing its attainment are associated with capacity sold in terms of productive hours, selling prices and costs, the latter classified under the three main headings of materials, labour and fixed overheads. It also recognises that payment for materials and wages are the largest recurring cash outlays.

You are advising the company about the nature, form and frequency of the main control reports to be introduced in order to monitor adherence to the profit plan. You have ascertained that the works manager is responsible for buying and that, as soon as production is ordered to begin on a job, the appropriate quantities of material, as contained in product specifications, are immediately issued from stores. The cost centre supervisors are responsible for labour and performance and for excess material usage (machine hour rates have no application to the company).

You are required to draft suitable forms of report for the information of and use by the cost centre supervisor, the works manager and the managing director respectively, indicating the frequency with which each should be prepared. Each report should deal only with the factors to be controlled.

15.7 Birtwhistle Ltd manufactures soft drinks which are sold to retailers in cases of 144 bottles. The company installed a standard costing system in February 19X4. Exhibit 1 gives the standard cost and revenue data applicable to that month.

Exhibit 1
Standard cost and revenue data, February 19X4

	Per case	
	£	£
Standard selling price		10.00
Materials: 10 lb at 20p	2.00	
Labour: 4 hours at 75p	3.00	
Overheads: Standard recovery rate	4.00	9.00
Standard profit		1.00

The overheads are all fixed and consist of administrative costs of £4,000, advertising of £10,000 and factory overheads of £26,000. The budgeted volume for February 19X4 is 10,000 units which represents the maximum possible production given the small staff which is retained in the winter months.

During March the actual results for February became available and from them the management accountant calculated the following variances:

Exhibit 2
Standard cost variances, February 19X4

	Favourable	*Adverse*
Sales volume variance		10,000
Materials price variance		360
Labour efficiency variances		1,518
Fixed overhead variances:		
Expenditure		2,000
Volume		4,000

No other variances occurred.

The management accountant had pressed for the introduction of standard costing, claiming that it would be instrumental in increasing the company's performance. When Exhibits 1 and 2 were presented to the management meeting the report was not received with much enthusiasm. The following observations were made by managers present at the meeting:

Managing director: 'What's the point of a fixed overhead volume variance? The overheads are fixed aren't they? By the way, what were the actual results?'

Purchasing Manager: 'The materials price variance is the result of a tax increase of 5%. I managed to prevent our supplying company passing on the whole of the increase by pointing out that we are its best customer. Anyway, it's only a 2% variance, so that doesn't matter. If you want my opinion, the standard is too tight and I don't think I should be judged against it.'

Sales Manager: 'February had particularly bad weather with lots of snow, and that's the cause of the sales variance. In fact, the trade association have calculated that total market sales were 12% down on what was predicted. In January our sales fell by only 10% which must have been better than the other companies we compete with. And don't forget, I could have sold 500 more cases if the factory could have provided them. And don't forget another thing, without that extra £1,000 worth of advertising sales would have been lower still.'

(a) Reconstruct the actual results for February 19X4 to satisfy the managing director's request.

(b) Explain for the managing director how the fixed overhead volume variance is calculated and how it may be interpreted.

(c) Prepare a report on the company's performance for February 19X4. Give particular attention to the performance of the sales and purchasing managers in the light of the additional information which they have provided and anything else which you consider relevant.

15.8 Nelson plc has operated a standard costing system for some time. It produces only one product, the portobello valve, and the standard costs for the valve for the current period are reproduced below:

	£ (per unit)
Direct labour 2 hours at £4.5 per hour	9.00
Direct material 4 lb at £7.5 per lb	30.00
Variable overhead 2 hours at £1.5 per hour	3.00
Fixed overheads: 2 hours at £3	6.00
	48.00

The budgeted fixed overheads for the period were £30,000, based upon a budgeted level of production for the period of 5,000 units. The standard selling price for the valve was £75.

Recently the actual results for the period became available and are shown below:

		£
Sales (4,700 units)		361,900
Direct labour: 9,750 hours	46,310	
Direct material: 24,000 lb	174,000	
Variable overhead:	16,550	
Fixed overhead	33,000	269,860
Profit		92,040

The production process for the valve is semi-automated and the flanging machine which is used is regularly inspected by the maintenance staff of Nelson.

The inspection is merely a visual check together with a discussion with the operatives working the machine. If all appears to be running well, no maintenance work is ordered. Nelson's maintenance staff do not maintain the flanging machine themselves, but call in the manufacturer's fitters. The manufacturers make a fixed charge of £500 for a visit whether or not any maintenance work is needed. In the past when maintenance has been needed the cost of repair (including all parts and labour from the manufacturer) has averaged £5,000. Normally, a repair requires the flanging machine to be stopped for 16 hours. If no repair is needed, the stoppage time for the machine is negligible. The contribution generated per hour by the flanging machine is £30. Over the last ten years the manufacturer's fitters have been called out on average once a month and on only twelve occasions did they find anything which needed repair. Nelson's production manager has estimated that the likely saving from repairing a faulty flanging machine would be £12,000 in present value terms.

There is some dissatisfaction with the way the flanging machine's maintenance is conducted. Nelson's maintenance manager has been criticised for not calling in the fitters often enough but replies: 'It costs a fortune to stop production, and anyway, the operatives always say that the machine gobbles up material, but the manufacturers keep checking it and nothing is wrong. Why should I call in the manufacturers?'

(a) Calculate cost and sales variances for Nelson for the period in question.

(b) Prepare calculations to show whether the manufacturer's fitters should be called in to examine the flanging machine. Comment briefly upon the maintenance policy of Nelson.

In addition to the information given in the question you are told that the maintenance department of Nelson is a cost centre and the manager's salary is related to the level of costs achieved in the year (the lower the costs, the more the manager is paid).

(c) Discuss and illustrate the effects of the cost centre policy on other departments in the firm and on the environment of the firm.

(d) Comment on the desirability of making the maintenance department a cost centre. What alternative policy could you suggest? Explain why your policy would be an improvement.

15.9 Wiley Ltd is a firm of sportswear manufacturers specialising in padded gloves and other protectors for a variety of sports. One of the major lines are cricketers' batting pads and a great deal of effort is put into monitoring the costs of this item. The standard cost card for the production of a pair of batting pads is shown below:

	£
Materials: Cloth (10 ft^2 @ £0.20/ft^2)	2.00
Stuffing (2 kg @ £0.50/kg)	1.00
Buckles and straps (one set)	2.00
Labour	4.00
Variable overhead	6.00
Contribution	10.00
Selling price	25.00

Wiley has always exercised firm control over labour and overhead costs but has felt somewhat 'in the lap of the gods' when it comes to materials costs. Over the first four months of the year, when much of the production takes place, 22,000 pairs of pads were produced at the following cost of materials:

	£
Cloth 245,000 ft^2	48,000
Stuffing 45,000 kg	24,000
Buckles and straps 22,490 sets	47,229
	119,229

On reviewing the materials cost variances it was pointed out that:

1. Though stocks of buckles and straps transferred to and used by the batting pads department had been recorded as 22,490, 200 in fact were transferred to the wicketkeepers' pads' department. It has also long been held that, as an easily concealed and useful item, an allowance of approximately 1% of standard usage should be made for theft – even though such an allowance is undesirable.
2. Management was surprised to see the standard cost card showing 10 ft^2 of cloth per pair of pads. It was always felt that an extra square foot should be allowed for trim loss, though after some recent modifications the average amount of trim loss per pair of pads was nearer 0.50 ft^2. With the benefit of hindsight a more realistic purchase price would have been £0.19 per ft^2, 20p being a somewhat pessimistic estimate.
3. At the start of each year a decision has to be made over the type of stuffing to use. The three alternatives are referred to as S1, S2 and S3, they are of comparable price and quality but require very different handling techniques and so once the decision over the material is made it is difficult to change the decision. Material S3 was chosen though, as the following figures show, S1 would – with hindsight – have been better.

	Original estimate of price (£/kg)	*Revised estimate of price* (£/kg)
S1	0.55	0.54
S2	0.52	0.60
S3	0.50	0.55

(a) Calculate traditional price and usage variances for each of the three types of material used.

(b) Explain the limitations of traditional variance analysis.

(c) Produce a revised analysis in the light of the three notes given for:
(i) buckles and straps;
(ii) cloth;
(iii) stuffing.

(d) Determine whether it is worth Wiley spending £750 on a simple financial modelling package designed to improve the chances of correctly estimating the price of stuffing. The cost of making the wrong decision over materials is assumed to be equal to the amount of the possibly avoidable planning variance. From past experience, without the package Wiley has selected the right material six times out of ten. They feel that with the package they will be able to improve this to eight times out of ten. The firm uses a ten year time horizon and a discount rate of 10% for analysing such investments (the appropriate discount factor being 6.14).

(e) Set out the factors to be taken into account when deciding whether to investigate a variance.

Further reading

Amey, L., 'Towards a new perspective on accounting control', *Accounting, Organizations and Society*, 1979, pp. 247–58.

Becker, E. A. and Kim, K. J., 'Direct material variances: review of the mix and yield variances', *Issues in Accounting Education*, Spring 1988.

Bromwich, M., 'Standard costing for planning and control', in Arnold, J., Carsberg, B. and Scapens, R. (eds.), *Topics in Management Accounting*, Philip Allan, 1980.

Clark, J., 'A new approach to labour variances', *Management Accounting*, December 1982.

Demski, J. S., 'Analysing the effectiveness of the traditional standard cost variance model', *Management Accounting*, October 1967.

Demski, J. S., 'Variance analysis using a constrained linear model', in Solomons, D. (ed.), *Studies in Cost Analysis*, 2nd edn., Sweet & Maxwell, 1968.

Dew, R. and Gee, K. P., 'Frequency of performance reporting', *Accounting and Business Research*, Summer 1972.

Dopuch, N., Birnberg, J. E. and Demski, J., 'An extension of standard cost variance analysis', *The Accounting Review*, July 1967.

Harvey, D. W. and Soliman, S. Y., 'Standard cost variance analysis in a learning environment', *Accounting and Business Research*, Summer 1983.

Horngren, C. T., 'The analysis of capacity utilisation', *The Accounting Review*, April 1967.

Kaplan, R. S., 'The significance and investigation of cost variances: survey and extensions', *Journal of Accounting Research*, Autumn 1975.

Peles, Y. C., 'A note on yield variance and mix variance', *The Accounting Review*, April 1986.

Solomons, D., 'The analysis of standard cost variances', in Solomons, D. (ed.), *Studies in Cost Analysis*, 2nd edn., Sweet & Maxwell, 1986.

Chapter 16

Divisional performance

Issues in managerial accounting have so far been discussed without attempting to draw any distinction between the character, size and internal structure of individual organisations. We have, in effect, presumed a common interest by all organisations in the issues we have raised. That such a common interest may not necessarily exist is perhaps obvious when we remember that firms can be controlled by a single owner–manager, by a board of directors responsible to thousands of shareholders or by a variety of intermediate structures; that firms can produce a single product or a vast array of very different goods and services which are sold all over the world; that firms operate in monopolistic, highly competitive or other forms of market. All these factors, and more besides, tend to generate their own individual problems requiring their own individual solutions.

In this chapter we pay particular attention to the distinctive character of the (often large) divisionalised company and to some of the problems presented by such an organisation for managerial planning, decision making and control. Most of the issues have been raised, either explicitly or implicitly, in previous chapters; for example, a major problem in accounting for divisions is how to measure their performance. One frequently used measurement method is return on investment (ROI). This measure bears a strong similarity to the accounting rate of return explained in Chapter 12. Similarly, the sort of relevant costing issues discussed in Chapters 5, 8, 9, 10 and elsewhere are also relevant to a study of divisionalised companies.

Large companies such as ICI, Hanson, Unilever and BAT Industries produce and sell a wide variety of different products, often in many different countries and continents. Because of the sheer complexity of operations in companies of this size and the difficulty of a head office exercising direct control of operations, their decision making is decentralised and their operations are usually divisionalised. There is in practice no single, universally accepted definition of a division. In some organisations, 'divisions' and 'departments' are used interchangeably, but as a general rule divisions are responsible for the profit earned from producing and selling a group of products. Thus companies are typically split into different divisions either in accordance with the products made, which is the more usual (e.g. division A might produce clothes, division B might produce toys, and so on), or on the basis of geography (e.g. division A which produces clothes, toys and books might be located in the United Kingdom; division B which also produces clothes, toys and books might be located in France, and so on). For very large companies, whose operations encompass totally different aspects of trade, divisionalisation might even be organised on an industry basis. Conglomerate companies such as Hanson plc and BTR plc are divisionalised in such a way.

The heart of divisionalisation is the delegation of decision making and authority to divisional managers and the retention of overall control by head office. The degree of head office involvement in divisional decision making depends on the structure as well as the strategic objectives of the organisation. Some large UK companies, such as Cadburys plc and United Biscuits plc, are very closely involved with the planning and control activities of their various divisions, whose targets are likely to be phrased in terms of meeting long-term objectives, for example improving their market share over a five year period. Other companies, of whom GEC plc, Hanson plc and BTR plc would be examples, give their different divisions greater autonomy in decision making but require them to meet strategic shorter-term financial goals. These organisations manage their divisions more by emphasising the importance of financial numbers than by adopting a patient approach to the achievement of longer-term strategic goals. The majority of UK companies follow a strategy which falls between these two approaches – i.e. they attempt to give their divisions a longer-term orientation in pursuing particular objectives, whilst at the same time demanding more immediate financial returns. Available evidence suggests that in these cases the more short-term 'numerical' emphasis will predominate.

Divisions usually represent individual responsibility centres within the total organisation – and responsibility usually extends to the return earned on assets employed by the division.

There are many advantages claimed for divisionalisation in large companies with a wide range of activities including the following:

1. Because of the greater degree of authority granted to divisional managers, they may be motivated to achieving a better level of performance, both for their own divisions and for the firm as a whole.

2. As communication channels are narrowed, potential communication problems are cut down if divisional managers need not continually report their actions to head office.

3. Because divisional managers have a more intimate knowledge of their own divisions, they are more likely to understand, and be capable of dealing with, the problems peculiar to their divisions.

4. Perhaps most importantly, because divisional managers handle their own problems, top management is given more time and opportunity to focus its attention on the strategic decisions which necessarily affect the entire company, for example decisions about which general areas of the company's activities should be expanded and which should be contracted in the long term. Decisions such as these require an overview of all the company's

activities and, by their nature, cannot usually be delegated to divisional managers. As we have noted, most divisionalised companies undertake a diversified range of operations. Such diversification provides the company with a portfolio of activities which results in a reduction in the company's overall level of risk, as we explained in Chapter 4. The maintenance of a well balanced portfolio of activities must ultimately be the responsibility of top management.

It should not be thought that divisionalisation is without its problems. Consider the continuing situation facing the top management of ICI plc, one of the largest divisionalised UK companies, and one of the largest companies in the world. In 1987 ICI employed worldwide 128,000 people, generated total sales of £11,123 million, invested £2 million every day in new plant, and at the end of the year showed a historical cost pre-tax profit of £1,312 million. This profit was generated from the operations of nine individual divisions (or business sectors); agriculture, fibres, general chemicals, industrial explosives, paints, pharmaceuticals, other chemical products, petrochemicals and plastics. Manufacturing facilities are located in the United Kingdom, West Germany, Holland, France, Italy, Canada, USA, Brazil, Mexico, Australia, New Zealand, Papua New Guinea, Japan, Malaysia, India and Pakistan.

How do the top managers of a company like ICI, located at the company's head office in London, plan, control and, above all, coordinate the activities of the various divisions in the very varied social, economic and political environments in which the company operates? Head office may, for example, lay down broad policies for the whole group in relation to the objectives and goals of the company; it may well develop specific long-term plans to achieve these goals and perhaps set out targets to be met in the form of market shares, sales revenues and profits, and it may well take overall responsibility for the raising of corporate capital. It will certainly take responsibility for the coordination of the company's total activities. These are primarily general management issues. But how do the company's top managers ensure that individual divisional managers are pursuing goals which are best for the company as a whole, rather than for their own personal gain or satisfaction? How do they ensure that there is no conflict of goals between individual managers? For example, there may be a general loss of profitability within the company if autonomous divisions attempt to maximise their own profitability while, at the same time, decreasing the net profit of the total company. This is the problem of suboptimisation, to which we have referred in earlier chapters and to which we return later in this chapter. In the remainder of this chapter we shall look at areas of concern which are peculiar to divisionalised companies. We begin by examining different methods of assessing a division's financial performance.

16.1 Divisional profit measures

Profit, determined by a variety of different accounting measurements, is the measure most widely used to assess an organisation's performance. All listed companies in

Table 16.1 Divisional profit statement

		£
	Sales revenue	150,000
	Less Variable cost	110,000
Performance measure (1)	← *Contribution margin*	40,000
	Less Controllable fixed costs	5,000
Performance measure (2)	← *Controllable profit*	35,000
	Less Non-controllable fixed costs	10,000
Performance measure (3)	← *Divisional profit before Head Office allocation*	25,000
	Less Allocated head office costs	5,000
Performance measure (4)	← *Divisional pre-tax profits*	20,000

the United Kingdom must, for example, publish the earnings (or profits) attributable to each individual share in the company, and this earnings per share statistic is widely used by financial analysts and other external users as a leading measure of the company's success. Most organisations also require their divisions to achieve certain profit targets – thus ensuring that the company, and the divisions (or business units) which make it up, are evaluated by similar criteria. These decentralised units are, unsurprisingly, known as *profit centres*. For our purposes we shall define a profit centre as a business unit which has responsibility for both its revenues and its controllable costs – i.e., it sells most of its output to external customers and makes its own purchasing and production decisions.

Many organisations take further the concept of profit responsibility by requiring their managers to be responsible not simply for an absolute level of profit, but also for an amount of profit which is related to the investment (controllable by the manager) in the business unit. Under this evaluation method, managers must seek to achieve an adequate return on investment (ROI). We will deal with ROI measures in the following section of this chapter. (We should note here that other forms of business unit exist in practice. Thus managers of *cost centres* will be held responsible only for the incurring of costs under their control, and will be rewarded accordingly if they succeed in minimising those costs; and managers of *revenue centres* will have control only over the amount of revenue generated.)

The trickiest issue in applying the profit centre concept is in the choice of an appropriate profit measure. The choice of measure is very important because it may influence the decisions taken by the manager (e.g. if the manager has to cover his controllable fixed costs before striking a profit he will, *ceteris paribus*, be more concerned with the absolute level of the division's fixed costs, than will a manager who is asked to maximise a division's contribution margin). Table 16.1 shows a simple profit statement for a division from which we might extract at least four possible performance measures in the form of different profit figures.

Let us consider the possible usefulness of each of the four performance measures in turn:

1. Contribution margin – £40,000

This figure is useful in showing how much contribution the divisional manager has made to the fixed costs over which he has control. However it suffers as a performance evaluation measure for the very reason that if managers are able to influence their cost structures by adjusting the balance of fixed and variable costs, they can adjust the contribution margin to their own advantage. Thus, at the very least, managers should be evaluated by a profit figure struck after charging controllable fixed costs.

2. Controllable profit – £35,000

This figure indicates the success of managers in using all the resources under their authority, and thus is perhaps the best single measure of managerial performance. It excludes the fixed costs over which a manager has no control, and thereby supposes that it is possible to determine clearly which fixed costs are controllable and which are not. In practice this split may be difficult to determine. Expenses such as depreciation and employees' wages may be classified as non-controllable only if divisional managers cannot influence the purchase and sale of fixed assets, and the levels of employment within the division. But in many organisations these decisions may be largely discretionary.

3. Divisional profit before head office allocations – £25,000

This figure represents the success of the division in generating profits towards meeting head office costs, and, as such, is probably a better evaluator of the *division*, than of the *manager*. This is a most important point. It would be unfair to evaluate divisional managers on the results of decisions over which they have no control, but equally it is necessary to evaluate divisions' long-term contribution to head office costs after charging all expenses relating to each division, irrespective of the instigator and the time of the decision. If the divisional profit before head office allocations is insufficient to meet its share of allocations, questions concerning the long-term future of the division may be asked.

4. Divisional pre-tax profits – £20,000

This amount shows the 'bottom-line' profit of the division after all costs, identifiable and allocated, have been charged to it. We might query the purpose of allocating head office costs to divisions in order to arrive at a proper basis for evaluation. What do such allocations tell us? It is of course a truism that the total of all divisional profits must be greater than head office costs – otherwise the business will fail – but whether such allocations give useful information for evaluation is debatable. The root of the problem is, of course, the arbitrariness of the allocations. If divisional activities do not directly *cause* central costs, how are we to agree upon a defensible allocation mechanism for their *effect*? (And if divisional activities do cause central costs, how are we to quantify the costs attributable to the particular divisions?) It can of course be argued that if divisions bear a 'fair share' of central overheads, they will press to contain the growth in such central support activities. But the problems attendant on quantifying how fair the share should be seem to outweigh this consciousness-raising. Divisional managers should be evaluated only on the activities, the effects of which they can control, and thus performance measurement – divisional profit before central allocations – seems a more appropriate basis of evaluating divisional profit performance. Having examined the validity of different measures of profit centre performance, we now turn our attention to the measurement of the performance of *investment centres* (i.e. situations in which a division's responsibility extends beyond absolute profits, to the relative relationship between its profits and its investment base). Investment centres can be defined as divisions for which managers have the authority to determine both the nature of short-term operating decisions and also the amount and type of long-term investment decisions.

16.2 Return on investment

Return on investment (ROI) is probably the most widely used accounting technique for evaluating the performance of divisions within a firm. In principle, it is very similar to the accounting rate of return measure discussed in Chapter 12. The ROI statistic attempts to draw together in a single percentage figure those quantitative aspects of a division's performance which are relevant for planning and control purposes. 'Profitability' indices as expressed through ROI are then used as common measuring units to compare the performance of different divisions within the same firm – even though divisions may operate in very different environments and produce and sell very different ranges of products. A word of caution should be inserted immediately. Although a single ROI would normally encompass the overall results of the business, it is important to realise that individual activities may be achieving returns different from the average. If this is the case, then, ideally, both the selection and monitoring of investments should be based on a range of rates.

It should also be stressed that ROI is not an absolute measure of profit, but rather a *relative* one. For example, a division which makes a profit of £2 million does not necessarily contribute more to the overall success of the firm than a division making a profit of £1 million. The difference in profit between divisions may be explicable simply in terms of differences in size. Thus division X showing a profit of £2 million with resources of £10 million is generating an ROI of 20%, whereas division Y, which shows a profit of £1 million with resources of £4 million, is generating a higher ROI of 25%. As we shall see, the determination of both aspects of the ROI statistic, profit and investment, presents both conceptual and practical measurement problems to even the most alert management accountant.

At its most basic level, divisional return on investment can be presented simply as net profit for the division, divided by investment in divisional assets:

$$\text{ROI} = \frac{\text{Net profit}}{\text{Investment in net assets}}$$

The ROI formula can be broken further into two measures of divisional performance: the margin achieved on the division's sales (profit margin) and the turnover of assets or investment turnover (sales divided by investment). This decomposition gives:

$$\text{ROI} = \frac{\text{Sales}}{\text{Investment in net assets}} \times \frac{\text{Net profit}}{\text{Sales}}$$

The profit margin on sales does not, of itself, produce success for a division, though the ability to reduce costs and thus increase margins is an important determinant of success. Profit must be related to the amount of resources used in its generation and therefore the more sales that can be generated from a given amount of resources (i.e. a given investment in net assets) the more opportunity the division will have to generate its profit margins. Alternatively we might say that the fewer the assets needed by a division, the more assets will be made available for profitable use elsewhere in the firm. The ratio of sales to net assets is an important factor in divisional success.

A simple illustration should help to clarify the contribution of both parts of the ROI equation to the measurement of a division's performance. Suppose a firm has two divisions, division X and division Y, which produce and sell two different products. Division X deals in soap power, division Y in colour TV sets. Division X generates a net profit margin on sales of 5%, whereas division Y has a margin of 25%; thus in terms of profit margins on sales division Y is certainly more successful. But we have assumed that companies will wish to maximise the return they generate on cash invested, not the return on sales. We need to know how effectively the investment base of each division has been used in generating these margins. Suppose we are told that X, the low margin division, turns over its assets three times each year (i.e. has a ratio of sales to net assets of three) whereas Y turns over its assets three times every five years, or 0.6 times each year. We now have information to allow us to build up a more complete picture of the relative performance of each division.

In ROI terms we have:

$$\begin{aligned}\text{Division X ROI} &= \text{Asset turnover} \times \text{profit margin}\\ &= 3 \times 5\%\\ &= 15\%\end{aligned}$$

$$\begin{aligned}\text{Division Y ROI} &= \text{Asset turnover} \times \text{profit margin}\\ &= 0.6 \times 25\%\\ &= 15\%\end{aligned}$$

This type of analysis shows how it is possible, by using the ROI statistic, to compare the efficiency with which different divisions, dealing in different products, use their net assets. In this case each division is earning the same 15% for the firm. Whether or not such a book return is satisfactory or even meaningful depends upon other issues; for instance if top management has specified a target return of 20% to be achieved by each division, then, clearly, 15% is inadequate. If this is the case then thought should be given to possible alternative uses of divisional assets. Target ROIs should try to reflect the different risks attaching to the different operations of divisions. It is by no means obvious that all divisions within the same company should be judged on their ability to meet the same target percentage figure. Furthermore, as explained in Chapter 12 and discussed subsequently in this chapter, rates of return based on conventional accounting measures may be deficient and misleading indicators of performance. Indeed maximising ROI may lead managers to disregard the interests of the company in selecting projects which will simply increase their own divisions' ROI.

We might, at this preliminary stage, best sum up the debate on the usefulness of ROI as follows. As a measurement of performance ROI has the following advantages:

1. It provides a relative measure which takes proper account of all the assets invested in the division.
2. The data necessary for its computation are compatible with those contained in conventional financial reports, and this aids the interpretation of the ratios by managers.
3. Because the ROI ratio can be subdivided into a series of explanatory ratios it is a useful analytical device for examining various aspects of performance.

In summary, ROI is a defensible and practical approach to the evaluation of divisional performance as long as it is used in a matter which reflects an awareness of its limitations. Ideally, it would be used as one of a range of measures in order to review performance in the widest possible perspective. We will look at one possible alternative to ROI later in this chapter.

16.3 Some problems with return on investment measures

Simple and widely used as the ROI statistic is, there are nevertheless many problems in its computation and interpretation which must be addressed by management. These problems fall roughly into three categories, which are by no means mutually exclusive. They are:

1. The problem in measuring revenues when some sales are made from one division to another within the firm. This is more commonly known as the *transfer pricing* problem.
2. The problem in determining and measuring appropriate expenses in arriving at divisional net profit. This problem is obviously compounded by the transfer pricing problem.
3. The problem in determining and measuring the asset base to be used to signify divisional investment.

In effect, the first two problem areas relate to the return element of the ROI statistic, whereas the third relates to the investment element of the statistic. We shall look at each of the three in turn.

16.4 Transfer pricing

The transfer pricing problem arises when some of a division's output is sold to another division or if some of its services (e.g. computer services) are provided to another division. In such cases, certain very specific problems emerge as to how these interdivisional sales or transfers of goods and services should be priced. (For example, ICI incurred interdivision transfers valued at £322 million in 1987.)

The problem affects both the selling and the buying division; the pricing of transfers represents sales revenue to the selling division, and variable cost to the buying division. For example suppose division G manufactures a component part which is subsequently assembled in division H as part of a finished product. Suppose for illustrative purposes that the entire output of G is 'sold' to H. The income statements of the two divisions can be represented in notational form as follows:

	Manufacturing Division G	*Assembly Division H*
Sales revenue	$P_G \times Q$	$P_H \times Q$
Less Variable costs	$-VC_G \times Q$	$-[(P_G \times Q) + (VC_H \times Q)]$
Fixed costs	$-FC_G$	$-FC_H$
Net profit	π_G	π_H

where P_G is the selling price (transfer price) per unit of G's goods; P_H is the selling price per unit of H's goods; Q is the quantity sold; VC_G is the variable cost per unit of producing and selling G's goods; VC_H is the variable cost per unit of producing and selling H's goods, additional to the cost of the component from G; FC_G is the fixed costs of G; FC_H is the fixed costs of H; π_G is the net profit of G, and π_H is the net profit of H.

Note that the price of the transferred good P_G influences the profit figures of both divisions – as a selling price in G and as part of the variable cost in H. Note also that these transactions may be represented purely by book-keeping entries. In some cases involving transfer prices, cash does not change hands directly between divisions. The establishment of an agreed transfer pricing system is critical, as transfer prices are used directly in the evaluation of the profitability of both G and H. Other reasons why the setting up of efficient transfer pricing systems are important are:

1. As transfer price multiplied by volume equals revenue to the selling division, it is possible for even small differences in the transfer price to lead to (relatively) large changes in divisional profit if the division makes many interdivisional sales.

2. Different divisional profit figures may lead to different degrees of motivation of divisional management, which in turn could result in an under-achievement of targets, and even in a loss of the advantages of divisionalisation.

3. Different transfer prices may deceive top management into believing, and acting on its belief, that individual divisions are more or less profitable than is actually the case.

By now the nature of the transfer pricing issue should be clearer. The issue is one of developing a system which both allows a performance measure to reflect the division's use of resources and, at the same time, ensures that there is an optimal allocation of the firm's resources. Suppose the following situation. Division B sells a product to outside customers at £9 per unit. It buys a major component for this product from division A for £7 per unit and incurs additional finishing costs of £3 per unit. Division B therefore loses £1 per unit and would decide to discontinue or seek an alternative source of supply. If the transfer price charged by A was reached as shown below this might not be a wise decision from the company's viewpoint, and the transfer price should therefore be changed to encourage B to produce.

		£
Transfer price:	Variable costs	4
	Allocated fixed costs	1
	Profit	2
	Transfer price	7

The effect on the company's profit for every unit of the product sold to outside customers is an increase of £2 comprising the ultimate selling price received by B (£9), less the variable costs incurred by A (£4) and B (£3). B must be encouraged to produce. The transfer price must be lowered. Any figure below £6 would encourage B to accept the component, any figure above £4 would motivate A to supply that component. The conflict between head office and divisional objectives shows the need to attain goal congruence within the divisionalised structure. There are dangers that the performance of the whole company may be suboptimal.

The transfer pricing issue is a difficult one to resolve. If there is no external market for the goods or services involved, there is no obvious method of pricing transfers which consistently serves the twin functions of preserving divisional autonomy and ensuring firm-wide optimisation. There are in fact many possible alternatives available for the pricing of transfers. The price may, for example, represent the revenue which the selling division could receive if the good or service was sold on the open market, if such a market is available. This is the system employed by ICI (whose 1987 report notes that products are transferred at 'prevailing external market prices'). Or the price could be based in some measure on the costs of producing the goods. If so, should only marginal costs be considered, or should prices be set equal to the 'full' costs of production plus some margin for the selling division's profit? Or the price might represent a 'halfway house' arrangement based upon negotiation between divisions and top management. We now turn to a consideration and illustration of each of these approaches to transfer pricing.

Market-based prices

Management's task in designing an appropriate transfer pricing system may be eased if there is an active, competitive outside market in the transferred goods. If this situation prevails the use of market prices will provide a good basis for pricing transfers insofar as prices will at least be objective and verifiable and, perhaps most importantly, will provide a measure of opportunity cost, i.e. if the selling division transfers goods to the buying division, the best alternative it forgoes is the revenue it could have received through sale on the open market. Equally the market price represents the best alternative the buying division forgoes if it does not purchase on the open market.

In order that the market-based system can work efficiently it is imperative that individual divisions have the freedom to act independently, i.e. selling divisions may sell either internally or externally as they wish, and buying divisions may have the same choice in their purchase decisions. This freedom helps to ensure that divisional profits are, as far as possible, not generated artificially. It may, however, involve the incurring of additional transaction costs which might detract from the advantages of the market-based system. For this reason some firms which use market prices for transferred goods deduct a small amount for 'normal' transaction costs.

How likely in practice is the existence of an active competitive market in similar products? It is the nature of the market which determines whether a unique market price exists. Very few markets are perfectly competitive and very few products are perfect substitutes for each other. If product specifications differ then it cannot really be said that the conditions for using market prices hold. Perhaps the biggest drawback to the use of market-based prices concerns the potential to create unused capacity in the selling division. For example, if division B decides suddenly to buy externally because the outside price is lower than the cost of purchase from Division A, the selling division may be left with unsold stock and with capacity which may be unused in the future.

Cost-based prices

The optimal transfer price for the firm as a whole is represented by the opportunity cost of the transferred good or service to the selling division. We have seen that opportunity cost is measured by market price if a competitive intermediate market exists. If no competitive intermediate market exists, opportunity costs are not measured by market prices, but rather by the marginal or incremental cost to the selling division. If resources are not freely available within the firm, opportunity cost will be measured by the incremental cash flow of the selling division (the additional cash flows up to the point of transfer) *plus* any imputed cost for the scarce resources used by the selling division. This imputed cost (internal opportunity cost – see Chapter 10) ensures that the transferred good is priced at the best level relative to all alternative uses, and relative to all constraints on the company's optimisation. If the transfer price is set below total opportunity cost, the selling division will maximise its ROI, to the probable detriment of the firm's overall position, by producing no units of the good or service to be transferred because it will be making an apparently negative contribution on each unit. If the transfer price is set above total opportunity cost, the buying division's marginal costs will be higher than the incremental cost to the firm as a whole of producing the transferred good or service, which will probably result in a higher than optimal selling price and a lower than optimal output level in the buying division. (See Chapter 8 for an explanation of the relationships between costs, selling prices and output levels.)

There is, however, a substantial practical problem with the use of opportunity cost-based transfer prices. By using only incremental costs to price his goods the manager of the selling division is prevented from covering his fixed costs and from generating a profit. The selling division incurs a 'loss' equivalent to the fixed costs if all its output is sold to the buying division. This means that in effect the selling division ceases to be a profit centre and becomes instead a cost centre, with the attendant motivational loss which may result from removal of 'profit maximising' status.

A possible solution to this problem is effectively to ignore strict economic analysis in pricing transfers and to charge a price which is based, in some measure, on recovering fixed costs and allowing a 'fair' margin for profit. But here again controversial issues abound. How, for instance, is 'fairness' to be defined? Should it be taken to mean a fair margin on costs? Or a fair return on capital? And what method of (arbitrary) allocation is to be used to assign total fixed costs to individual products? Indeed many of the benefits of cost control in divisions may be lost if selling divisions are allowed to pass on their operating inefficiencies via the inclusion in the transfer price of a substantial overhead element.

One possible way out of the dilemma posed by the lack of a competitive market in the transferred good, is to coordinate the output of the selling division with the purchase requirements of the buying division. Such coordination would seek to prevent any wastage of production capacity in the selling division, and would involve the buying division in a two-tier cost, and the selling division in a two-tier price. First, the buying division would contract for a proportion of the selling division's capacity, and would incur a *fixed* rent for using the facility; second, it would incur a cost equal to the selling division's variable cost of production for each unit purchased.

The following example illustrates some of the problems associated with the various forms of market-based and cost-based transfer pricing. Hillsborough plc has a producing division (1) that supplies several component parts to another producing division (2) which produces the company's main product. These component parts are listed below with relevant cost information:

Component	*Variable cost per unit* (£)	*Quantity produced*
A	4	20,000
B	6	20,000
C	10	30,000
D	1	10,000

The fixed costs of division 1, which would be avoided if the division was closed, amount to £160,000. These costs consist of the salary of the division managers, indirect labour costs, the costs of using machinery, etc. In calculating unit costs, the total fixed cost of £160,000 is allocated between the 80,000 units to be produced to arrive at a full cost per unit. The calculations are:

Component	*Variable cost per unit* (£)	*Fixed cost per unit*	*Full cost per unit* (£)
A	4	2	6
B	6	2	8
C	10	2	12
D	1	2	3

In establishing transfer prices, full cost is used. In division 2, which uses the four components, the manager has authority to buy inside the company or to buy from an outside supplier. The outside prices are expected to remain constant over the future. At the present time, the outside prices are as follows:

Component	*Outside price* (£)
A	6.00
B	8.50
C	12.50
D	2.90

The manager of division 2 notices that the outside purchase price per unit for component D is 10p lower than the transfer price and places an order with an outside supplier. Division 1 stops producing component D, reallocates the fixed costs to the remaining units, and adjusts the full cost transfer prices.

If there is little communication between the two divisions, we can begin to see the actions which the manager of division 2, acting in the interest of his own division, is likely to take. By recomputing the transfer prices of the remaining three components on the basis of an allocation of the £160,000 fixed costs among 70,000 components (A, B and C) we now have:

Component	*Variable cost per unit*	*Reallocated fixed cost per unit (£160,000 ÷ 70,000)* (£)	*Full cost per unit* (£)
A	4	2.29	6.29
B	6	2.29	8.29
C	10	2.29	12.29

On the basis of these figures the manager of division 2 will place an outside order for component A, as the outside buying price of £6 is lower than the readjusted full cost transfer price of £6.29. Suppose he does this, and division 1 then ceases production of A. The recomputed transfer prices for B and C on the basis of an allocation of the fixed costs of £160,000 among 50,000 (B and C) are then:

Component	*Variable cost per unit*	*Reallocated fixed cost per unit (£160,000 ÷ 50,000)* (£)	*Full cost per unit* (£)
B	6	3.20	9.20
C	10	3.20	13.20

The situation now is such that the adjusted transfer prices of B and C are higher than the outside prices. The manager of division 2 is now likely to order these two components from outside and division 1 will have no production (or at least no sales!).

The principle underlying this simple and simplistic situation is an important one. By including allocated fixed costs in the transfer price, the buying division may tend to use outside suppliers, thus creating unused capacity in the selling division. The question may be raised as to whether division 1 should be eliminated altogether. The calculations in Tables 16.2 and 16.3 show that it is better to keep the division (resulting in a saving of total costs of £24,000), even if the fixed costs of division 1 could be avoided if the division was closed.

The full cost transfer price system does not encourage behaviour which is in the best interests of the company as a whole. Unless production is shut down completely, the marginal cost to the company of producing one unit of a component is its variable cost only, and provided that the manager of division 1 can charge the manager of division 2 a price in excess of the variable cost, the manager of division 1 is making a positive contribution towards the fixed costs of £160,000.

However, as the fixed costs of division 1 are avoidable on closure of the division, the division must charge a transfer price which generates a contribution each period of at least £160,000 (the level of avoidable fixed costs). If division 1 fails to do this, Hillsborough plc may consider it to be in the interests of the firm to close the division.

Division 1 might best achieve this aim by adopting a two-tier price structure as explained previously, i.e. it might charge division 2 each period with a flat-rate proportion of its fixed costs, depending upon the extent of division 2's demands on its capacity, plus a rate per unit sold to division 2, based on division 1's variable costs.

It should be remembered that even if the financial analysis of divisions 1 and 2 does suggest that division 1 should be closed down and that division 2 should buy components from an outside supplier, there may be other non-quantitative factors which need to be considered. A decision to switch supply sources is often difficult and costly to reverse. It should not be made without consideration of future requirements and possible price changes. In addition external purchase may result in division 2 losing a degree of control over the supply of vital components. But more important may be the social and indeed legal factors associated with such a decision. For example, the decision to cease taking components from division 1 may result in redundancies (and redundancy costs). Large companies have responsibilities to employees which cannot, and in our view should not, be ignored when policy decisions, such as the possible switch of suppliers, are considered.

Table 16.2 Cost of operating division 1 if all components are manufactured

Component	*Quantity*	*Variable cost* (£)	*Total* (£)
A	20,000	4	80,000
B	20,000	6	120,000
C	30,000	10	300,000
D	10,000	1	10,000
			510,000
		Add Fixed cost	160,000
		Total cost	670,000

Table 16.3 Cost of buying parts outside

Component	*Quantity*	*Price* (£)	*Total* (£)
A	20,000	6.00	120,000
B	20,000	8.50	170,000
C	30,000	12.50	375,000
D	10,000	2.90	29,000
		Total cost	694,000

Negotiated prices

Because of the problems associated with both market-based and cost-based prices, and in particular because of the rigid centralisation of policy associated with the latter, top management is frequently asked to act as an arbiter in fixing interdivisional prices. This arbitration leads to the generation of negotiated and flexible transfer prices. However, negotiated prices are artificial in the same way that full cost prices are artificial, and indeed suffer the further disadvantage that their use can make divisional performance more difficult to measure realistically and independently. The use of negotiated prices removes the discipline imposed by adhering to transfer prices that are based on measures determined in the market place and which, as we have seen, provide an appropriate basis for interdivisional transactions.

16.5 Transfer pricing in practice

In recent years surveys have been carried out regarding transfer pricing in industry. The following brief comments highlight several practical points which are useful in gaining a broad perspective on the transfer pricing problem. The development of transfer pricing policies is seen as a means both of motivating divisional managers and facilitating local decision making, as well as offering tax planning advantages if divisions are located in the 'right' country or region.

The surveys have also uncovered certain drawbacks. Transfer pricing policies can encourage divisions to increase their own profits artificially at the expense of corporate profits, and can take up much managerial time through lengthy disagreements on prices. Nor do prices set to optimise corporate profitability necessarily motivate divisional managers. In general the surveys have consistently shown that transfer prices lag behind actual costs, and that divisional managers get too involved in earning income from other divisions instead of from external customers.

16.6 The determination of divisional expenses

Concern with transfer pricing is not the only important issue in determining a division's expenses for the purposes of calculating its ROI. Two further, interrelated questions arise: should divisions be charged for their use of central head office resources, and should divisions be charged, by way of an inputed interest cost, for the capital employed by the division? Each of these issues is now dealt with in turn.

Charge for central costs in ROI calculations

Most large organisations incur a block of costs, usually located at a head office, which directly or indirectly are intended to benefit all divisions within the organisation. These costs may be of two kinds: they may relate to the services provided to divisions, in the form of computing facilities, training programmes, legal advice etc.; or they may relate to the costs of the central *administration*, e.g. the salary of the managing director, the costs of heating the administration's offices, and the rent of head office premises. These costs have the distinguishing feature that, generally speaking, their level is seldom controllable by divisional managers. It is difficult to envisage the sorts of decisions which divisional managers are likely to take which could directly influence the amount of time which the firm's managing director devotes to particular divisions or indeed to particular aspects of overall policy.

The question then arises as to whether these central costs should be allocated to individual divisions. The answer, as always, depends upon the use to which divisional income figures are to be put. As we argued earlier in this chapter, the valuation of the performance of the divisional manager should be undertaken on the basis of the division's controllable profit (sales revenue less all controllable costs), as this measures the manager's success in generating a profit (and thus an ROI) in terms of the resources under his control. Whether the ROI is sufficient depends upon the standard expected from the division. The divisional manager should not be assessed on the basis of divisional profit after allocating central costs.

While recognising the importance of covering central service and administration costs, we believe that this can best be achieved if head office encourages divisional managers to maximise controllable ROI.

Charge for using capital

The use of ROI as a means of evaluating divisional performance has not been universally accepted. Academic accountants in particular have challenged its usefulness, and have advocated in its stead an alternative evaluation method known as the *net residual income* (NRI) method.[46] The NRI method was developed in America by the General Electric Co. in the 1960s to assess the performance of its divisional managers, and to prevent suboptimisation within the company, the argument being that managers who maximise controllable residual income will be more likely to behave consistently with a corporate objective of maximising cash flows, than those who maximise ROI. The net residual income of a division represents the excess of its controllable operating income over its cost of capital (or minimum desired rate of return) multiplied by its capital employed.

The cost of capital is determined by top management and ideally should reflect the different risks of the divisions. A numerical example may help to clarify the issues involved.

Suppose that division A has net assets of £2,000,000 and generates a controllable annual profit of £300,000, thus producing an ROI of £300,000/2,000,000 × 100% = 15% p.a. The company's overall target return is 12% p.a. On the basis of ROI, division A may be unwilling to invest in a project producing a return less than 15% p.a. as this would result in a reduction in its ROI, whereas under the NRI concept any project would be acceptable provided a positive income figure remains when the imputed interest charge is deducted from the division's profit, as follows:

Division A income statement (summary)

	£
Controllable profit	300,000
Less Imputed interest charge (12% × £2,000,000)	240,000
Net residual income	60,000

In this case, as the net residual income is positive after charging interest on the division's assets of £2,000,000 at the rate of 12% fixed by the company, the division

[46] See, e.g. Solomons, D., *Divisional Performance: Measurement and Control*, Irwin, 1965.

should expand its operations, provided that it earns a return of at least 12% p.a. on the incremental investment, even though the rate earned on the investment may be lower than the division's present ROI of 15% p.a. It must, however, be borne in mind that in addition to all the problems of determining appropriate transfer prices, divisional expenses and divisional assets associated with the measurement of ROI, the net residual income concept involves the further task of determining an agreed imputed interest charge for each division. However, the concept of charging divisions for their use of capital is likely to make managers more aware of the costs of finance, with the attendant benefits to the company of such awareness.

The use of imputed interest charges in the evaluation of divisional performance has been the subject of much debate, and a discussion of the issues involved is outside the scope of an introductory text.[47] We might sum up the general conclusions of the debate by saying that the NRI method is needed only if divisional managers have control over the size of new investments. If top management determines the level of divisional investment in assets (e.g. if the investment in net assets in our example of £2,000,000 was fixed by head office) then no interest charge should be made either for assessing the performance of the division or of its manager. The manager of division A should simply attempt to maximise the controllable operating income or, put another way, to maximise the return on the *fixed* divisional investment of £2,000,000.

As we noted earlier some parallels exist between ROI and NRI and the different methods of investment appraisal discussed in Chapters 11 and 12:

1. Net residual income uses a similar approach to net present value as an appraisal method. The aim is to accept all projects showing a positive return (cash surplus) when discounted at the (division's) cost of capital.
2. ROI is similar to the internal rate of return method of investment appraisal. The decision rule using ROI is to accept all projects showing a percentage return greater than the division's minimum required rate.

16.7 The determination of the asset base

The choice of assets to be included in the base for evaluating divisional performance should be consistent with the choice of profit measure. Thus controllability should be the determining factor. Controllability relates to decisions. If divisional managers can take investment decisions which influence the size of the division's asset base, then such assets are controllable and should enter the division's ROI calculation. We will examine three particular problems which arise when choosing an appropriate investment base.

[47] See e.g. Emmanuel, C. R. and Otley, D. T., 'The usefulness of residual income', *Journal of Business Finance and Accounting*, Winter 1976; and Scapens, R. W., 'Profit measurement in divisionalised companies', *Journal of Business Finance and Accounting*, Autumn 1979.

Definition of investment

Investment in a division can be measured by using various combinations of assets and liabilities (both fixed and current, short-term and long-term). For example investment can be defined as the division's total assets (fixed plus current assets), net assets (total assets less total liabilities), fixed assets plus net current assets or a number of other variants. In general, most companies, based on the argument that the primary purpose of ROI measurement is to evaluate the effectiveness of a division's operating management in using the assets entrusted to it, define divisional investment as total assets. This argument is supported by the observation that the appropriate amount of long-term indebtedness is an issue which is almost always handled at the company headquarters level. Alternatively if liabilities are traceable back to a particular division they should be accounted for by that division.

Valuation of assets

Most fixed asset valuation measures have both strengths and weaknesses and the main alternatives for inclusion in ROI calculations are:

1. *Net book value*: the major problem in using a depreciation-adjusted denominator is that this method will produce a continuously increasing ROI even if divisional profits remain constant over time. This problem is greatly compounded when assets, as is usually the case, are valued at historic cost. The net book value method could therefore encourage divisional managers to retain assets beyond their economic life in order to achieve higher ROI results.
2. *Gross book value*: this base still fails to overcome the problem of using an historic valuation, although the use of the higher value would prevent the rising return problem resulting from a depreciated asset base. In a very crude sense the use of gross values could be viewed as incorporating an inflation adjustment, but there is no valid reason why original cost should have such a link to current values over time.
3. *Current value*: this would produce the most meaningful asset valuation, although the cost of obtaining the information could be high. Nevertheless ratios based on current, or opportunity values, should provide the best comparative statistics both on the performance of different segments within the organisation, and of one company with another.

Allocation of joint assets

These problems arise because the assets directly traceable to the divisions of the business, when aggregated, do not equal the whole capital invested in the business. Therefore a decision has to be made as to whether or not to allocate joint (or corporate held) assets to divisions. It is generally agreed that allocation of the cost of the physical assets used by head office is inappropriate, but that allocation of centrally held cash and debtors is feasible. Cash may be allocated if a basis for reflecting different demands can be determined; debtors on the basis of their origin.

Discussion topics

1. Explain the advantages and disadvantages of divisionalisation from the viewpoint of any large multinational company.
2. Discuss some of the accounting measurement problems inherent in the use of the ROI statistic.
3. Do you believe that all divisions within the same organisation should seek to attain the same ROI? Explain your arguments with reference to a hypothetical (or actual) company with many different divisions dealing in quite dissimilar activities.
4. 'The net residual income criterion offers more promise as a measure of divisional success than the ROI method.' Discuss.
5. 'The determination of appropriate transfer prices is the single most important motivational tool in encouraging divisional performance, where divisions of the same company deal actively with each other.' Discuss.
6. 'There is no simple (or difficult) answer to the problems of transfer pricing. Common sense in setting prices is the only way to proceed.' Discuss.
7. Explain some of the problems associated with the allocation of non-controllable fixed costs and head office expenses to individual divisions.

Exercises

16.1 Purcell and Tallis are associated companies. Purcell manufactures a raw material for use solely by Tallis. Tallis processes the material into a product for sale in a specialised market. Cost and other data for 19X9 are given below. As part of a plan to establish responsibility centres, the group management gives the management of Purcell and Tallis a high degree of freedom in their budgeting and operations. They are told that for the purposes of management accounting in each company the raw material produced by Purcell is to be transferred to Tallis at a price of £10 per ton (this having been calculated to give Purcell an acceptable rate of return on the group investment in it).

The management of Tallis is told to buy its raw material from Purcell at this transfer price and to plan its output and sales on this basis. Purcell's management is told to produce as much as Tallis demands. Both managements are instructed, within these rules, to maximise their accounting profits.

The following data for 19X9 are available:

Purcell	
Total fixed costs (£)	500,000
Variable costs per unit of output (£)	4
Full capacity output (units)	100,000
Tallis	
Total fixed costs (£)	130,000
Variable costs per unit of output excluding material bought from Purcell (£)	3
Full capacity output (units)	100,000
Estimated demand conditions for final product	

Sales (units)	*Price* (£)
100,000	13
90,000	14
80,000	14.5
70,000	15
60,000	15.25
50,000	15.5

One unit of raw material from Purcell is required for each unit of output of final product. It can be assumed that, in both companies, fixed costs are constant and that variable costs have a linear relation to output, within any relevant range of output. There is no other market available for Purcell's product. Policies followed in 19X9 will have no effect on future demand or costs. Stocks are not to be increased or reduced.

You are required on the basis of the data provided and appending appropriate calculations to:

(a) Prepare Tallis's budgeted income statement for 19X9 if its management observes the group directive.

(b) Prepare Purcell's budgeted income statement for 19X9 on the assumption that Tallis plans as shown in (a) and informs Purcell how much raw materials it proposes to buy in that year.

(c) State, supporting your answer with reasons and appropriate figures, whether the consolidated group budget based on the budgets of (a) and (b) represents the best plan for the group. If not, provide a group budgeted income statement based on the optimal plan.

(d) State what conclusions you can draw from the results of (c).

(Work to the nearest 10,000 units of product in budgeting output and sales.)

16.2 A company has two divisions. Eastern division manufactures a unique timing device. It is never sold outside the company and it cannot be obtained from any other source. Western division incorporates this device in a finished product which it sells. One device is used for each unit of product. Most of eastern division's costs are fixed and for any output up to 1,000 units its total costs are £6,000. Thereafter total costs increase at the rate of £1,000 for every additional 1,000 units made. In the hope of optimising the division's results, eastern division's manager has set a transfer price of £5 per unit.

Western division's costs in assembling the timing device in the finished product and selling it are, in addition to the transfer price of the timing device, £12,000 for any output up to 1,000 units and £2,000 for every 1,000 units thereafter. Western division finds that it can increase its sales only by spending more on promotion or reducing selling prices. Western division's sales forecast is:

Sales in units	*Net sales revenue per thousand units* (£)
1,000	19,000
2,000	17,000
3,000	15,000
4,000	12,500
5,000	9,600
6,000	7,700

All costs, output rates and sales are per working day.

(a) Prepare a schedule of western division's costs (including purchases from eastern division), sales revenue and net income at the indicated sales levels.

(b) State what level of sales maximises western division's net income and calculate eastern division's net income and the net income of the company at that level.

(c) Assume that the company's divisional structure and transfer pricing is abandoned and prepare a further schedule of costs, sales, and net income for the company as a whole, at the indicated sales levels.

(d) State what level of sales maximises the company's net income and explain why it differs from that calculated under a divisional organisation.

(e) State what transfer pricing policy will maximise the company's net income under the divisional organisation.

16.3 A large provincial garage is installing a responsibility accounting system. There will be three profit centres: parts and service, new cars, and used vehicles. Forecourt sales rights have been let to another company. Departmental managers of each profit centre have been told to run their activities as though they were in business on their own account.

However, there will be interdepartmental dealings. For example:

(i) the parts and service department prepares new cars for final delivery and repairs used vehicles prior to resale;
(ii) the used vehicle department's major source of stock has been cars traded-in in part-payment for new cars.

The managing director asks the accountant to prepare a statement explaining the problems of transfer pricing and the principles to be followed. Clarity is of paramount importance because the statement will be relied upon to settle disputes. The managing director also wishes to be advised of any problems which might arise after the rules have been put into effect.

You are required to draft the statement requested. Specify and exemplify the rules to be used within the company for transfer prices in the case of the transfers cited.

16.4 Willoughby plc, manufacturer of tractors and other heavy farm equipment, is organised along decentralised lines, with each manufacturing division operating as a separate profit centre. Each division head has been delegated full authority on all decisions involving the sale of the division's output, both to outsiders and to other divisions of Willoughby plc. Division C has in the past always purchased its requirement of a particular tractor-engine component from division A. However, when informed that division A was increasing its price to £150, division C's management decided to purchase the engine component from outside suppliers.

The component can be purchased by C for £135 on the open market. Division A insists that owing to the recent installation of some highly specialised equipment and the resulting high depreciation charges it would not be able to make an adequate profit on its investment unless it raised its price. A's management appealed to the top management of Willoughby plc for support in its dispute with C and supplied the following operating data:

C's annual purchases of tractor-engine component (units)	1,000
A's variable costs per unit of tractor-engine component (£)	120
A's fixed costs per unit of tractor-engine component (£)	20

(a) Assume that there are no alternative uses for internal facilities. Determine whether the company as a whole will benefit if C purchases the component from outside suppliers for £135 per unit.

(b) Assume that internal facilities of A would not otherwise be idle. By not producing the 1,000 units for C, A's equipment and other facilities would be assigned to other production operations, and would result in annual cash operating savings of £18,000. Should C purchase from outsiders?

(c) Assume that there are no alternative uses for A's internal facilities, and that the price of outsiders drops by £20. Should C purchase from outsiders?

(d) Assume that A could sell the 1,000 units to other customers at £155 per unit with variable selling costs of £5 per unit. Should C purchase the 1,000 components from outsiders at £135 per unit?

16.5 Wilks Ltd has two divisions. Division 1 is responsible for slaughtering and cutting unprocessed meat. Division 2 processes meat such as hams, bacon, etc. Division 2 can buy meat from division 1 or from outside suppliers. Division 1 can sell at the market price all the unprocessed meat that it can produce. The 19X0 income statement for the company is given in the table below.

Wilks Ltd: income statement for the year ended 31 December 19X0

	£	£	£
Total sales			180,000
Cost of goods sold:			
Opening stocks		0	
Manufacturing costs:			
Raw materials, division 1	50,000		
Labour, division 1	30,000		
Overhead, division 1	20,000		
Processing supplies, division 2	15,000		
Labour, division 2	20,000		
Overhead, division 2	10,000	145,000	
Cost of goods available for sale		145,000	
Less Closing stocks at cost:			
Division 1		0	
Division 2		10,000	135,000
Gross margin			45,000
Operating expenses:			
Sales and administrative, division 1	11,000		
Sales and administrative, division 2	12,000		
Head office overhead	14,000		
			37,000
Net profit before tax			8,000

Closing stocks of £10,000 are valued at the cost of production incurred in division 1. These stocks are as yet unprocessed. The market value unprocessed is £12,000. The sales for the year can be broken down as follows.

	£
Division 1	40,000
Division 2	140,000
	180,000

The market value of the unprocessed meat actually transferred from division 1 to division 2 (exclusive of the closing stock) was £100,000.

(a) Prepare division income statements that might be used to evaluate the performance of the two division managers.

(b) Explain the transfer pricing policy you have used in preparing the statements and state whether it is suitable for decision making purposes.

16.6 Vaughan Ltd comprises three divisions. Divisions A and B manufacture components which they sell externally and transfer to division C. Raw materials are purchased for a central store from which they are issued to the operating divisions. The company operates a system of decentralised decision taking. It wishes to set transfer prices for components and materials such that divisional managers are motivated to take decisions likely to increase the wealth of shareholders. The following information is available on current divisional activities:

1. *Division A*: Manufactures component A, requiring per unit: 8 labour hours, 6 lb of material A and 4 lb of material B. The division can sell an indefinitely large quantity externally at the going price of £70 per unit.
2. *Division B*: Manufactures component B, requiring per unit: 6 labour hours, 4 lb of material A and 6 lb of material B. The division can sell up to 20,000 units p.a. at the selected price of £80 per unit.

   Division C: Manufactures three products:

	Product X	*Product Y*	*Product Z*
Required per unit:			
Material B (lb)	8	4	6
Component A (units)	4	6	2
Component B (units)	2	6	4
Labour hours	20	12	16
Selling price per unit (£)	350	560	250
Maximum annual demand (units)	10,000	6,000	8,000

Resources available per annum are:
Labour: Division A 200,000 hr at £1 per hr
Division B 160,000 hr at £1 per hr
Division C 120,000 hr at £0.50 per hr
Material A – 200,000 lb at £2 per lb.
Material B – as much as required at £5 per lb.

(a) Formulate the decision problem for the whole firm as a linear programming problem. Do *not* give a numerical solution.
(b) Explain how the desired transfer prices might be set. What can you say about their level without making calculations?

16.7 Eichner Ltd manufactures and distributes golf balls under the brand name superjacks. The company has adopted a divisionalised structure with a manufacturing division which produces the balls and supplies them in bulk to a distribution division which is responsible for packaging and marketing. Both divisions have considerable autonomy and both are evaluated as profit centres.

The manufacturing division has fixed costs of £25,000. The average variable cost is $£1.50 + 0.0001q$ per dozen balls. The distribution division has fixed costs of £10,000 and constant variable costs of £2 per dozen balls. Eichner Ltd has recently commissioned a market research project which has revealed that the demand for superjacks is such that a 25p reduction in the price of a carton of one dozen balls will result in demand increasing by 500 units. The existing price is £5 per dozen and the company is selling 20,000 cartons per year. The management of Eichner has not previously considered increasing the price because of competition from other manufacturers. However, they believe that a 25p increase in price would produce similar, though reversed, results to those resulting from a price reduction.

(a) Determine the price and output levels that would result in Eichner maximising its profits.

(b) Suggest a transfer price such that the divisional managements, acting independently, would arrive at the conclusions indicated in (a) above and show how total corporate profit would be allocated between the divisions.

Now suppose that the chief executive of the manufacturing division has found a chain store that is prepared to purchase the unpacked balls in bulk at a price of £5 per dozen direct from the manufacturing division.

(c) Determine the transfer price that will ensure optimal decisions, from the corporate viewpoint, are taken by the individual divisional executives.

(d) Calculate the new corporate profit and show how it is divided between the divisions.

Further reading

Abdel-Khalik, A. Rashad and Lusk, E. J., 'Transfer pricing – a synthesis', *The Accounting Review*, January 1974.

Amey, L. R., 'Divisional performance measurement and interest on capital', *Journal of Business Finance*, Spring 1969.

Bromwich, M., 'Measurement of divisional performance: a comment and an extension', *Accounting and Business Research*, Spring 1973.

Cats-Baril, W., Gatti, J. F. and Grinnell, D. J., 'Transfer pricing in a dynamic market', *Management Accounting*, February 1988.

Choudhury, N., 'Incentives for the divisional manager', *Accounting and Business Research*, Winter 1985.

Dearden, John, 'Measuring profit centre managers', *Harvard Business Review*, September–October 1987.

Eccles, R. G., 'Control with fairness in transfer pricing', *Harvard Business Review*, November/December 1983.

Emmanuel, C. R. and Gee, K. P. 'Transfer pricing: a fair and neutral procedure', *Accounting and Business Research*, Autumn 1982.

Emmanuel, C. R. and Otley, D. T., 'The usefulness of residual income', *Journal of Business Finance and Accounting*, Winter 1976.
Ezzamel, M. A., 'On the assessment of the performance effects of multidivisional structures', *Accounting and Business Research*, Winter 1985.
Hirshleifer, J., 'On the economics of transfer pricing', *Journal of Business*, July 1956.
Lawson, G. H., 'Measuring divisional performance', *Management Accounting*, May 1971.
Reece, James S. and Cool, W. R., 'Measuring investment centre performance' *Harvard Business Review*, May–June 1978.
Scapens, R. W., 'Profit measurement in divisionalised companies', *Journal of Business Finance and Accounting*, Autumn 1979.
Solomons, D., *Divisional Performance: Measurement and Control*, Irwin, 1965.
Tomkins, C. R., *Financial Planning in Divisionalised Companies*, Haymarket, 1973.
Tomkins, C. R., 'Financial planning and control in large companies', in Arnold, J., Carsberg, B. and Scapens, R. (eds), *Topics in Management Accounting*, Philip Allan, 1980.
Wright, M. and Thompson, S., 'Divestment and the control of divisionalised firms', *Accounting and Business Research*, Summer 1987.

Chapter 17

Summary and review

Our main concern in this book has been to identify and discuss the sort of accounting information which should be provided for managers of business organisations. This emphasis reflects our view that the purpose of *all* accounting is to provide information that assists its users to make good decisions. If this is not its purpose, then accounting is likely to be sterile and of little social or economic value, and decision makers may well develop other, perhaps more informal, sources of useful information.

In Part 1 we discussed topics central to our view of accounting and, in particular, of management accounting. Although such an extensive coverage of basic principles is not found in all books on management accounting, we believe that it is essential to an understanding of the role of management accounting as part of an enterprise's total information system. In Part 2 we applied these principles to a number of problems typically faced by managers, for which they require information from the firm's accounting system. We have not attempted to cover all the problem areas confronting managers: had we done so, the book would have been excessively long. Nevertheless we feel that the choice of areas covered in Part 2 is sufficiently comprehensive to illustrate the application to management problems of the basic principles of accounting information systems developed in Part 1.

In this final chapter we review both the main objectives of the book and the principles suggested for the preparation of management accounting information. We also summarise the pertinent problems involved in the provision of management information as we have identified them. We conclude with a discussion of the current state of management accounting and with some suggestions about the directions in which it might develop.

17.1 Review of the objectives of the book

We outlined our main objectives in Chapter 1. They are as follows:

1. To provide a framework for the analysis of accounting problems, i.e.

problems of identifying the appropriate information which aids users' decisions.

2. To use the framework to identify principles which specify the particular information that should be made available to decision makers.
3. To apply these principles to a variety of managerial problems, and to suggest methods for solving those problems.
4. To describe accounting procedures that are used by practising management accountants and to compare them with the procedures implied by our analysis.

We attempted to achieve the first and second objectives in Part 1 and the third and fourth in Part 2. In so doing, we identified three main interdependent areas of management activity: decision making, planning and control. Each of these areas is reviewed briefly in the next section.

17.2 The main principles

In order to review the key principles in the identification of good management accounting information it is helpful to consider separately the three areas of management activity mentioned above. For management *decision making* our central theme has been to argue in favour of opportunity cost or relevant cost as the most appropriate measure of the economic costs and consequences of decisions. By opportunity cost or relevant cost is meant the incremental or differential effect on a firm's cash flows of pursuing a particular course of action. We considered the application of the opportunity cost concept to a number of decisions including accept/reject decisions, output level decisions, pricing policy, the optimal use of scarce resources and decision making in divisions of organisations. We discussed the application of the concept to both short- and long-term decisions, the latter involving the determination and incorporation into the analysis of an interest rate, or cost of capital, to take account of the time value of money. Underlying our entire analysis is an objective of wealth maximisation or, more precisely, the maximisation of the discounted present value of an organisation's future net cash inflows.

Management *planning* is important because it provides the link between making decisions and controlling their implementation. Decisions which appear optimal may be of little benefit to a firm if they are not properly implemented. Plans, or budgets, embody the expected outcomes of particular decisions and should be prepared in a form which is consistent with the achievement of the desired outcomes. They should also be prepared in a way that facilitates management control.

Simply stated, *control* comprises the frequent comparison of actual results with planned performance and the subsequent investigation of variances. Because control implies comparison it is important that like be compared with like if the analysis is to be meaningful. Thus control systems should be in a form consistent with the models used for planning. As we explained in Chapters 13 and 15, there are many different purposes of control systems. Two of these bear repeating here. The first is to motivate those responsible for implementing an organisation's plans. The second is to provide an organisation with information that will enable it to improve the quality of its performance in the future. A good control system will include frequent consideration and, if necessary, revision of organisational plans.

In this context it should be clear that decision making, planning and control are all parts of a dynamic, iterative process. A good management accounting system should reflect the interdependences between the three areas. To decide upon an optimal plan is merely the first step in a procedure that will continue and involve regular changes as long as the firm exists.

17.3 Some problems reviewed

Throughout the book we have attempted to direct attention to problems which are likely to arise in the development and implementation of management accounting systems. Some of the more important of these problems are reviewed below.

The first problem, which affects all decisions, is the existence of risk and uncertainty (discussed in some detail in Chapter 4 and subsequently referred to on numerous occasions). All decisions are concerned with choices between future courses of action and the future is never certain. Thus all decisions are based on data that, to some degree, are uncertain. Although it is possible to specify the uncertainty involved in estimates and to adopt strategies which reduce the impact of uncertainty, for example by using portfolio analysis, it should be remembered that uncertainty can usually be decreased only at the cost of a lower expected return and can never be eliminated. In consequence, all decisions involve a possible trade-off between risk and return. Such a choice depends upon individual preferences and cannot be determined by an inanimate decision model.

A second difficulty in the development of management accounting systems is the existence of factors which cannot readily be expressed in financial terms. This is a particular problem for organisations in the public sector where social costs and benefits are often more important than in the private sector. For example, it is difficult to justify the existence of a police force, motorway or even an urban transport system purely on the grounds of readily identifiable financial costs and benefits. The directly identifiable financial costs of such services normally outweigh their directly identifiable financial benefits. Yet the fact that they are provided suggests the existence of other, less easily measured benefits. The same difficulties arise, although to a lesser degree, in private sector organisations. The decision to provide a 'subsidised' works canteen may, in fact, be a sound long-term financial investment for a firm. It may result in lower wages having to be paid, in a reduction in the rate at which employees leave and a consequent reduction in re-employment and retraining costs, and in a decrease in the number of working days lost through ill health, resulting from an inadequate diet. Such benefits, however, are difficult to quantify and their incorporation in a decision analysis may, in some situations, occupy a substantial amount of management time. We return to this issue in more detail at the close of this chapter.

A further problem relates to the relationship between a firm's management accounts and its external accounting reports, i.e. the reports it issues to its shareholders and to other groups outside the enterprise who have an interest in its performance (we took up this issue initially in Chapter 12). In some situations, the adoption of courses of action which seem desirable according to the decision models which we have advocated in this book may result in a deterioration in an enterprise's performance as measured in its external reports, particularly in the short term. Suppose, for example, that a firm is considering whether to invest £200,000 in a substantial advertising campaign. The advertising cost would be incurred in the coming year and would result in additional net cash inflows of £50,000 in the year after the campaign and in each subsequent year indefinitely. The firm's cost of capital is 10% p.a. In investment appraisal terms the project is very attractive; it has a net present value of +£300,000 (£50,000/0.1 – £200,000) and an internal rate of return of 25% (£50,000/£200,000 × 100). However, in the firm's external reports adoption of the project will probably lead to a decrease in reported income in the coming year, when some or all of the costs of the advertising campaign are recognised. It is true that the reported income of subsequent years will be higher than would have been the case without advertising, but some investors may decide to sell their shares at the end of the coming year on the basis of that year's reported results. The crux of the problem is this. If managerial decision making (which is based on *future* expectations) results in a course of action which, although worthwhile in the long run, reflects adversely on a firm's performance in the short run measured in its external reports, then users of the reports may make decisions which are not in their best long-run interests. Furthermore, since external reports are based on past performance and generally cover periods no longer than one year, they may not articulate well with managerial decision making processes which emphasise the future and often involve a consideration of periods considerably longer than one year. This means that managers should bear in mind the impact of their decisions on externally reported performance and, in some cases, modify the decisions accordingly.

17.4 The current and future state of management accounting

In this book we have attempted to explain at an introductory level the current state of management accounting as it is reflected in the literature of the subject. Much of the current literature on management accounting is influenced substantially by work on applied economics and applied operations research which was undertaken largely in the two or three decades up to the early 1970s, and by studies on the design of information systems which have been undertaken primarily since then.

A major problem facing researchers and writers in the management accounting area is that surprisingly little reliable empirical evidence exists concerning the use of management accounting systems in practice. Until more evidence is available it will be difficult for management accounting writers to ascertain which of their recommendations are useful to managers and which are not. An example of the difficulty is in the area of fixed overhead allocation. Virtually all management accounting writers argue, as we have done, that allocating costs which are fixed as arbitrary and may be misleading. But the limited empirical evidence which is available suggests that many firms operate cost accounting systems that involve simplistic allocations of fixed costs to products, decisions and so on. Until we know how widespread this practice is, for what decisions it is used and how the information is used in making particular decisions, it is not possible to evaluate the usefulness of fixed cost allocation for decisions in the real world.[48]

Closer liaison is clearly required between those who practise management accounting and those who make recommendations about management accounting systems. At the end of the day recommendations about 'best' management accounting systems, however plausible they may appear, are of little importance if they are not adopted in practice. However, we do know that there are major changes taking place in the world of business, and in particular in the nature of manufacturing technology. Perhaps the biggest challenge which faces management accounting is its ability to adapt to changes in the firm's operating environment. Accounting systems, such as those which we have discussed throughout this book, have been developed during periods when the primary aim of the firm's production managers has been to maximise the length of production runs of the same (standard) product, and so to minimise unit costs. Thus the management accountant has developed reporting tools, such as standard costing, which reflect a production setting of long runs with standard elements. The emphasis of standard costing is on rewarding the lowest *unit* costs of production, for example via the generating of favourable labour efficiency variances and favourable material use variances. This environment has demanded purely financial information from the management accountant – information which records actual and budgeted costs and revenues from particular decisions. It has not concerned itself greatly with the more qualitative issues of product quality, number of defective units, amounts of warranty expense, customer loyalty, speed of processing orders etc. As a consequence the accountant has not been called upon to develop recording and measurement techniques which address these qualitative issues.

The world of the 1990s and beyond is, however, unlikely to be so simple. No longer will most firms engage in long production runs of standard products, irrespective of the saleability of the output. In the 1990s the consumer will be king, and, as Japanese manufacturers have shown for the last decade, the production setting will have to change to reflect this. In effect the aim of production will be to meet, and to anticipate, changes in consumer taste and demand. Consumers will probably require more new production lines, a greater variety of products within each line, and more design features within each individual product. To meet those constantly changing consumer requirements firms will have to change their design and production technology to allow them to bring products quickly to market and then to produce at lower volumes in a cost-effective way. Flexibility and speed of change of machine use will be the order of the day and, indeed, many organisations are currently investing heavily in flexible manufacturing systems, in CADCAM

[48] There is, however, a recent series of cases developed at the Harvard Business School which addresses issues in product costing, and which deals with problems of fixed cost allocation.

systems, and in fully automated, computer integrated plants. All of these technologies allow the firm, in varying degrees, to adapt speedily and cheaply to changes in market preferences. As the emphasis moves away from long standard production runs and becomes one of *minimising* stock levels and *minimising* the total (rather than the unit) cost of production, the management accountant will have to reflect these changes in his or her measurement systems. This may not be easy. The change required in the mind set may be quite substantial.

The new production setting dictated by external factors will require measures of cost, quality, flexibility, service and innovation. These will, more and more, become the bases on which firms compete. At the moment, the training and practice of most accountants is rooted in the first of these bases – that of cost. The challenge over the next ten years will certainly be one of refining and specifying appropriate cost measurements (opportunity costing will be as important in the future as in the past), but will entail a closer knowledge on the part of the accountant of just where the firm's competitive advantage lies (Is it known as a quality firm? Does it compete on cost alone?), so that relevant measurements can be developed. It is likely that many of these measures will be non-financial. Thus we envisage that management accountants will concern themselves with measures of quality (changes in design, percentage of defects, percentage of items re-worked), with measures of productivity (value-added per employee, total factor productivity), with measures of innovation (number of high performance products introduced, delivery times from inception to customer), with better use of inventory (elimination of set-up times, less use of floor space, introduction of just in time theories), and measures of workforce satisfaction (training levels, measures of absenteeism, employee suggestions for continuous improvement) and with measures of customer loyalty (number of customers retained over a specified period, number of new customers gained). These, and other allied issues, are not obviously paramount within the current domain of accounting measurement, but they are likely to be a *sine qua non* of successful business in future years. If management accountants do not soon get to grips with these issues, their role as primary providers of useful information for business decisions may be usurped by others.

Discussion topics

1. Discuss the main principles involved in developing information for management decision making, planning and control.
2. Outline the problems created by the existence of risk and uncertainty in decision making.
3. 'Many decisions are made primarily on the basis of factors which cannot readily be expressed in financial terms. Decision models based on the maximisation of financial returns are of little help in such situations.' Discuss.
4. 'Enterprise reports to external users focus on the past. Information for managerial decision making focuses on the future. Thus consistency between information for external users and information for managers is unlikely.' Explain this statement and discuss its implications.

5 Explain and discuss the view that empirical evidence about the use of management accounting systems in practice is of crucial importance to management accounting theoreticians.

6 Discuss the difficulties which management accountants may experience in developing non-financial performance measures.

7 Do you believe it is the accountant's role to depart from his or her traditional responsibility of providing cost-based information?

Further reading

Bhaskar, K. N., 'Quantitative aspects of management accounting', in Bromwich, M. and Hopwood, A. G. (eds), *Essays in British Accounting Research*, Pitman, 1981.

Choudhury, N., 'In search of relevance in management accounting research', *Accounting and Business Research*, Winter 1986.

Demski, J. S., *Information Analysis*, 2nd edn, Addison Wesley, 1980.

Emmanuel, C. and Otley, D., *Accounting for Management and Control*, Van Nostrand Reinhold, 1985.

Hart, H., 'A review of some recent major developments in the management accounting field', *Accounting and Business Research*, Spring 1981.

Johnson, H. T., and Kaplan, R. S., *Relevance Lost: The Rise and Fall of Management Accounting*, Harvard Business School Press, 1987.

Kaplan, R. S., 'Measuring manufacturing performance: a new challenge for managerial accounting research', *The Accounting Review*, October 1983.

Kaplan, R. S., 'The evolution of management accounting', *The Accounting Review*, July 1984.

Otley, D., 'Developments in management accounting research', *The British Accounting Review*, Autumn 1985.

Scapens, R. W., *Management Accounting: A Review of Contemporary Developments*, Macmillan, 1985.

Zimmerman, I., 'The cost and benefits of cost allocations', *The Accounting Review*, July 1979.

Appendix

Compounding and discounting tables

INTEREST RATE 3.0 %

YEAR	FUTURE VALUE	PRESENT VALUE	SINKING FUND		ANNUITY	
			FUTURE VALUE	ANNUAL AMOUNT	PRESENT VALUE	ANNUAL AMOUNT
n	$(1+i)^n$	$V_{\overline{n\rceil}}$	$S_{\overline{n\rceil}}$	$S_{\overline{n\rceil}}^{-1}$	$A_{\overline{n\rceil}}$	$A_{\overline{n\rceil}}^{-1}$
1	1.0300	0.970874	1.0000	1.000000	0.9709	1.030000
2	1.0609	0.942596	2.0300	0.492611	1.9135	0.522611
3	1.0927	0.915142	3.0909	0.323530	2.8286	0.353530
4	1.1255	0.888487	4.1836	0.239027	3.7171	0.269027
5	1.1593	0.862609	5.3091	0.188355	4.5797	0.218355
6	1.1941	0.837484	6.4684	0.154598	5.4172	0.184598
7	1.2299	0.813092	7.6625	0.130506	6.2303	0.160506
8	1.2668	0.789409	8.8923	0.112456	7.0197	0.142456
9	1.3048	0.766417	10.1591	0.098434	7.7861	0.128434
10	1.3439	0.744094	11.4639	0.087231	8.5302	0.117231
11	1.3842	0.722421	12.8078	0.078077	9.2526	0.108077
12	1.4258	0.701380	14.1920	0.070462	9.9540	0.100462
13	1.4685	0.680951	15.6178	0.064030	10.6350	0.094030
14	1.5126	0.661118	17.0863	0.058526	11.2961	0.088526
15	1.5580	0.641862	18.5989	0.053767	11.9379	0.083767
16	1.6047	0.623167	20.1569	0.049611	12.5611	0.079611
17	1.6528	0.605016	21.7616	0.045953	13.1661	0.075953
18	1.7024	0.587395	23.4144	0.042709	13.7535	0.072709
19	1.7535	0.570286	25.1169	0.039814	14.3238	0.069814
20	1.8061	0.553676	26.8704	0.037216	14.8775	0.067216
21	1.8603	0.537549	28.6765	0.034872	15.4150	0.064872
22	1.9161	0.521893	30.5368	0.032747	15.9369	0.062747
23	1.9736	0.506692	32.4529	0.030814	16.4436	0.060814
24	2.0328	0.491934	34.4265	0.029047	16.9355	0.059047
25	2.0938	0.477606	36.4593	0.027428	17.4131	0.057428
26	2.1566	0.463695	38.5530	0.025938	17.8768	0.055938
27	2.2213	0.450189	40.7096	0.024564	18.3270	0.054564
28	2.2879	0.437077	42.9309	0.023293	18.7641	0.053293
29	2.3566	0.424346	45.2189	0.022115	19.1885	0.052115
30	2.4273	0.411987	47.5754	0.021019	19.6004	0.051019

INTEREST RATE 4.0 %

YEAR	FUTURE VALUE	PRESENT VALUE	SINKING FUND FUTURE VALUE	SINKING FUND ANNUAL AMOUNT	ANNUITY PRESENT VALUE	ANNUITY ANNUAL AMOUNT
n	$(1+i)^n$	$V_{\overline{n}\|}$	$S_{\overline{n}\|}$	$S_{\overline{n}\|}^{-1}$	$A_{\overline{n}\|}$	$A_{\overline{n}\|}^{-1}$
1	1.0400	0.961538	1.0000	1.000000	0.9615	1.040000
2	1.0816	0.924556	2.0400	0.490196	1.8861	0.530196
3	1.1249	0.888996	3.1216	0.320349	2.7751	0.360349
4	1.1699	0.854804	4.2465	0.235490	3.6299	0.275490
5	1.2167	0.821927	5.4163	0.184627	4.4518	0.224627
6	1.2653	0.790315	6.6330	0.150762	5.2421	0.190762
7	1.3159	0.759918	7.8983	0.126610	6.0021	0.166610
8	1.3686	0.730690	9.2142	0.108528	6.7327	0.148528
9	1.4233	0.702587	10.5828	0.094493	7.4353	0.134493
10	1.4802	0.675564	12.0061	0.083291	8.1109	0.123291
11	1.5395	0.649581	13.4864	0.074149	8.7605	0.114149
12	1.6010	0.624597	15.0258	0.066552	9.3851	0.106552
13	1.6651	0.600574	16.6268	0.060144	9.9856	0.100144
14	1.7317	0.577475	18.2919	0.054669	10.5631	0.094669
15	1.8009	0.555265	20.0236	0.049941	11.1184	0.089941
16	1.8730	0.533908	21.8245	0.045820	11.6523	0.085820
17	1.9479	0.513373	23.6975	0.042199	12.1657	0.082199
18	2.0258	0.493628	25.6454	0.038993	12.6593	0.078993
19	2.1068	0.474642	27.6712	0.036139	13.1339	0.076139
20	2.1911	0.456387	29.7781	0.033582	13.5903	0.073582
21	2.2788	0.438834	31.9692	0.031280	14.0292	0.071280
22	2.3699	0.421955	34.2480	0.029199	14.4511	0.069199
23	2.4647	0.405726	36.6179	0.027309	14.8568	0.067309
24	2.5633	0.390121	39.0826	0.025587	15.2470	0.065587
25	2.6658	0.375117	41.6459	0.024012	15.6221	0.064012
26	2.7725	0.360689	44.3117	0.022567	15.9828	0.062567
27	2.8834	0.346817	47.0842	0.021239	16.3296	0.061239
28	2.9987	0.333477	49.9676	0.020013	16.6631	0.060013
29	3.1187	0.320651	52.9663	0.018880	16.9837	0.058880
30	3.2434	0.308319	56.0849	0.017830	17.2920	0.057830

INTEREST RATE 5.0 %

YEAR	FUTURE VALUE	PRESENT VALUE	SINKING FUND FUTURE VALUE	SINKING FUND ANNUAL AMOUNT	ANNUITY PRESENT VALUE	ANNUITY ANNUAL AMOUNT
n	$(1+i)^n$	$V_{\overline{n}\rvert}$	$S_{\overline{n}\rvert}$	$S_{\overline{n}\rvert}^{-1}$	$A_{\overline{n}\rvert}$	$A_{\overline{n}\rvert}^{-1}$
1	1.0500	0.952381	1.0000	1.000000	0.9524	1.050000
2	1.1025	0.907029	2.0500	0.487805	1.8594	0.537805
3	1.1576	0.863838	3.1525	0.317209	2.7232	0.367209
4	1.2155	0.822702	4.3101	0.232012	3.5460	0.282012
5	1.2763	0.783526	5.5256	0.180975	4.3295	0.230975
6	1.3401	0.746215	6.8019	0.147017	5.0757	0.197017
7	1.4071	0.710681	8.1420	0.122820	5.7864	0.172820
8	1.4775	0.676839	9.5491	0.104722	6.4632	0.154722
9	1.5513	0.644609	11.0266	0.090690	7.1078	0.140690
10	1.6289	0.613913	12.5779	0.079505	7.7217	0.129505
11	1.7103	0.584679	14.2068	0.070389	8.3064	0.120389
12	1.7959	0.556837	15.9171	0.062825	8.8633	0.112825
13	1.8856	0.530321	17.7130	0.056456	9.3936	0.106456
14	1.9799	0.505068	19.5986	0.051024	9.8986	0.101024
15	2.0789	0.481017	21.5786	0.046342	10.3797	0.096342
16	2.1829	0.458112	23.6575	0.042270	10.8378	0.092270
17	2.2920	0.436297	25.8404	0.038699	11.2741	0.088699
18	2.4066	0.415521	28.1324	0.035546	11.6896	0.085546
19	2.5270	0.395734	30.5390	0.032745	12.0853	0.082745
20	2.6533	0.376889	33.0660	0.030243	12.4622	0.080243
21	2.7860	0.358942	35.7193	0.027996	12.8212	0.077996
22	2.9253	0.341850	38.5052	0.025971	13.1630	0.075971
23	3.0715	0.325571	41.4305	0.024137	13.4886	0.074137
24	3.2251	0.310068	44.5020	0.022471	13.7986	0.072471
25	3.3864	0.295303	47.7271	0.020952	14.0939	0.070952
26	3.5557	0.281241	51.1135	0.019564	14.3752	0.069564
27	3.7335	0.267848	54.6691	0.018292	14.6430	0.068292
28	3.9201	0.255094	58.4026	0.017123	14.8981	0.067123
29	4.1161	0.242946	62.3227	0.016046	15.1411	0.066046
30	4.3219	0.231377	66.4388	0.015051	15.3725	0.065051

INTEREST RATE 6.0 %

YEAR	FUTURE VALUE	PRESENT VALUE	SINKING FUND FUTURE VALUE	SINKING FUND ANNUAL AMOUNT	ANNUITY PRESENT VALUE	ANNUITY ANNUAL AMOUNT
n	$(1+i)^n$	$V_{\overline{n}\vert}$	$S_{\overline{n}\vert}$	$S_{\overline{n}\vert}^{-1}$	$A_{\overline{n}\vert}$	$A_{\overline{n}\vert}^{-1}$
1	1.0600	0.943396	1.0000	1.000000	0.9434	1.060000
2	1.1236	0.889996	2.0600	0.485437	1.8334	0.545437
3	1.1910	0.839619	3.1836	0.314110	2.6730	0.374110
4	1.2625	0.792094	4.3746	0.228591	3.4651	0.288591
5	1.3382	0.747258	5.6371	0.177396	4.2124	0.237396
6	1.4185	0.704961	6.9753	0.143363	4.9173	0.203363
7	1.5036	0.665057	8.3938	0.119135	5.5824	0.179135
8	1.5938	0.627412	9.8975	0.101036	6.2098	0.161036
9	1.6895	0.591898	11.4913	0.087022	6.8017	0.147022
10	1.7908	0.558395	13.1808	0.075868	7.3601	0.135868
11	1.8983	0.526788	14.9716	0.066793	7.8869	0.126793
12	2.0122	0.496969	16.8699	0.059277	8.3838	0.119277
13	2.1329	0.468839	18.8821	0.052960	8.8527	0.112960
14	2.2609	0.442301	21.0151	0.047585	9.2950	0.107585
15	2.3966	0.417265	23.2760	0.042963	9.7122	0.102963
16	2.5404	0.393646	25.6725	0.038952	10.1059	0.098952
17	2.6928	0.371364	28.2129	0.035445	10.4773	0.095445
18	2.8543	0.350344	30.9057	0.032357	10.8276	0.092357
19	3.0256	0.330513	33.7600	0.029621	11.1581	0.089621
20	3.2071	0.311805	36.7856	0.027185	11.4699	0.087185
21	3.3996	0.294155	39.9927	0.025005	11.7641	0.085005
22	3.6035	0.277505	43.3923	0.023046	12.0416	0.083046
23	3.8197	0.261797	46.9958	0.021278	12.3034	0.081278
24	4.0489	0.246979	50.8156	0.019679	12.5504	0.079679
25	4.2919	0.232999	54.8645	0.018227	12.7834	0.078227
26	4.5494	0.219810	59.1564	0.016904	13.0032	0.076904
27	4.8223	0.207368	63.7058	0.015697	13.2105	0.075697
28	5.1117	0.195630	68.5281	0.014593	13.4062	0.074593
29	5.4184	0.184557	73.6398	0.013580	13.5907	0.073580
30	5.7435	0.174110	79.0582	0.012649	13.7648	0.072649

INTEREST RATE 7.0 %

YEAR	FUTURE VALUE	PRESENT VALUE	SINKING FUND FUTURE VALUE	SINKING FUND ANNUAL AMOUNT	ANNUITY PRESENT VALUE	ANNUITY ANNUAL AMOUNT
n	$(1+i)^n$	$V_{\overline{n}\rceil}$	$S_{\overline{n}\rceil}$	$S_{\overline{n}\rceil}^{-1}$	$A_{\overline{n}\rceil}$	$A_{\overline{n}\rceil}^{-1}$
1	1.0700	0.934579	1.0000	1.000000	0.9346	1.070000
2	1.1449	0.873439	2.0700	0.483092	1.8080	0.553092
3	1.2250	0.816298	3.2149	0.311052	2.6243	0.381052
4	1.3108	0.762895	4.4399	0.225228	3.3872	0.295228
5	1.4026	0.712986	5.7507	0.173891	4.1002	0.243891
6	1.5007	0.666342	7.1533	0.139796	4.7665	0.209796
7	1.6058	0.622750	8.6540	0.115553	5.3893	0.185553
8	1.7182	0.582009	10.2598	0.097468	5.9713	0.167468
9	1.8385	0.543934	11.9780	0.083486	6.5152	0.153486
10	1.9672	0.508349	13.8164	0.072378	7.0236	0.142378
11	2.1049	0.475093	15.7836	0.063357	7.4987	0.133357
12	2.2522	0.444012	17.8885	0.055902	7.9427	0.125902
13	2.4098	0.414964	20.1406	0.049651	8.3577	0.119651
14	2.5785	0.387817	22.5505	0.044345	8.7455	0.114345
15	2.7590	0.362446	25.1290	0.039795	9.1079	0.109795
16	2.9522	0.338735	27.8881	0.035858	9.4466	0.105858
17	3.1588	0.316574	30.8402	0.032425	9.7632	0.102425
18	3.3799	0.295864	33.9990	0.029413	10.0591	0.099413
19	3.6165	0.276508	37.3790	0.026753	10.3356	0.096753
20	3.8697	0.258419	40.9955	0.024393	10.5940	0.094393
21	4.1406	0.241513	44.8652	0.022289	10.8355	0.092289
22	4.4304	0.225713	49.0057	0.020406	11.0612	0.090406
23	4.7405	0.210947	53.4361	0.018714	11.2722	0.088714
24	5.0724	0.197147	58.1767	0.017189	11.4693	0.087189
25	5.4274	0.184249	63.2490	0.015811	11.6536	0.085811
26	5.8074	0.172195	68.6765	0.014561	11.8258	0.084561
27	6.2139	0.160930	74.4838	0.013426	11.9867	0.083426
28	6.6488	0.150402	80.6977	0.012392	12.1371	0.082392
29	7.1143	0.140563	87.3465	0.011449	12.2777	0.081449
30	7.6123	0.131367	94.4608	0.010586	12.4090	0.080586

INTEREST RATE 8.0 %

YEAR	FUTURE VALUE	PRESENT VALUE	SINKING FUND FUTURE VALUE	SINKING FUND ANNUAL AMOUNT	ANNUITY PRESENT VALUE	ANNUITY ANNUAL AMOUNT
n	$(1+i)^n$	$V_{\overline{n}\rceil}$	$S_{\overline{n}\rceil}$	$S_{\overline{n}\rceil}^{-1}$	$A_{\overline{n}\rceil}$	$A_{\overline{n}\rceil}^{-1}$
1	1.0800	0.925926	1.0000	1.000000	0.9259	1.080000
2	1.1664	0.857339	2.0800	0.480769	1.7833	0.560769
3	1.2597	0.793832	3.2464	0.308034	2.5771	0.388034
4	1.3605	0.735030	4.5061	0.221921	3.3121	0.301921
5	1.4693	0.680583	5.8666	0.170456	3.9927	0.250456
6	1.5869	0.630170	7.3359	0.136315	4.6229	0.216315
7	1.7138	0.583490	8.9228	0.112072	5.2064	0.192072
8	1.8509	0.540269	10.6366	0.094015	5.7466	0.174015
9	1.9990	0.500249	12.4876	0.080080	6.2469	0.160080
10	2.1589	0.463193	14.4866	0.069029	6.7101	0.149029
11	2.3316	0.428883	16.6455	0.060076	7.1390	0.140076
12	2.5182	0.397114	18.9771	0.052695	7.5361	0.132695
13	2.7196	0.367698	21.4953	0.046522	7.9038	0.126522
14	2.9372	0.340461	24.2149	0.041297	8.2442	0.121297
15	3.1722	0.315242	27.1521	0.036830	8.5595	0.116830
16	3.4259	0.291890	30.3243	0.032977	8.8514	0.112977
17	3.7000	0.270269	33.7502	0.029629	9.1216	0.109629
18	3.9960	0.250249	37.4502	0.026702	9.3719	0.106702
19	4.3157	0.231712	41.4463	0.024128	9.6036	0.104128
20	4.6610	0.214548	45.7620	0.021852	9.8181	0.101852
21	5.0338	0.198656	50.4229	0.019832	10.0168	0.099832
22	5.4365	0.183941	55.4568	0.018032	10.2007	0.098032
23	5.8715	0.170315	60.8933	0.016422	10.3711	0.096422
24	6.3412	0.157699	66.7648	0.014978	10.5288	0.094978
25	6.8485	0.146018	73.1059	0.013679	10.6748	0.093679
26	7.3964	0.135202	79.9544	0.012507	10.8100	0.092507
27	7.9881	0.125187	87.3508	0.011448	10.9352	0.091448
28	8.6271	0.115914	95.3388	0.010489	11.0511	0.090489
29	9.3173	0.107328	103.9659	0.009619	11.1584	0.089619
30	10.0627	0.099377	113.2832	0.008827	11.2578	0.088827

INTEREST RATE 9.0 %

YEAR	FUTURE VALUE	PRESENT VALUE	SINKING FUND FUTURE VALUE	SINKING FUND ANNUAL AMOUNT	ANNUITY PRESENT VALUE	ANNUITY ANNUAL AMOUNT
n	$(1+i)^n$	$V_{\overline{n}\vert}$	$S_{\overline{n}\vert}$	$S_{\overline{n}\vert}^{-1}$	$A_{\overline{n}\vert}$	$A_{\overline{n}\vert}^{-1}$
1	1.0900	0.917431	1.0000	1.000000	0.9174	1.090000
2	1.1881	0.841680	2.0900	0.478469	1.7591	0.568469
3	1.2950	0.772183	3.2781	0.305055	2.5313	0.395055
4	1.4116	0.708425	4.5731	0.218669	3.2397	0.308669
5	1.5386	0.649931	5.9847	0.167092	3.8897	0.257092
6	1.6771	0.596267	7.5233	0.132920	4.4859	0.222920
7	1.8280	0.547034	9.2004	0.108691	5.0330	0.198691
8	1.9926	0.501866	11.0285	0.090674	5.5348	0.180674
9	2.1719	0.460428	13.0210	0.076799	5.9952	0.166799
10	2.3674	0.422411	15.1929	0.065820	6.4177	0.155820
11	2.5804	0.387533	17.5603	0.056947	6.8052	0.146947
12	2.8127	0.355535	20.1407	0.049651	7.1607	0.139651
13	3.0658	0.326179	22.9534	0.043567	7.4869	0.133567
14	3.3417	0.299246	26.0192	0.038433	7.7862	0.128433
15	3.6425	0.274538	29.3609	0.034059	8.0607	0.124059
16	3.9703	0.251870	33.0034	0.030300	8.3126	0.120300
17	4.3276	0.231073	36.9737	0.027046	8.5436	0.117046
18	4.7171	0.211994	41.3013	0.024212	8.7556	0.114212
19	5.1417	0.194490	46.0185	0.021730	8.9501	0.111730
20	5.6044	0.178431	51.1601	0.019546	9.1285	0.109546
21	6.1088	0.163698	56.7645	0.017617	9.2922	0.107617
22	6.6586	0.150182	62.8733	0.015905	9.4424	0.105905
23	7.2579	0.137781	69.5319	0.014382	9.5802	0.104382
24	7.9111	0.126405	76.7898	0.013023	9.7066	0.103023
25	8.6231	0.115968	84.7009	0.011806	9.8226	0.101806
26	9.3992	0.106393	93.3240	0.010715	9.9290	0.100715
27	10.2451	0.097608	102.7231	0.009735	10.0266	0.099735
28	11.1671	0.089548	112.9682	0.008852	10.1161	0.098852
29	12.1722	0.082155	124.1354	0.008056	10.1983	0.098056
30	13.2677	0.075371	136.3075	0.007336	10.2737	0.097336

INTEREST RATE 10.0 %

YEAR	FUTURE VALUE	PRESENT VALUE	SINKING FUND FUTURE VALUE	SINKING FUND ANNUAL AMOUNT	ANNUITY PRESENT VALUE	ANNUITY ANNUAL AMOUNT
n	$(1+i)^n$	$V_{\overline{n}\vert}$	$S_{\overline{n}\vert}$	$S_{\overline{n}\vert}^{-1}$	$A_{\overline{n}\vert}$	$A_{\overline{n}\vert}^{-1}$
1	1.1000	0.909091	1.0000	1.000000	0.9091	1.100000
2	1.2100	0.826446	2.1000	0.476190	1.7355	0.576190
3	1.3310	0.751315	3.3100	0.302115	2.4869	0.402115
4	1.4641	0.683013	4.6410	0.215471	3.1699	0.315471
5	1.6105	0.620921	6.1051	0.163797	3.7908	0.263797
6	1.7716	0.564474	7.7156	0.129607	4.3553	0.229607
7	1.9487	0.513158	9.4872	0.105405	4.8684	0.205405
8	2.1436	0.466507	11.4359	0.087444	5.3349	0.187444
9	2.3579	0.424098	13.5795	0.073641	5.7590	0.173641
10	2.5937	0.385543	15.9374	0.062745	6.1446	0.162745
11	2.8531	0.350494	18.5312	0.053963	6.4951	0.153963
12	3.1384	0.318631	21.3843	0.046763	6.8137	0.146763
13	3.4523	0.289664	24.5227	0.040779	7.1034	0.140779
14	3.7975	0.263331	27.9750	0.035746	7.3667	0.135746
15	4.1772	0.239392	31.7725	0.031474	7.6061	0.131474
16	4.5950	0.217629	35.9497	0.027817	7.8237	0.127817
17	5.0545	0.197845	40.5447	0.024664	8.0216	0.124664
18	5.5599	0.179859	45.5992	0.021930	8.2014	0.121930
19	6.1159	0.163508	51.1591	0.019547	8.3649	0.119547
20	6.7275	0.148644	57.2750	0.017460	8.5136	0.117460
21	7.4002	0.135131	64.0025	0.015624	8.6487	0.115624
22	8.1403	0.122846	71.4027	0.014005	8.7715	0.114005
23	8.9543	0.111678	79.5430	0.012572	8.8832	0.112572
24	9.8497	0.101526	88.4973	0.011300	8.9847	0.111300
25	10.8347	0.092296	98.3471	0.010168	9.0770	0.110168
26	11.9182	0.083905	109.1818	0.009159	9.1609	0.109159
27	13.1100	0.076278	121.0999	0.008258	9.2372	0.108258
28	14.4210	0.069343	134.2099	0.007451	9.3066	0.107451
29	15.8631	0.063039	148.6309	0.006728	9.3696	0.106728
30	17.4494	0.057309	164.4940	0.006079	9.4269	0.106079

INTEREST RATE 11.0 %

YEAR	FUTURE VALUE	PRESENT VALUE	SINKING FUND FUTURE VALUE	SINKING FUND ANNUAL AMOUNT	ANNUITY PRESENT VALUE	ANNUITY ANNUAL AMOUNT
n	$(1+i)^n$	$V_{\overline{n\rvert}}$	$S_{\overline{n\rvert}}$	$S_{\overline{n\rvert}}^{-1}$	$A_{\overline{n\rvert}}$	$A_{\overline{n\rvert}}^{-1}$
1	1.1100	0.900901	1.0000	1.000000	0.9009	1.110000
2	1.2321	0.811622	2.1100	0.473934	1.7125	0.583934
3	1.3676	0.731191	3.3421	0.299213	2.4437	0.409213
4	1.5181	0.658731	4.7097	0.212326	3.1024	0.322326
5	1.6851	0.593451	6.2278	0.160570	3.6959	0.270570
6	1.8704	0.534641	7.9129	0.126377	4.2305	0.236377
7	2.0762	0.481658	9.7833	0.102215	4.7122	0.212215
8	2.3045	0.433926	11.8594	0.084321	5.1461	0.194321
9	2.5580	0.390925	14.1640	0.070602	5.5370	0.180602
10	2.8394	0.352184	16.7220	0.059801	5.8892	0.169801
11	3.1518	0.317283	19.5614	0.051121	6.2065	0.161121
12	3.4985	0.285841	22.7132	0.044027	6.4924	0.154027
13	3.8833	0.257514	26.2116	0.038151	6.7499	0.148151
14	4.3104	0.231995	30.0949	0.033228	6.9819	0.143228
15	4.7846	0.209004	34.4054	0.029065	7.1909	0.139065
16	5.3109	0.188292	39.1899	0.025517	7.3792	0.135517
17	5.8951	0.169633	44.5008	0.022471	7.5488	0.132471
18	6.5436	0.152822	50.3959	0.019843	7.7016	0.129843
19	7.2633	0.137678	56.9395	0.017563	7.8393	0.127563
20	8.0623	0.124034	64.2028	0.015576	7.9633	0.125576
21	8.9492	0.111742	72.2651	0.013838	8.0751	0.123838
22	9.9336	0.100669	81.2143	0.012313	8.1757	0.122313
23	11.0263	0.090693	91.1479	0.010971	8.2664	0.120971
24	12.2392	0.081705	102.1742	0.009787	8.3481	0.119787
25	13.5855	0.073608	114.4133	0.008740	8.4217	0.118740
26	15.0799	0.066314	127.9988	0.007813	8.4881	0.117813
27	16.7386	0.059742	143.0786	0.006989	8.5478	0.116989
28	18.5799	0.053822	159.8173	0.006257	8.6016	0.116257
29	20.6237	0.048488	178.3972	0.005605	8.6501	0.115605
30	22.8923	0.043683	199.0209	0.005025	8.6938	0.115025

INTEREST RATE 12.0 %

YEAR	FUTURE VALUE	PRESENT VALUE	SINKING FUND FUTURE VALUE	SINKING FUND ANNUAL AMOUNT	ANNUITY PRESENT VALUE	ANNUITY ANNUAL AMOUNT
n	$(1+i)^n$	$V_{\overline{n}\vert}$	$S_{\overline{n}\vert}$	$S_{\overline{n}\vert}^{-1}$	$A_{\overline{n}\vert}$	$A_{\overline{n}\vert}^{-1}$
1	1.1200	0.892857	1.0000	1.000000	0.8929	1.120000
2	1.2544	0.797194	2.1200	0.471698	1.6901	0.591698
3	1.4049	0.711780	3.3744	0.296349	2.4018	0.416349
4	1.5735	0.635518	4.7793	0.209234	3.0373	0.329234
5	1.7623	0.567427	6.3528	0.157410	3.6048	0.277410
6	1.9738	0.506631	8.1152	0.123226	4.1114	0.243226
7	2.2107	0.452349	10.0890	0.099118	4.5638	0.219118
8	2.4760	0.403883	12.2997	0.081303	4.9676	0.201303
9	2.7731	0.360610	14.7757	0.067679	5.3282	0.187679
10	3.1058	0.321973	17.5487	0.056984	5.6502	0.176984
11	3.4785	0.287476	20.6546	0.048415	5.9377	0.168415
12	3.8960	0.256675	24.1331	0.041437	6.1944	0.161437
13	4.3635	0.229174	28.0291	0.035677	6.4235	0.155677
14	4.8871	0.204620	32.3926	0.030871	6.6282	0.150871
15	5.4736	0.182696	37.2797	0.026824	6.8109	0.146824
16	6.1304	0.163122	42.7533	0.023390	6.9740	0.143390
17	6.8660	0.145644	48.8837	0.020457	7.1196	0.140457
18	7.6900	0.130040	55.7497	0.017937	7.2497	0.137937
19	8.6128	0.116107	63.4397	0.015763	7.3658	0.135763
20	9.6463	0.103667	72.0524	0.013879	7.4694	0.133879
21	10.8038	0.092560	81.6987	0.012240	7.5620	0.132240
22	12.1003	0.082643	92.5026	0.010811	7.6446	0.130811
23	13.5523	0.073788	104.6029	0.009560	7.7184	0.129560
24	15.1786	0.065882	118.1552	0.008463	7.7843	0.128463
25	17.0001	0.058823	133.3339	0.007500	7.8431	0.127500
26	19.0401	0.052521	150.3339	0.006652	7.8957	0.126652
27	21.3249	0.046894	169.3740	0.005904	7.9426	0.125904
28	23.8839	0.041869	190.6989	0.005244	7.9844	0.125244
29	26.7499	0.037383	214.5828	0.004660	8.0218	0.124660
30	29.9599	0.033378	241.3327	0.004144	8.0552	0.124144

INTEREST RATE 13.0 %

YEAR	FUTURE VALUE	PRESENT VALUE	SINKING FUND		ANNUITY	
			FUTURE VALUE	ANNUAL AMOUNT	PRESENT VALUE	ANNUAL AMOUNT
n	$(1+i)^n$	$V_{\overline{n\rceil}}$	$S_{\overline{n\rceil}}$	$S_{\overline{n\rceil}}^{-1}$	$A_{\overline{n\rceil}}$	$A_{\overline{n\rceil}}^{-1}$
1	1.1300	0.884956	1.0000	1.000000	0.8850	1.130000
2	1.2769	0.783147	2.1300	0.469484	1.6681	0.599484
3	1.4429	0.693050	3.4069	0.293522	2.3612	0.423522
4	1.6305	0.613319	4.8498	0.206194	2.9745	0.336194
5	1.8424	0.542760	6.4803	0.154315	3.5172	0.284315
6	2.0820	0.480319	8.3227	0.120153	3.9975	0.250153
7	2.3526	0.425061	10.4047	0.096111	4.4226	0.226111
8	2.6584	0.376160	12.7573	0.078387	4.7988	0.208387
9	3.0040	0.332885	15.4157	0.064869	5.1317	0.194869
10	3.3946	0.294588	18.4197	0.054290	5.4262	0.184290
11	3.8359	0.260698	21.8143	0.045841	5.6869	0.175841
12	4.3345	0.230706	25.6502	0.038986	5.9176	0.168986
13	4.8980	0.204165	29.9847	0.033350	6.1218	0.163350
14	5.5348	0.180677	34.8827	0.028667	6.3025	0.158667
15	6.2543	0.159891	40.4175	0.024742	6.4624	0.154742
16	7.0673	0.141496	46.6717	0.021426	6.6039	0.151426
17	7.9861	0.125218	53.7391	0.018608	6.7291	0.148608
18	9.0243	0.110812	61.7251	0.016201	6.8399	0.146201
19	10.1974	0.098064	70.7494	0.014134	6.9380	0.144134
20	11.5231	0.086782	80.9468	0.012354	7.0248	0.142354
21	13.0211	0.076798	92.4699	0.010814	7.1016	0.140814
22	14.7138	0.067963	105.4910	0.009479	7.1695	0.139479
23	16.6266	0.060144	120.2048	0.008319	7.2297	0.138319
24	18.7881	0.053225	136.8315	0.007308	7.2829	0.137308
25	21.2305	0.047102	155.6196	0.006426	7.3300	0.136426
26	23.9905	0.041683	176.8501	0.005655	7.3717	0.135655
27	27.1093	0.036888	200.8406	0.004979	7.4086	0.134979
28	30.6335	0.032644	227.9499	0.004387	7.4412	0.134387
29	34.6158	0.028889	258.5834	0.003867	7.4701	0.133867
30	39.1159	0.025565	293.1992	0.003411	7.4957	0.133411

INTEREST RATE 14.0 %

YEAR	FUTURE VALUE	PRESENT VALUE	SINKING FUND FUTURE VALUE	SINKING FUND ANNUAL AMOUNT	ANNUITY PRESENT VALUE	ANNUITY ANNUAL AMOUNT
n	$(1+i)^n$	$V_{\overline{n}\vert}$	$S_{\overline{n}\vert}$	$S_{\overline{n}\vert}^{-1}$	$A_{\overline{n}\vert}$	$A_{\overline{n}\vert}^{-1}$
1	1.1400	0.877193	1.0000	1.000000	0.8772	1.140000
2	1.2996	0.769468	2.1400	0.467290	1.6467	0.607290
3	1.4815	0.674972	3.4396	0.290731	2.3216	0.430731
4	1.6890	0.592080	4.9211	0.203205	2.9137	0.343205
5	1.9254	0.519369	6.6101	0.151284	3.4331	0.291284
6	2.1950	0.455587	8.5355	0.117157	3.8887	0.257157
7	2.5023	0.399637	10.7305	0.093192	4.2883	0.233192
8	2.8526	0.350559	13.2328	0.075570	4.6389	0.215570
9	3.2519	0.307508	16.0853	0.062168	4.9464	0.202168
10	3.7072	0.269744	19.3373	0.051714	5.2161	0.191714
11	4.2262	0.236617	23.0445	0.043394	5.4527	0.183394
12	4.8179	0.207559	27.2707	0.036669	5.6603	0.176669
13	5.4924	0.182069	32.0887	0.031164	5.8424	0.171164
14	6.2613	0.159710	37.5811	0.026609	6.0021	0.166609
15	7.1379	0.140096	43.8424	0.022809	6.1422	0.162809
16	8.1372	0.122892	50.9804	0.019615	6.2651	0.159615
17	9.2765	0.107800	59.1176	0.016915	6.3729	0.156915
18	10.5752	0.094561	68.3941	0.014621	6.4674	0.154621
19	12.0557	0.082948	78.9692	0.012663	6.5504	0.152663
20	13.7435	0.072762	91.0249	0.010986	6.6231	0.150986
21	15.6676	0.063826	104.7684	0.009545	6.6870	0.149545
22	17.8610	0.055988	120.4360	0.008303	6.7429	0.148303
23	20.3616	0.049112	138.2970	0.007231	6.7921	0.147231
24	23.2122	0.043081	158.6586	0.006303	6.8351	0.146303
25	26.4619	0.037790	181.8708	0.005498	6.8729	0.145498
26	30.1666	0.033149	208.3327	0.004800	6.9061	0.144800
27	34.3899	0.029078	238.4993	0.004193	6.9352	0.144193
28	39.2045	0.025507	272.8892	0.003664	6.9607	0.143664
29	44.6931	0.022375	312.0937	0.003204	6.9830	0.143204
30	50.9502	0.019627	356.7868	0.002803	7.0027	0.142803

INTEREST RATE 15.0 %

YEAR	FUTURE VALUE	PRESENT VALUE	SINKING FUND		ANNUITY	
			FUTURE VALUE	ANNUAL AMOUNT	PRESENT VALUE	ANNUAL AMOUNT
n	$(1+i)^n$	$V_{\overline{n\rceil}}$	$S_{\overline{n\rceil}}$	$S_{\overline{n\rceil}}^{-1}$	$A_{\overline{n\rceil}}$	$A_{\overline{n\rceil}}^{-1}$
1	1.1500	0.869565	1.0000	1.000000	0.8696	1.150000
2	1.3225	0.756144	2.1500	0.465116	1.6257	0.615116
3	1.5209	0.657516	3.4725	0.287977	2.2832	0.437977
4	1.7490	0.571753	4.9934	0.200265	2.8550	0.350265
5	2.0114	0.497177	6.7424	0.148316	3.3522	0.298316
6	2.3131	0.432328	8.7537	0.114237	3.7845	0.264237
7	2.6600	0.375937	11.0668	0.090360	4.1604	0.240360
8	3.0590	0.326902	13.7268	0.072850	4.4873	0.222850
9	3.5179	0.284262	16.7858	0.059574	4.7716	0.209574
10	4.0456	0.247185	20.3037	0.049252	5.0188	0.199252
11	4.6524	0.214943	24.3493	0.041069	5.2337	0.191069
12	5.3503	0.186907	29.0017	0.034481	5.4206	0.184481
13	6.1528	0.162528	34.3519	0.029110	5.5831	0.179110
14	7.0757	0.141329	40.5047	0.024688	5.7245	0.174688
15	8.1371	0.122894	47.5804	0.021017	5.8474	0.171017
16	9.3576	0.106865	55.7175	0.017948	5.9542	0.167948
17	10.7613	0.092926	65.0751	0.015367	6.0472	0.165367
18	12.3755	0.080805	75.8364	0.013186	6.1280	0.163186
19	14.2318	0.070265	88.2118	0.011336	6.1982	0.161336
20	16.3665	0.061100	102.4436	0.009761	6.2593	0.159761
21	18.8215	0.053131	118.8101	0.008417	6.3125	0.158417
22	21.6447	0.046201	137.6316	0.007266	6.3587	0.157266
23	24.8915	0.040174	159.2764	0.006278	6.3988	0.156278
24	28.6252	0.034934	184.1678	0.005430	6.4338	0.155430
25	32.9190	0.030378	212.7930	0.004699	6.4641	0.154699
26	37.8568	0.026415	245.7120	0.004070	6.4906	0.154070
27	43.5353	0.022970	283.5688	0.003526	6.5135	0.153526
28	50.0656	0.019974	327.1041	0.003057	6.5335	0.153057
29	57.5755	0.017369	377.1697	0.002651	6.5509	0.152651
30	66.2118	0.015103	434.7451	0.002300	6.5660	0.152300

INTEREST RATE 16.0 %

YEAR	FUTURE VALUE	PRESENT VALUE	SINKING FUND FUTURE VALUE	SINKING FUND ANNUAL AMOUNT	ANNUITY PRESENT VALUE	ANNUITY ANNUAL AMOUNT
n	$(1+i)^n$	$V_{\overline{n}\rvert}$	$S_{\overline{n}\rvert}$	$S_{\overline{n}\rvert}^{-1}$	$A_{\overline{n}\rvert}$	$A_{\overline{n}\rvert}^{-1}$
1	1.1600	0.862069	1.0000	1.000000	0.8621	1.160000
2	1.3456	0.743163	2.1600	0.462963	1.6052	0.622963
3	1.5609	0.640658	3.5056	0.285258	2.2459	0.445258
4	1.8106	0.552291	5.0665	0.197375	2.7982	0.357375
5	2.1003	0.476113	6.8771	0.145409	3.2743	0.305409
6	2.4364	0.410442	8.9775	0.111390	3.6847	0.271390
7	2.8262	0.353830	11.4139	0.087613	4.0386	0.247613
8	3.2784	0.305025	14.2401	0.070224	4.3436	0.230224
9	3.8030	0.262953	17.5185	0.057082	4.6065	0.217082
10	4.4114	0.226684	21.3215	0.046901	4.8332	0.206901
11	5.1173	0.195417	25.7329	0.038861	5.0286	0.198861
12	5.9360	0.168463	30.8502	0.032415	5.1971	0.192415
13	6.8858	0.145227	36.7862	0.027184	5.3423	0.187184
14	7.9875	0.125195	43.6720	0.022898	5.4675	0.182898
15	9.2655	0.107927	51.6595	0.019358	5.5755	0.179358
16	10.7480	0.093041	60.9250	0.016414	5.6685	0.176414
17	12.4677	0.080207	71.6730	0.013952	5.7487	0.173952
18	14.4625	0.069144	84.1407	0.011885	5.8178	0.171885
19	16.7765	0.059607	98.6032	0.010142	5.8775	0.170142
20	19.4608	0.051385	115.3797	0.008667	5.9288	0.168667
21	22.5745	0.044298	134.8405	0.007416	5.9731	0.167416
22	26.1864	0.038188	157.4150	0.006353	6.0113	0.166353
23	30.3762	0.032920	183.6014	0.005447	6.0442	0.165447
24	35.2364	0.028380	213.9776	0.004673	6.0726	0.164673
25	40.8742	0.024465	249.2140	0.004013	6.0971	0.164013
26	47.4141	0.021091	290.0883	0.003447	6.1182	0.163447
27	55.0004	0.018182	337.5024	0.002963	6.1364	0.162963
28	63.8004	0.015674	392.5028	0.002548	6.1520	0.162548
29	74.0085	0.013512	456.3032	0.002192	6.1656	0.162192
30	85.8499	0.011648	530.3117	0.001886	6.1772	0.161886

INTEREST RATE 17.0 %

YEAR	FUTURE VALUE	PRESENT VALUE	SINKING FUND FUTURE VALUE	SINKING FUND ANNUAL AMOUNT	ANNUITY PRESENT VALUE	ANNUITY ANNUAL AMOUNT
n	$(1+i)^n$	$V_{\overline{n}\rceil}$	$S_{\overline{n}\rceil}$	$S_{\overline{n}\rceil}^{-1}$	$A_{\overline{n}\rceil}$	$A_{\overline{n}\rceil}^{-1}$
1	1.1700	0.854701	1.0000	1.000000	0.8547	1.170000
2	1.3689	0.730514	2.1700	0.460829	1.5852	0.630829
3	1.6016	0.624371	3.5389	0.282574	2.2096	0.452574
4	1.8739	0.533650	5.1405	0.194533	2.7432	0.364533
5	2.1924	0.456111	7.0144	0.142564	3.1993	0.312564
6	2.5652	0.389839	9.2068	0.108615	3.5892	0.278615
7	3.0012	0.333195	11.7720	0.084947	3.9224	0.254947
8	3.5115	0.284782	14.7733	0.067690	4.2072	0.237690
9	4.1084	0.243404	18.2847	0.054691	4.4506	0.224691
10	4.8068	0.208037	22.3931	0.044657	4.6586	0.214657
11	5.6240	0.177810	27.1999	0.036765	4.8364	0.206765
12	6.5801	0.151974	32.8239	0.030466	4.9884	0.200466
13	7.6987	0.129892	39.4040	0.025378	5.1183	0.195378
14	9.0075	0.111019	47.1027	0.021230	5.2293	0.191230
15	10.5387	0.094888	56.1101	0.017822	5.3242	0.187822
16	12.3303	0.081101	66.6488	0.015004	5.4053	0.185004
17	14.4265	0.069317	78.9792	0.012662	5.4746	0.182662
18	16.8790	0.059245	93.4056	0.010706	5.5339	0.180706
19	19.7484	0.050637	110.2846	0.009067	5.5845	0.179067
20	23.1056	0.043280	130.0329	0.007690	5.6278	0.177690
21	27.0336	0.036991	153.1385	0.006530	5.6648	0.176530
22	31.6293	0.031616	180.1721	0.005550	5.6964	0.175550
23	37.0062	0.027022	211.8013	0.004721	5.7234	0.174721
24	43.2973	0.023096	248.8076	0.004019	5.7465	0.174019
25	50.6578	0.019740	292.1049	0.003423	5.7662	0.173423
26	59.2697	0.016872	342.7627	0.002917	5.7831	0.172917
27	69.3455	0.014421	402.0323	0.002487	5.7975	0.172487
28	81.1342	0.012325	471.3778	0.002121	5.8099	0.172121
29	94.9271	0.010534	552.5121	0.001810	5.8204	0.171810
30	111.0647	0.009004	647.4391	0.001545	5.8294	0.171545

INTEREST RATE 18.0 %

YEAR	FUTURE VALUE	PRESENT VALUE	SINKING FUND FUTURE VALUE	SINKING FUND ANNUAL AMOUNT	ANNUITY PRESENT VALUE	ANNUITY ANNUAL AMOUNT
n	$(1+i)^n$	$V_{\overline{n\|}}$	$S_{\overline{n\|}}$	$S_{\overline{n\|}}^{-1}$	$A_{\overline{n\|}}$	$A_{\overline{n\|}}^{-1}$
1	1.1800	0.847458	1.0000	1.000000	0.8475	1.180000
2	1.3924	0.718184	2.1800	0.458716	1.5656	0.638716
3	1.6430	0.608631	3.5724	0.279924	2.1743	0.459924
4	1.9388	0.515789	5.2154	0.191739	2.6901	0.371739
5	2.2878	0.437109	7.1542	0.139778	3.1272	0.319778
6	2.6996	0.370432	9.4420	0.105910	3.4976	0.285910
7	3.1855	0.313925	12.1415	0.082362	3.8115	0.262362
8	3.7589	0.266038	15.3270	0.065244	4.0776	0.245244
9	4.4355	0.225456	19.0859	0.052395	4.3030	0.232395
10	5.2338	0.191064	23.5213	0.042515	4.4941	0.222515
11	6.1759	0.161919	28.7551	0.034776	4.6560	0.214776
12	7.2876	0.137220	34.9311	0.028628	4.7932	0.208628
13	8.5994	0.116288	42.2187	0.023686	4.9095	0.203686
14	10.1472	0.098549	50.8180	0.019678	5.0081	0.199678
15	11.9737	0.083516	60.9653	0.016403	5.0916	0.196403
16	14.1290	0.070776	72.9390	0.013710	5.1624	0.193710
17	16.6722	0.059980	87.0680	0.011485	5.2223	0.191485
18	19.6733	0.050830	103.7403	0.009639	5.2732	0.189639
19	23.2144	0.043077	123.4135	0.008103	5.3162	0.188103
20	27.3930	0.036506	146.6280	0.006820	5.3527	0.186820
21	32.3238	0.030937	174.0210	0.005746	5.3837	0.185746
22	38.1421	0.026218	206.3448	0.004846	5.4099	0.184846
23	45.0076	0.022218	244.4868	0.004090	5.4321	0.184090
24	53.1090	0.018829	289.4945	0.003454	5.4509	0.183454
25	62.6686	0.015957	342.6035	0.002919	5.4669	0.182919
26	73.9490	0.013523	405.2721	0.002467	5.4804	0.182467
27	87.2598	0.011460	479.2211	0.002087	5.4919	0.182087
28	102.9666	0.009712	566.4809	0.001765	5.5016	0.181765
29	121.5005	0.008230	669.4475	0.001494	5.5098	0.181494
30	143.3706	0.006975	790.9480	0.001264	5.5168	0.181264

INTEREST RATE 19.0 %

YEAR	FUTURE VALUE	PRESENT VALUE	SINKING FUND FUTURE VALUE	SINKING FUND ANNUAL AMOUNT	ANNUITY PRESENT VALUE	ANNUITY ANNUAL AMOUNT
n	$(1+i)^n$	$V_{\overline{n\rceil}}$	$S_{\overline{n\rceil}}$	$S_{\overline{n\rceil}}^{-1}$	$A_{\overline{n\rceil}}$	$A_{\overline{n\rceil}}^{-1}$
1	1.1900	0.840336	1.0000	1.000000	0.8403	1.190000
2	1.4161	0.706165	2.1900	0.456621	1.5465	0.646621
3	1.6852	0.593416	3.6061	0.277308	2.1399	0.467308
4	2.0053	0.498669	5.2913	0.188991	2.6386	0.378991
5	2.3864	0.419049	7.2966	0.137050	3.0576	0.327050
6	2.8398	0.352142	9.6830	0.103274	3.4098	0.293274
7	3.3793	0.295918	12.5227	0.079855	3.7057	0.269855
8	4.0214	0.248671	15.9020	0.062885	3.9544	0.252885
9	4.7854	0.208967	19.9234	0.050192	4.1633	0.240192
10	5.6947	0.175602	24.7089	0.040471	4.3389	0.230471
11	6.7767	0.147565	30.4035	0.032891	4.4865	0.222891
12	8.0642	0.124004	37.1802	0.026896	4.6105	0.216896
13	9.5964	0.104205	45.2445	0.022102	4.7147	0.212102
14	11.4198	0.087567	54.8409	0.018235	4.8023	0.208235
15	13.5895	0.073586	66.2607	0.015092	4.8759	0.205092
16	16.1715	0.061837	79.8502	0.012523	4.9377	0.202523
17	19.2441	0.051964	96.0218	0.010414	4.9897	0.200414
18	22.9005	0.043667	115.2659	0.008676	5.0333	0.198676
19	27.2516	0.036695	138.1664	0.007238	5.0700	0.197238
20	32.4294	0.030836	165.4180	0.006045	5.1009	0.196045
21	38.5910	0.025913	197.8474	0.005054	5.1268	0.195054
22	45.9233	0.021775	236.4385	0.004229	5.1486	0.194229
23	54.6487	0.018299	282.3618	0.003542	5.1668	0.193542
24	65.0320	0.015377	337.0105	0.002967	5.1822	0.192967
25	77.3881	0.012922	402.0425	0.002487	5.1951	0.192487
26	92.0918	0.010859	479.4306	0.002086	5.2060	0.192086
27	109.5893	0.009125	571.5224	0.001750	5.2151	0.191750
28	130.4112	0.007668	681.1116	0.001468	5.2228	0.191468
29	155.1893	0.006444	811.5228	0.001232	5.2292	0.191232
30	184.6753	0.005415	966.7122	0.001034	5.2347	0.191034

INTEREST RATE 20.0 %

YEAR	FUTURE VALUE	PRESENT VALUE	SINKING FUND FUTURE VALUE	SINKING FUND ANNUAL AMOUNT	ANNUITY PRESENT VALUE	ANNUITY ANNUAL AMOUNT
n	$(1+i)^n$	$V_{\overline{n}\vert}$	$S_{\overline{n}\vert}$	$S_{\overline{n}\vert}^{-1}$	$A_{\overline{n}\vert}$	$A_{\overline{n}\vert}^{-1}$
1	1.2000	0.833333	1.0000	1.000000	0.8333	1.200000
2	1.4400	0.694444	2.2000	0.454545	1.5278	0.654545
3	1.7280	0.578704	3.6400	0.274725	2.1065	0.474725
4	2.0736	0.482253	5.3680	0.186289	2.5887	0.386289
5	2.4883	0.401878	7.4416	0.134380	2.9906	0.334380
6	2.9860	0.334898	9.9299	0.100706	3.3255	0.300706
7	3.5832	0.279082	12.9159	0.077424	3.6046	0.277424
8	4.2998	0.232568	16.4991	0.060609	3.8372	0.260609
9	5.1598	0.193807	20.7989	0.048079	4.0310	0.248079
10	6.1917	0.161506	25.9587	0.038523	4.1925	0.238523
11	7.4301	0.134588	32.1504	0.031104	4.3271	0.231104
12	8.9161	0.112157	39.5805	0.025265	4.4392	0.225265
13	10.6993	0.093464	48.4966	0.020620	4.5327	0.220620
14	12.8392	0.077887	59.1959	0.016893	4.6106	0.216893
15	15.4070	0.064905	72.0351	0.013882	4.6755	0.213882
16	18.4884	0.054088	87.4421	0.011436	4.7296	0.211436
17	22.1861	0.045073	105.9306	0.009440	4.7746	0.209440
18	26.6233	0.037561	128.1167	0.007805	4.8122	0.207805
19	31.9480	0.031301	154.7400	0.006462	4.8435	0.206462
20	38.3376	0.026084	186.6880	0.005357	4.8696	0.205357
21	46.0051	0.021737	225.0256	0.004444	4.8913	0.204444
22	55.2061	0.018114	271.0307	0.003690	4.9094	0.203690
23	66.2474	0.015095	326.2369	0.003065	4.9245	0.203065
24	79.4968	0.012579	392.4842	0.002548	4.9371	0.202548
25	95.3962	0.010483	471.9811	0.002119	4.9476	0.202119
26	114.4755	0.008735	567.3773	0.001762	4.9563	0.201762
27	137.3706	0.007280	681.8528	0.001467	4.9636	0.201467
28	164.8447	0.006066	819.2233	0.001221	4.9697	0.201221
29	197.8136	0.005055	984.0680	0.001016	4.9747	0.201016
30	237.3763	0.004213	1181.8816	0.000846	4.9789	0.200846

INTEREST RATE 21.0 %

YEAR	FUTURE VALUE	PRESENT VALUE	SINKING FUND FUTURE VALUE	SINKING FUND ANNUAL AMOUNT	ANNUITY PRESENT VALUE	ANNUITY ANNUAL AMOUNT
n	$(1+i)^n$	$V_{\overline{n\mid}}$	$S_{\overline{n\mid}}$	$S_{\overline{n\mid}}^{-1}$	$A_{\overline{n\mid}}$	$A_{\overline{n\mid}}^{-1}$
1	1.2100	0.826446	1.0000	1.000000	0.8264	1.210000
2	1.4641	0.683013	2.2100	0.452489	1.5095	0.662489
3	1.7716	0.564474	3.6741	0.272175	2.0739	0.482175
4	2.1436	0.466507	5.4457	0.183632	2.5404	0.393632
5	2.5937	0.385543	7.5892	0.131765	2.9260	0.341765
6	3.1384	0.318631	10.1830	0.098203	3.2446	0.308203
7	3.7975	0.263331	13.3214	0.075067	3.5079	0.285067
8	4.5950	0.217629	17.1189	0.058415	3.7256	0.268415
9	5.5599	0.179859	21.7139	0.046053	3.9054	0.256053
10	6.7275	0.148644	27.2738	0.036665	4.0541	0.246665
11	8.1403	0.122846	34.0013	0.029411	4.1769	0.239411
12	9.8497	0.101526	42.1416	0.023730	4.2784	0.233730
13	11.9182	0.083905	51.9913	0.019234	4.3624	0.229234
14	14.4210	0.069343	63.9095	0.015647	4.4317	0.225647
15	17.4494	0.057309	78.3305	0.012766	4.4890	0.222766
16	21.1138	0.047362	95.7799	0.010441	4.5364	0.220441
17	25.5477	0.039143	116.8937	0.008555	4.5755	0.218555
18	30.9127	0.032349	142.4413	0.007020	4.6079	0.217020
19	37.4043	0.026735	173.3540	0.005769	4.6346	0.215769
20	45.2593	0.022095	210.7584	0.004745	4.6567	0.214745
21	54.7637	0.018260	256.0176	0.003906	4.6750	0.213906
22	66.2641	0.015091	310.7813	0.003218	4.6900	0.213218
23	80.1795	0.012472	377.0454	0.002652	4.7025	0.212652
24	97.0172	0.010307	457.2249	0.002187	4.7128	0.212187
25	117.3909	0.008519	554.2422	0.001804	4.7213	0.211804
26	142.0429	0.007040	671.6330	0.001489	4.7284	0.211489
27	171.8719	0.005818	813.6759	0.001229	4.7342	0.211229
28	207.9651	0.004809	985.5479	0.001015	4.7390	0.211015
29	251.6377	0.003974	1193.5129	0.000838	4.7430	0.210838
30	304.4816	0.003284	1445.1507	0.000692	4.7463	0.210692

INTEREST RATE 25.0 %

YEAR	FUTURE VALUE	PRESENT VALUE	SINKING FUND FUTURE VALUE	SINKING FUND ANNUAL AMOUNT	ANNUITY PRESENT VALUE	ANNUITY ANNUAL AMOUNT
n	$(1+i)^n$	$V_{\overline{n}\rceil}$	$S_{\overline{n}\rceil}$	$S_{\overline{n}\rceil}^{-1}$	$A_{\overline{n}\rceil}$	$A_{\overline{n}\rceil}^{-1}$
1	1.2500	0.800000	1.0000	1.000000	0.8000	1.250000
2	1.5625	0.640000	2.2500	0.444444	1.4400	0.694444
3	1.9531	0.512000	3.8125	0.262295	1.9520	0.512295
4	2.4414	0.409600	5.7656	0.173442	2.3616	0.423442
5	3.0518	0.327680	8.2070	0.121847	2.6893	0.371847
6	3.8147	0.262144	11.2588	0.088819	2.9514	0.338819
7	4.7684	0.209715	15.0735	0.066342	3.1611	0.316342
8	5.9605	0.167772	19.8419	0.050399	3.3289	0.300399
9	7.4506	0.134218	25.8023	0.038756	3.4631	0.288756
10	9.3132	0.107374	33.2529	0.030073	3.5705	0.280073
11	11.6415	0.085899	42.5661	0.023493	3.6564	0.273493
12	14.5519	0.068719	54.2077	0.018448	3.7251	0.268448
13	18.1899	0.054976	68.7596	0.014543	3.7801	0.264543
14	22.7374	0.043980	86.9495	0.011501	3.8241	0.261501
15	28.4217	0.035184	109.6868	0.009117	3.8593	0.259117
16	35.5271	0.028147	138.1085	0.007241	3.8874	0.257241
17	44.4089	0.022518	173.6357	0.005759	3.9099	0.255759
18	55.5112	0.018014	218.0446	0.004586	3.9279	0.254586
19	69.3889	0.014412	273.5558	0.003656	3.9424	0.253656
20	86.7362	0.011529	342.9447	0.002916	3.9539	0.252916
21	108.4202	0.009223	429.6809	0.002327	3.9631	0.252327
22	135.5253	0.007379	538.1011	0.001858	3.9705	0.251858
23	169.4066	0.005903	673.6264	0.001485	3.9764	0.251485
24	211.7582	0.004722	843.0329	0.001186	3.9811	0.251186
25	264.6978	0.003778	1054.7912	0.000948	3.9849	0.250948
26	330.8722	0.003022	1319.4890	0.000758	3.9879	0.250758
27	413.5903	0.002418	1650.3612	0.000606	3.9903	0.250606
28	516.9879	0.001934	2063.9515	0.000485	3.9923	0.250485
29	646.2349	0.001547	2580.9394	0.000387	3.9938	0.250387
30	807.7936	0.001238	3227.1743	0.000310	3.9950	0.250310

INTEREST RATE 30.0 %

YEAR	FUTURE VALUE	PRESENT VALUE	SINKING FUND FUTURE VALUE	SINKING FUND ANNUAL AMOUNT	ANNUITY PRESENT VALUE	ANNUITY ANNUAL AMOUNT
n	$(1+i)^n$	$V_{\overline{n}\rceil}$	$S_{\overline{n}\rceil}$	$S_{\overline{n}\rceil}^{-1}$	$A_{\overline{n}\rceil}$	$A_{\overline{n}\rceil}^{-1}$
1	1.3000	0.769231	1.0000	1.000000	0.7692	1.300000
2	1.6900	0.591716	2.3000	0.434783	1.3609	0.734783
3	2.1970	0.455166	3.9900	0.250627	1.8161	0.550627
4	2.8561	0.350128	6.1870	0.161629	2.1662	0.461629
5	3.7129	0.269329	9.0431	0.110582	2.4356	0.410582
6	4.8268	0.207176	12.7560	0.078394	2.6427	0.378394
7	6.2749	0.159366	17.5828	0.056874	2.8021	0.356874
8	8.1573	0.122589	23.8577	0.041915	2.9247	0.341915
9	10.6045	0.094300	32.0150	0.031235	3.0190	0.331235
10	13.7858	0.072538	42.6195	0.023463	3.0915	0.323463
11	17.9216	0.055799	56.4053	0.017729	3.1473	0.317729
12	23.2981	0.042922	74.3270	0.013454	3.1903	0.313454
13	30.2875	0.033017	97.6250	0.010243	3.2233	0.310243
14	39.3738	0.025398	127.9125	0.007818	3.2487	0.307818
15	51.1859	0.019537	167.2863	0.005978	3.2682	0.305978
16	66.5417	0.015028	218.4722	0.004577	3.2832	0.304577
17	86.5042	0.011560	285.0139	0.003509	3.2948	0.303509
18	112.4554	0.008892	371.5180	0.002692	3.3037	0.302692
19	146.1920	0.006840	483.9734	0.002066	3.3105	0.302066
20	190.0496	0.005262	630.1655	0.001587	3.3158	0.301587
21	247.0645	0.004048	820.2151	0.001219	3.3198	0.301219
22	321.1839	0.003113	1067.2796	0.000937	3.3230	0.300937
23	417.5391	0.002395	1388.4635	0.000720	3.3254	0.300720
24	542.8008	0.001842	1806.0026	0.000554	3.3272	0.300554
25	705.6410	0.001417	2348.8033	0.000426	3.3286	0.300426
26	917.3333	0.001090	3054.4443	0.000327	3.3297	0.300327
27	1192.5333	0.000839	3971.7776	0.000252	3.3305	0.300252
28	1550.2933	0.000645	5164.3109	0.000194	3.3312	0.300194
29	2015.3813	0.000496	6714.6042	0.000149	3.3317	0.300149
30	2619.9956	0.000382	8729.9855	0.000115	3.3321	0.300115

Index